The Unauthorized Inside Story of the Sitcom that Broke ALL the Rules

SOAP

A.S. BERMAN

WITT/THOMAS/HARRIS PRO

presents

SOAP

A Revolutionary New Com

Children Under 16 not ad

KTLA — CHANNEL 5 — S
5800 Sunset Blvd., Entrance

To **Susan Harris, Tony Thomas and Paul Junger Witt**, for taking the biggest gamble of their young careers, and sticking with it when the going got tough. And to **Marsha Posner Williams** for remembering what others have forgotten ever since.

This book is dedicated to **Richard and Judy Berman**, and **Pamela Norman Berman**. The first two prepared me for this world, and the last gave me the best reason not to leave it.

Foreword

One night in September 1977, several days after the sitcom *Soap* premiered on ABC, a 24-year-old woman called Catharine was walking with a friend near the corner of Hawthorne and Highland in Los Angeles. Her friend left the scene shortly after a Cadillac drove up to block their way, but Catharine stopped when one of the two men in the car got out and showed her a badge, demanding to see her ID.

An exceedingly lucky Catharine Lorre two years before her run-in with the Hillside Stranglers.

Claiming that her wallet had been stolen, she gave the man her citizenship papers that said she'd been born in Germany, and that her father was the late film star Peter Lorre. Though he'd made a career in America playing villains on radio and in the movies, he was still best known at the time for his role as a child killer in the 1931 Fritz Lang classic *M*. Two family photos that had fallen out of Catharine's purse clinched it—both showed her with her father. "Be careful now," the bogus cop's companion told her. "You shouldn't be out walking like this at night. Be good."

The young woman quickly left the scene for the bus stop on Sunset she'd been bound for in the first place. She had just missed the "special attentions" of Angelo Buono Jr and Kenny Bianchi, cousins who would later be known as the Hillside Stranglers; they would kill the first of 10 women just one month later. Had it simply been Catharine's relationship to a film star that had persuaded them to change their minds about killing her, or was this something of a professional courtesy the real-life killers had paid the daughter of a man who had brought their fantasies to life on the big screen?

Obscure as this incident is, it stands as a jarring lesson in the importance that Americans assign to television and film, and the difficulty that many have separating fictional characters and situations from the real world. It was a lesson that the cast, crew and producers of *Soap* learned months before its Sept. 13, 1977 premiere.

The golden ticket. Actually, they were green...and other colors, too.

Given nearly 40 years of hindsight, it's easy to see that *Soap* was never going to be greeted with that giggle and yawn reserved for other shows that aired that year. While 1977 would see the debut of critical darling *Lou Grant*, it also brought us the premieres of *CHiPs*, *Eight is Enough*, and two series that epitomized both extremes of the banal-daring continuum: *The Love Boat* and *Three's Company*. While this last would attract its fair share of criticism for continuing a trend in "jiggle television" (itself a phrase racier than anything glimpsed at the time) begun by *Charlie's Angels*, it never reached the levels of hysteria inspired by *Soap*.

To understand the controversy, as well as the attitudes of the producers who refused to knuckle under to mounting pressures from special interest groups, ABC affiliates and advertisers, you must understand the real-life events that engulfed the world at the time. To that end, you will find marginalia throughout this book illustrating the wars, murders, race baiting, homophobia and hypocrisies that plagued the '70s and '80s during *Soap*'s original run. Just as one cannot understand WWII without knowing something of the war that preceded it, one cannot understand the Tates and the Campbells without knowing something about Anita Bryant, Vietnam and Jonestown.

Above all, this book seeks to reveal something of the creative process that transformed a series of swiftly written scripts into a rich cultural experience week after week. (Though some behind-the-scenes tensions are acknowledged here, this work focuses on the making of *Soap* and not the conflicts that inevitably result from any high-pressure situation.)

Great pains have been taken to examine each episode in detail, yet the meat grinder that is television syndication makes this particularly difficult in the case of *Soap*. While producers brought episodes in around the 23-minute mark to accommodate the commercials ABC affiliates inserted into the first-run time slot, those episodes were trimmed in syndication to make room for additional commercials. To make things even more confusing, these scenes were restored in the early VHS Columbia House release, yet some were ignored by Sony, which used the shorter syndicated versions for some of its DVD box sets starting in 2003. The decision was made to base episode entries in this book on the syndicated versions as these are what have been most widely circulated. It is hoped that the behind-the-scenes information provided here more than makes up for this.

The Columbia House tapes really did become collector's items as they contain the complete shows; the DVDs do not.

Finally, as frequently happens with the writing of any book, the author ended up with far more information than could be included here. *Soap* fans are encouraged to seek out interview transcripts, photos and other information at **The Soap Archive (soaparchive.wordpress.com/)**.

A.S. BERMAN
Phoenix, Ariz.

COVER + INTERIOR DESIGN
Pamela Norman Berman

TEXT © 2013 AS Berman

PHOTOS (265, 352, 353, 344) by Mark Lipczynski, **marklipczynski.com**

PHOTOS (58, 401, 442) courtesy of Marsha Posner Williams

ILLUSTRATIONS (265, 352, 353, 344) by Judy Evans Steele

This book is not affiliated in any way with ABC or Witt Thomas Harris Productions. All photos and/or copyrighted material appearing in this book remains the work of its owners; every effort has been made to give credit. No infringement is intended in this work of journalism.

Published by
BearManor Media
bearmanormedia.com

Printed by **lightningsource.com**

SOAP! THE INSIDE STORY OF THE SITCOM THAT BROKE ALL THE RULES
AS Berman, author.
p.cm.

Includes bibliographical references and index.

ISBN 1-59393-687-7

I. Television and popular culture, 2000-2013 2. Biography.
3. Television and popular culture-history. I. Title.

Contents

- **10** Introduction
- **13** The '70s in America
- **48** Controversy
- **72** Season One
- **164** Season Two
- **248** Season Three
- **328** Season Four
- **415** Bios + Where are they now?
- **436** Children of *Soap*
- **441** Bibliography
- **443** Acknowledgments
- **445** Index

Introduction

On Jan. 20, 2011, television writer Susan Harris was inducted into the Academy of Television Arts & Sciences Hall of Fame, along with Diahann Carroll, Cloris Leachman and others, in a ceremony at the Beverly Hilton Hotel. While her introduction at the event would be filled with some token "Give 'em hell, Harris" kudos about a little sitcom called Soap, it would be The Golden Girls series that would be guaranteed to soak up the greatest praise. After all, who doesn't love The Golden Girls? Sure the old gals were often misbehavin', but few get worked up over oldies feeling their oats. Funny! Fabulous! Safe.

Soap creator Susan Harris was inducted into the ACTAS Hall of Fame in 2011.

Looking around the room, hearing about what a phenomenal career she'd had, there was probably a moment when she looked out at her peers and realized that three months shy of 30 years ago, the industry pulled the plug on her *Soap*. This after a four-year battle with forces within the industry and without. ("I never even won an Emmy for writing," she will tell the author seven months later. "I won the Writer's Guild Lifetime Achievement Award never having been even nominated for a Writer's Guild award, either.")

There's a lot of history in that Beverly Hilton Hotel. It was here that in 1975 ABC tried to schedule a bury-the-hatchet breakfast meeting between *Barney Miller* creator Danny Arnold and the network's chief censor, Alfred Schneider, after the two came to loggerheads over censorship of that series. (Schneider would perform a similar function for *Soap* just a few years later, with somewhat less-confrontational results.)

After all these years, here was the industry giving Harris an honored place in the annals of television, alongside the more than 100 other people who've been inducted since the Hall of Fame's creation in 1984.

The previous year, Dick and Tommy Smothers were given a similar treatment, the irony of which couldn't have been lost on Harris. The Smothers Brothers waged a two-year war with CBS in the late '60s over increasing levels of censorship that ended in a legal victory for the pair. They had been taken back into the fold in 2010 now that they were "safe" commodities. There's nothing like official recognition to co-opt a revolution.

Unlike the Smothers Brothers, Susan Harris hadn't given up television for touring the country's performance venues after the end of *Soap*. Dick and Tommy had struck a powerful blow for First Amendment rights with their on-air bits about the Vietnam conflict and the political pony-trading that went on behind the scenes of network television. Yet Harris had the added challenge of blowing through the barriers that had made female showrunners such a rarity when she launched *Soap* with Paul Junger Witt and Tony Thomas in 1977. There were plenty in the business who would be only too happy to see her give it all up for a nice house in the country.

To understand the part that Susan Harris and her compatriots played in the industry, and why *Soap* was, and remains, one of the most controversial—and influential—programs in American television, you have to understand the tumultuousness of the times, and America's ambivalence toward television's place in society.

When *Soap* began, the faces of Burt, Mary, Jessica and the rest peered back at America from a variety of magazine covers.

The '70s In America

During the decade of its bicentennial, the United States of America was showing every sign of coming apart at the seams. Not surprising, really, as the '60s had been largely spent demolishing every ideal the society professed to hold dear. Every bit of turmoil abroad that Americans had quietly thought "can't happen here" *had* happened there. A sitting president gunned down in Dallas—the opening salvo in a wave of political assassinations; riots (the Watts neighborhood in LA being one of the country's worst); huge military losses overseas that would lead to complete defeat; and the emergence of a nuclear threat in Cuba, just 90 miles off the US coast. By 1969, putting a man on the moon—what had once seemed an act of dreamy optimism—now felt like a desperate move to escape a country, and a world, gone mad. If anything, the '70s would be worse.

The year 1970 got off to a horrifying start with the May 4th massacre of four Kent State University students in Ohio by members of the National Guard, destroying yet another point of American pride; until then, it had never so publicly unleashed the military on its own unarmed citizens. That the National Guard wasn't technically considered part of the military did little to comfort shocked onlookers, or to bring back the dead.

The military disregarded the Posse Comitatus Act—the 1878 legislation that severely limits domestic military operations—three years later when the Pentagon secretly dispatched military advisers, armored personnel carriers and 400,000 rounds of ammunition to put down the 1973 takeover of the small South Dakota town of Wounded Knee by approximately 200 members of the American Indian Movement. That the insurrection came in response to numerous beatings and murders perpetrated by the administration of Dick Wilson, the FBI-supported chairman of the Oglala Sioux Tribal Council on the Pine Ridge Reservation, would not be widely known for some time. In the meantime, the full extent of the FBI's abuses were already coming to light.

The 1975-76 hearings by a committee chaired by Sen. Frank Church (D-Idaho) revealed that another of America's cherished ideals—that a democracy should avoid the temptation to maintain a secret police force—had been a trifle optimistic. Though it had been long known that the FBI under J. Edgar Hoover had used its investigative powers to pass sensitive information about progressive leaders such as Martin Luther King Jr to political allies, the sheer breadth of these activities were finally, if briefly, glimpsed in the Church Committee's findings. However, revelations about warrantless wiretaps and the secret opening of private citizens' mail by the FBI were quickly overshadowed by those of the CIA's attempts to assassinate world leaders—another American "we don't do that" quickly bit the dust.

Yet the Church Committee finding that caused the most outrage among civil rights and anti-war activists back home was the revelation of the FBI's counter-intelligence program (COINTELPRO). Though it would be years before its implications were fully realized, the bullet points alone were astounding. Begun in 1956, the program saw the FBI conduct "a sophisticated vigilante operation aimed squarely at preventing the exercise of First Amendment rights of speech and association, on the theory that preventing the growth of dangerous groups and the propagation of dangerous ideas would protect the national security and deter violence," according to the report.

The **JANUARY** issue of the *National Lampoon* features the image of a black-and-white dog called "Cheeseface" with a gun pointed at his head, accompanied by the headline "If You Don't Buy This Magazine, We'll Kill This Dog." Three years later the offices of the *National Lampoon* received word that somebody had tracked the dog to the farm where he lived and shot him.

Through illegal surveillance, smear campaigns, wrongful arrests (often using local law enforcement), and the planting of agent provocateurs and informers, the FBI targeted subversive groups such as the Black Panther and Socialist Workers parties. The results were devastating. In addition to assisting with a wave of political murders (the 1969 killing of Black Panther national spokesman Fred Hampton in Chicago perhaps the most infamous), the FBI also sewed enough discord within groups to cause their members to kill each other, and occasionally, themselves. It seems the nation was only spared further abuses by the death of "FBI Director for life" Hoover in 1972, though President Richard Nixon wasn't averse to using the bureau to get his way. After all this, his 1974 resignation over the Watergate affair seemed almost quaint by comparison.

Political killings of the '60s (including those of Fred Hampton, left, and Robert F Kennedy) cast a long shadow over the '70s.

It was from this chaos that the men and women who would bring forth *Soap* sprang.

'I Don't Want to Fight for This'

Some people, despite going on to achieve great things, never really got over the tumult of the 1960s.

"Our band was supposed to play the Ambassador Hotel the night that Bobby Kennedy was shot" in 1968, remembers *Soap* director JD Lobue of his days with the band The Gordian Knot, fronted by "Midnight Train to Georgia" songwriter Jim Weatherly. "But because we had gotten another paying job, we decided to take that instead. I was listening to the election results from the California Primary. While we were on stage we were between songs and I heard that he had been shot [at the Ambassador Hotel], and we just walked off stage. And that's when I dropped out of politics for a long time."

The Gordian Knot performed for the likes of Natalie Wood and Robert Wagner, Robert Mitchum, Richard Harris, James Coburn and others. They also toured with The Dave Clark Five and shared the bill with The Byrds, The Mamas and Papas, and others. (Future *Soap* Director JD Lobue is pictured at top of photo above.)

Adding to his disillusionment: the rate at which America was burning through its young men for its conflict in Vietnam. Fresh out of college, Lobue faced being shipped out shortly. Desperate, he told his manager, "I don't want to fight for this." His manager referred him to famed four-star Air Force general and head of Strategic Air Command Curtis LeMay. "I got on the phone with LeMay and he says, 'Well son, here's what I think you should do. Join the Air Force.' I said, 'But I'm trying to avoid getting into combat.' He says, 'This is the best way for you to at least direct your own future—join the Air Force. You won't be in combat in the infantry.' And I'm thinking this guy is crazy! To try to avoid military service by joining the military didn't seem viable to me."

Six weeks before he was due to report to the draft board, Lobue received a deferment after marrying his first wife, who had two children from a previous marriage. "So that kept me from being killed in the jungles of Vietnam."

Actor Billy Crystal (*Soap*'s Jodie Dallas) had his own brush with the draft in 1970, he told Oprah Winfrey in the June 2004 issue of *O, The Oprah Magazine*. "I was dying: My life could be decided by Defense Secretary Melvin Laird, with 365 ping-pong balls and a hopper. The first 200 numbers called: Goodbye, you're goin' to 'Nam. By the time I got home that day, the first hundred had been called. I dialed Mom and said, 'What happened with the lottery?' She said, 'There's a two-hour *Bonanza* on. I didn't see it.' Later I was watching *The Joe Franklin Show*, and they were running a ticker tape of the lottery numbers. I was free. I'd just been offered a permanent teaching job on Long Island, but I didn't take it. Instead, I called two friends and said, 'Let's form a comedy group.'

Soap Director JD Lobue

Others did not dodge the bullet so easily.

During the Spring of 1969, a young University of California-Davis student named Sal Viscuso (later to become *Soap*'s Father Timothy Flotsky) was dealing with more than the usual opening-night jitters in the green room while waiting to go on in a production of *The Madwoman of Chaillot*. It was the same night that the latest set of draft lottery numbers were being drawn; he received No. 24.

"Low 20s were really bad numbers, meaning you were likely to get drafted," he remembers. "So I started to panic."

The following year, as he began his graduate work at the New York University School of the Arts, he found himself sorting through the 12 character references he'd managed to solicit from people in order to apply for conscientious objector status.

"My dad and I stopped talking because he felt that I was unpatriotic," Viscuso admits. "He had served in World War II in the amphibious division; he would get down in the ocean in the South Pacific and defuse all those bombs. So he was a hero, and he thought I was a coward. And I remember hanging up the phone on him in the fall of '70 knowing that I had my life on the line, and that it didn't matter that he didn't get me. I had an envelope of 12 letters from people who did, who knew who I was and who I'd become in my dad's absence. I remember sending him the packet, and later going to the bulletin board at NYU and seeing a note: 'Call your father.' In that conversation we reconciled and he said he was going to support me any way he could."

In one of the most surreal aspects of the draft, young men saw their lives decided on television by the selection of ping-pong balls from a hopper...by people not subject to the draft.

Vietnam wasn't just an abstract boogeyman to Viscuso; it had already destroyed the life of a cousin who returned from service in 1968 at the age of 19. Irony of irony, the actor was playing a clueless Nazi soldier in Bertolt Brecht's antiwar play *Schweik in the Second World War* when he learned what had happened. "I got a call from Pauly in New York saying I'm back home. He told me that he'd been blinded when he was shot. I went berserk, pretty much destroyed the apartment. I have no memory of how I got on stage that night, let alone how I did that last performance. That really got to me. Whether you know it or not, it transforms you. You either become a coward or you say, 'Go fuck yourselves! Fuck you! You are not taking me!'"

Facing what seemed certain death or maiming for no particular reason, men of draft age had established a type of underground railroad peopled by doctors and psychiatrists who appreciated the insanity of it all, and knew how to improve one's chances of escaping the system. "The draft counselor taught me how to buy time," says Viscuso. "Don't send in the appeal until the 29th day, then send

1974

FEB 2 Media heiress Patty Hearst, 19, is kidnapped from her home by members of the American terrorist group the Symbionese Liberation Army. After being subjected to rape and abuse by the group, she participates in a series of SLA actions until her September 1975 arrest.

NOV 13 Union activist and chemical technician Karen Silkwood dies in a one-car accident after leaking information about dangerous conditions at the Kerr-McGee nuclear plant in Oklahoma to *The New York Times*.

it overnight mail so they get it on the 30th and it buys you another 30 days. So I went without eating sometimes—I spent money on postage with return receipts and all that."

After being told by a shrink that "you're a different kind of crazy" from the one the government would reject for service, Viscuso turned to a sympathetic physician who suggested making himself physically unfit for duty.

During the summer of 1971, while working at the Hunt's ketchup cannery in California's San Joaquin Valley in the blazing heat, "I would drop these giant cans of tomato juice on my too-small, squeezed-tight tennis shoes and spray my feet with water with these high pressure hoses they used to clean out the tanks." It worked. And it cost him.

"I had my foot wrapped up in a plastic bag, I hadn't washed it in a week. In the waiting room where the physical was going to be, people moved away from me because my foot smelled so bad. I was totally straight with [the examining doctor]. He said you realize you have to get this operated on, we really can't do anything with you. I drove back to Davis that night, took a bath—the nail fell off by itself. Needless to say I had already won the deferment and I got out. I was used to adversity. I survived Catholic school, survived a broken family, I survived the army being after me for five years."

In September 1979, within weeks of Viscuso leaving *Soap*, his cousin Pauly shot himself in Chicago; he was 30. "He couldn't take it anymore. He'd been blind 11 years and I hadn't been here to get his call. In the fall of '69, a year after he was blinded, he called me, and in the course of that conversation I realized that he was in a bad way. My college roommates kept me up all night till we could call a priest the next morning to go to his house. But 10 years later, I didn't know that he'd been trying to reach me. That stuff gets under your skin, do you understand? It makes you determined to not capitulate."

The '70s on American Television

Meanwhile, American television reflected none of this. You could still smile along with the down-home doings in *The Andy Griffith*

Show's Mayberry thanks to the follow-up series *Mayberry RFD* (though Sheriff Andy Taylor and Opie were strangely absent). *The Beverly Hillbillies* continued to butt hayseeds with city slickers, and *The Brady Bunch*, God love 'em, were still wrestling with grave societal issues such as tattling and bullies.

It was bland fare to be sure, but American television had always been so by design. Throughout the '50s and '60s, networks had launched a plethora of shows designed to gather the broadest audiences possible, refusing to run the risk of offending anybody. Yet, by the end of the 1960s, advertisers were increasingly anxious to reach younger, sophisticated big city audiences. Though shows such as *Green Acres* and *The Beverly Hillbillies* were pulling in healthy ratings for CBS, then-executive Fred Silverman pulled the plug on them and others, freeing up room on the schedule for a slew of modern replacements.

On Jan. 12, 1971, CBS unveiled Norman Lear's *All in the Family*, a controversial series that in many ways was *Soap*'s twin. While *All in the Family* would seldom push the boat out sexually (though it delved into everything from impotence to abortion), its cutting wit and willingness to address widely held prejudices put audiences, advertisers and competing networks on notice: compromises were going to be few and far between.

From then on, all the networks put their old-guard series to sleep and set their sights instead on edgy entertainment. *All in the Family* begat *Maude* in 1972, which joined the premiere of *M*A*S*H*, also on CBS. Over on NBC, Lear and production partner Bud Yorkin launched *Sanford & Son* that same year. This was pretty much the first American series to feature a mostly black cast exploring modern situations, followed by *Maude* spin-off *Good Times* in 1974. Before the decade was over, American TV would be invaded by the fetishistic fantasy *Wonder Woman* (1975), the sexy PIs of *Charlie's Angels* (1976), and the prime time adult situations on *Dallas* (1978).

In many ways, *All in the Family* was *Soap*'s twin, though it reaped kinder reviews.

If this was all a bit much to absorb for the typical American family, the shift toward more frank discussions and depictions of sex, race

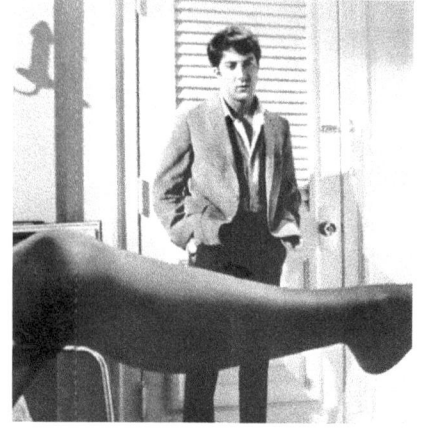
The Graduate (1967)

and modern life were perfectly in keeping with developments in the rest of the cultural landscape. If anything, television was still a little shy. At the local cinema, the 1960s had begun with unchallenging outings such as *The Nutty Professor* (1963) and *Mary Poppins* (1964), only to slide off the rails with the likes of *Rosemary's Baby* and *The Graduate* (both 1967), and *Midnight Cowboy* (1969, written by *Soap* actress Jennifer Salt's father, Waldo). By the 1970s, the gloves were off completely. There was everything from the classic eroticism of *Last Tango in Paris* (1972) and *Caligula* (1979) to the grindhouse depravity of *I Spit on Your Grave* (1978) and *The Last House on the Left* (1972). On the book rack: *The Sensuous Woman* (1971) kept company with *The Stepford Wives* (1972).

In fact, every artistic medium had grown up a bit... with the exception of television. Surely the small screen could drop the veil ever so slightly, network executives thought. They would learn better soon enough.

The Family Friendly Viewing Hour

In the late fall of 1975, American television slipped down a rabbit hole that was as inevitable in a nation with such a stubborn puritanical streak as it was shortsighted, and ultimately, short lived.

> "What we are trying to do is not to offend the most uptight parent that we can imagine watching with his children."
> —DICK KIRSCHNER, CBS's West Coast program practices chief.

After years of viewer dissatisfaction with ever increasing amounts of sex and violence on television, Congress finally leaned on the Federal Communications Commission, which in turn leaned on the networks to clean up their acts. Fearing potential government regulation, the National Association of Broadcasters adopted "the Family Viewing Policy," which prohibited the airing of "entertainment programming inappropriate for viewing by a general family audience" between the hours of 7 p.m. and 9 p.m. ET.

One of the first problems to present itself was the fact that the people who worked for the networks' "standards and practices" departments—those that dealt with programming complaints—had no guidelines to pass along to writers and producers. The US Supreme Court had famously gotten away with an amorphous definition of obscenity ("I know it when I see it" said Justice Potter Stewart about 1964's *Jacobellis v. Ohio*), but the networks could not afford to be so vague. Broadcasters had been spared federal regulation by the Family Viewing Policy—nobody wanted to jeopardize that by airing something that could inflame the public. Yet no one was sure where the boundaries of "family viewing" were.

Even more problematic, pre-existing programs also had to live up to these new standards. *Rhoda*, the immensely popular *Mary Tyler Moore Show* spin-off launched on CBS the previous year, saw Valerie Harper's title character dealing with the challenges of being a new wife. It was one of the first programs to brush up against the "Family" ceiling.

Shortly after being assured by CBS Vice President for Programs Fred Silverman that *Rhoda* wouldn't have to make any changes now that it had moved from 9:30 to the 8 p.m. Family Hour slot, the creative team was confronted by the network's Program Practices department, and *they* wanted changes. According to Geoffrey Cowan's excellent 1978 book *See No Evil*, *Rhoda* writer Allan Burns was told simply, "No matter what the Program Department told you, you can't get away with everything you did last year." (Later that year, Silverman would leave CBS to become president of entertainment for rival ABC, and chief corporate architect of *Soap*.)

The new policy turned network executives against producers, producers against writers, and networks against each other. Nearly every aspect of television programming was affected, from syndication deals to program story lines. How exactly did you measure what was "inappropriate"? To be on the safe side, networks moved any programs that could be considered potentially violent to 9 p.m. and later. Yet, once violent programming had been resettled south of the 8 o'clock hour, there was no place left for even slightly challenging (read: socially relevant) comedies to go.

Under the Family Viewing Policy, *Rhoda*'s writers were told "you can't get away with everything you did last year."

Soap's Mother, *Fay*

In 1975, the Family Viewing Policy destroyed creations great and banal in equal measure. While the US began the year with its first

continued on page **26**

The Mom Who Said She Could Write Better TV... *and Did*

There's always been a satisfying symmetry to the idea that Susan Harris, the television writer who challenged attitudes about the American family was, herself, the head of that longtime conservative boogeyman: a one-parent household. You can practically hear the television executives of the day posing the question: How can a single mother ever relate to the idea of "family friendly viewing"?

Born in Manhattan, Susan Spivak moved to Mount Vernon, NY, at 3, brought up by an accountant and a homemaker. Right from the beginning she saw what society had in mind for her.

"I was a child of the '50s, so there wasn't that much expected of girls. You were expected to get married and have children; a career was not even discussed. Generally, daughters were told to become teachers until you got married and had children."

Though she majored in English literature at Cornell University, and later at NYU, she wrote no more than the average young person, summing up her output as "Little poems and tortured diaries in college."

Around 1964 she moved to Los Angeles and married actor Berkeley Harris (*The Virginian*, *Texas*) the following year. Two years later they had a son, Sam. But, as she confided to the audience at her Hall of Fame induction speech in 2011, "In the late '60s I was very fortunate—my husband left me for another woman. An actress." By 1969 they had divorced.

Secretarial work was just about the only thing she could find to pay the bills initially, but she knew it wasn't work that she could rely on indefinitely. "I was a single mother, I had a 2 year old and no money, or money that was going to run out very, very quickly, and I had to do something. I didn't want to leave my son in day care.

"One night I was watching television and thought, 'I can do that.' I got some scripts, just to see the form, and with a friend picked a show that seemed to have the loosest structure."

That show was 1969's *Then Came Bronson*, an NBC action series starring Michael Parks as a man who ditches his job as newspaper reporter to seek out the meaning of life exploring America on his Harley. Parks' *Bronson* became another in a long tradition of TV characters—e.g., *The Millionaire* (1955-1960), *The Incredible Hulk* (1977-1982)—who do little more than act as agents of change for the people they meet.

Not only did it have the loosest structure on television, *Then Came Bronson* had an additional attraction for Harris. Her writing partner—future actress Lisabeth Hush—"knew the creator of that series, who gave our spec script to the producer. It just so happened they were desperate for a script for their last show."

Harris didn't have too far to look for a story idea. When her son had been about 6 months old, she had been taking night classes at UCLA in short-story writing; one of the stories she came up with became the basis for the TV script she and Hush wrote.

Writing partner Lisbeth Hush in *The Virginian*.

The sale of that episode, "The Ninety-Nine Mile Circle" (for $4,500, according to a 1978 *New York Times* piece), was enough to land Harris her first agent. After that, she met "Garry Marshall who really helped me in learning the comedy form, and got me my first job on *Love American Style*. They decided to take a chance on me because I was untested as far as comedy went." Marshall, creator of such TV hits as *Happy Days* and *Laverne & Shirley*, promised the producers that if her script was unusable, he'd rewrite it. "I wrote one for them, then they asked for 10 more. That was it. It really *was* that easy—I was very lucky." »

» Luck occasionally gets you in the door, but in Hollywood it rarely sustains you for long if you don't have some brains and terrier-like tenacity to back it up.

Learning at the Side of the Master

If the management at ABC was somehow whisked off to see Christmases past ala Scrooge, doubtless they would cry out in horror the moment they glimpsed fledgling television writer Susan Harris meeting Norman Lear. The godfather of smart American situation comedy was also the future thorn in the side of CBS, the network that he'd helped to elevate to the top spot.

Though Harris doesn't recall exactly how she met Lear, she does remember that "I was invited to see the pilot of *All in the Family*. Once I saw that, that changed everything for me because this was not Shirley Jones burning the pot roast in *The Partridge Family*, this was real stuff that you could sink your teeth into; you could write *people*. And so I was asked to do an episode, and I was asked to do more, and I was asked to do *Maude* and I did that. That was a very important period for me because I could see what was possible."

She would famously write a two-part *Maude* episode in November 1972 in which the 47-year-old title character (Bea Arthur) considers getting an abortion, but that sober premise belies the writer's humorous, and more importantly, human, approach. Maude's "liberated" grown-up daughter, Carol (Adrienne Barbeau), tries to convince her mother that she doesn't have to have the baby if it's not something she wants to do.

Maude is convinced her husband, Walter (Bill Macy), wants the child, when in reality he doesn't but can't bear to deprive his wife of another son or daughter. (Keep an eye out for a friend of Walter's neighbor, Arthur (Conrad Bain), who sets the father-to-be straight on the merits of vasectomy—Robert "Chester Tate" Mandan.)

Though the humor is fairly low key, the attention paid to the emotions involved in such a decision is not. Even in 1972 we can see Harris refining a technique that would come to characterize the rest of her career, switching between humor and emotion from one line to the next. Toward the end of the episode, for example, Walter and Maude are playing gin rummy in bed, her husband winning easily each time, driving her nuts. The next moment they're gently admitting to each other that neither feels able to cope with raising a child at their age.

"Maude's Dilemma" aired just a few months before the landmark *Roe v. Wade* US Supreme Court decision made abortion legal. Predictably, a repeat airing could pick up no sponsors, and 39 CBS affiliate stations refused to air it.

Even at this point, Alberto-Culver, which sold everything from beauty products to food stuffs, told The Associated Press that it had a policy that prevented it from sponsoring any program "in which such controversial subjects as drug addiction, deviate sex practices and abortion are treated facetiously or as material for comedy." Proving, it seems, that they hadn't seen the episodes in question.

Though Norman Lear was used to pressure groups objecting to depictions of life as it is truly lived, this was Susan Harris' first real brush with an audience backlash. It would not be her last.

In a *New York Times* interview that same year, Carroll O'Connor psychoanalyzed his *All in the Family* character Archie Bunker. In the process, he may have come as close as anyone ever has to explaining the psychology of those who feel it their duty to object to the world they see portrayed on their televisions.

"Archie's dilemma is coping with a world that is changing in front of him. He doesn't know what to do except lose his temper, mouth his poisons, look elsewhere to fix the blame for his own discomfort. He isn't a totally evil man. He's shrewd. But he won't get to the root of his problem, because the root of his problem is himself and he doesn't know it."

Backlash against Susan Harris' *Maude* "abortion" story line was her first brush with pressure groups.

continued from page 21

ever female governor—Connecticut's Ella Grasso—a truly liberated woman was quite literally not ready for prime time.

Though relatively young, producers Tony Thomas and Paul Junger Witt had a fair number of credits to their names, having hit a grand slam with one of their first official collaborations at Screen Gems Television. The 1971 ABC TV movie *Brian's Song*, starring James Caan and Billy Dee Williams, won Witt, then 28, and screenwriter William Blinn, Emmy awards.

Thomas and Witt soon decided to strike out on their own, and hit upon reviving one of the most respected names in television: Danny Thomas Productions. "Dad's company was just lying dormant and I went to him and said I'd like to start it up, and that Paul and I would like to run it," explains Thomas. "He said great, do it. So we took what little structure there was there and tried to build the company again, and we did briefly with a couple of shows and some movies for television."

Lee Grant in *Fay*

Toward the end of their work under that company's name, Witt and Thomas hooked up with writer Susan Harris in 1975 for a little NBC series called *Fay*. Based on characters created by Harris (she was credited as writer and executive story consultant), the sitcom follows the title character (Lee Grant), an easygoing, intelligent woman in her 40s recently divorced from attorney Jack (Joe Silver), as she jumps back into the dating world. In other words, she was what the title character in *Rhoda* would become *next* year.

When NBC execs saw the pilot in February, they loved it, doubtlessly seeing it as a sexier take on *The Mary Tyler Moore Show*. By the fall, after repeatedly bashing heads with the standards and practices department over *Fay*'s suitability for its 8:30 p.m. "Family Viewing Policy friendly" time slot, they would kill it after airing just four or five episodes. If ever a show suffered from appalling timing, *Fay* was it.

"It was way ahead of its time," Grant admitted to Henry Colman in 2010 during an Archive of American Television interview. "It was like the next thing to *That Girl*."

More importantly, it was the first time Susan Harris received full rein to play in her own TV sandbox, creating the characters and coming up with story lines. Though she stuck closely to the television mores of the day, she gave both barrels to the double standards and petty injustices that have always plagued women in America.

When Fay takes her boss on a date to help get over his loneliness—though we're given little evidence to suggest anything untoward has happened—she's admonished for "dipping your pen in the company ink." In another episode, she and her ex-husband try to help their daughter, Linda, and son-in-law get over a profound disagreement about whether they should have another child. After hiding behind a professed desire to go back to school, Linda finally tells her husband that she just doesn't want another child, and that's that. To a television culture that still clung to the idea that it was 1950, this was a big deal.

Paul Junger Witt

More famously, when her friend's fiancé (played by *One Day at a Time*'s Schneider, Pat Harrington) starts coming on to her, Fay tells him, "Stop right now or I will do something unpleasant, in which case you will have to take up a whole new hobby." (Interestingly, Harrington's sudden interest in one of her scars prompts Fay to say, "Well, it happened over 36 years ago so I'm over the initial shock"—pretty much word for word what Mary Campbell will tell a randy professor about her own scar in *Soap* episode 2.8.)

Tony Thomas

On Aug. 15, 1975, a network executive sent Paul Junger Witt a letter giving him the lay of the land in the brave new world of the Family Viewing Hour. After telling him that the episodes he and Thomas felt were the strongest would have to be canned because they in some way mentioned or alluded to sex, the exec ended this way, according to Cowan's *See No Evil*:

"Paul, I cannot emphasize enough the importance of this issue. It makes no sense at all to put the most sophisticated, sexy comedy in TV history on the air if families are going to be afraid to watch it.

So for the time being, we will have to settle for just being the most sophisticated, funny comedy in TV history."

Fay, Family Viewing Hour, and the Finger

Throughout her discussion of *Fay* with Colman, Lee Grant refers to the Family Viewing Hour as "Children's Hour", a distinction that explains not only why *Fay* was caught in the crossfire of politics masquerading as conscientious programming, but also why the policy itself met such a swift end.

Had the series begun just a couple of years earlier or later, *Fay* likely would've enjoyed a short but hassle-free life. While some of its subject matter might've raised an eyebrow or two, those episodes that survive today rarely raise their head above the parapet.

Yet, on Oct. 30, 1975, *Fay* met its inevitable end. Not only had it been unable to remain utterly devoid of subject matter relevant to adults, but it also had been broadcast opposite ratings behemoth *The Waltons* on CBS.

"I walked into rehearsal...and I was evicted," Grant told Colman. "The furniture was out on the studio lot...A stage hand told me that it was canceled. And they had me set for the Johnny Carson show that night to sell the show. So I went to the Johnny Carson show and said look, I'm here but it's been canceled. What do I do? And he says let's go on. Let's do it."

Meanwhile, Sal Viscuso, one of the 8.5 million Carson viewers that night, was settling down with his wife after working hard all week on *Fay*'s 8 p.m. lead in, *The Montefuscos*. "And as Lee Grant came on, they blanked out half the screen because she was flipping off Marvin Antonowsky who was the head of NBC at the time, telling him to fuck off for taking off her show," Viscuso remembers. Grant, in turn, blamed *The Montefuscos* in part for her show's cancellation, he says. "And while we're watching this around a quarter to 12, we get a call from the [*Montefuscos*] producers in LA. It was Bill Persky saying I've got bad news, *we* were canceled. It was horrible."

Dinah Manoff—Grant's daughter and *Soap*'s "Elaine Lefkowitz"— remembers that night very well. "I always remember my mom

> " I don't see *Soap* being a knee-jerk reaction to *Fay*, it just was that Fred [Silverman] widened the field and said go for it."
>
> —TONY THOMAS, Executive Producer

going on Johnny Carson and flipping off the network; I remember that really clearly. I also remember her loving the job, I mean really having a great time. She enjoyed it and loved Susan and Paul."

As Grant told Colman of her bird flippage, "It was a tremendous relief. So much better than my pulling over to the side of the road and crying, to have the opportunity to say these fools did such and such and such, and do you know what I feel about them? So it was over, and over in a very healthy, fun way."

Lee Grant and the Spirit of Defiance

By this time, Grant of all people knew just how petty and vindictive Hollywood could be. In 1951, just one day after she said at a memorial service that the House Un-American Activities Committee (HUAC) had hounded co-worker J. Edward Bromberg into suffering the heart attack that killed him, the twentysomething actress was blacklisted from working in television and film (with just a few exceptions) for the next 12 years. Though a courageous agreement between Actor's Equity and stage producers allowed blacklisted actors to work in theater, Grant only performed on stage in about one production a year, with the rest of her time devoted to raising husband Arnold Manoff's two sons from a previous marriage (and later their daughter, Dinah), and teaching at the Herbert Berghof Studio in New York. As a result, "the Golden age of television passed me right by," she told Colman.

Just one day after speaking at the memorial service of actor J. Edward Bromberg (center), Lee Grant found herself blacklisted.

Well into the 1960s, when the U.S. government was decrying the horrors of the neighbor-snitching-on-neighbor culture in East Germany, HUAC was reaching the tail end of its own Stasi-like campaign of terror. Even with that public face of red baiting, Sen. Joseph McCarthy, dead since 1957, his House counterparts still refused to let go of Grant. As far as she knew, her only company on the blacklist by that time was character actor Morris Carnovsky and actress Uta Hagen. Only when she testified against her husband would HUAC let her off the hook. As she told Colman, "I don't give a shit about acting if acting means I have to turn in somebody. I don't care. I've got a life. I've got a great life. And the battle meant more to me than acting ever would."

✱ Like *Soap* and *Fay*, Metalious' best-selling novel was pilloried more for the media's portrayal of this story about small town life than for the raciness of the book itself.

It was only a year later when HUAC asked a favor of Nat Lefkowitz, head of the William Morris Agency at the time and an ally of Grant's, that they agreed to strike her from the blacklist. The next week she returned to television and film, only to find that she had to prove herself all over again; 12 years is a lifetime in the public eye.

In 1964, with a 6-year-old Dinah to support, Grant reluctantly gave up acting in one of Joseph Papp's "Shakespeare in the Park" productions in Central Park to take the role of Stella Chernak in *Peyton Place*,* the ABC television series based on Grace Metalious' scandalous 1956 novel. It was this role that would land Grant her first Emmy win just two years later.

By then, the original novel had been out for nearly 10 years, and the once-shocking story had been massaged into banal respectability by a dull 1957 movie starring Lana Turner, with Hope Lange playing the role Grant would (with some alterations) in the series. After suffering the national ignominy of the blacklists, it was nice to be recognized for her work in *Peyton Place*, which had become something of a national obsession, airing three days a week. When she was later offered the title role in *Fay*, things at last seemed to be finally going Grant's way.

As she put it on that episode of Carson later, "That's life and death on television in the Family Hour, folks. And I just want you to know it because I left 12 crying actors." Whether or not that included herself we may never know.

After the smoke had cleared, Harris, Witt and Thomas were still trying to understand what had happened to their little modern comedy about a divorcee figuring it all out.

"In *Fay* we broke ground, having a woman who's divorced," says Harris. "We took a lot of heat from the network about a single woman having an affair, so we broke ground then, and we just continued to do that on *Soap* later. In other words, we always spoke to a certain reality of life that had not been touched at all on television. Television's consciousness was way behind life at that time."

Meanwhile, the Family Viewing Policy would be quashed by US District Court Judge Warren Ferguson in 1976. He thought the FCC had overstepped its bounds by convincing the networks to create their stringent rules to avoid regulation. The policy would be completely scrapped by the fall of 1977; fortuitous timing for Witt, Thomas and Harris' next group project: *Soap*. Still, the wounds from their experiences on *Fay* would take a while to heal.

"*Fay* was heartbreaking," Paul Junger Witt admits. "It was a show that we deeply believed in and felt we had executed well, and felt, had we been given more time, and been able to make a couple of adjustments, we could have ultimately been quite successful. We were yanked, we felt, kind of quickly. Now producers and writers always feel that way, and networks have difficult decisions to make. We were grown-ups and we understood that."

Perhaps most heartbreaking of all is the fact that this sitcom that first showed the world what the Witt Thomas Harris triumvirate could do has been all but lost. Though a few episodes were taped by viewers during its run and passed from collector to collector over the years, *Fay* has never received a proper home video release. The masters, if they still exist, are probably locked away somewhere in the storage rooms of Danny Thomas Productions, says Tony Thomas. A last, posthumous victory for the short-lived Family Viewing Hour.

Television Loosens up...a Bit

However traumatic the demise of *Fay* had been, the one thing of which producers Witt and Thomas were certain was that they wanted to work with writer Susan Harris again. In the meantime, the pair returned to the TV-movie genre that had brought them such success with *Brian's Song*, and soon realized that despite the Family Viewing Hour fiasco, television was growing up.

"There was a progression that one could look at through movies of the week, which were at their peak at that time; boundaries were being pushed dramatically," Witt remembers. "I don't mean the push was dramatic but dramas, especially long-form miniseries and movies of the week, were expanding the material and controversial issues that could be covered."

As early as 1972, ABC had been the first network to give the country a sympathetic portrayal of homosexuality with *That Certain*

ABC's TV movie *That Certain Summer* (1972) featured one of the first sympathetic portrayals of homosexuality on U.S. television.

Summer, a TV movie starring Hal Holbrook as a divorced father who lives with his lover (Martin Sheen). The following year, the television adaptation of *Go Ask Alice*, the controversial tale of a teen girl who gets mixed up in sex and drugs, was also screened as an ABC Movie of the Week. It wasn't just the TV-movie format offering unprecedented creative freedom, either, it was the networks.

Despite a puritanical streak that was still wrestling with the idea that you could show one mattress in the bedroom of a married couple on television without having society crumble, America's airwaves had loosened up considerably by the 1970s. This was due in large part to the increased competition between the three major networks, which found themselves vying for ad revenues that seemed to know no bounds. To capture the greatest number of eyeballs, and thus command the highest advertising rates, the networks continually tried to push the envelope without the public crying foul.

Born Innocent (1974) is thought to be the TV movie that spawned the Family Viewing Hour.

In 1974, NBC aired a daring TV movie about the horrors of a reform school for girls called *Born Innocent*. Though conceived as a stark but responsible glimpse into an important and little discussed part of life, the movie quickly became infamous for its harsh depictions of violence, particularly the explicit on-screen-rape-by-broom-handle of the main character, played by a 15-year-old Linda Blair. It had been one thing to see the actress possessed by a pea-soup-spewing demon in *The Exorcist* the year before, but for the viewing public at 8 p.m. on a Tuesday night, this was clearly too much. As the newspaper ads proclaimed, "She's a woman in prison. She's 14 years old. She's learning fast what you have to learn to survive there." NBC, too, after hundreds of withering phone calls and the horrible discovery that the rape scene may have inspired a copycat crime in San Francisco with victims aged 9 and 7, learned fast. (*Born Innocent* is largely thought to have been the production that spawned the Family Viewing Policy the following year.)

However, NBC, ABC and CBS continued their quest to produce "must see TV". ABC already had a track record of exploring the road less traveled. Not only did it spin-off one of the most controversial novels for television (*Peyton Place*, 1964-69), but it also produced the first supernatural soap opera (*Dark Shadows*, 1966-71). And with the introduction of the ABC Movie of the Week in 1969, it popularized the long-form television program with such classics as Steven Spielberg's first feature, *Duel* (1971), and that year's aforementioned *Brian's Song*.

Meanwhile in 1971 at CBS, the network's new head of programming, Fred Silverman, replaced lowest-common-denominator programming such as *Hee Haw*, *The Beverly Hillbillies* and *Mayberry RFD* with innovative shows like *M*A*S*H*, *The Mary Tyler Moore Show*, and most importantly, *All in the Family*.

In an industry that manufactures "legends" with the frequency that China pumps out widgets, Silverman was, and remains, the real deal. To date the only person to have held executive positions at all three major networks, Silverman was snapped up by CBS shortly after getting his master's degree from Ohio State University, and never looked back. In 1975, he jumped ship to ABC where he became president of entertainment, and proceeded to take that network to the top of the ratings with sexy new shows like *Charlie's Angels* (1976-81) and *Three's Company* (1977-84). Advertisers had recently begun to move from wanting to attract as many viewers as possible to hankering after 18 to 24 year olds, and Silverman's new shows delivered. After the launch of *Three's Company* in March 1977, while news magazines were busy debating the merits and debasements posed by what quickly came to be known as "jiggle TV", Silverman knew something that only a few other people in the world knew: ABC was developing a series that would make the adventures of Jack Tripper & Co. seem like a school play in comparison.

Fred Silverman, the only person to have held executive positions at all three major networks.

'This is the Story of Two Sisters...'

Ever since *Fay*, a ritual had developed around the home of Susan Harris. Nights and weekends she, Paul Junger Witt and Tony Thomas would work around her kitchen table.

"For me it was wonderful because I had a young child and I could be at home," she remembers. "We did a lot of our finest work around the kitchen table." It was around that table that the idea for *Soap* began to form. Before the characters, before any of the plots, what occurred to her first was the appeal of writing one long, continuous story.

"I did not want to be tied to the sitcom format," she says; creating a conflict and resolution in a 22-minute, three-act structure can be excruciating week after week. "I said to Paul and Tony, how about we do something that's a continuing saga? And that's where it started. Then we came up with the idea of the two sisters and the two families and their differences, and it evolved."

No matter how many characters came and went, *Soap* would always focus on its heart: two sisters, Mary (Cathryn Damon) and Jessica (Katherine Helmond).

While *Soap* would grow to include one of the largest casts in television history, it was the relationship of sisters Jessica Tate and Mary Campbell that would serve as the cornerstone of the series. In hindsight, it might have been the disintegration of that relationship that helped to hasten *Soap's* untimely demise.

By this point, the producers both knew that whatever type of series their new project turned out to be, "Susan was the only one who could put it on the page," says Thomas. In 1976 they had formed a new production company—Witt Thomas Harris—and realized that whatever first emerged from its doors would be what Hollywood judged them on now, no matter how successful they had been in the past. It's that kind of town.

"This was our flagship, so we had never done anything in our careers that was more important to us," says Witt. "We had this extraordinary working relationship amongst the three of us. I don't know if you've seen this thing that's been all over the Internet, the twins speaking their own language—we were kind of triplets that had their own comedic language. We understood each other to an extraordinary degree. We had different strengths but we complemented each other. We all had the same goal, we all understood our characters and loved them, and we all brought a perspective to it."

✽ As Carsey-Werner Productions (beginning in 1983), the pair would produce a string of television hits including *The Cosby Show, Roseanne* and *That '70s Show*.

Recalls Silverman, "When the idea for *Soap* was presented to me by Marcy Carsey and Tom Werner*, who were running comedy at

> 31.
>
> BENSON
>
> Benson, who knows everything about everyone in the Tate family due to his persistant eavesdropping on the kitchen phone, does his best to hold the Tate family together although he is forever asking himself why. He personally supervises the settling in of Noyen Nu and little Joey Nu Tate in the Tate household. They revive his hope that David Tate might still be alive. But Benson is soon faced with problems in his own family. His daughter, Ruby, moves to New York from New Orleans. Ruby's mother, an octoroon, who left Benson before the birth of their daughter, raised Ruby as white and never told her that she herself, and her father were in fact, black. Benson is faced with a dilemma when he discovers that his daughter is engaged

A peek at the 36-page *Soap* "bible" the producers wrote for ABC (including some plot points that never made it to air).

ABC Entertainment for the network, I just thought it was terrific. I knew of Susan Harris' work for Norman Lear on *Maude*. Those were really cute, novel concepts with a first-rate comedy writer and creator, which is a hell of a combination."

The trio quickly produced a 36-page document outlining the history of the Tates and the Campbells, including the secrets each member of the families was concealing, and what might happen in the first five years of the series. (This "*Soap* bible" is a fascinating combination of series blueprint and whimsical storytelling, sometimes reflecting keen psychological insights and a high-schooler's sense of humor in the same sentence.)

"Once [Silverman] saw that bible he said great," says Thomas. "So we took that bible and went with it, but we were always thinking 'go past it, don't do the expected.' Certainly as a team it was our nature. Susan did the abortion show on *Maude*, she was always pushing. And Paul and I are as rebellious as one can be, at least in those days. We would want to do something different, so it was in our nature to push the envelope."

Silverman says he took the *Soap* concept to Fred Pierce, president of ABC Television at the time. "But it didn't require much selling. He loved the show as much as I did. I think everybody recognized that this was a quality effort and that we should move forward with it."

Yet, just as with the flap over NBC's *Born Innocent*, it's difficult to understand why the producers—who had been gutted two years earlier over the cancellation of the only-slightly-racy *Fay*—didn't foresee the controversy that would plague the completely irreverent *Soap*.

"I don't know," Harris says honestly. "First of all it was a different network and a different time. And ABC just loved the idea, they loved the scripts, and took a real chance on us."

How big a chance would become clear soon enough.

Laying the Groundwork

Meetings around Susan Harris' kitchen table grew less frequent the closer *Soap* moved toward production at ABC Television Center in Hollywood, though the writer worked at home as often as possible to keep an eye on her son.

"The three of us talked about everything that she was going to write fairly thoroughly before she wrote," Tony Thomas remembers. "She would say 'I got it, I got it!' Otherwise we would pitch jokes together; we would talk about the dynamics of the scene. On *Soap*, because we were really new and we were really spending days and days and days together just talking about big series arcs and big character arcs, it was a collaboration of the three of us coming up with the potential for humor, and lots of times actual jokes she would jot down. But in the end, without Susan crafting it all into those scripts, we had nothing."

While Harris wrote, Witt and Thomas "were just collecting paychecks and leaving early," deadpans the former, neatly demonstrating who had the driest wit in the production office.

One of the people who saw the trio craft *Soap* from the very beginning was Harris' secretary, and later *Soap*'s associate producer, Marsha Posner (now Marsha Posner Williams).

"She would handwrite her scenes and then hand them to me to type up in the proper format, so I would be the first person to read what this incredible writer had written, which was just joyful for me," says Posner. A driven woman with an almost computer-like memory—she remains the go-to person for sorting out what hap-

Tony Thomas (left), Marsha Posner and Carl Lauten staging a scene during Season 1.

pened 36 years ago on *Soap*—Posner knew first-hand what it was like to make a name for yourself as a woman in an age when you were more likely to be handed a coffee cup to refill than a decent paycheck.

Born and raised in Scottsdale, Ariz., Posner first drove to LA around 1972, "and within 24 hours I was back in Phoenix. I was scared to death, I didn't know what to do, I didn't know anybody. I stayed two or three more weeks, I came to Hollywood, I lasted two weeks and I went back to Arizona."

Back home, her ability to type 120 words a minute landed her several job offers for secretarial work. After some soul searching, she returned to Hollywood for a third time, her first two years there being some of the most harrowing she had known—sleeping in her car was not unknown to her. While earning a few dollars dancing with men for money (and no, that's not a euphemism—oh the innocent '70s), one of her co-workers told her about an indie film she was working on. *If You Don't Stop It... You'll Go Blind* (1975) was little more than a string of dirty jokes, but somebody needed to write them up. For the next two years "all I did was read and type jokes for a living because they made a *second* movie."

A few weeks after she quit that job, someone called from the office of Danny Thomas Productions asking her to fill in as secretary for four weeks for Steve Gordon, creator of Thomas' show at the time,

✳ Among other things, Denoff and producing partner Bill Persky were involved with everything from The Dick Van Dyke Show to That Girl.

The Practice. "She said can you start Monday for $200 a week plus overtime? I hung up the phone, I called my father and said guess what, I've made it! I'm going to MGM Studios—Danny Thomas!"

Though she hated secretarial work, Posner managed to make such a good impression on Gordon that after the four weeks, she became secretary to *The Practice*'s executive producer, industry legend Sam Denoff.* Three months later, *The Practice* was canceled.

"The producers of the show were Paul Witt and Tony Thomas," says Posner. "And Tony said I know you got a layoff notice from MGM but forget it, you're coming with us. They moved into offices at 20th Century Fox and we did seven episodes of a show called *Loves Me, Loves Me Not*. That didn't work. The next thing I know, we're casting for the pilot of *Soap*."

Kip Gilman and Susan Dey in *Loves Me, Loves Me Not*

One of the perks of being Susan Harris' secretary was being the first to see her words on the page. During the day Posner was frequently reminded just how close she was to the writer's office. "Sometime's I'd be typing and I'd start laughing, and she'd run out and say, 'What are you laughing at?!'"

This desperation to know which parts of her script had worked speaks to an aspect of Harris' personality that has often been held up as a contradiction by journalists over the years. As a TV Guide reporter put it in a 1980 piece: "*Soap* being one of the loonier shows on TV, I expected its creator to be more fun. But Susan Harris seems bound up, terribly serious, almost grim." Yet this seriousness is perfectly in keeping with her character, and that of most successful satirists, such as her longtime role model Paddy Chayefsky*. To successfully write about the human condition, even humorously, you have to take the accompanying quirks seriously—you have to give a shit.

✳ Chayefsky is best remembered today for his screenplay for the 1976 movie *Network* ("I'm mad as hell and I'm not going to take it anymore"). All of his films tackled the pathos of everyday life with a bittersweet humor.

"I'm funny on paper; I'm not particularly funny in person," Harris admits. "When *Soap* became a hit, I remember one luncheon we had. After the lunch, the head of Sony or Columbia or whatever called my agent and said, 'She's not funny.' They sat next to me and they were really disappointed. People had those expectations. They would see *Soap* and they would figure I would be a barrel of laughs and that was just never the case, so I was just constantly disappointing people."

It was this dichotomy in Harris' approach to life and work that gave her scripts the ability to, as Posner puts it, "make you laugh and make you cry in the space of two minutes like nobody's business."

Once the script for the pilot was completed (sometime during the first two months of 1977), most of the cast and crew were assembled. It would be shot around March, Ted Wass estimates.

By far one of the biggest "gets" for the new series was director Jay Sandrich. With more than 20 years of television experience, including working on roughly two-thirds of *The Mary Tyler Moore Show*'s seven-year run, he was one of the most respected directors in the business. Though everyone who worked with Sandrich on *Soap* loves him to this day, most say that he seldom suffered fools gladly; he had a schedule to keep and you weren't leaving the set until he got what he wanted.

Jay Sandrich (right), holding his 1973 Emmy for his work on *The Mary Tyler Moore Show*, was one of *Soap*'s biggest "gets".

Sandrich had worked briefly with Witt Thomas Harris the season before on a pilot (long lost to memory) which, like most pilots, didn't get picked up to series. By the time *Soap* was starting up, *The Mary Tyler Moore Show* was winding down.

"They'd asked me to do Betty White's show*—she is one of my favorite people in the whole world—but the script wasn't ready and I got the *Soap* script. I had to make a decision; it was very hard to leave [Mary Tyler Moore's production company] MTM. It was particularly hard to say to Betty, 'I'm not going to be there to do your pilot.' But I read the *Soap* script and I thought it's so different, it's either going to be a real embarrassment or it's going to be something that's wonderful, depending on how we cast it. The fortunate thing was we had time to cast. Sometimes you get into pilots and you have three or four weeks, but we had good time to cast this show. Part of it was, as a group, we were pretty much in

❋ Cowan's *See No Evil* suggests that part of the reason the show didn't do as well as expected is because Fred Silverman, then head of rival ABC Entertainment, had snapped up the contracts of some of the MTM writers who would've otherwise worked on the series.

sync." Meanwhile, *The Betty White Show* would be canceled by CBS after just 14 episodes.

As JD Lobue remembers it, Sandrich had known him for only a few days before he asked Lobue to be his associate director on *Soap*. "I said Jay, thank you, I'm really flattered, but you know I'm directing these days and I'm trying to cut back on the AD work. He says, well do me a favor, just come in and meet these people. I think you'll like them."

Lobue went into his first meeting with Harris, Witt and Thomas "just as arrogant as my youth could deliver," he laughs now. "After a few minutes I said you know, I don't really want to be your AD on this show. I think it was Tony who said well, what are you doing here? I said I want to *direct* your show. And they kind of looked at each other like who the hell is this? I said I'll tell you what. I'll be your AD on the first 13 shows, your first order, and you ask Jay at the end of 13 weeks if I'm qualified to direct the show and we'll go from there. It must've worked because before I got to my home, I had a message waiting that they wanted to hire me as the AD. But I learned some humility over the years, believe me."*

Populating Dunn's River

Despite the menagerie of intriguing characters milling around inside Susan Harris' head, *Soap*'s lone minor, Billy Tate, was one of the first people cast.

Jimmy Baio, 15 at the time that *Soap* began, had been under contract with ABC for two other pilots—*Freeman*, starring Stu Gilliam as a ghost that only Baio's character can see, and a pilot with John Byner (the future Det. Donohue)—before he was given the role of Billy. Though ABC wanted him in the series, Sandrich and the producers initially weren't so sure.

"When Jay met my mom, he said Jimmy was great but he's just too young," Baio remembers. "They really need somebody older because it's a risqué show and a lot's going to be going on, so they don't want a minor. And then with me being under contract with the network, the network spoke with them and then they changed their minds."

* Ironically (considering the hassle the religious right would give *Soap* later on), before *Soap* Sandrich asked Lobue to be associate director on the "This Side of Eden" episode of *Insight* "which was sort of a quasi-religious morality play that aired on Sundays," Lobue recalls. (They met the week before when Sandrich came by to watch Lobue direct an episode called "Arnstein's Miracle.") "Ed Asner was God, Walter Matheau was Adam, and Carol Burnett was Eve. My first experience with the comedy format was with Jay on that show as his associate."

Even before *Soap*, Jimmy Baio (Billy) was well known, particularly to girls who were egged on by vaguely suggestive teen-magazine spreads like this one.

Early on, Richard Mulligan was being discussed for the role of Chester, Sandrich says. "I said knowing Mulligan, and knowing how brilliant he is, he couldn't play that straight a character. I felt he'd be wonderful in the part he eventually played, so we switched that."

Shortly before Sandrich left *The Mary Tyler Moore Show*, an actor called Robert Mandan showed up to work on an episode of the spin-off, *Phyllis*, starring Cloris Leachman. "While I was there, I got a call to do a voice on *Mary Tyler Moore*," says Mandan. "They had a puppeteer, and the puppeteer got frightened and they couldn't hear him on the microphone. They called me and said can you do this voice? Well sure because it was *The Mary Tyler Moore Show* and they were about to wind up; they had maybe six more shows."

Despite significant experience on television and the stage, Mandan had come to something of a crossroads in his career just a few years before. Around 1973, he spent about two years working to transition into the psychology field. Part of that involved enrolling in a master's degree program. "The first course I took was in statistics," he says. "I hated it. I didn't think it had anything to do with helping people, myself included. And they said you have got to finish the course because you couldn't get a degree otherwise. So I did some thinking about that and I called my agent—I still had an agent—and said, 'Get me outta here!'"

Robert Mandan had quite a track record before *Soap*, including appearing on *Barney Miller* two years before *Soap*'s debut. The two series were shot in studios that stood side by side.

After shooting 13 episodes of the Stacy Keach/Carl Franklin cop show *Caribe* in Miami, he returned to LA only to find a dearth of work opportunities. "I saw an ad for Stella Adler who was teaching a class, so I got into her class, which I'm grateful I did and sorry I didn't do it when I was a kid. Then I started doing some guest spots. I did *One Day at a Time*, got another agent out of that, and I did *Phyllis* with Cloris Leachman."

After working with Sandrich on *Mary Tyler Moore*, Mandan asked him what he was doing during the summer hiatus. "He said I'm doing one of the funniest shows I've ever seen, it's the only thing I'm doing." The director also told him he'd be perfect as one of the fathers on the show. "He called the production office and I did a reading for *Soap*. On a Friday I did a screen test and on the Monday I went to work on the show.

Beginning with the 1971 off-Broadway debut of *The House of Blue Leaves*, Katherine Helmond began to perfect a character not unlike *Soap's* Jessica Tate.

"The audition went extremely well. Matter of fact, I left and they were still applauding inside the room. Knowing these people, it wasn't something they normally do. My wife was with me and I went outside and she was just 'Was that for you?' I said I guess so, I'm the only one leaving the room. And the other actors that were sitting in the waiting room were like 'Oooh, what was that?' It was very exhilarating. I don't think I'd ever had any audition quite like that."

The actress who would play his on-screen wife never had a similar crisis of career—she grew up in the theater and became one of its best-loved stars—but none of those plaudits, or the occasional television dramas, earned her nearly enough to keep the wolf from the door. Says Katherine Helmond, "Finally my manager said we've got to get you into a sitcom."

As her manager was able to get the scripts in advance of her auditions, "I was able to bring a character into the readings, so I think that was a big help, especially when it came to *Soap*. I went in there with no sitcom experience when I read for them. It was just putting one foot in front of the other. I think it was a natural progression with my trying to do the best job I could with every job I got."

Helmond was working in New York when casting began for *Soap*, so back she flew to meet with the producers. "I just picked out two scenes that I thought showed the character. I went in and read my two scenes and nobody laughed. I thought, Oh dear. I said, 'Look, if I'm on the wrong foot, just tell me and I'll try another way to read it.' And Susan Harris said it's so crazy and so real, I didn't quite take time to laugh. And so from that day I got the job." Jessica "seemed to them to be the most difficult role in the sense that I had to jump from almost slapstick comedy to tragedy, sometimes from one line to the next. I think they thought that was going to be the most difficult thing to do."

What the *Soap* producers might not have realized was that Helmond had found her biggest success on stage to date in John Guare's black comedy *The House of Blue Leaves*, in which she perfected this very talent. Starting with the play's 1971 off-Broadway debut, Helmond played Bananas, the mentally ill wife of a man who wants to institutionalize her so he can be with his lover. Very quickly the actress found the believability in this character who said outrageous things one moment and fought her illness long enough to survey the shambles of her life the next. The subsequent acclaim she found in the role (including winning the Clarence Derwent award for "most promising female performer") brought Helmond to the fore in New York, and allowed her to recreate that role in Los Angeles where new opportunities abounded. It's also not hard to see Jessica Tate meeting Bananas' fate had she not enjoyed the strong support of her sister, Mary.

To the best of her recollection, Helmond was the first person cast on *Soap* (who wasn't already under contract with ABC). Though Harris can't remember for sure, she says "she might've been. It would make sense.

"We knew immediately when Katherine Helmond came in and read that she was Jessica. There was just no question about it. The same thing with Richard Mulligan. There were some like that, and others that took a long time to find. A lot of them came from New York, a lot of stage people." This makes perfect sense, "because it really is like putting on a play. You're doing it in front of a live audience every week—it's very similar."

One of *Soap*'s greatest casting challenges turned out to be finding the perfect Corinne. "I know we had trouble finding the part that Diana Canova played," says Sandrich. "She originally had come in to read for Jennifer [Salt's] part. We needed somebody for the part that Diana played that was very likable, because the part was pretty trampy, and Diana was so likable."

However, Canova would be the next-to-last person cast. It was Jennifer Salt who first read for Corinne. As she remembers it, "I was doing an actual screen test and they said would you mind doing Eunice as well, so I did both." It was a meeting that nearly didn't happen at all.

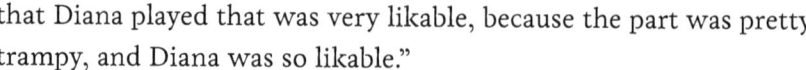

Jennifer Salt

"I had auditioned for Paul Witt in the past and came close to getting another part in a different pilot they'd made. And the funny thing is my agent said to me, 'Oh, I don't know why you're bothering to go.' I said I have a migraine and is there a way to reschedule? And she said, 'No, but who cares? It's ridiculous. I wouldn't worry about it. It's some horrible *Mary Hartman, Mary Hartman* rip-off.' So I did think to myself that doesn't sound right. Paul Witt was a swell guy and I went to the audition."

In all, the producers took about six months casting the pilot, which was fraught with frustrations not uncommon to other shows. Two other pilots were shot—two other actors played Peter Campbell and two other actresses Mary Campbell (including *Mary Hartman, Mary Hartman* regular Salome Jens)—before the final pilot with Robert Urich and Cathryn Damon was completed.

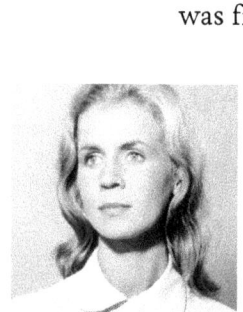

Katherine Helmond remembers auditioning with Damon and feeling that, at last, she'd finally found her on-screen sister. "I thought we did make a good team together; she had a very good sense of humor. I also thought she was a good opposite of me. You know how sometimes in a family there are three or four kids and none of them seem like they came from the same father? You think gee, where did this kid come from? I thought that was a funny element to add to the script. We didn't look alike, we didn't function alike. And yet we were very fond of each other and very supportive of one another."

Salome Jens (above) and another actress (unknown, below) were cast as Mary before Cathryn Damon (right) snagged the role.

Like Jimmy Baio, Billy Crystal, too, was already under contract with ABC when he was cast as Jodie Dallas, Jay Sandrich remembers. "I knew Billy was a really good actor, much more than a comedian."

From the vantage point of 2013, it's nearly impossible to appreciate the pressure a straight actor must have felt being cast as a homosexual in a 1977 program. Based on various media interviews and his own published memoirs, it's likely that he still harbors psychological scars from the experience. (He was also the only person involved with *Soap* who declined to be interviewed for this book.) It didn't help that the actor came to the role after quitting the very first episode of *Saturday Night* (later renamed *Saturday Night Live*) after his 6-minute sketch was cut short at the last minute. Aside from an episode of *All in the Family*, he had little experience on television, and was now being asked to make his first regular TV appearance as a gay man. Only three years earlier homosexuality had still been listed in the *Diagnostic and Statistical Manual of Mental Disorders*.

After quitting the first episode of *Saturday Night Live* on principle, Billy Crystal got his second chance on *Soap*.

Whatever challenges Crystal faced, there was no responsibility on his part to safeguard the dignity of an entire group of people. He was not a gay man and did not write the scripts. Robert Guillaume's portrayal of Benson was another matter.

Perhaps the actor who came closest to portraying the smarter-than-his-boss black servant before Robert Guillaume was Eddie Anderson. (Anderson would die on Feb. 28, 1977, around the same time production began on *Soap*.) The actor brought his character, Rochester, from the Jack Benny radio show to television (1950-65), where he continued to perpetually deflate Benny's on-camera ego. Still, it was one thing to play a smart black man in pre-1960s America when the country had its black citizenry firmly under heel. It was quite another to do that in the '70s, when some whites were still trying to reconcile themselves to integration and the implications of the 1968 Fair Housing Act (illustrated wonderfully by Danny and Polly's predicament in *Soap* episode 3.19), and many blacks were dead set against being stereotyped as servants. (More on this in the "Robert Guillaume's Tightrope Walk" section of entry 2.20.)

As the caustic servant/smartest person in the room, Benson stood to potentially offend both sides of the racial divide.

"They had been searching for someone to play Benson for a long time," says Robert Guillaume. "In other words they had everyone else cast already but they couldn't do anything until they filled that role."

Sandrich recalls seeing Guillaume on stage in a New York production of the musical *Jacques Brel is Alive and Well and Living in Paris*. "We just read everybody [for the part] and we could not find anybody to work, so we said let's bring Robert out and work with him. We brought him out to do an audience run-through the night he arrived. The audience response to him was terrific."

The only challenge was the network's refusal to cast Guillaume in the role. The producers appealed to Silverman, who ultimately agreed the actor was the man for the job.

In his autobiography, Guillaume explains how he approached his first audition for Benson with the dictum "Do Nothing"—he refused to try too hard and risk second-guessing his instincts. "Other auditioners had been either too militant or too obsequious," he wrote. "That's why they were considering a Japanese woman instead." Wow.

Basing his reading of the character on the aloofness of his brother James, and his grandmother's take-no-guff attitude, he found the perfect voice. James "was the oldest of four children and he had this dry sense of humor," Guillaume told the author in 2008. "He used to tease us unmercifully, and when we would complain to my grandmother who was raising us, she would say James, you leave those kids alone. And he would reply, 'I ain't doin' nothing,' as if he were totally innocent and couldn't understand why anybody would object to what he was saying."

As it turned out, the only part harder to cast than Benson was that of Burt's split-personality son, Chuck.

"We couldn't find any ventriloquists who could play the part—this really sweet guy who was such a great ventriloquist—so we were going to use an actor and have a voice off stage read the dummy's lines," Sandrich remembers. On the very last day of casting, in came Jay Johnson.

After giving up on the idea of simply using an actor, the producers had resorted to advertising in the newspaper to find a ventriloquist that would work, and Johnson arrived in response to that ad. "Hundreds and hundreds of people were looking to get this part; it was all new. No one knew what to do with a guy and a puppet. They knew

The casting of Jay Johnson saved audiences from four years of hearing somebody read Bob's lines from off stage.

how to get an actor that would play the part and they would loop it in later, but for me doing it live as it was happening, it was more unique than anyone thought."

Sandrich "said it's only going to work if the actors on the set can interact in real time," Johnson recalls. "So you need to find a ventriloquist who can do it live so that the actors on the set have something to go back and forth with. You can't get your timing, you can't post [produce] that. You can't have the guy sitting off the set."

"As a director I would sometimes really forget Jay was there and I would talk to Bob, give Bob notes," Sandrich laughs. "Every once in a while, just for fun, I would whisper something in Bob's ear."

By the time Diana Canova auditioned for the part of Corinne, every part had been cast, with the exception of Benson, she remembers.

"My agent at the time, Arnold Rifkin, called me on a Friday and said he had just read the funniest script he had ever seen, and I was to go to the audition right away. I remember being the only one there in my usual attire: jeans, a T-shirt and no makeup. The other girls there were mostly dressed like hookers. I guess when they saw the breakdown of Corinne, a 'nymphomaniac,' they figured she was fast and loose. I didn't see her that way."

Diana Canova's girl-next-door attire and demeanor on the day of her audition helped her land the role of Corinne.

Canova quickly absorbed the material for the pilot and launched into Corinne's off-the-cuff excuse to Jessica for not coming home the night before: "Turkey truck overturned and there were these turkeys all over the road."

Says Canova, "I remember making Jay Sandrich, our amazing director (and the nicest man ever), laugh in the room. By the time I got home, my agent was calling me to get back in the car and go to ABC in Century City to read for Freddie Silverman, as I was going to the network. So I did. I started rehearsal the following Monday. Susan Harris later told me I was the only one who came in looking like a normal girl—that got me the part. And I suppose the fact that I could make them laugh with the turkey speech. I was a very lucky girl."

Controversy

In many ways *Soap* was the canary in the coal mine as far as American mores were concerned. The wildfire response that the sitcom received months before it even premiered said more about the times than about the show.

If one theme prevailed throughout 1970s America, it was "No one is listening." Despite mounting protests, the country's involvement in Vietnam continued to spiral out of control. President Nixon doggedly held on to office despite the Watergate scandal that threatened to consume every official he had appointed.

And the religious right continued to watch as the values they cherished—prayer in school, abstinence before marriage, and the view of homosexuality as sin, among others—were repeatedly contravened. School prayer had been virtually obliterated by 1971's Supreme Court ruling in *Lemon v. Kurtzman*, and modern television had made a joke of abstinence, even as gay characters were slowly being introduced to the small screen. How could it be that what they'd been told was a Christian nation was now failing on so many levels to reflect what they saw as fundamental Christian values, particularly on television?

Rise of the Pressure Group

Though the phrase "if you're not paying for it, you're the product" has a special relevance today thanks to the dealings of online entities like Google and Facebook, it is a concept that goes back to early newspapers and radio.

Throughout the golden age of radio (roughly the '30s to the '50s), a single company would finance an entire show, work mentions of its products into the entertainment, and slap its name on the title for good measure (e.g., *The Chase & Sanborn Hour*). However, by the early 1950s this model proved impractical for television as it was far too expensive for a single advertiser to finance an entire show. Thus was born the "scatter" model we have today wherein several sponsors purchase commercial time during a given program. Not only did this free up sponsors to place their messages in front of the viewers of several different shows, it also afforded them a certain "plausible deniability" when confronted by viewers angered by a specific broadcast.

The following sponsor's reply to a viewer's complaint, quoted in Kathryn C. Montgomery's book *Target: Prime Time*, gives you some idea of what concerned viewer's were up against:

"...For instance, our commercial might be scheduled in *Marcus Welby*, but we would not know whether the show content involves heart trouble, diabetes or abortion." In other words, get stuffed.

It was the very disingenuousness of this "our hands are tied" argument that would eventually galvanize *Soap*'s critics into action. Too often they'd seen advertisers call the tune when it came to television content. It's difficult to say now just what anti-*Soap* activists knew about network executives at the time. Still, you can imagine their reaction if they realized that ABC head Fred Silverman, the man responsible for defending *Soap* to its critics, was the same executive responsible for pulling the plug on several inoffensive, cornball shows such as *The Beverly Hillbillies* over at CBS just six years earlier, solely to cater to advertisers' needs to attract younger, more affluent viewers. Though networks had recently instituted "open door" policies that invited advocacy groups to visit with executives to air their concerns, and the standards and practices people did their best to maintain "ongoing relationships" with them, the staunchest activists soon realized that nothing really changed.

More galling still, conservative viewers seemed to be the only ones *not* influencing programming. In the early '70s, groups like Justicia, inspired by Cesar Chavez, successfully pressured networks to improve their depictions of Hispanics on television, in part by threatening the renewal of their broadcast licenses. As ABC's West Coast Vice President Tom Kersey told Montgomery in *Target: Prime Time*, "One of our stations was worth between $35 million and $40 million."

During the development of ABC's 1972 TV movie *That Certain Summer*, gay rights groups including the Gay Activist Alliance began to test their own powers in the television market. In a detail funnier than much of what passed for television comedy at the time, organizations such as the GAA often knew what was in the pipeline

1977

MAY 25: The Unabomber strikes for the first time, wounding a security guard at Northwestern University.

at all three networks well in advance because of the number of gay activists in the industry itself. Often actions such as network office occupations could be coordinated in response to a forthcoming offending TV episode before executives even knew the broadcast was planned.

This whole move to influence television content had begun back in 1972 when that perennial boogeyman of the right, Planned Parenthood, served as a consultant to a two-episode arc of *Maude*—the "Maude gets an abortion" episodes written by *Soap* creator Susan Harris—designed to address concerns about skyrocketing world population numbers. Set in motion by The Population Institute's move to enlist Hollywood's help in spreading the population-control message, the *Maude* episodes promised to be some of the most controversial television aired by CBS. The network persuaded Norman Lear to shoe-horn in a satisfied mother character—who's pregnant yet again—just to add balance to the pro-abortion stance the episodes took. (If anything, the self-satisfied idiot "Lorraine" and her bratty offspring likely struck many as a further argument for termination on demand, and was just as likely a tweak of the nose of the network orchestrated by Harris and Lear.)*

The message was clear: Gays, minorities and pro-life groups all seemed to get somewhere with the networks, yet conservative grievances were fobbed off with condescending letters. It was a pattern that conservatives, particularly religious conservatives, recognized from the political arena. It was only a matter of time before the various right-wing elements left out in the cold coordinated their efforts and finally put the screws to the networks.

* As a result of the controversy the *Maude* abortion episodes sparked, Montgomery points out in *Target: Prime Time*, Lear created a position at Tandem Productions tasked with dealing directly with pressure groups during the development of programming, defusing issues before they became big problems, and even using those groups as a sort of marketing force.

A Nation (within a Nation) Awakes

In the Internet age where a contrary opinion is a click away, it's hard to recall just how isolated American communities were from one another, and how much suspicion and animosity that separation bred. Local newspapers echoed local sentiment, as did local

TV news broadcasts. And high-circulation magazines such as *The Saturday Evening Post*—kept anodyne so as to appeal to the broadest readership—suggested that the mores found in small-town America were held by Americans everywhere.

This illusion of homogeneity began to crumble in the 1960s as technology enabled local network affiliates to beam everything from Vietnam war footage to Haight-Ashbury love-ins into homes everywhere. These events suggested to conservatives throughout the land that something was very wrong in America. Young people were burning their draft cards, spouting communist rhetoric, and in the case of the Weather Underground, placing bombs in the nation's capital. Meanwhile, both houses of Congress passed (an ultimately doomed) Equal Rights Amendment in 1972, and the Supreme Court toppled a national ban on abortion in 1973's *Roe v. Wade* decision. And television—the nation's unblinking eye—broadcast every blow.

As we've seen, television itself had taken a turn for the controversial in the '70s. The only attempt to limit the amount of sex and violence on TV—the Family Viewing Policy—had been quashed just two years after its implementation.

Rev. Jerry Falwell's Moral Majority would become a major thorn in *Soap's* side.

The conservative elements in the country, realizing that they already enjoyed a culture within the culture at large, decided to create their own media system. In 1960, minister Pat Robertson established the Christian Broadcasting Network. Two years later he launched a telethon that would evolve into *The 700 Club*, a two-hour Christian variety program that, starting in 1978, offered a fundamentalist-Christian take on the day's news and political stories.

Another minister, Lynchburg, Va.'s Jerry Falwell, deeply affected by the numbers of Christians who came to his "I Love America" rallies around the country in the mid-1970s, saw that he could consolidate them into a strong political base. Though the Moral Majority political group he subsequently launched in June 1979 has been blamed for the beating *Soap* took from activists, those protests were in fact some of the most ecumenical efforts in this nation's history.

The Article That Launched a Thousand Protests

For many years, the received wisdom has been that the backlash against *Soap* was touched off by a single 600-word, back-of-the-book piece in the *Newsweek* magazine dated June 13, 1977 (three months to the day before *Soap*'s premiere) written by television beat reporter Harry F. Waters. The headline: "99 and 44/100% Impure."

"This was before the show went on the air, after we had announced it to our affiliates," says Fred Silverman, then-president of ABC Entertainment. "They were saying what a ribald comedy it is. Somehow or other [*Newsweek*] got a hold of a story line for the show that was not an official story line. Somebody made it up. It involved a priest who had an affair and I think he was gay—it was just a total fabrication. We had no intention of doing anything close to that. And some of the affiliates jumped all over that as a result of the *Newsweek* article."

Silverman's hardly alone in this memory; a good half-dozen people involved with the show cited that same article as the beginning of the whole public relations nightmare. Nearly all remembered it containing exaggerations about what future *Soap* episodes would contain. Not surprisingly, the Wikipedia entry for *Soap* even goes so far as to suggest "Whether Waters' errors and misrepresentations were intentional or accidental is unresolved."

For decades, cast and crew blamed this 1977 article for the controversy that engulfed *Soap*. The writer of the piece never knew.

"We knew the shot we were taking with *Soap* and we were prepared for just about everything, other than being blindsided by this piece that was written before the show aired about elements of the show that never existed," says Paul Junger Witt. "That hurt us,

> "If you do an article three months before a show's coming on, and you describe it as fairly out there, well, what's wrong with that? That's called journalism."
>
> — HARRY F WATERS, author of the 1977 *Newsweek* piece

the perception of the show. Some of the affiliates became nervous about it; some of them moved the show or dropped it."

These recollections, from former ABC executives and *Soap* producers on down, appear to be, at least in part, mistaken. Though it seems likely that the *Newsweek* piece *was* the partial cause of the public backlash, and Waters may have been remiss in his journalistic duty to quote someone from the other side of the controversy, the piece was accurate in its recounting of plot details, from the pilot right through the projected story lines for coming years:

"Jessica's promiscuous daughter will try to seduce a Jesuit priest (in church), the gay blade takes up with a pro football player and meets a stepbrother who is a schizophrenic ventriloquist, and some Tates discover that they have actually been sired by Campbells—and vice versa." Check, check, check and check. (Technically it's a Campbell—actually a Dallas—sired by a Tate, but who knows what would've been revealed had the series continued.)

Indeed, the only real quibble hangs on our definition of the verb *seduce*. While Corinne definitely meets the first Merriam-Webster definition, "to persuade to disobedience or disloyalty"—in this case to Father Tim's vow of celibacy—she certainly did not "entice to sexual intercourse" in the church itself.

Though the *Newsweek* piece is faithful to the series, it fails to do justice to the writing or the actors on *Soap*, slagging off the former as possessing "the subtlety of a chain saw" and the latter as offering little more than a "mug and smirk as if they were auditioning for a Harvard Hasty Pudding show." Guillaume's Benson is said to "deliver the obligatory racial put-downs, but not even Redd Foxx could wring laughs from his lines." Really? Personal tastes aside, the one other explanation for this scathing review may lie in the possibility that the pilot Waters saw was one of two versions taped prior to the final one the rest of the nation would see three months later. The photo accompanying the *Newsweek* article, which depicts Diana Canova and Billy Crystal alongside an unknown actress playing Mary, makes this seem all the more likely.

The author managed to track down Harry F. Waters with the help of the *Newsweek* editor at the time the *Soap* piece was written:

Edward Kosner. Despite not having seen a copy of his article since it left his desk in 1977, Waters had a fair recollection of what he'd said. "We have a fact-checking department at *Newsweek*," he says. "They've got 14 very tough women who check stories; that never would've gotten through the checking if I hadn't said exactly what the truth was. Fred Silverman and I discussed this later; Fred and I became good buddies. Fred had no problem with that story."

More surprising, Waters had no idea that it is his one *Newsweek* article that's always been blamed for sparking the whole *Soap* controversy. "If I had that kind of power, I would be a president," he says with a laugh. "That pilot was being shown to more people than me. It was being shown to advertisers. A show like that is going to attract controversy, not from one source. *Advertising Age*, *Variety*, they all were covering *Soap*.* *Soap* was designed to engender that kind of controversy, and all the trade publications covered that controversy. The fact that it lasted four years and was such a fairly dumb show tells me that the controversy probably was part of the reason it *did* last four years, because there will always be an audience that will turn on a show that's controversial. *Jersey Shore* is a perfect example of how you can never be too crude or too dumb. The farther out you go, you can always get an audience."

The previous week's *Newsweek*

Reaction (to a Show No One had Seen)

The first salvo in the public backlash against *Soap* arrived the same month *Newsweek* published that article. The Southern Baptist Convention, the second largest Christian organization in America after the Catholic Church, issued its "Christian Life Commission Recommendations on Television and Morality" in June. Though the document doesn't mention *Soap* by name, it urges the Southern Baptist churches throughout the land to, throughout "the month of September...encourage our members to exercise careful moral judgment regarding television, determining in advance which programs

❋ Waters remembers reading about *Soap* in the industry trades of the day before he ever tackled it, including in the now-defunct *Broadcasting* magazine. However, it may well have been *Newsweek* that brought this inside-the-industry banter into the mainstream, alerting the more conservative elements in the country to what they could look forward to come September.

Though the (comparatively) over-sexed *Three's Company* had been running since March, it was clear that *Soap* had been the breaking point for the SBC.

to watch and which programs not to watch in the knowledge that if we do not control television, television will control us." As *All in the Family* had been running since 1971, *Charlie's Angels* since 1976, and *Three's Company* since March 1977—essentially the only other controversial shows on the 1977 schedule—the timing of the SBC document points squarely at *Soap* as its target. Section 4 of this five-section document is particularly instructive considering what was to come:

"(4) We recommend that the Southern Baptist Convention encourage our people to use the month of October for special communication with those who are responsible for television programming. (A) Communicate with the advertisers who will pay attention when Christians buy products whose makers sponsor good programs and refuse to buy products whose makers sponsor bad programs. (B) Communicate with network officials: pray for them; write them; call them; reason with them; plead with them; commend them for the good; hold them responsible for the bad; and remember that ancient Rome at first had no earthly intention of paying any real attention to the early Christians. (C) Communicate with the local television station officials; write them; call them; visit them; share both your moral support and your moral outrage with them; and remind them of their moral obligation to the community. (D) Communicate with your Senators and Congressperson, the chairman of the Federal Communications Commission, and the chairman of the Federal Trade Commission to plead for their support on behalf of the rising tide of public concern for morality in television programming. Let Southern Baptists communicate our convictions about television."

Point (D) is particularly interesting considering the whole Family Viewing Policy had been meant to head off congressional regulation in the first place.

That same month, Methodist minister Donald Wildmon launched the National Federation for Decency, predecessor of today's American Family Association—in Tupelo, Miss. This in response to the lack of programming he felt suitable for his children. Though Wildmon's group would flounder throughout 1979, it would get an enormous boost the following year with the election of conservative icon Ronald Reagan. The advice he would give in 1981 voices a sentiment other television activists had already begun to adopt during *Soap*'s run: "...forget writing to the networks. As long as the money is coming in, they don't care what you think.... The real clout that churches have is against people who pay the bills—the advertisers, the sponsors." (Though Wildmon's star would begin to sink in 1981 after internecine battles with fellow activists and his targeting of increasingly more innocuous programs, the damage to *Soap* and other shows would already be done.)

During this time, another rare act of ecumenicalism saw the United Methodist Church, the National Council of Churches, the United Church of Christ and the US Catholic Conference mobilize their 138,000 member churches into action, generating an estimated 22,000 letters of protest to ABC.

As the time grew closer to *Soap*'s debut, protesters began to show their displeasure right outside the Witt Thomas Harris production offices. Late one evening, Marsha Posner, then Harris' secretary, was working late in the office by herself when the phone rang. Groggily, she answered it.

"And this guy says to me, 'I want the address of where I can write a letter protesting against this show.' It had just been a really long frigging day for me, and I thought I have nothing to lose. So I said to this guy, 'Listen, I'm happy to give you an address and you're more than welcome to write a letter, but can I ask you a question: Have you ever *seen* the show?'"

Of course she already knew the answer to this; the show had yet to air. In other words, thank you very much *Newsweek* magazine. When asked why he wanted to protest *Soap*, the caller rattled off a list of sins he'd read the program was guilty of.

"So do you believe everything that you read," she asked him. "Are you not capable of forming your own opinion? I talked to this guy for 15 minutes and at the end of the conversation, he said, 'Well, I have to tell you, you have totally convinced me to wait and watch the show myself and make up my own mind.' I said that's all I'm asking. That's what the channel changer's for. You don't like it,

1977

On **JUNE 28**, the US Supreme Court prohibits universities from imposing quota systems for admissions, but allows programs that benefit minorities (*University of California Regents v. Bakke*).

JUNE 29: Bob Crane, best known as the wisecracking American POW Col. Robert Hogan on *Hogan's Heroes* (1965-1971), is murdered. Though Hollywood had always been rife with rumors about Crane's off-screen activities, it wasn't until the 1993 book *The Murder of Bob Crane* by Robert Graysmith that the public learned about his obsession with filming his many sexual conquests.

Marsha Posner and Robert Guillaume, decades after the angry phone calls over *Soap*.

watch something else, but don't do something just because somebody else tells you to do it. Be your own person, make up your own mind. Isn't that only fair?" She laughs. "I'm such a liberal."

Unfortunately, members of the National Gay Task Force *had* seen the first two episodes, which had been given to them to screen by ABC, and proceeded to pitch their own media fit. Understandably, the confusion over whether Jodie was a transvestite, a gay man, or both infuriated them. Particularly enlightening was the response of ABC's East Coast vice president for broadcast standards, Richard Gitter, to the NGTF, quoted in *Target: Prime Time*. "ABC is receiving conflicting messages regarding homosexuality. On the one hand, certain church groups criticize us for too positive a portrayal of homosexuality in *Soap*, while you argue that our portrayal is negative and stereotypical, and likely to constitute a setback in the Gay Rights movement." One can practically feel Gitter's frustration with a society that was (and in many ways remains) as schizophrenic as Chuck Campbell.

Some Last Minute Tinkering

In an Aug. 22, 1977 piece in the trade journal *Broadcasting*, Fred Silverman admitted that some of the criticisms leveled against the pilot had been taken on board. "We're getting more flesh-and-blood characters, with more humanity, without sacrificing the comedy," Silverman explained.

The most notable change came with the handling of Jessica's affair with Peter. In an earlier version of the pilot, Jessica and Peter were shown in bed together rather than simply showing Jessica already dressed when the scene opens. Also gone was Corinne's greeting to Peter after her mother's departure: "Hi. Take off your clothes and let's go to bed." The number of times Jessica and Peter say "boff" (see P. 75) was also reduced.

Yet these cosmetic changes did little to reassure the reluctant stations amongst ABC's 195 affiliates, particularly in the more conservative parts of the country. At the time of the *Broadcasting* article, "seven or eight" affiliates had not yet cleared the show for airing in their markets, Silverman said. Additionally, Cy Bahakel issued a statement saying his six ABC-affiliated stations—mostly in traditionally conservative markets including Montgomery, Ala. and Jackson, Tenn.—would also pass on *Soap*. Some station heads, such as WFTV (Orlando) General Manager Walter Windsor, considered airing the show if they could run it around 11:30 p.m. rather than in the 9:30 p.m. slot. Brian Cobb, general manager for Nashville's WNGE-TV, told *Broadcasting* that he expected a "great big hassle" over the show in his market, adding that he planned to run a message requesting written feedback from his audience, a brave move considering the "whinge" predicted in the station's call letters.

"The charge was led by the head of Group W, the Westinghouse Stations, Don McGannon," Silverman told the author in 2008. "He hadn't even seen the pilot and was already saying we're going to cancel the show, we're going to disaffiliate. And then before you know it there were a lot of pressure groups, a lot of citizen censors who jumped on the bandwagon."

The changes made to the first two episodes came on the heels of an impassioned address by Silverman to affiliates via a closed-circuit broadcast the month before, assuring them that *Soap* would show the ramifications of any immoral behavior, according to Geoffrey Cowan's *See No Evil*:

"...Silverman promised that Jessica would undergo 'extreme suffering' as the result of her brief extramarital affair and would emerge as a better person; Chester, her philandering husband, would undergo a crisis and exhibit 'unexpected depth of character'; and Jodie, the gay son, would not go through with his sex-change operation and instead would 'meet a girl and find there are other values worth considering.'" The ABC head may have gone a bit too far by painting *Soap* as something approaching a morality play, calling it "socially redeeming" in that "no character in *Soap* is ever rewarded for immoral behavior...The clear message is not 'Do what they do' but 'Laugh, enjoy and learn what not to do.'" Yet decades later, Silverman told the author, "Literally, we spent the whole summer defending the show and sticking to our guns, saying we were not going to bend to any pressure."

By Cowan's estimation, about 20 stations—mostly in the South—refused to carry the show before its premiere, with an additional 15 deciding to run it at 11 p.m. or later.

Any Publicity is Good Publicity?

Newsweek writer Harry Waters keeps coming back to the question of how Fred Silverman, one of the shrewdest network heads of his time,* could've been so naïve as to think *Soap* would've squeaked by uncommented on, or that he would ever even wish for that to happen. After all, Waters had known Silverman for a long time.

"Fred would be on the line saying to those writers, 'We don't want another *Mary Hartman*. Let's push it as far as we can. And at that time, I guess that's pushing it. Today it doesn't seem that way. Fred was a guy who wanted a show to be a hit and the fact—what I've learned from this conversation—is that it was on *four years* and that it really did do the plotlines I suggested [in the article]. Which tells me that was kind of the goal of the show. They wanted attention. I don't think the attention that came to them was either surprising or hurtful. I think they were smart enough to want it."

Of course "they" in this context were the executives at ABC who lived and died by ratings. Those who *were* both surprised and hurt by the negative publicity were the people who worked so feverishly to put the first few episodes together in the first place.

While the *Newsweek* piece didn't do the show any favors, Jay Johnson thinks part of the resulting furor could've been headed off by the Powers That Be. "Looking back on it, what really happened was some of our executive producers were not, and maybe still aren't, social creatures. They were business people and they were writers and artists, they weren't social. I think a couple of them ticked off a couple of reporters, just from their attitude."

In other words, though the *Soap* story lines that *Newsweek* wrote about were accurate, there are many ways to couch the coverage, Johnson points out. "If you take comedy and reduce it down to its elements, most of the time it is cruel, harsh and painful, because most comedy comes from that. So all the things we're talking about, yes, we are going to have a possessed baby, yes we were going to have a

Fred Silverman

❋ So wily was Silverman, he developed a strategy as head of ABC in which he signed exclusive contracts with the stars of hit programs on rival networks such as Redd Foxx (*Sanford & Son*), Harvey Korman (*The Carol Burnett Show*), as well as some rival top-notch writers, according to *See No Evil*. The result—many of the shows they had once headlined collapsed or lost ratings.

homosexual, yes there was going to be a scene where Corinne tries to seduce a priest in the confessional, and all these things. But if you just say that's what we're going to do, that sounds awful. That sounds like we're completely mad and we're ruining America. But when you add 'and it's a comedy', you have to then understand that that's not the impact it's going to have. It's going to be done for a laugh, it will be defused. I just think that the first reporters concentrated on the plot itself without ever saying 'this is going to be hysterically funny.' That would've changed it all."

Ted Wass ("Danny") recalls just how quickly ABC's reaction to the controversy changed. "At one point I remember before we went into production, or early on into production, we were hearing that ABC was taking like 20,000 letters a week and everybody was really loving it. Then the climate changed because the groups that were writing those letters figured out that they shouldn't be writing to ABC, they should be writing to Madison Avenue, they should be writing to all those big advertising companies. Once those letters started going to the advertising companies, that's when it got really tense. That's when all of the sudden it was oh jeez, *now* there's a problem. Because up to that point it was yeah, fine, stir the pot for us, make it a big controversy, it'll just ensure a big tune-in. But once they started to go for the pocketbook…"

Yet there is something that everybody involved with *Soap* acknowledges at some point. As director JD Lobue puts it, "People got uptight about this little half-hour comedy on television when there were so many more important things going on in the country at that time."

Soap Premieres

After three months of insanity, everybody involved with the show was eager to finally see the finished product when it debuted on ABC on Sept. 13, 1977.

"I remember sitting around and everybody wanted to have a party and nobody was offering a place," says Bob Seagren, who played Jodie's football player boyfriend, Dennis Phillips. "So I kind of put my hand up and said, 'Well, I've got a house.'"

1977

On **APRIL 25**, St. Paul, Minn., becomes the second US city to repeal its gay rights laws, following last year's action in Dade County, Fla.

A former Olympic athlete who'd captured the gold medal in pole-vaulting during the 1968 games, Seagren had done pretty well for himself since, and had a "pretty good size" house in Westwood, a nice Los Angeles community bordered by Bel-Air, Beverly Hills, Brentwood and Century City. Pretty much the entire cast and the producers turned up for the premiere night party.

"I was the least known of anybody in that cast, and certainly was the lowest paid of anybody in that cast," says Seagren, who estimates about 60 people showed up in all. "It was kind of funny that we ended up at my house for the big premiere night." Part of the reason for the turnout, he reasons now, had to do with the 6-foot projection-screen TV he had at the time. "It had the three big round tubes that projected up, so maybe that was one of the reasons; everybody could see this great big screen. It showed well and I think everybody had a good time."

Jay Johnson remembers "It was Fred Silverman, it was all the ABC network people, it was all the producers, all the cast, all the crew. The *Soap* pilot comes on, something everybody on the show had

Soap premiered Sept. 13, 1977... and immediately afterward was dissected on-air by a panel of religious figures on the local Los Angeles ABC affiliate.

already seen at least once. "It was actually half of what was shot. It was shot as an hour show and they only showed the first 30 minutes. So to all of us looking at it, it was OK, but it's only setting up the jokes. We're all kind of congratulating each other."

And then?

"And then the local news comes on, and it's Jerry Dunphy who was the big Ted Baxter of Los Angeles. He comes on and says, 'You've just seen it, there it is. What do you think?' And he turned to a rabbi, a Catholic priest and another religious fundamentalist, and there was a panel of people discussing *Soap*! That was the first time I realized how surreal this whole thing was, that a show was being turned into a panel issue on the nightly news."

Also at the party was Sal Viscuso whose character, Father Tim, hadn't even been introduced yet. "And Fred Silverman was standing next to me. He says, 'You know, Sal, enjoy this because we might not get you on the air.'"

Over the next few weeks, as ABC tried to pacify its advertisers and communicate with the public through the media, the pressure groups kept up their onslaught. *Soap*'s old friend, the Southern Baptist Convention, went straight to the press with a revelation that ABC executives probably would've rather kept quiet considering the hellish ride the show had endured over the last three months.

According to a press release issued by the SBC on Sept. 22, 1977, Anacin-maker American Home Products received $40,000 worth of *free* ad time during the second episode of *Soap* broadcast Sept. 20. "We did not pay one penny. They gave us a free ride," the

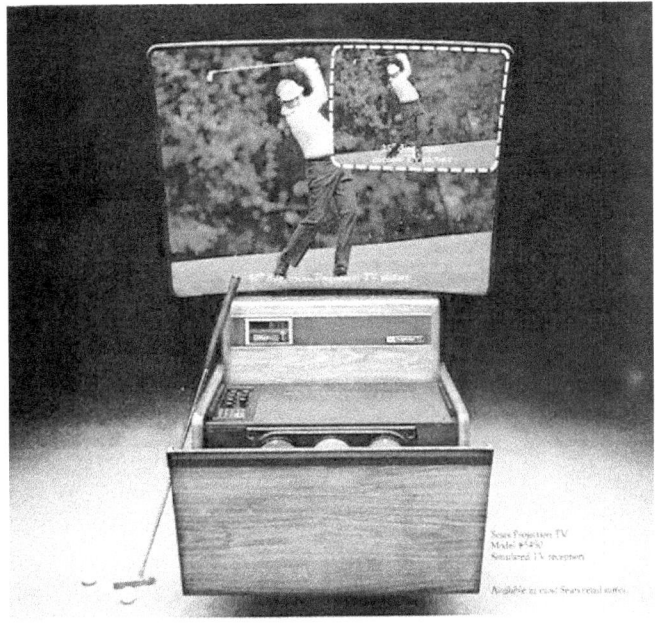

Much of the cast and crew gathered at Bob Seagren's (Dennis Phillips) home to watch the premiere on his big-screen projection TV.

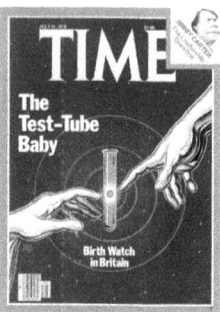

1977

On **JULY 25**, Louise Brown, the first person conceived through in vitro fertilization, was born in Manchester, England. Presumably the "test tube baby" simultaneously gratified and enraged the conservatives who agitated for the cancellation of *Soap*. It brought the world one step closer to doing away with the sinful act of sex and all of those "adult themes," while usurping God's unique ability to bring forth new life.

SBC quoted Dan Rogers, chairman of the AHP's John F. Murphy advertising agency, as saying. This quote, and much of the rest of the information in the piece, comes courtesy of another helpful SBC "Christian Life Commission Report," which was sent to many media outlets. The press release also points out that a 30-second spot on *Soap* at this time was going for $75,000, which manages to suggest that the sponsor received a free ride on ad time that had already been marked down nearly 50%. Finally, it closes with a helpful list of all the sponsors that had ads appear on either of the first two episodes of *Soap*: Lee Filter Division; Mem Company (English Leather); Bic Pen Corp.; Vlasstc Foods Inc. [probably pickle merchant VLASIC Foods]; Max Factor; Jovan Inc.; the aforementioned AHP; Manischewitz Light Wines; Preference by L'Oreal; and Presto Industries for the alarmingly named "Presto Fry Baby."

That same day, another release was issued by the SBC informing the faithful that its Sunday School Board was in the process of divesting itself of 2,500 shares of ABC stock worth nearly $100,000 because "the board does not approve of programming related to the abuse of human sexuality, violence and perversion." In case there was any question about what triggered this sudden hot line call to EF Hutton, Pastor Grady C. Cothen cuts through the subtlety. "During the controversy over the sex-oriented program *Soap*, we discovered the 2,500 shares in an examination of our portfolio held by one money manager..." As a final twist of the knife, Cothen informed the SBC that the program "should disgust intelligent people."

The September Winds Continue to Blow

It's difficult to appreciate the mood that ran through the production offices of Witt Thomas Harris throughout September and October. The wave of controversy that had been building since the June *Newsweek* story had broken over them all since *Soap*'s premiere, and things didn't seem to be getting any better.

"To tell you the truth, it kind of shocked me because when we did the pilot and it had not gone on the air, I thought gosh, this is such clever writing," says Katherine Helmond. "And oh boy, my part is wonderful. This should really go on for years. And then the pilot went on the air and oh my goodness, all of the newspapers and the magazines—we were just bombarded with stuff, that it was just shocking and it was degenerate and terrible. At the time I guess it broke through a lot of no-nos in television. For one thing, I was a married woman that had an affair with a tennis teacher. I think that was the first time you really saw a nice lady from a nice family openly having an affair. And then my daughter got involved with a priest that left the priesthood, and one daughter got involved with a convict; it was just one thing after another.... But I don't think we ever got the support that we deserved. I think that Susan's writing really deserved better than what was given to her."

A Dec. 12, 1977 *People* magazine profile of Helmond and artist husband David Christian took great pains to fan the flames with descriptions of *Soap* as "raunchy," possessing "sledgehammer double entendres" and plot lines "that often read like *Screw* magazine rejects." (Suggesting to those with lives beyond the pages of *People* magazine that the reporter knew little about *Screw* beyond its title.)

While Christian was certainly on to something when he lamented *Soap*'s double-standard on having Jessica chastised for her older woman/younger man affair with Peter while Chester failed to receive a comeuppance for his philandering, it was Helmond's grandmother who put it best in a story Helmond told the *People* reporter. "Before the premiere she called to ask if I would be doing anything dirty like taking off my clothes...After she saw the show she called and said, 'It's all talk and no action.'"

When it became clear that the media had already made up its mind about how *Soap* would be portrayed to the American people, cast members were told to avoid talking to reporters for the first six months of the series, Johnson says, undercutting what should've been a joyous time for them all. "We were on a show that was getting all the attention and we couldn't take advantage of, or even discuss, that. We just weren't allowed to enjoy any of that because anything we said was probably going to be turned around. So the best thing was to say nothing and stay out of the spotlight and don't go to those premieres. They might ask you questions that maybe you'll answer."

> ❝ It is true that some of [my] characters speak coarsely. That is because people speak coarsely in real life. Especially soldiers and hardworking men speak coarsely, and even our most sheltered children know that. And we all know, too, that those words really don't damage children much. They didn't damage us when we were young. It was evil deeds and lying that hurt us. After I have said all this, I am sure you are still ready to respond, in effect, 'Yes, yes—but it still remains our right and our responsibility to decide what books our children are going to be made to read in our community.' This is surely so. But it is also true that if you exercise that right and fulfill that responsibility in an ignorant, harsh, un-American manner, then people are entitled to call you bad citizens and fools. Even your own children are entitled to call you that."
> —KURT VONNEGUT JR., from a 1973 letter to Charles McCarthy, head of the school board that governed North Dakota's Drake High School, which burned copies of Vonnegut's book *Slaughterhouse-Five*.

1977

AUG. 26: Albino Luciani becomes Pope John Paul I, succeeding Pope Paul VI 20 days after the death of that pontiff. Luciani will be dead by *Soap* episode 2.3.

Perhaps nobody was more surprised by the outpouring of displeasure than the heads of ABC. Just a few months earlier, they had made it very clear that they considered *Soap* one of the flagship programs of their new fall season. This was the impression Robert Mandan had when the cast was introduced at a gathering of affiliate heads earlier that year.

"I can remember we were back in the kitchen waiting to go on. We went on and came down the flight of stairs, but we were in the kitchen. And Marlo Thomas was standing behind me and said, 'God, you always end up in the kitchen, don't ya?' You couldn't really hear what preceded you but when you hit the top of those stairs, all of those station managers and people were on their feet screaming. Our pictures were flashed around the walls of the convention hall. You had to go whoah, these guys are looking forward to this show because it's going to be their show of the season.

"There was a lot of false controversy that got started around *Soap*. In actuality, almost all of the scenes we did had been done on late night in *Mary Hartman, Mary Hartman*. They'd done the gay thing, they'd done a lot of stuff. But it wasn't in prime time."

Not that everybody viewed the controversy in quite such negative terms. "To tell you the truth, I was 22 years old, I had just gotten out of college, I thought it was great," stage manager Carl Lauten says with a laugh. "You wanted to be controversial, in a good way though. If you could be in something that was cutting edge and unique and well thought of in an intelligent way, I'd take that over *Three's Company* any day."

However, being a part of *Soap* was, in some circles, akin to being a McCarthy-era communist. Marsha Posner, who had paid her dues so completely when she moved to Hollywood, got a good taste of this when she returned to her native Phoenix her first year on the show.

"I had worked in local television there for two years as a secretary. I knew a lot of the people in local TV there, so I went back and I happened to meet the president of the NBC station there who I knew. I said to him, 'Guess what, I'm working in television in Hollywood; I'm working on a show called *Soap*! Isn't that great?' He looked at me and said, 'I wouldn't let my grandmother touch that show with a 10-foot pole.' And I thought, Ohhhkay. I guess we got that straight. So that was the end of that relationship."

Fortunately, other grandmothers weren't nearly so judgmental. "I'm from Mobile, Alabama," says Lauten. "My grandmother's Methodist. She had friends of hers who came up and said, 'I don't know how your grandson can work on such trash.' And she said, 'Well, have you ever seen the show?' And they'd say no. 'You have nothing to say to me then,'" is how she'd respond.

For years, success in television had been quantified by eyeballs; if you could cultivate a large audience, you were golden. True, efforts had been made by the networks to attract more sophisticated viewers (i.e., those with deeper pockets) in recent years, but big ratings were still a strong thing to have on your side. Yet the night of the *Soap* premiere, there was already a sense among cast and producers that high numbers weren't going to be enough to win the day.

"I think we had a 55 share," Johnson says of the premiere. "Fifty-five percent of all televisions were turned to *Soap* that night. We never did that again, unfortunately, but we certainly had that audience the first night. I kept thinking this is being blown out of proportion, this is just a show. Just relax and enjoy it. This is not news, this is just us."

A Backlash with a Subtext

However much free-speech advocates are tempted to characterize those who led the fight against *Soap* as a bunch of narrow-minded busy bodies, the benefit of hindsight shows that there was more going on than might have been apparent at the time.

There may be no greater example of a *Soap* critic who ultimately did more good than harm than Dr. Everett Parker, director of the office of communications for the United Church of Christ from 1954-1983. Though he would be remembered by *Soap* fans for his characterization of the series in the Sept. 26, 1977 issue of *Time* magazine as "A deliberate effort to break down any resistance to whatever the industry wants to put into prime time," Parker was no simple, out-of-touch moralist.

Dr. Everett Parker

1977

On **SEPT. 8**, INTERPOL criminalizes the pirating of video tapes, something that is still cited in the "FBI Warning" at the beginning of DVDs and other video formats today. **SEPTEMBER** also sees the publication of Jay Anson's *The Amityville Horror: A True Story*.

In the 1960s he led an effort to force broadcasters in the south to meet legal guidelines of fairness regarding blacks and other minorities. This culminated in a tense confrontation between the management of NBC affiliate WLBT-TV in Jackson, Miss., and Parker and his allies. WLBT was notorious for its treatment of blacks on the air, often mysteriously dropping an interview when the person being interviewed was black (claiming "technical difficulties"), refusing to sell ad time to black political candidates—the stories of wrongdoing were endless. Yet Parker and his associates managed to take the station to court within a few weeks of the murder of Jackson civil rights activist Medgar Evers on June 12, 1963.

"We determined that WLBT just had to lose its license," Parker told the author in 2008. "And to get the FCC to revoke a license was like asking heaven to open up and let everybody in." After lengthy legal battles, the FCC ultimately was ordered to revoke the station's license in 1971.

"It was a terrible time," says Parker. "Standing up for any minority was just the same as putting a gun to your head. I remember this much. When Mrs. Parker and I got out of Mississippi into Tennessee, we got out and kissed the ground. It was that dangerous. There are many people who can't believe I wasn't shot because that's the way they did it—they shot ya if they didn't like what you were doing."

In his 95th year when we spoke in 2008, Parker admitted that he couldn't really remember the fuss made over *Soap*. Yet something he said regarding his battle with WLBT goes some way toward explaining the attitude of those who picketed ABC over what they saw as its ramming of *Soap* down their throats in 1977.

"The networks are not something that anybody attacks without having thought about it a bit because they have a lot of power on their side, and they have billions of dollars and investments to protect. The networks are not on the side of the people….It's maybe the most powerful industry in the country and it's interested only in itself. Somebody has to take 'em on sometimes, and we did it."

Soap as Thin End of the Wedge

While the pre-launch news magazine coverage of *Soap* may have stoked initial opposition to the series, greater forces were at work.

More than sex, more than racial and LGBT issues, what really got up the noses of conservative critics the most was irreverence—humor at the expense of those values they held dear. From the heyday of radio right through the television broadcasts of the early 1960s, the players in nearly every mass medium had censored themselves so much, the "little old lady from Dubuke"* could be forgiven for believing every American from Rhode Island to California was straight, conservative, God fearing and military supporting, and liked their media as unchallenging as she did.

Though pre-'70s television comedy had simply been a continuation of the safe laughs—jokes about being cheap, fat or dumb—found on the radio, other parts of the media had grown considerably.

Fueled by newly-affordable printing technologies, underground "comix" (featuring counterculture artists such as Robert Crumb and Art Spiegelman) and left-leaning underground newspapers such as Austin's *The Rag* and the *Berkeley Barb* that were sold in head shops and record stores throughout the country, dealt with taboo subjects such as sex, gender issues and the war frankly, and in the vulgar idiom of the day.

On vinyl, so-called "party albums" transported the adults-only comedy of stand-ups like Redd Foxx, Richard Pryor and Lenny Bruce from big city nightclubs to teen and twentysomethings' basements. Adventurous radio DJs, too, weren't above putting on an 11 minute comedy set, simultaneously boosting their street cred and garnering themselves a decent cigarette break.

* The classic description put forth by Harold Ross, founder of *The New Yorker*, describing who his new magazine (launched in 1925) would NOT be for.

Not only did this expose more young people to comedy that challenged the bland variety of broadcast material, but it also made some realize that they weren't the only ones second-guessing the culture, the government and society as a whole. As these items turned up in their children's rooms, it also put parents on the defensive—the earthy parts of the world were invading their homes. Television, as it turned out, was the line they drew in the sand. And in 1977, *Soap* gleefully crossed it.

"We had just come out of the '60s in which there was a sexual revolution, so things were changing very quickly, and change always stokes fear, especially from certain elements of society who are resistant to it," Paul Junger Witt points out. "We were up against a prevailing attitude in certain parts of the country that was uncomfortable with women's equality, was uncomfortable to one degree or another with racial equality, was uncomfortable with homosexuals coming out of the darkness and into the light, was uncomfortable with what they saw as change threatening a traditional way of life. We didn't see it that way. We saw it as progress. I think the show mirrored that progress."

Whether the country was ready for that progress was another question.

Season One

With the nation's media lined up squarely against it on one side, and ad hoc groups protesting its very existence on the other, few television series have premiered with the cards so heavily stacked against them as *Soap*.

Though it would struggle in its first few episodes to define the sexuality of Jodie Dallas and to otherwise find its eventual trademark balance between farce and emotion, Season 1 of *Soap* remains one of the strongest first seasons in American television. And it all began with the story of two sisters...

 Pilot • First aired: Sept 13, 1977 • Written by Susan Harris • Directed by Jay Sandrich

Though still close, sisters Jessica and Mary live very different lives. Jessica married Chester Tate, a pompous businessman who will sleep with any woman but his wife. They have three children: Billy, 14, and his two older sisters, the prudish Eunice and the promiscuous Corinne. Jessica and Mary's delusional father, The Major, lives with the Tates. Their servant, Benson, appears to be the only sane person in the house. Mean-

NOTE: *Two episodes that share the same air date were originally aired as an hour-long segment.*

while, Mary married neurotic Burt Campbell, stepfather to Mary's sons Danny, who's mixed up in the mob, and younger brother Jodie, who's gay. And as becomes abundantly clear almost immediately, both families are up to their eyeballs in secrets.

Cast. Jimmy Baio (Billy Tate), Diana Canova (Corinne Tate), Billy Crystal (Jodie Dallas), Cathryn Damon (Mary Campbell), Robert Guillaume (Benson), Katherine Helmond (Jessica Tate), Robert Mandan (Chester Tate), Richard Mulligan (Burt Campbell), Arthur Peterson (The Major), Jennifer Salt (Eunice Tate), Robert Urich (Peter Campbell), Ted Wass (Danny Dallas), Rod Roddy (Announcer)

Highlights. Chester's bizarre hog-truck-accident excuse, and Corinne's addition of a turkey-truck disaster later on. Benson's simulated bombing sending The Major under the breakfast table, Jessica telling Peter that "to boff" sounds like a name you give a puppy: "Here Boff, here Boff."

Confused? You Won't Be? *'This is the story of two sisters...'*
▶ Chester has dangerously high cholesterol, hates fish, and is a diabetic. His excuse about being late home because of a hog truck will be reused for Burt much later (2.9) with a brilliant final line. The lavender scarf Eunice is hunting all over the house for will finally show up next episode.

▶ Though Benson says Billy's the only one in the family "worth a damn," we'll soon see that it's Jessica that he really cares most about.

▶ With Danny and Burt's kitchen-table argument, *Soap* is already employing one of its favorite bits of physical comedy—messing about with food.

▶ Right away, Benson is asserting his authority over his employers, making Chester reach for things he wants handed to him. This is also the first time we get Chester's trademark reply: "Shut up, Benson."

▶ Thus begins Danny's signature defense of brother Jodie: "I told you before, my brother is not a fruit! He's a practical joker with a wonderful sense of humor."

> ❝ Susan and I couldn't stop hugging and kind of elbowing each other [during filming of the pilot]. Actually it reminded me of my father's stand-up because we had crafted for some time that two-parter, and to hear that audience just go crazy. We were in the booth with the director; Jay [Sandrich] almost kicked us out: 'Would you guys shut up!' We were laughing and giggling and thrilled that the audience was loving it so much. We really were giddy with the fact that the material was going over so well."
>
> —TONY THOMAS
> Executive Producer

▶ Burt will spend much of the series feeling that the Tates are looking down on him for not having enough class. This episode we see that this persecution complex may have started much earlier, after his wife took their kids and moved to Hawaii 15 years ago "because she decides *I* don't have enough class, she can do better."

▶ Once Mary leaves the kitchen, Burt reveals (in a monologue) why he hasn't been able to be passionate with his wife in the bedroom: he killed her last husband, who was a criminal.

15 years: How long it's been since Burt's seen his own sons.

12 years: How long it's been since Benson spoke to Eunice.

NBC Can Be Controversial, Too!

Considering all of the chest-thumping that went on prior to *Soap*'s premiere, it's odd that virtually lost to history is the fact that the same night saw the debut of another bit of controversial television—*The Richard Pryor Show*—at 8 p.m., no less. Though sufficiently reined in by NBC executives, the controversial stand-up still managed to offend. As Pryor later observed, "One week of truth on TV could straighten out everything. But they're not going to write shows about how to revolutionize America. The top-rated shows are for retarded people." How little has changed.

Boff Wars

For every high-profile battle *Soap* would have with pressure groups over story lines, there were dozens of small skirmishes that producers had with the network over…lines. One of the first arose over Peter and Jessica's use of a bit of slang.

"We argued for days about the word 'boff,'" remembers Tony Thomas. "I mean just forever. And we had to shoot it nine different ways. We finally got boff in. And at the time it was funny. Now, I turn to my wife when we're watching TV—'I can't believe they're getting away with that.' *Golden Girls* was easier, that's for sure. But I think it's because first of all a lot of years had passed, and no one wanted to say those women could do any wrong."

1977

SEPT: *Mother Jones* magazine reveals that Ford Motor Co. declined to repair a defect in its Pinto vehicles for eight years, which resulted in hundreds of deaths by fire. (Its advertising agency, J. Walter Thompson, *did* drop a line from the end of a radio spot that read "Pinto leaves you with that warm feeling.")

Now Entering East Berlin: *Soap* and *Barney Miller* were shot in two different studios, side by side in the same building. And the casts of both shows had to labor under demanding conditions. Recalls Jay Johnson, "We would come in at 10 o'clock in the morning and [*Barney Miller*] had started a script. We'd rehearse all day, go home, come back the next day for the next rehearsal, and they would *still* be shooting the same scene at *Barney Miller*. It was this slow, tedious process that they would go on forever. However, just to let you know what it was like on our set, they called *us* East Berlin. All these nighters and rewrites and all that stuff, but they still thought they had it better than us."

Best Lines.

Billy [about Benson's home remedy]: Does it work for pimples?

Benson: Well, it's hard to say, 'cause it's not actually *for* pimples. You see, *we* don't get pimples. God said, "I won't give them pimples, I'll just screw up their hair."

Major [to Benson]: After breakfast, boy, maybe you'll sing a little song for me.

Jessica: Uh, daddy. Daddy dear, we don't call them "boy".

Major: What do you call them, boogies?

Jessica: No Daddy, *his* name is Benson.

Chester [after The Major has taken some pistol shots at their neighbor]: What I'd like to know is where does he get the bullets? [Benson enters the room, catches Chester's question, and quickly leaves.]

Rod Roddy's Wrapup. Will Jessica find out about Corinne and Peter? Will Corinne find out about Jessica and Peter? Will Burt tell Mary he killed her first husband? Will Billy's zit disappear before his first date? Will Benson make fish? These questions and many others will be answered on the next episode of *Soap*.

Jessica, right, reveals her affair to her usually unflappable sister, Mary.

1.2
First aired: Sept 20, 1977 • Written by Susan Harris • Directed by Jay Sandrich

Jessica confesses to Mary that she's taken a younger lover, and Chester finds himself on the messy end of blackmail when his plans to dump lover/secretary Claire go awry. Danny is told he must fulfill a murder contract if he wants to leave the mob, Burt accidentally bumps into the son he's been estranged from for 15 years, and Jodie tells everybody he's considering a sex-change operation.

Cast. Jimmy Baio (Billy), Diana Canova (Corinne), Billy Crystal (Jodie), Cathryn Damon (Mary), Robert Guillaume (Benson), Katherine Helmond (Jessica), Richard Libertini (The Godfather), Robert Mandan (Chester), Richard Mulligan (Burt), Arthur Peterson (The Major), Kathryn Reynolds (Claire), Jennifer Salt (Eunice), Robert Urich (Peter), Ted Wass (Danny), Rod Roddy (Announcer), Stephen Mendillo (Sheldon)

Highlights. Jessica's confession to Mary about the reason for her new "glow", Mary and Jodie's heart-to-heart in her bedroom, and everyone's reaction to Peter when he walks into the Tate living room and is introduced as Burt's long lost son.

Confused? You Won't Be. *'Boy, this is a lot for one day.'*
◉ This episode brings us our first peek at a Tate/Campbell get-together, which goes about as well we'd expect.

1977

SEPT. 20: The week after ABC introduced the Tates and the Campbells, it aired the *Happy Days* episode that featured Fonzie jumping a shark on water skis, giving birth to a phrase that remains with us to this day.

▶ Billy borrows $10 from Chester for a date, starting on the long road to Leslie Walker.

Oct. 28, 1962: Billy's birthday.

Today's Cliffhanger: Will the Tates and Campbells find out that Burt's long lost son is carrying on with Jessica and Corinne?

Chester's track record with women (according to Claire): He's been seeing "Pigeon" for weeks; the blonde in securities; the redheaded switchboard operator; the brunette in payroll. As Claire tells him: "I've watched you work your way up through half this building, Chester. I never knew if you were doing it by floor or hair color."

The Tate-Campbell Meal Scenes

"The very first two shows started out with some funny, funny stuff because we had a big family reunion in the Tate household, I think, with a big dinner," Robert Mandan remembers. "And the prop department had set all the food outside under plastic. By the time we got to the second show, all the food was spoiled. It had been sitting out in the hot Southern California sun. They were running around with hairspray trying to deodorize some of the stuff because it smelled bad, and they were running around going, 'Don't eat anything, don't eat anything, it's all spoiled!' And we were trying to shoot this dinner scene. Then, of course, we're throwing food and

it was wild. Sadly enough, that prop man, he was replaced immediately. It was like 'Is this going to be fun, or is this going to be horrible for the rest of the time that we're on the air?'"

Rod Roddy's Wrapup. Will Jodie have a sex-change operation? Will Danny take the contract and find out that Burt, his stepfather, killed his father? Will Jessica find out about Chester and his secretary, Claire? Will Chester find out about Jessica and Peter? Will Corinne find out about Jessica and Peter? Will Jessica find out about Corinne and Peter? Will Burt find out? Will Benson find out? Will Benson care? These questions and many others will be answered on the next episode of *Soap*.

Behind the Scenes. Recalls Director Jay Sandrich, Cathryn Damon "made me laugh with that line: 'Oh, you wear that belted.' Nobody had made it work for me and I really laughed when she did that line. (She was in New York and so we only had a videotape of her to go on.) I realized if she can do that one line, she can play the part. She was a wonderful actress."

Best Lines.
[Peter comes into the Tate home.]
Corinne: Peter!
Jessica: Peter!
Peter: Corinne?
Jessica: Corinne?
Peter: Jessica?
Corinne: Mother?
Burt: Jessica.
Mary: [putting it together] Oh my God.
Chester: Jessica?
Jessica: [hiding behind her makeshift veil] Peter.
Corinne: [looking annoyed] Mother?
Jodie: [seductively] Peeeeter.

Jodie impresses his mother with his dress sense as he prepares for his sex change.

Mary: Jodie, how many times do I have to tell you: leave my things alone! Look at that! My wig, my necklace, my best dress. [Takes in what she's seeing for a moment.] Oh! You wear that *belted*!

1.3
First aired: Sept 27, 1977 • Written by Susan Harris • Directed by Jay Sandrich

Jessica is horrified by the arrival of Peter and resolves to confess her affair to Chester, despite Mary's attempts to set her straight about just how faithful *Chester* has been. Despite an inability to resolve his bedroom problems with Mary, Burt does make some substantial progress in making peace with Danny, and more difficult still, Jodie. Yet, when Danny resolves to leave the mob and finally make peace with Burt, the godfather hits him with a 1-2 punch: Burt is the man who killed his father, and if Danny doesn't kill him, the mob will kill Danny.

Those in the audience weren't the only ones having trouble keeping a straight face.

Cast: Jimmy Baio (Billy), Diana Canova (Corinne), Billy Crystal (Jodie), Cathryn Damon (Mary), Robert Guillaume (Benson), Katherine Helmond (Jessica), Richard Libertini (The Godfather), Robert Mandan (Chester), Richard Mulligan (Burt), Arthur Peterson (The Major), Jennifer Salt (Eunice), Robert Urich (Peter), Ted Wass (Danny), Rod Roddy (Announcer)

Highlights. Burt and Danny burying the hatchet, however temporarily; *The Cookbook of Sex*; and Burt's heart-to-heart with Mary and Jodie about the reasons he's so put off by Jodie's sexuality.

Confused? You Won't Be. *'I mean I just got used to...'*

◉ This episode is all about adjustment. For Jessica, it's getting used to the fact that not only did she cheat on Chester, she cheated on him with her step-nephew-in-law. For Burt, it's wrapping his head around the fact that Jodie is a person, despite his homosexuality. For Danny, it's about learning to accept Burt because he makes his mother happy.

◉ Billy continues his quest for female companionship, borrowing the keys to the family car so he can "park" with his girlfriend.

◉ Burt's "The Flying Wallendas at the height of their career couldn't get into a position like that" on seeing one of the positions in the *Cookbook of Sex* is slightly unfortunate, as Karl Wallenda will plummet to his death on March 22 the following year at 73 while walking a tightrope between two towers of a hotel in San Juan, Puerto Rico.

Food fun: Burt gives Danny a faceful of mashed potatoes after the young man tells him that Jodie's not a fruit, starting a food fight between the Tates and the Campbells. The conflict continues between Burt and Danny at home until Mary threatens to leave if she finds one more speck of food anywhere but on a plate.

6 months ago: The last time Burt and Mary…you know.

'From now on, I'll try to look at ya as a person.' After two episodes that pretty much summed up many Americans' views of homosexuals as "fruits," this one does for homophobes what *All in the Family*'s Archie Bunker did for bigots: It allows Burt to put his reasons for hating Jodie on the table. It all starts with Mary demanding to know why Burt hates her son so much:

Jodie: It's because I'm gay, right Burt? I mean you hate me because I'm gay, right?

Mary: Well?

Burt: I guess if you need a reason, that's a good one.

Jodie: Burt, it's a terrible reason. I mean look at me, I'm a person.

Mary: Burt, look at him.

[Burt forces himself to turn around and look at Jodie, who puts on his best smile; Burt shudders.]

Burt: He gives me the creeps.

Jodie: Burt, what do you mean I give you the creeps?

Burt: I don't know; you're spooky.

Mary: He's not spooky. I do not find him in the least spooky.

Burt: Well maybe you're used to it.

Jodie: Burt, just think of me as a person, that's all. That's all I am. I'm a person sitting here. Burt, look at me. I'm a person…[Burt looks at him]….who happens to like men.

Mary: Burt!

1977

SEPT. 29: The U.S. stamp program is enacted to feed many unemployed and low-income Americans.

While Burt will never be completely comfortable with Jodie, this episode is the start of a fragile peace between them.

In fairness to Burt, Jodie's mannerisms during the first few episodes were kind of creepy.

Burt: No, wait a minute. I don't know. It's hard, this gay business. I'm not used to it. I mean all my life, I was never around them. When I was growing up, gay meant happy. I mean it's just hard to get used to it. And life was a lot easier then. I mean maybe when you guys were still in the closet, maybe it was not easy on you, but it was a hell of a lot easier on us. I mean it used to be you'd walk down the street and a guy would smile at you, you'd smile back. Today you smile back and you either get arrested or invited dancing. So it takes getting used to. It's hard getting used to a guy who likes guys and not girls. And now you're going to get a sex-change operation and be a girl. Now I've got to get used to a guy who's now a girl who likes guys and not girls who used to be a guy who liked guys and not girls! But...I'll try. From now on, I'll try to look at ya as a person.

Jodie: And I'll try to look at you the same way.

Says Susan Harris, "I still get thanked for that character [Jodie] by gay people. I think it was the first time there was a homosexual on television who was portrayed as a human being. I would say out of all the characters, that was the one that had the most impact on people for that very reason."

Best Lines.

Jessica: Mary, I'm so ashamed I could die. Do you realize what I've done? I've had an affair with my nephew. I think that's against the law.

Mary: He's not your nephew.

Jessica: I mean I just got used to adultery and now I have to get used to uh, to uh...

Benson: Incest.

Jessica: Mary, I've never done this before, ever. See what it was, I was lonely. I mean Chester's never here and the kids are never here

1977

OCT. 3: The night before this episode aired, NBC gave the now-dead Family Viewing Policy its own salute by airing *Murder in Peyton Place*, a 100-minute film loosely based on the "scandalous" Grace Metalious novel of the 1950s. (*Soap's* network, ABC, aired its own successful series based on the book in the 1960s.)

and I've done all the clever things I could with shelving paper, so Mary, I did *that*. But I'm never going to do it again, Mary. Ever.

Mary [to Burt]: I've tried everything. Short nightgowns, long nightgowns, new nightgowns, no nightgowns. I have powdered myself, perfumed myself—bees are attracted to me and you're not.

Rod Roddy's Wrapup. Will Burt and Danny become friends, or will Danny kill Burt, thus putting somewhat of a strain on the relationship? Will Jodie get a sex-change operation? Will Corinne and Jessica find out that not only do they have the same tennis teacher, but that neither of them are learning to play tennis? Will Jessica be able to stop? Will Burt be able to start? These questions and many others will be answered on the next episode of *Soap*.

Marc Summers, who would go on to host the '80s Nickelodeon game show *Double Dare*, was the "warm-up guy" on *Soap*, Jay Johnson remembers. His job was to keep the audience laughing between takes. Johnson would play a similar role later on *Night Court*.

 First aired: Oct 4, 1977 • Written by Susan Harris + Tony Lang • Directed by Jay Sandrich

Corinne's still sleeping around, Billy's still trying to get a steady girlfriend, and Jodie's still talking about a sex change (though now we see why). Chester's secretary Claire gives him an ultimatum—leave Jessica or she'll spill the beans about what she knows to the SEC. Meanwhile, Burt is overjoyed with what he thinks is a newfound understanding he's reached with Danny, oblivious to the fact that his klutzy stepson is actually trying to kill him.

Cast. Jimmy Baio (Billy), Diana Canova (Corinne), Billy Crystal (Jodie), Cathryn Damon (Mary), Robert Guillaume (Benson), Katherine Helmond (Jessica), Robert Mandan (Chester), Richard Mulligan (Burt), Arthur Peterson (The Major), Kathryn Reynolds (Claire), Jennifer Salt (Eunice), Bob Seagren (Dennis), Robert Urich (Peter), Ted Wass (Danny), Rod Roddy (Announcer), Olivia Barash (Molly), Marianne Bunch (Pigeon)

Confused? You Won't Be. 'We're a perfectly nice, normal family.'
▶ The series has mercifully done away with the captions telling us where we are and what time it is. Billy continues his quest for

female companionship, landing the annoying Molly whom he strong arms into going steady with him, though it costs him his swimming medal.

▶ Eunice tells everybody she's flying to Washington to cover a press conference, though we'll see this may not be technically true next episode.

▶ Our first glimpse of Jodie at work, he's directing a commercial for Ball 4 starring hunky quarterback Dennis Phillips.

▶ Danny's frustrated attempts to kill Burt with anything he can get his hands on is the beginning of a type of humor that will turn up in several places in *Soap*'s run, most effectively in Chuck's desperate attempts to animate various foods in the Campbell kitchen after Jodie hides Bob in the fridge (1.20).

Today's reveal: Corinne is adopted, and her mother was a skank, too.

Introducing...Dennis Phillips, Jodie's boyfriend.

300: The number of calories Eunice allows herself daily. "If I brush my teeth twice a day, that puts me a little over."

12 years: How long Claire's been Chester's secretary.

Jacqueline Bisset: Who Jodie will look like after the sex change, according to his doctor.

Chester and Benson

There has never been a TV relationship between black worker and white boss quite like that between Benson and Chester. There is a long tradition of worker/boss humor, of course, most notably PG Wodehouse's famous thick-headed gentleman Bertie Wooster and his brainy butler, Jeeves. And the Jack Benny radio show of the '30s, '40s and '50s featured the black valet Rochester van Jones (played by Eddie Anderson, who died about seven months before *Soap* premiered). Rochester dealt good-naturedly with his pompous, penny pinching boss Jack Benny by frequently getting the last laugh. Jack would occasionally get exasperated with his valet, but neither Rochester nor Jeeves ever exuded the same utter contempt for their employers that Benson did for Chester. Similarly, neither employer so clearly detested their servant as Mr. Tate.

"Rochester was never as right or as intelligent or as smart as Benson," says Robert Mandan. "He was kind of instinctually smart. Benson was smart, I always felt. He ran the house.

"We had set up between Bob [Guillaume] and I these things where he'd say I'm not doing that or whatever, and I would say very haughtily (my only retort to him because I was made totally helpless) 'Oh shut up, Benson.' That was it. One day, I don't remember who it was that said it, 'Well, let's not do that anymore.' I went, 'What? It's a running gag!' 'Well, it's not funny anymore.' I thought maybe not to you but it certainly would be to the audience. But we dropped it, and I was always sorry about that because I thought that really established their relationship. That he wasn't going to control Benson in any way whatsoever and was just left with this helpless 'shut up.' He couldn't fire him because he knew Jessica would be on his case about that."

The way valet Rochester (right) frequently made fun of boss Jack Benny's vanity and foibles made him a sort of Benson 1.0.

Best Lines.

Jessica [to Chester]: We can't fire Benson. Nobody but Benson would put up with us.

Billy [about sex education]: I don't know why they have to teach us about animals. Benson told it better.

Chester: Well, I'm sure that Benson, in his primitive way, explained things to you, but I think it's a good idea if you had the right view of things.

Jessica: The white view? Chester, do whites and blacks do it differently?

Chester: I said the *right* view, Jessica.

'Oh shut up, Benson.'

Jodie [after Dennis admits he's been seeing a woman]: A woman. Does she know?

Dennis: I haven't told her yet.

Jodie: Well Dennis, when you touch her and throw up, I think she's going to be suspicious.

Rod Roddy's Wrapup. Will Jessica and Corinne ever stop to wonder why they're both learning to play tennis in Peter's apartment? Will Jessica leave Peter and try to make her marriage work? Will Chester leave Claire and risk getting sent to jail? Will Jodie get a sex-change operation and try to compete with his boyfriend's girlfriend? Will Burt get to eat his sandwich or will Danny kill him first? These questions and many others will be answered on the next episode of *Soap*.

Shooting an Episode

No one disputes that *Soap* shot on a rigorous five-day schedule, but people's memories today vary with some contemporaneous accounts covering the first two seasons.

In an article on Jay Sandrich from the May 1978 issue of *American Film* magazine, production is said to begin on a Saturday with taping taking place on Wednesday evenings. Cast and crew receive the next week's script on Thursday; on Fridays they do the first run-through. Harris finalizes the script on Friday evenings, with actors having the lines memorized by Monday. (Today, Sandrich doesn't remember it this way. "My memory is we taped on Wednesday and started the next show on Thursday. But we did not work over the weekend.")

The following is how stage manager Carl Lauten and several members of the cast remember it:

Monday: Cast and crew come in around noon to read and block out the new script. They would then rehearse the first act and go home.

Tuesday: Cast and crew return at 10 a.m., rehearse the second act, go to lunch, and review how the first act went. At 3:30 p.m., the cast would have a formal run-through of the script. Susan would rewrite any troublesome scenes.

Wednesday: Cast and crew report at 10 a.m. for more rehearsal. At 4 p.m., they have another run-through of the script, this time for the Standards and Practices people from the network.

Thursday: By 9 a.m., they would run through the entire episode again, this time incorporating the camera to make sure everything—blocking, lighting, etc.—looked all right. From 4 p.m. to 5 p.m., the cast would don the clothes they would wear for the episode, allowing the wardrobe department a chance to make sure everything looked OK. Everyone would call it a day by 6 p.m.

Friday: Shooting day. Everybody would arrive at noon and spend about 15 minutes on each scene. Lunch would be from 2 to 3, with different actors being called away to hair and makeup starting around 2, in order to ensure all will be ready in time. From 5 p.m. to 6 p.m. the dress rehearsal would be taped in front of a live audience. From 6:30 to 7:30, cast and crew would go to dinner, where they would receive notes from the producers about what needed to be changed for the next taping (in front of another live audience) at 8. The director would put together a first cut of the episode, which would be submitted to the producers, who would give their suggestions for changes to the video editor, says director JD Lobue. The editor would share those notes with the director for his input before a final cut was produced.

"If you give that schedule to any sitcom today they'd say it can't be done, that it's never been done," says Lauten.

Soap's competition for this episode as seen in TV Guide.

1977

OCT. 13: Taking of Lufthansa Flight 181. Four members of the Popular Front for the Liberation of Palestine terrorist group hijacks this flight bound for Frankfurt, forcing the pilot to change course for Cyprus, and ultimately, Somalia. Like actions before theirs, the group demanded the release of key members of West Germany's Red Army Faction, aka the Baader-Meinhof group.

1.5

First aired: Oct 13, 1977 • Written by Susan Harris + Tony Lang • Directed by Jay Sandrich

This episode, everybody seems to be grappling with the unavailable man in their life. Mary drags Burt to Dr. Medlow's office to get to the root of his impotence problem; Claire continues to pull Chester's strings; and Jodie and Eunice discover that they're both seeing unavailable men on the sly—Eunice is dating married Congressman Walter McCallam, and Jodie's still with Dennis. But Corinne seems to be the one with the biggest problem: She's in love with the celibate priest Father Timothy Flotsky, a childhood sweetheart who left her for the priesthood. When she vows to try to forget him by finally telling Peter she'll move in with him, her heart is broken even more by what she finds at his place—Jessica.

Cast. Diana Canova (Corinne), Billy Crystal (Jodie), Cathryn Damon (Mary), Robert Guillaume (Benson), Katherine Helmond (Jessica), Robert Mandan (Chester), Richard Mulligan (Burt), Jennifer Salt (Eunice), Bob Seagren (Dennis Phillips), Robert Urich (Peter), Sal Viscuso (Father Tim Flotsky), Ted Wass (Danny), Rod Roddy (Announcer), Byron Webster (Dr. Medlow), Nita Talbot (Mrs. Fine)

Highlights. Eunice and Jodie bonding over their pursuit of unobtainable men at the restaurant; Burt's insane behavior at the psychiatrist's office, and his instant "are they good looking" when the doctor explains about sexual surrogates ("Is there a choice? Ya got pictures?"); Corinne's heartfelt appeal to Father Tim in the confessional; and her reaction to seeing her mother in a clinch with Peter.

Confused? You Won't Be. *'Ministers do it, why can't you?'*
▶ Burt grew up in Pittsburgh. Eunice tells Jodie she didn't like him when she was younger because he used to steal her clothes, something he still does (1.1). Burt's first visit to a shrink is not his last this season (1.19).

▶ Like much of *Soap*'s story lines, the whole Father Tim/Corinne one is a nod to contemporary culture, in this case the Colleen McCullough novel *The Thorn Birds*, published in April 1977. This tale of a young woman who grows to love an Australian priest would become a popular ABC miniseries in 1983 starring Richard Chamberlain and Rachel Ward (left).

Burt's first visit to Dr. Medlow is the beginning of the series-long struggle he will have with his hold on his own mental stability.

⏵ Despite some physical comedy that hasn't aged well (Benson proving that Chester is faking his arm problem by making him catch a grapefruit), this episode is pretty solid, with Richard Mulligan and Diana Canova stealing the show in their respective scenes.

Introducing... Father Timothy Flotsky.

"Father Flotsky's Triumph"

There's something almost Dickensian about the name of the man who captured Corinne's heart: Father Flotsky. It practically cries out "schlub". Yet the name also served another purpose: a declaration that the producers who were raked over the coals just a few years ago on *Fay* had no intention of toning down their material now. For the hip crowd, the name Flotsky called to mind only one person.

"It was an homage to Lenny Bruce, who pushed boundaries, who spoke publicly what we very often thought privately," says Paul Junger Witt. Specifically, the name comes from "Father Flotsky's Triumph," a classic bit from Bruce's 1958 album *Interviews of Our Time*. Ostensibly a parody of the 1938 movie *Prison Break* and, more broadly, every old movie with a moral, "Father Flotsky's Triumph" follows

1977

OCT. 17-18: The so-called "German Autumn" sees West Germany explode with instances of terrorism inspired by

the already imprisoned founders of the Red Army Faction (aka the Baader-Meinhof group). By the end, Andreas Baader, Jan-Carl Raspe and Gudrun Ensslin will either commit suicide or be murdered in their cells, depending on how you read the evidence. Ulrike Meinhof died in prison the previous year.

5

The number of men Corinne confesses to having been with since her last confession two months ago

---

a naive priest's attempts to put down a prison riot led by a prisoner called Dutch(!). In the process, Bruce skewers a number of society's ills, including the country's jailing of blacks at the height of the civil rights movement. On the other hand, the whole bit ends with the prison's gay hospital attendant agreeing to defuse the situation in return for being named the official Avon representative for the prison.

The controversy begins...now. *Corinne hits on Father Flotsky in the confessional.* Pretty much the first scene that *Soap*'s opponents latched on to in order to prove how horrible the show was is also one of the sweetest in the series. Corinne, a young woman who we've recently learned is adopted, is struggling to understand why Flotsky, someone who's flirted with her since 5th grade, has abandoned her for the church. Though it may not be entirely fair for her to blame her promiscuity on his lack of availability, it demonstrates a lot of self-insight for a sitcom character.

For his first appearance on *Soap*, Sal Viscuso says he couldn't have asked for a better introduction. The audience was "laughing so hard at the confessional scene, if you look carefully you can see me laugh, which I wish I could've gone back and redone. But we reshot it at the end of the night and sent the audience home because they said they just couldn't hear the words because there was so much laughter."

$50/hour: How much Burt and Mary are paying Dr. Medlow.

Mr. & Mrs. Murray Fleischman: The fake names Burt gives Dr. Medlow.

For the *Soap* Bible Tells Us So. Tim and Corinne attended elementary and junior high school together, and were voted cutest couple in 9th grade. However, Mrs. Flotsky, convinced that Tim "had the calling," placed him in St. Elmo's Jesuit Seminary. He returned to town to teach at the local parochial school, only to find Corinne hanging around, pretending to be contemplating conversion to the church.

Rod Roddy's Wrapup. Will Corinne ever leave Father Tim alone? Will Corinne ever forgive her mother for Peter? Will Corinne ever forgive Peter for her mother? Now that Jodie is going to become his boyfriend's girlfriend, will his boyfriend get rid of his girlfriend? Since Burt seems unwilling to talk, will the psychiatrist ever be able to cure his impotency? Since Danny seems to be a klutz, will he ever be able to kill Burt? Will Burt be cured or killed? These questions and many others will be answered on next week's episode of *Soap*.

Best Lines.

Corinne: You love me and I love you, so why can't we be together? It's not fair.

Tim: Because *He* won't allow it.

Corinne: Don't be ridiculous. I mean what did you do, have a personal conversation with Him and He said, "No Tim, no whoopee"?

Sal Viscuso and Robert Urich in an '88 episode of *Spencer for Hire*

Corinne [after catching Peter and Jessica kissing at his apartment]: This is really the limit mother. When I was 8, you took away my cap pistol. When I was 13, you took away my eye shadow. But this!

1.6 First aired: Oct 25, 1977 • Written by Susan Harris • Directed by Jay Sandrich

No sooner does Chester pull Billy out of the doldrums after Molly dumps him than he learns daughter Corinne is leaving to shack up with Peter Campbell. Jessica tries to square things with her daughter, but Corinne's still heartbroken over Father Tim, and appeals to him at church. The only person who's happy this episode is Burt, who's just learned that his son Chuck is coming for a visit from Hawaii (along with his dummy, Bob, but the less said about that the better). If he'll live to actually see Chuck is questionable, though, as Danny's given one last chance by the Godfather to kill his stepfather.

Richard Libertini's Godfather is equal parts sympathetic and menacing.

Cast: Jimmy Baio (Billy), Diana Canova (Corinne), Billy Crystal (Jodie), Cathryn Damon (Mary), Robert Guillaume (Benson), Katherine Helmond (Jessica), Richard Libertini (The Godfather), Robert Mandan (Chester), Richard Mulligan (Burt), Arthur Peterson (The Major), Jennifer Salt (Eunice), Sal Viscuso (Father Tim), Ted Wass (Danny), Rod Roddy (Announcer), Ian Wolfe (Monsignor)

Highlights. Corinne and Eunice trying to one-up each other over the complexity of their respective romantic relationships (Corinne wins when she explains that Peter's also having an affair with their mother); Burt explaining to Mary, Jodie and Jessica about Chuck & Bob; Father Tim's reaction to Corinne in church while reading from the Bible in Latin; and the Godfather's avuncular conversation with Danny in his rooftop Manhattan greenhouse.

Confused? You won't be. *'In life, people make mistakes.'*
▶ Burt gave Bob to Chuck when he was a kid. He took Bob to school with him, and into the Army, where he served in "special services" in Vietnam, where he and Bob also entertained the troops. Burt explains that Chuck gets upset if people refer to Bob as a "dummy," ostensibly setting up just how real Chuck believes Bob is. In actuality, this also reflects the attitude of many professional ventriloquists, including Jay Johnson (Chuck), who prefer to refer to their companions as "puppets."

▶ Diana Canova continues to be the one who pulls at the heartstrings, not only with the emotions that wash over her face while Jessica apologizes to her about what happened with Peter, but also with her second appeal to Father Tim in church. As Chester tells Billy at the beginning of this episode, there are many, many beautiful women in the world, but in this case, not many can simultaneously convey the cheeky nature and childlike innocence wielded by Canova in these scenes.

Best friend Benson: Benson tells Corinne to call him if she needs anything, though he adds that stops at doing her laundry.

And introducing... Chuck & Bob, and the Godfather's superior, Mr. Lefkowitz, all in name only.

The controversy begins...now. *Corinne bits on Father Flotsky in church...again.* Though Corinne telling Father Tim that she'll be thinking of him when she's "with" Peter seems calculated to tweak the noses of those who got flustered by the confessional scene last episode, we're again presented with a scene that's more heartbreaking than heretical. Sal Viscuso remembers being called to the producers' office to be told that the network was having a problem with that whole scene. "They felt like even though I don't touch

2 MONTHS AGO
When Chester gave Jessica a tennis racket, sparking her affair with Peter (In a moment of relief, Jessica tells Mary "This is all Chester's fault")

her, I don't say anything—it's all in Latin—my looks were suggesting clearly that I was responding to her. If you look at that carefully, you can tell she was getting to me. They basically had to negotiate where I was going to look at her and where I wasn't."

Diana Canova about Corinne: "I loved her immediately. She was warm and funny and a bit mixed up, but really totally sincere. She was in love. I would have played the family dog (if we had had one) to be in this show."

Chuck & Bob: Dunn's River's Most Wanted

One of the inspired creative streaks of the series was its penchant for putting the popular culture of the moment under a microscope and supplying its own fractured riff on the day's craze, which is exactly how Chuck & Bob were born.

For that added touch of authenticity, the prayer book Father Tim reads from is actually the very one Sal Viscuso used for his confirmation in the 1950s at St. Mary Star of the Sea on Court Street in Brooklyn (above).

Once Susan Harris and the producers had decided that Peter Campbell was going to meet a sticky end, they had to come up with someone to do him in. That's when Harris thought of one of the great archetypes of insanity: the demented ventriloquist.

The year before, novelist William Goldman (*The Princess Bride*, *Marathon Man*) had published a smart psychological potboiler called *Magic*. Now best remembered for the 1978 Richard Attenborough adaptation it inspired starring Anthony Hopkins, *Magic* recounts the now-classic tale of Corky Withers, an unbalanced magician turned ventriloquist, and his dummy, Fats, whom he believes alive.

Harris "told me that she pretty much lifted the description of Corky right out of that book and put it into her bible for *Soap*," says Jay Johnson. "Ultimately, I really got to play that part of Corky from *Magic* in *Soap*, and had a better time doing it.

"I asked Susan later why she wrote this particular character into the script. In the original bible of *Soap*, Chuck & Bob were the killers of Peter Campbell. That's the reason that character was brought in, so eventually they could be pinned with the murder. The bible called for Bob turning state's evidence on the witness stand and implicating Chuck, and then going to prison. Then, sort of like *Alcatraz* and *The*

Recalls Jay Johnson, "When I first got to Los Angeles, that book [*Magic*] was given to me by someone who said, 'Boy you ought to read this.' So I read it and I remember putting the book down and immediately going to my manager that I had just signed with after moving from Texas. I put the book on his desk and said, 'They will make a movie out of this book, and I think I'm the only guy in the world probably who can play this part. This is the part I was made to play.' Very cocky. And he said, 'Well, I'll check into it, but people think they're right for stuff all the time.' So I got very close to that movie. Had Norman Jewison directed that film, I probably would've been part of the cast. I doubt they would've let me play Corky because I was so unbankable at that point. But then Richard Attenborough took over the film and I never had a shot."

Great Escape, while he's in prison, Chuck makes a puppet of himself and Bob and leaves it on the pillow and they escape. There was quite a story line with that, but eventually that character was to escape and always be a threat and never be seen again. But after my first couple of shows, they got tremendous mail and great positive reaction. So they abandoned that plotline toward the end of the year and hired me as a regular."

Here is an excerpt from the *Soap* bible about the Peter Campbell trial:

"Chuck maintains that his dummy did the actual killing and insists he tried to stop him, and then was forced to cover up. It is a colorful trial as a distraught Chuck begs his dummy to 'fess up.' The dummy, who is no dummy, is impervious to his pleas and sits among the spectators, woodenly silent."

And under the section "Back Burner Plots":

"Chuck will eventually escape from Mattawan Prison for the Criminally Insane and terrorize all of Cos Cob," presumably the Connecticut neighborhood on which Dunn's River was based.

Though Chuck & Bob would be dropped as Peter Campbell's murderers, if you look at the early episodes closely, you can still see some remnants of that story line. Take, for example, Burt's mention of Chuck's time spent fighting in Vietnam.

"I think a lot of those early scenes were to accommodate the plot of Chuck & Bob going to court," Johnson says. "It may be that the original idea was that Peter was killed by stabbing and strangling, and the court would prove that was a military technique. I think a lot of those things were followed through, just because they applied to that arc."

"We never intended for Chuck & Bob to stay around as long as they did," admits Susan Harris. "It was just in and out. But they were so popular that we kept them. We also had the luxury of getting rid of somebody who just didn't work. There was an awful lot of freedom in that form to do really just about anything we wanted."

Rod Roddy's Wrapup. Will Corinne find happiness with Peter? Will Jessica find happiness without Peter? Will Corinne find happiness without Father Tim? Will Father Tim find happiness, or will Corinne drive him crazy? Will Danny invite Burt to the woods to kill him? Will Burt's other son, Chuck, and his little wooden doll, Bob, arrive from Hawaii? And if they do, will Burt live to see them? These questions and many others will be answered on next week's episode of *Soap*.

Best Lines.

Corinne [after Eunice admits she's in love]: You're in love? But you never go out.

Eunice [to Corinne, about Jessica and Peter]: I can't believe it. It took me 20 years to believe she did it with *daddy*.

Mary [reading the cable]: Burt, this is signed Chuck & Bob. Who's Bob?
Burt: That's nobody.
Mary: Well he's obviously somebody, Burt, because he's coming and he doesn't eat meat.
Jodie: Who doesn't eat meat?
Mary: Bob.
Jodie: Who's Bob?
Mary: I don't know. Somebody who's coming with Chuck.
Jodie: Who's Chuck?
Mary: Burt's son. Who's Bob?
Jodie: I don't even know who Chuck is. Who's Bob?
Burt: He's a dummy.
Mary: Burt, I didn't ask you for his IQ, I asked you who he was.
Burt: A dummy.
Jodie: Well your son Peter's no genius, either.
Jessica: Where's Peter?
Burt: He's a *dummy*!
Jessica: But he's sweet, Burt.

> "It was the first scripted television show I had ever done. I'd done a lot of variety shows and the specials, where they just needed an act to come in. But yeah, that was the first time I'd ever been cast in that situation. It was tough and easy and wonderful and hard and all those emotions you want to think when you first start. There were people who were friendly to me right away. There were people that were friendly, then became unfriendly. There were so many people in the cast that you could form your own kind of clique. I remember everybody being extremely nice to me, and any problems that happened just happened later. I was very focused on doing the best job I could, that's really what it was. If that meant being a little scared, that's what it was."
>
> —JAY JOHNSON on his first day on *Soap*

1.7 First aired: Nov 1, 1977 • Written by Susan Harris + Tony Lang • Directed by Jay Sandrich

As The Major escalates his one-man war against neighbor Mr. Kirby, Claire pulls out the big guns to force Chester to leave Jessica—she tells Jessica all about their affair! Burt's joy at being reunited with son Chuck (and his puppet, Bob) and being invited to go fishing in the Poconos with Danny are short-lived when Danny pulls a gun on him, threatening to kill him once and for all.

Cast: Jimmy Baio (Billy), Billy Crystal (Jodie), Cathryn Damon (Mary), Robert Guillaume (Benson), Katherine Helmond (Jessica), Jay Johnson (Chuck & Bob), Robert Mandan (Chester), Richard Mulligan (Burt), Arthur Peterson (The Major), Kathryn Reynolds (Claire), Jennifer Salt (Eunice), Ted Wass (Danny), Rod Roddy (Announcer), Alan Oppenheimer (Mr. Kirby)

Highlights. Jessica trying to assuage The Major's former prisoner, Mr. Kirby, with offers of liquid refreshments; Chuck & Bob meeting Mary, Danny and Jodie for the first time; Burt and Danny's death-defying meeting at the top of a building under construction; and Benson's delight at seeing Chester come home, knowing that Claire and Jessica are talking in the dining room.

Confused? You Won't Be. *'I've always wanted to meet a Hawaiian ventriloquist.'*

▶ Benson's "Let's not waste all this good food. Let's invite the Campbells over, they can throw it around" is a reference to the food fight in 1.3. The Major has a long history of sparking international incidents, from attacking the German consulate in Manhattan to capturing the entire staff of Benihana's of Tokyo (on Pearl Harbor day, no less). This time, The Major captures Mr. Kirby, their neighbor (last mentioned in 1.1), who he thinks to be a Nazi spy. Despite numerous attempts to prove he's an American, Kirby can't tell The Major who played third base for the Yankees in 1931. Of course neither can Chester. (Oh, and the answer is Joe Sewell, by the way.)

▶ We get our first glimpse of Burt at work, courtesy of some construction stock footage and an impressive, girder-filled stage, complete with New York backdrop and a working crane (kind of).

▶ The instant animosity between Jodie and Bob probably stems from the former's hurt feelings over how easily Burt accepts Chuck's eccentricities while being revolted by Jodie's homosexuality.

Marsh Steel: Manufacturer of the girders.

$2,000: How much Claire spent wallpapering her apartment (on Chester's dime, of course).

Excuses Chester has given Claire for not leaving Jessica over the last 10 years: Billy had a perception problem; Eunice wouldn't get dressed or leave her room; Corinne had to be hospitalized because she couldn't keep solids down.

Chuck & Bob's intro song: Hello, hello, we're here to start the show. I'm Chuck. I'm Bob. Hello, hello, hello. Let's go, let's go, let's go. I'll sing and dance, he'll dance and sing. Wherever we go, whatever we do, we're going to go through it, together. Yeah!

Fun with Chuck & Bob: While it's Bob's cutting wit that people remember most, Chuck & Bob are masters of physical comedy, too. Chuck trying to help Bob turn his head back around after Danny twisted it defending Jodie is an excellent example—you actually feel for Bob!

42 STORIES

The drop from where Burt is working on the construction site

"I Love Anita Bryant"

Bob's verbal jab at Jodie is far more hurtful than Jodie's sawdust and knock-on-wood jokes. Few people divided the country in the 1970s quite like singer Anita Bryant, one of the most visible symbols of the Christian right that would soon dominate much of the 1980s.

Born in Oklahoma, Bryant spent her teens making significant headway in local beauty pageants, becoming second runner-up in the 1959 Miss America competition. She recorded several high-charting singles including "Paper Roses" and "In My Little Corner of the World." In 1969, she recorded several popular commercials for the Florida Citrus Commission (singing "Come to the Florida Sunshine Tree").

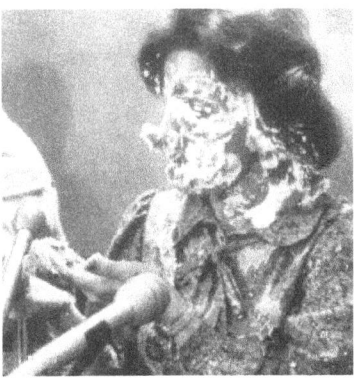

Anita Bryant pied by Minnesota activist Thom Higgins during a press conference in Des Moines on Oct. 14, 1977, the day after episode 1.5 aired.

However, it was her opposition to a Dade County, Fla. ordinance that banned discrimination based on a person's sexual orientation that really grabbed the headlines. Heading a group called Save Our Children, she appealed to Christian fundamentalists to vote to repeal the ordinance in a referendum on June 7, 1977, suggesting that many of America's gays were bent on recruiting the nation's youth. It worked.

As Save Our Children took on a more national role, many public figures joined the cause, including Rev. Jerry Falwell, the televangelist who would, two years later, found the Christian political group Moral Majority—an organization that would exert significant political influence throughout the next decade.

Yet it was Bryant who would vow to export her crusade against homosexuality to the rest of the United States, and it was Bryant who gave the specter of homophobia a face. In a sense, it was her Florida campaign that served as the catalyst for a new gay rights movement that had seen precious little accomplished since the Stonewall riots of 1969. Florida groups concentrated on organizing boycotts of the oranges Bryant pushed ("Squeeze a fruit for Anita" being a popular lapel button at the time), while gays from New York and California to the far reaches of Australia and Scandinavia used the sunshine state skirmish as a rallying point.

Today's Cliffhanger: Will Danny kill Burt?

For the *Soap* Bible Tells Us So. Originally, Burt's ex-wife, Jewel, was supposed to accompany Chuck & Bob to Dunn's River. "Jewel wants money. And Jewel wants Burt."

Rod Roddy's Wrapup. Will Claire come up with a new plan to force Chester into leaving Jessica? Will Chester leave Jessica? If he does, will Jessica know it? Will The Major continue fighting World War II single-handedly? Will Bob, the wooden doll, relax and enjoy his stay with the Campbells, or will he continue to act warped? Now that Danny has the gun in his hand, will he pull the trigger and kill Burt? And if he does, will Burt finally stop laughing and take him seriously? These questions and many others will be answered on next week's episode of *Soap*.

1977

NOVEMBER After Dan Rather's interview with Weather Underground member Matthew Landy Steen on *60 Minutes*, the American terrorist organization is considered all but extinct. (Five members were arrested the same month for plotting to bomb the office of California State Senator John Briggs.)

Best Lines.
Bob [to Chuck]: I love your family. This is great. Your father just laughs and sputters, the dame just sits. One guy's a fruit and the other guy has an IQ slightly higher than kelp.

Benson [after witnessing Jessica's failure to acknowledge Claire's affair with Chester]: Mr Tate, I have seen dumb luck in my time. I have seen a guy fill an inside straight flush to beat four aces. I have seen a guy hit the daily double for two solid weeks…straight! But I have never, at no time, seen nothing like this!

1.8
First aired: Nov 8, 1977 • Written by Susan Harris + Tony Lang • Directed by Jay Sandrich

Unable to bring himself to kill Burt, Danny decides instead to go into hiding from the mob. Still reeling from that situation, Danny is forced to confront the fact that Jodie is gay, and may soon be his sister. Though the family tries to convince Mary that Danny is actually working as a spy for his country, she discovers just how dangerous her son's life is when the mob tries to kill him at the Tate home.

Cast: Jimmy Baio (Billy), Billy Crystal (Jodie), Cathryn Damon (Mary), Robert Guillaume (Benson), Katherine Helmond (Jessica), Jay Johnson (Chuck & Bob), Robert Mandan (Chester), Richard Mulligan (Burt), Arthur Peterson (The Major) Jennifer Salt (Eunice), Ted Wass (Danny), Rod Roddy (Announcer)

Highlights. Danny's reluctance about killing Burt, and Burt's selfless attempts to get him to do it; Mary and Bob bickering in the kitchen over his eggs; Danny and Jodie's frank discussion about his homosexuality, and Danny and Mary's sad parting; Bob's "I've been hit" after the drive-by, and Chester rushing to call the ambulance.

Confused? You won't be. *'I guess I have to say goodbye now. Could I say goodnight instead?'*
◉ This is the first time we're clear that Danny understands why Burt had to kill his father when he did. His "Boy, this is a lot for one day" after Jodie tells him that he and Dennis Phillips are lovers is the

same reaction he had to learning from the Godfather that his father was murdered, and that he must kill his father's murderer (1.2).

▶ Chuck & Bob continue wearing their loud Hawaiian shirts.

▶ When Danny says goodbye to Bob before he leaves home, it's the first time that anybody has acknowledged Bob without being prodded to do so first, foreshadowing the degree to which Danny will come to see Bob as a real person later on.

▶ Benson's "I feel like chinks" when Chester asks him where he'd like to go for dinner seems a tad coarse, not only by today's standards, but by those *Soap* displayed throughout the series.

▶ Chuck & Bob make the Campbells stop the car on the way to have dinner with the Tates because they want to fight in private… over the billing for their act. (Bob thinks his name should come first. He'll get his wish after Chuck thinks Bob's been shot by the people who were gunning for Danny.) Jodie and Eunice are now fast friends, thanks to their recent bonding over unobtainable men (1.5).

▶ This episode marks the beginning of the "if you have something crude to say, let Bob say it" policy. Presumably Bob has been recovering from his flight up till now.

▶ This is an emotional roller coaster of an episode, following up one of that day's frankest depictions of "coming out" on mainstream television with Cathryn Damon's coming to terms with the fact that Danny has to leave home. While much of these scenes' impact was down to the performances, Susan Harris' writing made it all a seamless tapestry of emotion. As associate producer Marsha Posner observes, "She'll make you laugh and make you cry in the space of two minutes like nobody's business."

Scotch and soda (neat): Bob's drink of choice at the Tate home.

Danny's disguise du jour: Bewhiskered telegram delivery man at the Tate house. (It doesn't work, as he narrowly misses being killed in a drive-by when he opens the door to leave.)

1977

NOV. 8: Harvey Milk, the first openly gay official to be elected in any large city, is elected to the San Francisco Board of Supervisors.

Now if I Had Said That...

Bob [to Chuck, after sizing up the shapely Jessica]: Big ones.

Bob [to Jessica about Chester]: I hope he's got plenty of money because it's probably all you're getting from him.

Danny Dallas and the Evolution of TV Characters

Part of the reason that Ted Wass went on to become such a successful director (*Spin City, Two and a Half Men*) is because of the intimate understanding of acting he developed during his days in front of the camera. Between his role as Danny and that of Nick Russo on *Blossom*, he discovered some of the fundamentals of character evolution on television.

"There were probably maybe half a dozen linchpin moments in the script that I would look at that I'd go these are the moments that define this character for me. And I would try to assemble the rest of the character around those moments. Being where I am now and how I approach the work and working with actors, I'm always encouraging them, particularly during a pilot, to be as open-minded about their characters as they possibly can be.

"The tendency is you find pieces of a character that you can really relate to strongly, that pull all of your passion. Sometimes as actors we tend to cling to those moments a little too tightly, and I've worked with actors (and I've done this myself) where, in the first few weeks of a series or during the directing of the pilot, an actor would say to me, 'I don't think my character would do that.'

Playing the (initially) one-note character of Danny taught Ted Wass the importance of allowing a character to grow.

"And I will say to them, 'I can tell you from experience, in years 3, 4, 5 and 6, you'll be wishing you didn't say that. You'll be wishing that right now you were trying to figure out under what circumstances your character *would* do that now, because as the series progresses, you'll wish you had more range.

You'll wish you could play more colors. You're going to wish that you could do many more different things.

"All you have to do is open a newspaper and read who does what to who—the least likely person does the least likely thing—and you're going to see that everything is possible.

"You start out on a series trying to forge as concentrated a character as you possibly can so you can really make it stick. As time goes on, you go, 'Oh jeez, those six linchpin moments, I've done them now so many times, episode after episode, year after year, I feel like I need to do something else.'

On *Soap*, "I was like dumb as a rock and in the mob or something and wanted to kill people and beat people up and pretend that I didn't know my brother was gay and all that stuff. As time goes on, I changed and [Jodie] changed—we all did."

Rod Roddy's Wrapup. Will Mary find out that Danny is running for his life from the mob or will she continue to believe he's a spy? Will Mary ever make eggs the way Bob likes them, or will the dummy have to go to a coffee shop for breakfast? Will Jodie really become Danny's sister? Will Danny, now that he has to run from the mob, live to see it? These questions and many others will be answered on next week's episode of *Soap*.

Best Lines.
Burt: Danny, listen to me! If they kill you, your mother's never going to survive; you're her little boy. I'm just her husband. I mean her first husband got killed—she's used to it.

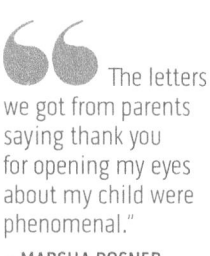

> The letters we got from parents saying thank you for opening my eyes about my child were phenomenal."
> —MARSHA POSNER, associate producer, on this exchange between Jodie and Danny

Jodie [after telling his brother he's gay]: Danny what's the big deal, huh? I mean now that you know, am I any different? We're not friends anymore?

Danny: You don't look gay.

Jodie: I'm still me. Hey, I'm still the Jodie who plays tennis with you. I'm still the Jodie who bowls with you. I'm still the Jodie who laughs with you. I'm still the Jodie who counts on you.

Danny: You're probably not gay.

Jodie: I am! And it shouldn't make any difference. And if it does and you don't love me because of it, then you've never loved me at all. [Starts to leave.]

Danny: Jodie! Look, all these years, I didn't want to hear it. I didn't want to listen to you. I was afraid that if I ever heard it, I couldn't look at you again.

Jodie: Well, can you?

Danny [gradually looks at Jodie]: Yeah.

Jodie [offers his hand]: Friends?

Danny: Are you kidding? [Hugs Jodie.] Are we still friends? Not only are you gay, you're a jerk.

Jodie: Thanks, big brother.

Danny: You're OK, little brother.

Bob [to Benson, who refuses to serve him]: Hey Sambo, the noon whistle did not blow. I said Scotch.

Benson [to Chuck]: One more word and he goes into the fireplace.

 **1.9** First aired: Nov 15, 1977 • Written by Susan Harris + Tony Lang • Directed by Jay Sandrich

Despite an irritating lack of support from lover Dennis Phillips, Jodie arrives at the hospital to go through with his sex change. This, much to the amusement of fellow hospital roommate Barney Gerber, and the titillation of Nurse Nancy. Burt finally unburdens himself to Dr. Medlow, which does wonders for his sex drive. Meanwhile, *Chester's* sex drive (or self-preservation instincts considering his table partner) succeeds in demonstrating to Jessica that all the stories about his philandering are true after all.

Cast: Diana Canova (Corinne), Billy Crystal (Jodie), Cathryn Damon (Mary), Robert Guillaume (Benson), Katherine Helmond (Jessica), Robert Mandan (Chester), Richard Mulligan (Burt), Udana Power (Nurse Nancy Darwin), Kathryn Reynolds (Claire), Jennifer Salt (Eunice), Bob Seagren (Dennis Phillips), Ted Wass (Danny), Harold Gould (Barney Gerber), Byron Webster (Dr. Medlow), Eric Mason (Johnny Dallas), Rod Roddy (Announcer)

Udana Power's Nurse Nancy (above) was the first of two female characters to come on to Jodie. The second, Carol David, won't appear until 1.21. An entry in the *Soap* bible strongly suggests the two characters were meant to be one.

Highlights. Barney Gerber and the delightfully flirtatious Nurse Nancy Darwin; Dr. Medlow's reaction to Burt telling him why he's impotent; Eunice, Corinne and Jodie trading secrets in the hospital room, and trying to get Benson to give up his own ("My secret is I know all your secrets"); Jessica telling Mary that she's so lonely she talks to Dinah Shore every day at 3 o'clock (on TV); and Mary's desperate attempt to keep her sister from seeing Chester kissing Claire in the restaurant.

Confused? You won't be. *'If we didn't have unhappy experiences, how would we know when we were having happy ones?'*

▶ Jodie tells Nurse Nancy that he's never "you know" with a woman.

▶ We finally get the backstory on what led up to Burt's killing of Mary's first husband, Johnny Dallas. (This is also the first flashback we get in the series.) Shortly after Burt's wife left him, Mary and Johnny came to his construction business and asked him to build them a house, and he instantly fell for Mary. After he was done with the house, Johnny Dallas forced Burt to make him a partner in the construction business. After mysterious accidents and intimidation, Burt decided he had nothing left to live for, and was about to jump from the top of a construction site when Johnny Dallas turned up…to kill him. While bargaining for his life, he accidentally pushed Johnny from the top of the construction site 30 stories up.

▶ Considering the "Jodie thinks he's an old Jewish man" story line to come (4.17), it's possible that the unassuming Barney Gerber may have achieved immortality after all, wedging himself neatly into Jodie's subconscious.

Danny's disguise du jour: Jodie's nurse. (No, *not* Nurse Nancy.)

42nd St: Where Johnny Dallas met his end.

Things Burt left out of the Dallas home he was building so that Mary would come talk to him: The kitchen sink; toilet; a functioning closet door; stairs.

Joe Namath, Mickey Mantle and OJ Simpson: Barney's guesses at who Dennis Phillips is.

How old Bob guesses Chester is

Best friend Benson: Benson brings Jodie a picnic basket including duck in rum sauce and banana bread. "Now don't think it's because I like you."

Jessica's Moment of Clarity

One of the most poignant scenes of the entire series happens in this episode when Jessica finally sees Chester for the philanderer he is. It also remains one of Katherine Helmond's favorite moments.

"I was just chatting away and having the best time with my sister, and then I spotted Chester. I turned around and looked and there he was, kissing someone. And then I turned back to the camera, my entire life had fallen to pieces. I had to make that jump from a kind of fun little luncheon to disaster. I thought that was a very powerful moment in *Soap* overall. It showed through Susan's writing how you can be bouncing along in life and then suddenly be cut down by life, too. She was very, very good at writing that kind of thing. It's like you walked into a bomb."

It was also a scene that really stuck with director Jay Sandrich. "Katherine Helmond was a constant amazement to me with what she could do. The scene calls for her to be crying. When she did it in the first rehearsal and turned back to the camera and there were tears in her eyes, I said to her—never expecting her to do it—is there any way for you to hold the tears as you turn toward the camera? And the night of the show, that's what she did. She turned and you saw the tears starting to form."

Rod Roddy's Wrapup. Will Jodie decide to be a woman, or will Nurse Nancy convince him to be *with* a woman instead? Since Burt couldn't with Mary because he thought he was a murderer, now that the psychiatrist has told him that he isn't a murderer and didn't do it, will he be able to? Will Danny run out of disguises or closet space? And what will Jessica, now that she's discovered what Chester is doing, do? These questions and many others will be answered on next week's episode of *Soap*.

Best Lines.
Nurse Nancy [to Jodie]: Your chart says you're here for a sex-change operation. Why in the world would you want a sex-change operation?

1977

NOV. 15: 13-year-old Megumi Yokota becomes one of at least 13 Japanese citizens abducted from her own country by North Korea to help train their spies. Unlike some others, she will die in her captive country years later. **NOV. 19:** Egyptian President Anwar Sadat becomes the first Arab leader to visit Israel when he goes there to discuss a peace settlement.

Barney: Boredom.

Nancy: Quiet.

Barney: I'm thinking of getting one myself next week. They say women live longer.

Nancy [after learning Jodie's never been with a woman]: How long are you going to be here?

Jodie: Two weeks.

Nancy: Oh great. That gives me plenty of time. I taught my cousin to drive in three days.

Jessica [after seeing Chester kissing Claire]: Oh my God. Mary, it's true. All of it's true. Everything everybody's been saying all these years is true. Oh Mary. I would faint if I knew how.

1.10 First aired: Nov 22, 1977 • Written by Susan Harris + Tony Lang • Directed by Jay Sandrich

Still grappling with seeing Chester and Claire at the restaurant, Jessica tells Mary that she thinks their family is cursed. Danny drops by the Campbell house, only to find the Godfather and his flunky there looking for him. And Dennis Phillips breaks it to Jodie that he's going to marry a girl, driving Jodie to give up not only on the sex change, but on his life.

Cast: Diana Canova (Corinne), Billy Crystal (Jodie), Cathryn Damon (Mary), Robert Guillaume (Benson), Katherine Helmond (Jessica), Richard Libertini (The Godfather), Richard Mulligan (Burt), Bob Seagren (Dennis Phillips), Sal Viscuso (Father Tim), Ted Wass (Danny), Harold Gould (Barney Gerber), Brandy Carson (Nurse), Michael Schwartz (Intern), Rod Roddy (Announcer)

Highlights. Jessica and Mary going through the family photos (much to Benson's displeasure), and sweet old Barney Gerber's talk about losing two wives and still hanging around to see if he might someday be happy again.

Confused? You Won't Be. *'You know what Mary? I think we're cursed.'*

◉ Feeling that the family is cursed, Jessica references *The Omen* (and later, *The Exorcist*), foreshadowing what is to come (2.19).

◉ Mary and Jessica's brother, Randolph, fathered an illegitimate child with a Swedish maid and disappeared in Ecuador, where he went to sell wall-to-wall carpeting. Nearly in the next breath, Jessica, making the case for their family being cursed, says that she has one illegitimate daughter who sleeps around, telling us something Corinne won't find out for a few episodes yet (1.15, 1.16).

◉ Burt finally tracks down Mary at home, ready to prove that his impotence is cured, when she tells him that with one thing and another, she's not in the mood.

◉ In a revealing chat with God, Father Tim tells the Almighty that being a priest saved him from being a motorcycle-obsessed high school loser, but that Corinne is severely tempting him.

◉ While the religious right continued to bang on about *Soap*'s risqué, blasphemous content, the series delivers an episode worthy of the plaudits usually reserved for Norman Lear. Fundamentalist dogma fears nothing quite so much as the addressing of life questions that have no easy answers, and this episode manages to tackle both the problems faced by young priests everywhere, and the cruelty of a society that drives thousands of gay men and women to suicide and sham marriages every year, all in just 23 minutes.

Georgie Smith: The name The Godfather uses when visiting Mary Campbell. (His "boss" has made it clear that if he doesn't find Danny, the Godfather will be killed in his place.)

Danny's disguise du jour: Rabbi Macabee, who's collecting money to send trees to Israel, narrowly missing being found out by the Godfather and his thug, who just showed up at the Campbell house looking for Danny.

Today's Cliffhanger: Will Jodie survive his overdose?

For the *Soap* Bible Tells Us So. The Godfather (referred to as "Capo" in the bible), was meant to get involved with Corinne after

68

Barney Gerber's age ("with a heart that beats like a struggling moth")

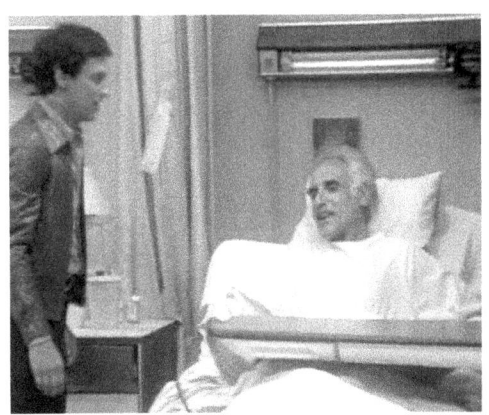

Barney Gerber's speech about life and love begins Susan Harris' *Soap* tradition of dialogue that's equal parts funny and sad.

Father Tim leaves her (somewhere around 2.16). Corinne was on the verge of getting the Godfather to forgive Danny when they discover Corinne and Tim's baby is possessed.

'And Soon I'll Have to Earn a Living from Having Been a Football Player…'

In an early case of "meta" casting in American television, professional football quarterback Dennis Phillips was played by 1968 Olympic gold medal champion pole vaulter Bob Seagren. Like Dennis, Seagren had his eye on his post-sports career. Unlike Dennis, Seagren had always been a shrewd businessman.

Olympic Gold Medalist Bob Seagren never considered becoming a professional actor, even while he played Jodie's boyfriend, Dennis Phillips.

"After the '68 Olympics, I came back and you start getting calls, people saying you should look into acting," Seagren remembers. "So I started going on some interviews and I got a commercial here or a little walk-on part in something else. In those days, to me it was more fun than anything else. I don't think I ever really considered myself an actor, or that that was going to be a career path for me. I've always been business oriented, I guess."

So much so, some of Dennis Phillips' troubled expressions might've been less about the closeted gay character's predicament and more about some of the actor's real-world business ventures. While he was on *Soap*, he was operating a travel agency, Happy Bookers in Beverly Hills, in anticipation of a much larger enterprise: the creation of an Olympic training center just outside of St. Petersburg, similar to the fantasy football camps today. However, it was around the time he was on *Soap* that Florida's coastal commission changed its guidelines for "buildable above sea level land," instantly whittling down Seagren's 160 acres to about 18. "So it really killed the project."

Still, Seagren and two other people bought into a 10-city franchise for Chicago-style pizza chain Josephine's, though they later changed the name to Harper's Livery after the historic building one of the restaurants was in. He also did some work for Puma shoes, convincing TV and film stars to wear the products—an early form of product placement.

It wasn't until he launched International City Racing in 2001 (renamed RUN Racing in April 2010) that he truly found his calling.

The events company organizes several big name races and parades throughout California, including the Long Beach Marathon, the LA County Half-Marathon, and Long Beach's Sea Festival. The seeds were sewn for his career change around 1979, he says.

"I just found it too boring sitting on a set, chitchatting, waiting to get up and rehearse or regurgitate a few memorized lines. Television wasn't an ego trip for me, I had my ego trip with athletics. So to see myself on screen—it wasn't making me a complete person."

Rod Roddy's Wrapup. Are the Tates and the Campbells cursed, or are they just having a run of bad luck? Is Danny's rabbi disguise good enough to fool the mob? Is it good enough for him to perform Passover services? Will Father Tim get a sign from God? A phone call? A Mailgram? Something? Will Jodie live? These questions and many others will be answered on next week's episode of *Soap*.

Best Lines.
Benson [about Jessica's family photos]: They are depressing. A bunch of ugly people in old clothes, and then you've got those dried up pressed flowers that fall out all over the place, and the pictures crumble and you cry. Every time you look at those pictures, I've got to do the floor.

Father Tim [to God]: …I understand tests and I know you've given some humdingers in your day, but are you going to send Corinne in once a week for the rest of my life? Because if you are, I think we're going to get to a week there that could embarrass everyone…

Jodie: Boy I can really pick 'em. No sense being a girl now. Actually, there's no sense in being. It's checkout time. Make life a lot easier for me. Mom. Burt. Anita Bryant.

Barney Gerber [to Jodie, about his first wife]: One day she wakes up, a little lump. Six months later, bing bing, the light goes out on my life. Oh boy. I'll tell you, I walked around for months, I was doubled over, like somebody slugged me. I went through the normal routine of daily living—I ate, I slept, I went to the bathroom. And in between these three major activities, Jodie, there was a lot of pain. I thought I'm never going to fall in love again.

> " I remember my agent called me and said there's a real controversial show that's getting a lot of attention, and there's a role in it that you might be interested in. Then, of course, he told me that I was going to be a gay football player and I kind of laughed. My agent said no big deal, and I wasn't worried about being typecast or anything. I was married and had kids, so I wasn't too threatened by it."
> —BOB SEAGREN
> (Dennis Phillips)

But a few years later, I met a redhead. Not like my wife, no, entirely different. So I ate, I slept, I went to the bathroom. One day I laughed, and one day I noticed I laughed. Then another day I hummed. Then soon after, I sang. I married her. Oh Jodie, if we weren't happy... in an entirely different way. It wasn't better, it wasn't worse, it was different. There I was, miserable Barney Gerber, happy again. You see, Jodie, you see how smart I was? I thought I'll never love again. I thought I'll never be happy again. I also thought I'll never have to say goodbye again. Ten years we were happy, Jodie. And then one day some maniac with bourbon in his blood and something on his mind runs through a red light and stops Barney Gerber right in mid-song.

That was 16 months ago. Since then, I have eaten, I have slept, occasionally I went to the bathroom. And I had a heart attack. So I said 'Gerber, that's all, you're finished, forget it. It's never going to happen again. Once was wonderful. Twice was incredible. A third time? What, you're kidding yourself. C'mon, a third time would be asking for a miracle.' But you know something, Jodie? I don't really believe that. If I believed that, I wouldn't be here in this hotel letting them sew Dacron into my heart to hold it together. I wouldn't be here begging my blood to visit my heart at least a few times a day. I wouldn't be here at all, Jodie, if I didn't believe there could be a third time. Listen, I know you don't feel so terrific right now, but wait, Jodie, wait. Someday, I guarantee you're going to hear somebody laughing, and you'll turn around...and it'll be you.

1.11

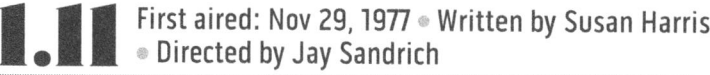

First aired: Nov 29, 1977 • Written by Susan Harris • Directed by Jay Sandrich

It's a full day for the Campbells. Burt and Mary are about to test the efficacy of Dr. Medlow's impotence cure when they're interrupted, first by a bumbling burglar and Danny in disguise, and next by the news that Jodie has tried to kill himself at the hospital. Corinne, still pining over Father Tim, threatens to kill Peter if he doesn't give up his "private lessons" with the women at the tennis club. Finally, Jessica confronts Chester about what she saw at the restaurant and confesses to her own fling (without naming names), only to be faced with Chester's steadfast refusal to admit he's ever cheated on her.

Cast: Diana Canova (Corinne), Billy Crystal (Jodie), Cathryn Damon (Mary), Katherine Helmond (Jessica), Jay Johnson (Chuck & Bob), Robert Mandan (Chester), Richard Mulligan (Burt), Robert Urich (Peter), Ted Wass (Danny), Rod Roddy (Announcer), Harold Gould (Barney Gerber), Jerry Houser (Burglar)

Highlights. Burt and the family confronting the burglar; the circus that is Jodie's family visiting him in the hospital; snaky Peter arranging a tryst silently with another woman while he's hugging Corinne in the pro shop; and Jessica's painful confrontation with Chester over her own affair, and his inability to admit to his.

Confused? You won't be. *'In your life, you're entitled to one really stupid thing.'*

▶ Burt's rant at the Arab-dressed Danny is laced with the usual stereotypes (Aladdin and camels, etc.), but seems to be meant to solidify his blue collar credentials. Compare with Benson's "chink" reference earlier (1.8).

▶ Jodie tells Barney "that story you told me really made me want to live, but I was just too sleepy to tell you" (1.10).

▶ Corinne's threat to kill Peter if she ever finds out he's cheating on her telegraphs one of *Soap*'s most famous plotlines. It all kicks off next episode.

▶ Jessica's confrontation with Chester over his affair with Claire is by turns painful, comical, and tells us more about both Chester and Jessica than we've ever known before. For the first time, Jessica isn't the flighty comic relief or the wounded wife; in her own humility, confessing to her affair, she finds the strength of her convictions, and realizes for the first time just how immature and devoid of empathy her husband really is.

Danny's disguise du jour: An Arab sheik in full keffiyeh, shades and beard.

Jessica's Affair: What's Good for the Goose...

When the topic of *Soap*'s controversial nature comes up, Jodie's homosexuality and Father Tim's temptation are usually the two topics people assume accounted for most of the backlash. The reality, however, may have been more *Soap*'s challenge to the patriarchal nature of American society.

"I remember an affiliate screening in which I would say the audience was at least 98% male, and they were very uncomfortable with women having extramarital relations," says Paul Junger Witt. "Now there is a degree of discomfort about that, but one of the oldest comedic elements has always been the cuckold, has always been the husband who fools around consistently. That kind of thing was always kind of acceptable on one level or another in traditional comedy, but women were held to a different standard. All of that was changing. We were trying to reflect what was happening in the country at the time and turn things on their heads."

Rod Roddy's Wrapup. Now that Burt can, will he and Mary ever find the time? Will Corinne really kill Peter if she catches him fooling around? Will Peter continue to fool around? Will Corinne catch him? Now that Danny's been both an Arab and a Jew, will he declare war on himself? Will Jessica really walk out on Chester, or will she call a cab? These questions and many others will be answered on next week's episode of *Soap*.

Best Lines.
Bob [after Jodie tells the family he's not going to have the sex-change operation]: Wonderful. You lose a daughter, you gain a suicidal sissy.

Corinne: I've given up a lot for you, Peter. I've given up my home and my family, someone who's very important to me. So if you're lying to me and I catch you, I swear, Peter, I'll kill you.

Jessica [confessing to her affair]: You were never here, Chester. I mean when you were here, somehow you weren't really here, just like Fluffy.

Chester: What?

Jessica: You remember Fluffy. The cat we had. I mean you know she would eat and she would wash herself and then she'd just lay around.

45
The number of pills Jodie took (Yet he still breaks aspirin in half because they're too big)

And I don't believe once in all those years that she ever really looked at any of us. I mean of course it was hard to tell with all that hair, you couldn't see if her eyes were open, which was of course why we called her Fluffy. I mean Chester, that's why I had an affair.

Chester: Because of Fluffy?

Jessica: Chester, it was short, it wasn't very spectacular, and it is over now. But you know for a little while, minutes maybe, somebody was really there.

Chester: You had an affair? You mean you slept with another man?

Jessica: Well, I mean Chester, that's usually what an affair is.

Chester: How could you? How could you do that to me? How many people know about this affair, Jessica? How many people have you bragged to about it?

Jessica: I never bragged about it Chester. I mean that isn't exactly something I felt like bragging about.

Chester: I trusted you, Jessica. All these years I trusted you. And you went out and had a cheap, dirty, sordid little affair.

Jessica: Well Chester, I don't think of it that way. I mean I did think of it that way for a while, but I don't anymore. I mean I prefer to think of it as something that happened.

Chester: Something that happened.

Jessica: Chester, what I did was wrong, and I'm not trying to minimize it by saying this. But I mean Chester, what I did for a few weeks you made into a career.

1.12
First aired: Dec 6, 1977 • Written by Susan Harris • Directed by Jay Sandrich

After staying out all night, Jessica returns to tell Chester that she'll put his infidelity "on the shelf" for now, but he'd better not fool around again. As Jodie and Barney prepare to leave the hospital, Nurse Nancy manages to get Jodie to agree to having a meal together, raising Burt's hopes that his gay days are over. Both Jessica and Corinne discover that Peter is still sleeping around. Corinne turns to Father Tim, and somebody puts paid to the philandering tennis pro once and for all while he's taking a shower.

Cast: Diana Canova (Corinne), Billy Crystal (Jodie), Cathryn Damon (Mary), Robert Guillaume (Benson), Katherine Helmond (Jessica), Jay Johnson (Chuck & Bob), Robert Mandan (Chester), Richard Mulligan (Burt), Udana Power (Nurse Nancy Darwin), Jennifer Salt (Eunice), Robert Urich (Peter), Sal Viscuso (Father Tim), Rod Roddy (Announcer), Harold Gould (Barney Gerber), Nita Talbot (Mrs. Fine), Shelley Morrison (Maid)

Highlights. The emotional final words between Jodie and Barney Gerber as they each prepare to leave the hospital; the way Nurse Nancy gets Jodie to agree to dinner with her; and the killing of Peter Campbell.

Confused? You won't be. *'When I came in here I had a life. I knew who I was, what I was going to do, what I wanted—I had someone. Now I don't know.'*

● Burt took Mary ice skating on their first date.

● Though *Soap* frequently put its own spin on TV shows and movies in the popular culture at the time, the killing of Peter Campbell actually anticipated the most famous shooting in TV history: the 1979-1980 killing of JR Ewing on *Dallas*. (Though the fact that he seems to have been shot, stabbed and bludgeoned by a flying brick keeps us squarely in the realm of absurdity.)

● Jessica's "You lied to me and you're cheating on Corinne; I could kill you" quickly shoehorns her into the list of suspects for Peter's murder, just as Corinne's threat did last episode.

The Pussycat Motel: Where Corinne's staying when Father Tim comes to prevent her from killing herself.

Grunt: The cologne that Burt tries to get Jodie to wear on his date with Nurse Nancy. (Burt wore it on his first date with Mary.)

Today's cliffhanger: Who killed Peter Campbell?

Breaking the news. "We were sitting around the table at the first reading of the show," associate producer Marsha Posner says.

5

The number of stupid things that Mary and Barney Gerber agree a person is entitled to do in their lifetime

"Everyone's sitting around the table and reading and we get to that murder scene. Just before we get ready to read that scene, Robert Urich says, 'I just want to say something before we read this: Please don't kill me. Please don't kill me!'"

For the *Soap* Bible Tells Us So. The timeline of events is a bit different in the bible, as is the way poor Peter Campbell dies. Jessica catches Peter in bed with Corinne. When Ingrid later reveals to the young girl that she was adopted, Corinne moves out of the Tate home and in with Peter, being sure to tell Chester that Jessica was sleeping with her boyfriend. Corinne later goes to the pro shop to find Peter "garrotted on the stringing machine." Meanwhile, Father Tim has been chastised by the church for suggesting they replace the communion wafer with Oreos to "bring young people back into the Church." A note at the bottom of the page reads: "This joke over the protest of Tony Thomas."

"I just want to say something before we read this [script]," said Robert Urich. "Please don't kill me."

Says Thomas now, "I vaguely remember the Oreo thing and I did not remember the footnote. There were times when one of us would say you can't do that. Obviously [Father Tim] was never going to do that in the show; it was just for the tone of the bible. But it was 'What are ya touching on that for?' I was a Catholic boy raised by nuns and Jesuits, and the Eucharist was certainly holy. Paul and Susan didn't have that reference—I think I thought we had crossed a line here if we're going to turn the communion wafer into an Oreo. In hindsight I don't think I would object to it. I guess at the time it really hit me the wrong way. We would always reread the pages out loud so we'd hear how it was sounding, and it was 'Oh God, why are we saying that?' It was just an old childhood thing that I had a knee-jerk reaction to. But I took great joy in Father Flotsky and all the trials and tribulations that we put him through."

Best Lines

Jessica: Well you see, Chester, I know what you've done and I have decided to, well, forgive wouldn't be exactly the right word because I'm not going to forgive you, but to put it on the shelf for now. But

Whodunit? *Soap* did with the murder of Peter Campbell more than a year before *Dallas*' "Who Shot JR" story line.

Chester, if it ever happens again, I'm afraid I won't be able to put it on the shelf. By then the shelf will be full.

Father Tim [after spotting a married man checking into a motel room with another woman]: And this guy never has anything to confess. Do you love it? His biggest confession is taking home paper clips from the office. Now look what he's taking home from the office.

Maid [to Father Tim]: Listen, you don't know what goes on in these rooms. And wait. Next month they're putting in movies. I don't know. Me, I go home to my husband. The fanciest we ever get is we open our eyes.

Peter [showering, hears noises from the other room]:
Corinne? Babe is that you? Jessica? Marsha? OK, who's there?
[A blade comes through the shower curtain, narrowly missing Peter.]
Peter: Evelyn, I know you're aggravated but you made your point.
[A brick is thrown in, hits him on the head. What sounds like two gun shots can be heard. Peter opens his eyes for a moment after the curtain comes away.] You. [Slumps over. A *Psycho* shower scene motif can be heard.]*

Rod Roddy's Wrapup. Jessica said she would leave Chester if he fools around again. Will he? Will she? Nurse Nancy said she and Jodie would do more than just eat dinner. Will they? Corinne once said she would kill Peter. Did she? Jessica once said she would kill Peter. Did she? Who killed Peter? These questions and many others will be answered on next week's episode of *Soap*.

> "They used to be all the time watching my neckline, and if I wore sweaters, there couldn't be any kind of bosom showing, no cleavage, nothing like that."
> —KATHERINE HELMOND

Recalls Marsha Posner, "When Peter Campbell gets killed in the shower, I was laughing out loud because he hears a door and he says, 'Jessica, is that you?' Nothing. 'Corinne, is that you? *Marsha*?' That was our little joke in those days."

1.13 First aired: Dec 13, 1977 • Written by Susan Harris • Directed by Jay Sandrich

Burt and Mary finally have sex, putting the former in such a celebratory mood, he wants to throw a party. He swings by Peter's place to invite him personally, only to discover him dead. Immediately after the funeral, Chief of Police Tinkler confronts the Tates and the Campbells at the Tate home, and tells them that they're all suspects.

Cast: Jimmy Baio (Billy), Diana Canova (Corinne), Billy Crystal (Jodie), Cathryn Damon (Mary), Robert Guillaume (Benson), Katherine Helmond (Jessica), Jay Johnson (Chuck & Bob), Gordon Jump (Chief of Police Tinkler), Robert Mandan (Chester), Richard Mulligan (Burt), Arthur Peterson (The Major), Jennifer Salt (Eunice), Sal Viscuso (Father Tim), Ted Wass (Danny), Rod Roddy (Announcer)

Highlights. Burt playing the grieving father immediately after the funeral; Burt, Jodie and Mary taking turns holding each other back from clobbering Tinkler; and the spontaneous applause when Burt tells Tinkler that Jodie was out with a girl last night. (He wasn't.)

Confused? You Won't Be. *'Would anyone here like to confess to the murder of Peter Campbell...?'*

◉ Father Tim says he's known the Tates and the Campbells since childhood. Though Chester knew that Jessica had been having an affair (1.11), the first he learns that the other man was Peter is from Chief of Police Tinkler this episode.

◉ Despite being pegged as suspects in the murder of Peter Campbell, Corinne and Eunice shield the men in their lives who could give them an alibi: Father Tim and Congressman McCallam, respectively.

◉ Jodie admits that he stood up Nurse Nancy.

◉ Tinkler informs us the Tates and the Campbells are Episcopalian.

◉ This is the first truly disappointing episode of the series, due largely to its riff on the clichéd "the murderer is in this room" scenes. The dialogue lacks the wit we've come to expect from Susan Harris.

And introducing...Chief of Police Tinkler.

Peter's Cause of Death: According to the coroner's report, he was stabbed, shot, strangled, suffocated and bludgeoned.

Chief of Police Tinkler reveals that Peter Campbell was strangled, shot, stabbed, suffocated and bludgeoned.

Between midnight and 7 a.m.: Peter Campbell's "precise" time of death, according to Chief of Police Tinkler.

The Suspects (according to Tinkler): 1. Chester: Was asleep in his bedroom at the time; 2. Jessica: Was asleep in the guest room; 3. Corinne: Was at a motel; 4. Benson, because he's black *and* a butler; 5. Eunice: was in a Washington DC hotel; 6. The Major: He has a gun. (Tinkler incorrectly dubs him suspect #7, and blows the numbering after this); 7. Danny: He's disappeared and he's connected with the underworld; 8. Jodie: Because he's a "homo" (Benson: That's almost as good as my reason); 9 and 10: Chuck & Bob (they're each other's alibi); 11: Mary: Because there's no reason in the world to suspect her; 12: Burt: Because he's the least likely suspect of all. [The only two let off the hook are Father Tim (because he's a priest) and "Rabbi Macabee" (Danny).]

Meta meta meta. [Billy, after being told to leave the room by Tinkler, indirectly addresses the absurdity of America's double-standard when it comes to sex and violence on television]: But that's not fair, why can't I stay? This is violence you're discussing, not sex!

Danny's disguise du jour: Rabbi Macabee again.

Susan Harris: An Average Day for the *Soap* Creator

"I got up very, very early because I also was a runner," says Susan Harris. "I made breakfast for my son and drove the carpool, then went to the studio and worked until I could get out of there. Rewrite nights notoriously go very, very late on most shows, at least they did then. I hated rewrite nights so I tried to make them as short as possible. I think the record was we got out once at 5:30 in the evening—very, very early. Because of the way it was set up, it really was easier to write than your traditional sitcom. We didn't have a story to lick every week, which made it much easier. I always hated stories and making stories work in 23 minutes. It's a very hard job and everything is sacrificed to the plot. So this really gave all of us a wonderful freedom that made it much easier. Not that it was easy; you still had to write 23 minutes of dialogue."

Best Lines.
Jessica: Well, when I go I want a *big* funeral with hundreds of people crying, you know, and television coverage and flags at half mast and the schools closed, and a riderless horse. Of course I don't know how you go about getting that.

Jessica [after being named as a suspect by Tinkler]: Don't be silly, I couldn't murder anybody. I couldn't even spank the children when they were bad.

Tinkler [indicating Benson]: He's a suspect.
Chester: Why?
Tinkler: For two reasons. Number one because he's black.
Benson [nodding]: That's fair.
Tinkler: The other reason is because he's the butler. We all know that in many, many cases like this, the butler did it.

Rod Roddy's Wrapup. Who killed Peter Campbell? Jessica? Chester? Corinne? Eunice? The Major? Benson? Burt? Mary? Jodie? Danny? Chuck? Bob? This question might be answered on next week's episode of *Soap*.

DRISTAN

All Corinne has on her when Father Tim shows up to stop her from committing suicide

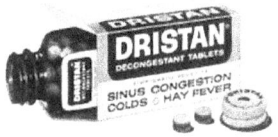

 First aired: Dec 27, 1977 • Written by Susan Harris • Directed by Jay Sandrich

As the mystery surrounding Peter's death continues to grow, the Tates suspect the Campbells, the Campbells suspect the Tates, and Billy is using the whole incident to increase his popularity at school. Meanwhile, Eunice "interviews" Congressman McCallam on an official flight while his wife gets more and more loaded. And Chief of Police Tinkler finally makes an arrest in the murder case...between mouthfuls of prime rib.

Cast: Jimmy Baio (Billy), Diana Canova (Corinne), Billy Crystal (Jodie), Cathryn Damon (Mary), Robert Guillaume (Benson), Katherine Helmond (Jessica), Jay Johnson (Chuck & Bob), Gordon Jump (Chief of Police Tinkler), Robert Mandan (Chester), Richard Mulligan (Burt), Arthur Peterson (The Major), Jennifer Salt (Eunice), Ted Wass (Danny), Edward Winter (Congressman Walter McCallam), Judith-Marie Bergan (Marilyn McCallam), Rod Roddy (Announcer)

Highlights. Chester finally realizing how all his years of cheating made Jessica feel, and apologizing for it; Burt strangling Bob (and Chuck's horrified expression) after one insult to his dead son too many; and McCallam confronting his wife in the airplane lavatory.

Confused? You Won't Be. *'I am sick of this murder.'*

▶ Again *The Exorcist* is invoked, this time by Chester, saying no one in their extended family could sit through it, let alone kill Peter Campbell.

▶ Burt is convinced Jessica is the killer, and cites her talking to her flowers as proof that she's deranged. (They talk back.)

▶ Congressman McCallam claims he's in favor of the Equal Rights Amendment.

▶ Benson informs Chester that all the servants on the block have started up a pool on who killed Peter, adding, "You've got more money on you than [Muhammad] Ali in the last fight."

▶ This episode is especially coarse, essentially living up to the reputation *Soap* had among those who'd never seen it up to this point. Marilyn refers to Eunice as being "in heat", the congressman asks Eunice "how many weeks" when she says she's in trouble—there's a sense that the producers are trying to deliver on *Soap*'s steamy reputation. This is jarringly at odds with the way this episode began, showing Chester and Jessica wrestling with another controversial subject—infidelity—but doing so with humor and compassion.

1948: The last time Jessica threw up.

Crapples. The Tate trees were infested by these pesky birds, according to Jessica. (She means grackles.) Danny passed around a petition to prevent the birds from being shot.

Danny's disguise du jour: Arabian sheik, again.

Chuck & Bob: Hanging On

"I was not hired to be a regular, I was hired to be a seven [episodes] out of 13, to come on and be written off before the end of the first year," says Jay Johnson. "I realized real quick that my life on that show would depend upon getting stuff to do until eventually I would get a story line, and that would keep the character going.

"I went in with maybe 20 ideas on a piece of paper and submitted those to Paul Witt. And then every six months or so, I would do the same thing to make it a point: Here's some ideas for story lines.

"I never knew when those bits might show up or *if* they might show up. Susan would write some of those things.

"I guess out of the 20 ideas I would submit, probably eight or 10 would make their way in."

Best Lines.
Eunice [after Corinne suggests Jodie might've killed Peter]: Jodie? Please. The man couldn't even kill himself.

Jay Johnson...possibly thinking up new ideas for Chuck & Bob to keep them both on the show.

Chester: But to discover that you were robbing the cradle. Do you know how that looks? Do you know what people say about that?
Jessica: Well, when men do it they say congratulations.
Chester: That's something else entirely, Jessica. Young girls are attracted to older men, it's a known fact. We can't help it.
Jessica: Yes you can. You could say no.

Chester [fuming about Peter]: I mean the guy has got energy, and tricks. How can you compete? He grew up on *Penthouse*. I grew up on *National Geographic*.

Burt: Maybe God looked down and said, 'Eh, Campbell's too happy. Let's cool him down, kill his son.'

Rod Roddy's Wrapup: Will Chester and Jessica really stop fooling around with other people and actually start fooling around with each other? Will Mrs. McCallam find out her husband is giving more than just an interview to Eunice. Will the airlines increase the size of their bathrooms to accommodate larger parties? Will Corinne be jailed, tried and convicted for the murder of Peter? Will the Tates ever invite Chief Tinkler to a roast beef dinner again? These questions and many others will be answered on next week's episode of *Soap*.

1.15
First aired: Jan 3, 1978 • Written by Susan Harris • Directed by Jay Sandrich

Corinne is taken to the local lockup with Jessica and Chester in tow, putting to an end Burt's *CSI*-like attempts to figure out the identity of Peter's killer. While Mary still worries that Jodie will try to commit suicide again, Danny, sick of living in fear, pays a visit to Mr. Lefkowitz but is discovered by his daughter, who promptly falls in love with him. Just as things appear to be returning to normal in Dunn's River, Chief of Police Tinkler receives a visit from Ingrid Swenson, who claims to be Corinne's real mother.

Ingrid sits in Ecuador awaiting an opportunity for revenge. (And Randolph just sort of sits around.)

Cast: Jimmy Baio (Billy), Diana Canova (Corinne), Billy Crystal (Jodie), Cathryn Damon (Mary), Robert Guillaume (Benson), Katherine Helmond (Jessica), Jay Johnson (Chuck & Bob), Gordon Jump (Chief of Police Tinkler), Robert Mandan (Chester), Dinah Manoff (Elaine Lefkowitz), Richard Mulligan (Burt), Jennifer Salt (Eunice), Inga Swenson (Ingrid), Ted Wass (Danny), Rod Roddy (Announcer), Bernard Fox (Randolph), Susan Harris (Babette)

Highlights. Susan Harris' cameo, and her reaction to Chester; Burt trying to recreate the murder in his basement (complete with bathtub, pistol and Danny's inflatable clown "Mr. Bozo") in order to solve it; Bob getting the best of Danny; Mary's heart-to-heart with Jodie; Elaine Lefkowitz's love-at-first-sight vibe mixed with her take-charge attitude; and Jessica's talk of "bad beans".

Confused? You Won't Be. *'My baby's gone to jail.'*
● Randolph, the missing brother of Jessica and Mary, remains in Ecuador (1.10) with the Swedish maid he ran away with: Ingrid.

▶ In a nod to the countless reports of former Nazis living out their days in accommodating Latin American countries after the war, we see a very old Hitler refresh Randolph's wine, give a Nazi salute, click his heels and depart.

▶ The mental illness that will plague Burt through much of the rest of the series starts to manifest itself in this episode; clearly whatever tiny grasp he had on sanity up to this point was destroyed with the murder of his son.

▶ Mary's heart-to-heart with Jodie about finding the love of your life ("what happens is they usually die") suggests that however evil Johnny Dallas was in his dealings with Burt, he must've meant a great deal more to Mary than he's willing to admit to himself.

▶ Chief Tinkler is doing his best Travis Bickle impression when Ingrid arrives at the police station; *Taxi Driver* premiered the previous year.

And introducing…Elaine Lefkowitz and Ingrid Swenson.

For the *Soap* Bible Tells Us So. Initially, Elaine Lefkowitz was Elaine Berman, daughter of "famous syndicate lawyer" Skinny Berman. Skinny is one of those rare instances when a single character in the bible ended up becoming two distinct characters in the series. In this case, Berman became both mob boss Charles Lefkowitz, father of Elaine; *and* E. Ronald Mallu, as it is Skinny Berman who defends Jessica when she is charged with Peter's murder. The name Lefkowitz is probably a tribute to Nat Lefkowitz, who was head of the William Morris Agency in the '70s.

Even more interesting, there is a strong possibility that this father and daughter were based on American mobster David Berman and his daughter, Susan. A partner of Bugsy Siegel, the Ukraine-born Berman ran successful operations ranging from extortion and gambling to bank robbery, in Iowa, New York City, Las Vegas and Minneapolis. Daughter Susan wrote a memoir about her life as a mobster's daughter called *Easy Street* (1981). Her father died on the operating table in 1957; Susan herself was shot in the head in 2000 while developing a series about the mob for cable channel Showtime that aimed to rival HBO's *The Sopranos*.

By June of this year, Dinah Manoff's star will begin to rise with the release of the movie *Grease*, with Manoff playing crowd favorite Marty Maraschino.

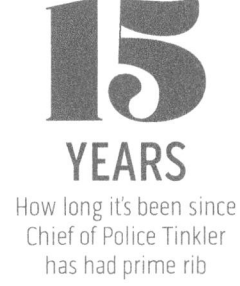

15 YEARS
How long it's been since Chief of Police Tinkler has had prime rib

While there's the temptation to think she was killed by the mob, there is another possibility. Kathie Durst, wife of Susan's college friend, Robert, disappeared in 1982. Nearly 20 years later, Susan was contacted by Westchester County, NY's district attorney to set up an interview about that cold case—Robert Durst, heir to his father's real estate empire, had always been suspected of his wife's death. Susan was killed just days before she was to be interviewed. (The 2010 movie *All Good Things*, starring Kirsten Dunst and Ryan Gosling, was based on the Durst case.)

Susan Berman, real-life mob boss' daughter and, judging by information in the *Soap* bible, possibly the model for Elaine Lefkowitz.

Susan Harris, Actress. As if writing and producing every episode of *Soap* wasn't enough, Susan Harris found herself in front of the camera as well in this episode, and in 1.17, as the brassy hooker Babette. (She even gets pride of place in the still used for the credits at the end of this episode.) As Harris remembers it, "We left minor parts for casting until Tuesday or Wednesday of the week, but then the read-throughs were on Mondays. So I would read the parts of whoever was missing. I read the part of Babette and Jay [Sandrich, the director] said, 'You should be Babette, you read that great.' So I became Babette." Harris laughs. "It was typecasting." As Katherine Helmond told the audience at the 1990 *Soap* reunion at the Museum of Broadcasting: "And when she did it, she said, after that week, 'I will never do this again.'"

$150,000: Corinne's bail.

Second door on the left upstairs:
Billy's bedroom.

Danny's disguise: Still a sheik.

Best Lines.
Cop: Aw c'mon, Babette. You know it's illegal.
Babette: Oh please, illegal. I told him he could go around the world for a hundred dollars. I'm a travel agent, for God's sake.
[Tinkler brings in Corinne, with the rest of the Tates in tow.]
Jessica: Oh please, Officer Tinkler, this is silly. It's hardly necessary to put a sweet young girl in jail.
Babette: That's just what I told 'em. [Recognizes Chester.] Chet! [She gets hauled away]

Jessica [to Chester]: Do you know her?

Chester: Who?

Jessica: That girl. That girl who said "Hi Chet."

Chester: No, she said "I bet." Probably arrested for gambling.

Mary: You have to meet people, date, find someone and hope you like them. Then if you do, hope they like you. Then if you make it that far, where you both like each other, you have to worry about will you still like each other when you drop the good behavior and you can be yourself. Then once you make it through that when you're both yourselves, and you both like each other, you're up against worrying about whether they'll leave. But once you're convinced that they won't leave and you won't leave, and you're very happy together and everything is finally wonderful, what happens is they usually die.

Jodie: Did you come here to cheer me up?

Mary: What I'm saying is things end, so things have to begin. There are no shortcuts. You either go through those beginnings or you wind up alone.

Billy: All my life, every time I walk into a room, people stop talking. Years ago everyone used to spell in front of me. Then once I could spell, they talked in Pig Latin. After that it was French. And then they didn't understand each other. I mean do you know what that's like? In school the teacher says I have trouble in comprehension. Of course I have trouble in comprehension—I live in a silent movie.

Jessica: We tell you things, Billy. We just do it the way Juan Valdez picks out his coffee beans.

Chester: Right.

Jessica: He just gives us the good beans. He never lets us see the bad beans. We just don't give you any bad beans.

Billy: Like Corinne being in jail?

Chester: Right.

Jessica: That would be a bad bean. Corinne getting married, on the other hand, would be a good bean.

Eunice: Corinne having a baby would be a good bean.

3 DAYS
How long it's been since Peter's murder

Jessica: Right. [Suddenly whispers to Eunice.] Unless of course she wasn't married in the first place, in which case that would be a very bad bean!

[*Later*]

Jessica [to Billy, preparing to tell him why she and Chester are suspects]: Now you remember what I told you about the good and the bad beans? Well, what you're about to hear is going to sound like some very bad beans. In fact, if Juan Valdez had beans like these, that man would shoot his donkey and burn the mountain.

Rod Roddy's Wrapup: Will Burt's investigation prove that Corinne is guilty, or will it prove that Burt is bonkers? Will Elaine talk to her father on Danny's behalf? Will her father let Danny go? If he does, will Elaine let Danny out the door? Is Ingrid Swenson really Corinne's mother, or is this some kind of traditional Swedish prank? These questions and many others will be answered on next week's episode of *Soap*.

1.16 First aired: Jan 10, 1978 • Written by Susan Harris • Directed by Jay Sandrich

On learning that Ingrid is her mother and that Jessica and Chester have been lying to her all this time, Corinne is devastated. Burt is still researching Peter's death (with the help of hairs plucked from Mary and Jessica, and pieces of Peter's bathtub), and Ingrid's private detective, Himmel, shakes loose some of the skeletons from the Tate and Campbell closets. Corinne is eventually cleared, but Chief Tinkler makes another arrest in the Peter Campbell murder case—Jessica!

Cast: Jimmy Baio (Billy), Diana Canova (Corinne), Billy Crystal (Jodie), Cathryn Damon (Mary), Robert Guillaume (Benson), Katherine Helmond (Jessica), Jay Johnson (Chuck & Bob), Gordon Jump (Chief of Police Tinkler), Robert Mandan (Chester), Richard Mulligan (Burt), Arthur Peterson (The Major), Jennifer Salt (Eunice), Inga Swenson (Ingrid), Ted Wass (Danny), William Daniels (Heinrich Himmel), Rod Roddy (Announcer)

Highlights. Heinrich Himmel's Gestapo-like grilling of the Campbells and the Tates, and Benson being the only one strong enough to stand up to him. Special props to Burt's increasing madness and Bob's interaction with Himmel.

Confused? You Won't Be. *'It just might be a hairy hunk of gloop that hangs one a ya.'*

▶ Continuing the gag about Ecuador being a haven for former Nazis, Ingrid engages the services of private detective Heinrich Himmel (a tad close to Nazi SS chief Heinrich Himmler) to clear Corinne's name.

▶ Himmel forces Mary to bring the rest of the Campbells up to date on who Ingrid Swenson is. When she and Jessica still lived at home, their brother Randolph got the Swedish maid, Ingrid, pregnant. Their mother, wanting the baby for herself, sent Ingrid and Randolph to Ecuador, then convinced the authorities that the former was an illegal alien, and the latter was plotting to overthrow the government. The baby, Corinne, was then given to Jessica and Chester to raise as their own.

▶ Mr. Rollo was the clown that entertained at Jessica and Mary's birthday parties until he died at one of the former's—more proof that Jessica might've been on to something when she said their family is cursed (1.10).

Jessica's Animated Expressions

Katherine Helmond in particular managed to express a wide range of emotions through her face, a skill developed during her time on the stage.

"I think on the stage you play a variety of roles, which you don't do in television," says Helmond. "You get one character and you play that for years. One of the things that I think supports the character on stage is facial expressions—the eyes, the attitude, the body expression. And actually it does carry beyond the first row. It may be that they can't see your eyes, but if you follow through with the entire body in attitude, then the audience all the way to the back gets it.

"I think that one of the reasons I did that was because I wanted to show the audience Jessica's process of thinking. I didn't want them to dismiss her as just stupid, but as a person that processed things in a different way. I think that all the facial expressions and the eye expressions and the follow through of the body conveyed the fact that she had to think very seriously about everything, and then came to a conclusion, which was not always the correct one, but was OK for her."

Best Lines.
Bob [explaining why Burt went to a shrink]: Impotence.
Himmel: Really?
Bob: Yeah.
Himmel. No kidding.
Bob: No, it's the truth.
Himmel: I love it. So classically American. A problem we never have in Germany. No impotence. No smog.
Bob: No Jews.

Tinkler: On my little search through your house I found the gun that shot Peter Campbell, I found the knife that stabbed Peter Campbell, and I found the brick that hit Peter Campbell. Now the gun was found in your drawer, the knife was found in your jewelry box, and the brick was found in your rose garden! Mrs. Tate, you are under arrest for the murder of Peter Campbell!

Rod Roddy's Wrapup. Will Corinne ever forgive Jessica and Chester for not telling her she was adopted? Will the courts accept Burt's findings as evidence, or will the judge rule it hair-say? Did Jessica kill Peter Campbell, or does she merely collect murder weapons? Will the Tates do without dessert, or will they eat Heinrich's pants? These questions and many others will be answered on the next episode of *Soap*.

1.17
First aired: Jan 17, 1978 • Written by Susan Harris • Directed by Jay Sandrich

While Jessica sits in jail, Burt continues to spiral deeper into his grief-fueled insanity. Ingrid pays a visit to the Campbell house and promises to destroy every member of both families. Danny finally buries the hatchet with Mr. Lefkowitz, little knowing that the mobster expects him to marry Elaine. Congressman McCallam is being blackmailed over his affair with Eunice, and Chester realizes that getting Jessica out of jail is going to be harder than he thought.

Cast: Billy Crystal (Jodie), Cathryn Damon (Mary), Robert Guillaume (Benson), Katherine Helmond (Jessica), Jay Johnson (Chuck & Bob), Gordon Jump (Chief Tinkler), Robert Mandan (Chester), Dinah Manoff (Elaine Lefkowitz), Richard Mulligan (Burt), Jennifer Salt (Eunice), Inga Swenson (Ingrid), Ted Wass (Danny), Edward Winter (Congressman McCallam), Rod Roddy (Announcer), Sorrell Booke (Mr. Lefkowitz), Susan Harris (Babette), Howard Hesseman (Mr. Franklin), Pierrino Mascarino (Henchman), Lee Weaver (Sergeant)

Highlights. The cheerfulness with which Jessica takes to her jailing; the delight that is Sorrell Booke's performance as Mr. Lefkowitz ("a finger!"); Danny being beat at checkers by Chuck & Bob; Ingrid's victory lap through the Campbell living room; and Benson bringing Jessica breakfast in jail.

Confused? You Won't Be. *'I've taken your Corinne and soon they'll take your life. Ha!'*

▶ Just before Tinkler takes her to the cells, Jessica admits to Chester that she's never spent the night alone before. Her only fear now is that if she is wrongfully convicted and executed, Shelly Winters will play her in the movie version. (Catherine Deneuve and Barbra Streisand are Jessica's choices for her role; Robert Redford should play Chester.)

▶ Elaine's treatment of Danny as little more than a boy toy will be reversed (briefly) later on.

▶ This episode begins two classic *Soap* routines: Bob outsmarting Danny, and Burt's "invisibility".

52603

The number on the little plate Jessica holds when Tinkler takes her picture at the police station

▶ Mr. Franklin was originally Corinne's lawyer. Buried in the insanity that is the attorney's grilling of his potential client is another nail in Chester's coffin—it was Chester who bought Jessica the gun that killed Peter for those nights when his "work" prevented him from coming home at night. Had he not fooled around, not only would there not have been a gun to kill Peter Campbell, his wife never would've had the opportunity to take up with him.

Jay Johnson on the Origin of the Checkers Game

"Originally, the script would say 'Chuck & Bob are sitting on the couch.' Danny's there for a scene later, and Mary says such and such. The scene was about Mary and Jodie talking about something, and occasionally Danny would throw in a line, and maybe midway through the scene Chuck would throw in a line. But soon I had no lines in the scene, I was really just there sitting in the living room.

"So at the top of the scene, Jay Sandrich said, 'Well, you can't just be sitting in the scene. What can you be doing?' And so he got the prop man to get a checkerboard and he staged a scene between Danny and myself. Danny wasn't the sharpest knife in the bin; he was a little bit of a pretty boy in the script. So he would make a move with his checker, and Bob would go, 'I don't think so,' and he would take it back. And he'd start to make another move and Bob would go, 'I don't think so.' And Chuck is obviously playing with Danny. And finally Danny moves his checker and Bob says, 'Perfect.' Bob gives him a nod and a wink, and Chuck jumps five checkers and wins.

"That was simply a director saying why don't you guys do that at the top of the scene, and it became a very funny moment in the show that wasn't written, it was just done on the fly to keep two characters alive. That was always a great gift that Jay Sandrich would give me. If there was nothing to do and nothing scripted, he would help me find something and help me learn that that's what you do, you just find your life."

Best friend Benson: Smuggles breakfast into Jessica's jail cell by posing as her lawyer. On the menu: Canadian bacon, blueberry muffins and grapefruit. "I knew you couldn't eat the food in here. What do you want for dinner?"

Robert Guillaume has a particular fondness for this scene. "I enjoyed that scene because it was an opportunity to display the affection between those two characters, and we even allowed for the possibility that something was going on between them that was deeper than what we saw," he says. "I enjoyed playing that part, too. That was the kind of thing that an actor comes to like very much. It's an extra bonus in what you're doing because it resonates far beyond what is being said."

200: The number of Bunsen burners Burt bought recently, proving he's lost his marbles. (They were on sale, Mary says defensively.)

3 minutes: How long Eunice "sees" Congressman McCallam during their meetings. (Granted, she was pretty upset when she said this.)

$50,000: The amount demanded by the blackmail letter McCallam received to keep pictures of him and Eunice out of the papers. (Possibly taken at the hotel in Atlanta, where he dressed up as a Roman gladiator and Eunice was the slave he'd just bought.)

Jay Sandrich: Working with the Master Part 1

Few if any television directors are as widely respected as Jay Sandrich. Though polite and soft spoken, Sandrich never allowed anything to get in the way of the performances of which he knew his cast, and his crew, were capable.

"I always reminisce about this moment," associate director (later director) JD Lobue says. "[*Soap* stage manager Carl Lauten and I] were in the control room and Jay was sitting in the back as I was blocking the cameras. Whenever I would do something, Jay would make a comment back. I stopped after a few minutes and said, 'You know what, I really appreciate you doing this for me. This is a real great opportunity, but I can't follow my train of thought with you giving me notes while I'm doing it.' He says, 'Oh JD, I'm so sorry,' and he left the booth.

The number of years Ingrid and Randolph have been in Ecuador

Carl looked at me and said, 'Are you out of your mind? You just ran Jay Sandrich out of his own control room!' I said, 'I did…oh my God, I can't believe that!' I went to him later and said, 'Jay, I really apologize for that.' He says, 'No, you're absolutely right. I was kibitzing from the back of the house and it wasn't fair to you.' That's the kind of guy Jay is." (Lauten disputes this actually happened. Nearly 40 years on, it's hard to say whose memory is correct. Still, it illustrates Sandrich's professionalism and sense of fair play, which no one disputes.)

Best Lines.

Jodie [about Burt]: Mom, he should see a psychiatrist.

Mary: Look, the man's son was murdered. That's an enormous shock. There's bound to be some reaction to it. He'll get over it.

Jodie: Mom, last night he told me that sometimes he thinks he's invisible.

Mary: He was joking with you. Invisible. [Laughs.]

Jodie: He was serious, mom. He told me that sometimes he can walk through a room and nobody sees him. He says it helps him greatly with his detective work.

Mary: And you believed it? He was joking with you. Look, this is all a reaction to grief. There is no reason in the world to worry about Burt.

[Cue enormous explosion.]

Franklin: Mr Tate, let me put this as candidly as possible. Now your wife, as we know, had the motive. The murder weapons were found in her room with her fingerprints all over them, and she had no alibi for that night. Plus which the judge, as you can see from the astronomical bail that he has set, hates rich people.

Chester: What you're saying is it will be a difficult case.

Franklin: Mr. Tate, Clarence Darrow in his prime, arguing this case against a mute prosecutor with a jury of Mrs. Tate's relatives, with you sitting as the judge, could not possibly hope to win. I'm sorry but I do have a career to think about. I cannot take this case.

Rod Roddy's Wrapup: Will Ingrid really destroy all the Tates and Campbells, or is this just some Swedish bragging? Does a blackmailer really have compromising pictures of Eunice and the congressman or is it merely a school chum playing a practical joke? Will Danny marry Elaine, or will he decide he'd rather be killed? If the case against Jessica was argued against a mute prosecutor with Chester as the judge, would Jessica really be found guilty? And if she is, will her worst fear be realized? Will Shelly Winters play her in the film? These questions and many others will be answered on the next episode of *Soap*.

1.18 First aired: Jan 24, 1978 • Written by Susan Harris • Directed by Jay Sandrich

Father Tim visits Corinne at Ingrid's apartment and tells her he's heading to Canada for a religious retreat in hopes of curing himself of his desire for her. Burt's moved his research from the basement to the bathtub, and confides in Mary that he has the power to become invisible (but not when he's wet). And while Chester hires top lawyer E. Ronald Mallu (and risks the wrath of secretary Claire) to do his best for Jessica's defense, Jessica admits to Mary that she feels unneeded and unloved.

Cast: Diana Canova (Corinne), Billy Crystal (Jodie), Cathryn Damon (Mary), Robert Guillaume (Benson), Katherine Helmond (Jessica), Jay Johnson (Chuck & Bob), Robert Mandan (Chester), Richard Mulligan (Burt), Kathryn Reynolds (Claire), Eugene Roche

(E. Ronald Mallu), Inga Swenson (Ingrid Swenson) (Father Tim), Ted Wass (Danny), Rod Roddy (Announcer), Lupe Ontiveros (Lady in airport)

Highlights. Corinne's "Please God, I need him more than you do" prayer after Father Tim leaves; Burt's "invisibility" talk with Mary in the bathtub steals the show; and Claire's freakout at the restaurant with Chester has been a long time coming.

Confused? You Won't Be. *'Whoever heard of anybody being invisible? Unless of course you have the ring of power.'*

▶ Father Tim's rationale for going on his religious retreat may have been a scripting or performance mistake as he tells Corinne "If I'm able to forget about you, Corinne, then they'll transfer me and make me stay away until you're too old to tempt me, and I'm too old to care." Surely that should be "*unable* to forget about you." Corinne kisses him goodbye on the lips, pissing him off as she said she'd kiss him on the forehead.

▶ "Darling, you're not yourself," Mary tells Burt, foreshadowing his replacement by an alien in Season 3.

▶ Chester has had to mortgage the house to put up Jessica's bail money.

▶ Jessica tells Mary that she tried to volunteer at the hospital but got booted out because she was depressing the patients. Her feelings of being unneeded around the house have been plaguing her for a while now.

A day and a half: How long Burt's been in the bathtub.

$200/month: How much Chester is paying for the garage that houses the car he bought for Claire. (Don't worry. Mallu's fee is so high, he's going to sell the car, the parking space and Claire's apartment to raise money.)

Best friend Benson: Benson catches Jessica at the airport just before she boards a plane for Rio de Janeiro. "Mrs. Tate, you're white and rich, they ain't gonna hang you," he assures her.

Strong grandmothers and the on-screen closeness of their characters led Katherine Helmond and Robert Guillaume to become lifelong friends.

Jessica and Benson: Portrait of a Friendship

The strong bond between Jessica Tate and the Tate family servant Benson remains one of *Soap*'s greatest relationships. Though the series is primarily known for its sympathetic portrayal of its gay character Jodie, the Benson-Jessica friendship did a great deal to combat the horrible stereotyping of black people in America in the wake of the nation's civil rights battles.

Katherine Helmond deftly gets to the heart of why the characters worked so well together: "Everybody else was deceiving Jessica, or covering up things so she wouldn't be upset, and she had been a really protected woman in a lot of ways. Benson was the only person that really stood by her in an adult way, and in a strong friendship way. And interestingly enough, out of practicing that every day at work, Bob Guillaume and I have become really terribly close friends. We see each other quite a bit and celebrate birthdays together and holidays together."

The actors hit it off pretty much the moment Guillaume set foot on the *Soap* stage, Helmond recalls. "I think it was because for one thing we both came from the South. We were also both very much

1978

FEB. 1: Director Roman Polanski flees rape charges in the U.S. by skipping bail and seeking asylum in France.

involved with our grandmothers raising us and our mothers out working. We had a lot in common."

Best Lines.

[Mary joins Burt in the bathtub and gently explains that he's been saying some strange things, including that he can become invisible.]

Burt: Come on Mary! Whoever heard of anybody being invisible? Unless of course you have the ring of power.

Mary: The ring of power? Burt, do you have it?

Burt: What?

Mary: This ring of power.

Burt: Don't be silly.

Mary: Well that's a relief. Because for a minute there I thought you were telling me that you had this ring thing that made you invisible.

Burt: No, no...I can be invisible without it.

Mary: You think you can be invisible?

Burt: Mary, it's the damndest thing. You see what happens is sometimes I go into a room and people say "Hi Burt," but then of course I know I'm not invisible. But other times I go into a room, think people can see me, but nobody says anything. Those are the times I'm invisible. I don't know how to control it yet, Mary, but when I can, when I can, I'm going to blow this investigation wide open! Can you imagine it? I can go anywhere. I can hear everything. I can see everybody, and nobody can see me. I will also be able to get into the movies free.

Mary: Burt, you cannot make yourself invisible.

Burt: No? All right. Watch. [Puts fingers to his temples, concentrates, snaps his fingers and relaxes, secure in the knowledge that he's invisible.] Well? Can you see me? See, I told ya!

Mary: Burt, you're not invisible.

Burt: [Muffling his voice with his hand] All right, where am I?

Mary: Right there!

Burt: You knew that before.

Mary: I can see you, I can see you!

Burt: Are you sure you can see me?

Mary: Yes!

Burt [realizes his error]: It doesn't work when you're wet. Listen Mary, I'll tell you what. After our bath, while you're making dinner, I'll kinda dry off and blowdry my hair, and then I'll become invisible for ya.

Jessica [to Mary]: I'm like Eunice's Raggedy Ann doll that sits on her bed. It's old and kind of worn out and nobody even looks at it anymore. But nobody has the heart to throw it away because, well, it's just been there so long.

Rod Roddy's Wrapup: Will Burt ever come out of the bathtub? And if he does, will he be all wrinkled? Will Father Tim's retreat in Canada cure him of Corinne, or will he take up hockey? Will Chester be able to pay E. Ronald Mallu's enormous fee for Jessica's defense? And now that Claire has called the SEC, will he have any money left over for his own defense? These questions and many others will be answered on next week's episode of *Soap*.

1.19 First aired: Feb 7, 1978 • Written by Susan Harris • Directed by Jay Sandrich

As E. Ronald Mallu desperately searches for character witnesses he can put on the stand in Jessica's defense, Jessica mounts her own defense with Corinne, explaining why she never told the girl she was adopted. It might've worked, too, if not for a few cynical words from Corinne's real mother, Ingrid. Meanwhile, Mary tries to get Burt psychiatric help for his invisibility delusion, and Eunice and McCallam's blackmailer kicks things up a notch, pushing Eunice to the edge…of a window ledge!

Cast: Diana Canova (Corinne), Billy Crystal (Jodie), Cathryn Damon (Mary), Robert Guillaume (Benson), Katherine Helmond (Jessica), Jay Johnson (Chuck & Bob), Robert Mandan (Chester), Richard Mulligan (Burt), Arthur Peterson (The Major), Eugene Roche (E. Ronald Mallu), Jennifer Salt (Eunice), Inga Swenson (Ingrid Swenson), Ted Wass (Danny), Edward Winter (Congressman McCallam), Rod Roddy (Announcer), Byron Webster (Dr. Medlow), Judith-

While the focus is on Ed Winter's Congressman McCallam, it is Judith-Marie Bergan's Marilyn McCallam who steals the show in this family.

Marie Bergan (Marilyn McCallam), Marvin Braverman (The Messenger)

Highlights. Burt revelling in his newfound invisibility in the living room scene (and Mary's mixed look of love and embarrassment when Burt suggests testing how his "invisibility" affects their lovemaking); Chester begging off testifying in Jessica's defense and asking if, given Claire's call to the SEC, Mallu offers "family rates"; the smooth way Burt convinces Dr. Medlow that Mary's the one with the problem, her momentary freakout when she thinks he *has* become invisible at Medlow's office, and Burt's own surprise that he can't walk through walls; Jessica's heart to heart with Corinne; Eunice's reaction to seeing the blackmail photos for the first time, and McCallam accidentally giving them to the messenger for the press instead of his speech.

Confused? You Won't Be. *'What we're looking for are good character witnesses.'*

▶ There's a tradition in episodic radio and television for a series to occasionally "reset" the show, allowing new viewers to easily get up to speed on who the characters are and what makes them unique. In this episode, Harris does this for nine characters in a single scene (10 if you count Bob), touching on Jodie's homosexuality and suicide attempt, Burt's invisibility, and Danny's mob ties among other things in just a few minutes.

▶ Burt cites his inability to become invisible while wet (1.18) as a reason he won't be able to demonstrate his invisibility to Dr. Medlow—he's perspiring because he's nervous. The last time we saw Dr. Medlow was when he cured Burt's impotence (1.11). Mary's "Burt hasn't been himself lately" to Dr. Medlow again foreshadows Burt's alien predicament in Season 3.

▶ Special props go to Judith-Marie Bergan who plays Congressman McCallam's clueless wife, Marilyn. Any actor can play the perpetual drunk; few can be at once shrewish and sympathetic the way Bergan can.

▶ Jessica's speech to Corinne about why she never told her she was adopted is an excellent example of Susan Harris working within the framework of mainstream comedy and drama, and then subverting it, in this case with a single sentence from Ingrid: "Everything she said, Corinne, she said to save her own neck".

Ben Evans: The Tate family photographer who's taken gorgeous pictures of Eunice…according to Eunice.

Mr. Magoo: What Jessica calls Mallu.

Getting to the Heart of Chester

Anyone who's ever played a bit of a rogue on television will tell you that there are more than a few people out there ready to take you to task for whatever terrible things your character has been up to. Yet this was never the case with Chester Tate, Robert Mandan points out. "When I was out, people would sort of look and go, 'There's Chester, isn't that nice?' I think they sensed the underlying pathos in Chester because I always approached him as being very, very sad with a very sad life.

"Susan Harris spoke to this when she was being interviewed. They asked how do you get to the things that are funny? And she said I go to the things that are sad and that gives the energy for comedy. And comedy of course is just an attitude, I think. But I always thought that Chester was this spoiled, sad little rich boy who didn't have anything, didn't have any guidance, didn't have any parents.

"I always feel that most enduring characters have a really dark side to them, which you don't want to see every week, but it feeds the energy of the character and the energy of the comedy. Otherwise, comedy is just shtick. If there's not some kind of emotional engine underneath it all, then it gets flat and bland and boring."

For the *Soap* Bible Tells Us So. Though we never learn this in the broadcast series, Eunice, Corinne and Billy have an older brother: David. According to the *Soap* bible, he was 26 at the time the series began, a class valedictorian and all-state basketball star.

1978

FEB. 11: The Rev. Moon's Unification Church marries 16 couples simultaneously in New York City.

David was drafted into the Vietnam conflict and has been missing in action for five years when *Soap* begins. Unknown to his family, he actually lived for quite a while with Noyen Nu, the daughter of a "South Vietnamese opium smuggling general". Soon after David disappeared, Noyen gave birth "to a blue-eyed baby".

With the exception of a few digs at Anita Bryant's anti-gay campaigns in Season 1, *Soap* would keep its distance from political controversy, suggesting that this story line was quashed in discussions fairly early: The fall of Saigon happened less than three years before the premiere of *Soap*, after all.

Though a note under the heading "Back Burner Plots" informs us that David would eventually return after having lived in Bangkok (this following his escape from a POW camp) with a wife, the daughter of an English missionary, it was his relationship with Noyen Nu that held the greatest potential for *Soap*. The jettisoning of the David Tate arc was one of *Soap*'s most unfortunate missed opportunities.

Best Lines.
Jessica: My mother once said to me, Jessica, with a face like that, you could get away with murder.

Mallu [about Jessica]: Put her on the stand? You might as well strap her in, shave her head and attach the electrodes right there.

Mallu [to Chester, after meeting the family]: I have for character witnesses Al Capone, Tinkerbell, Punch and Judy and the Invisible Man.

Jessica: I was afraid. Oh Corinne, I loved you the way I loved all my children, and I was afraid that if I told you who you were and where your real parents were, you'd leave and go to them. Which was not too unlikely at the time, Corinne, because you blamed daddy and me for your braces and your bra and your pimples and your period. I lived through your drinking shoe polish and eating a worm. I made ballerina costumes and baked birthday cakes, and I laughed at you when you dressed the dog in Eunice's clothes. And I cried with you when Johnny Carrington left you in the seventh grade for that hussy, Rita Lewis. Because you were my child. And you were no less my child than had you come from my womb. Corinne, love does not come from having shared the same body. Love comes from having shared a lifetime. I'm on trial for my life now and I know most people would say that's the most important thing in the world. But it's not. The most important thing in the world to me right now is that once I had a little girl, and now she's gone.

Mallu to Chester: "Put her on the stand? You might as well strap her in, shave her head and attach the electrodes right there."

Rod Roddy's Wrapup: Will Burt be committed? Or will life continue to be a snap for him? Will Corinne go to Jessica or stay with Ingrid? What will Corinne do on Mother's Day? Will Mallu defend Jessica without character witnesses, or will he put Al Capone, Tinkerbell and the Invisible Man on the stand? Will Eunice get off the ledge? Will Congressman McCallam get the pictures back? If he doesn't, will Eunice want to get off the ledge? These questions and many others will be answered on next week's episode of *Soap*.

1.20 First aired: Feb 14, 1978 • Written by Susan Harris • Directed by Jay Sandrich

McCallam gets the pictures back from the messenger and Mr. Lefkowitz tells Danny that he must marry Elaine, this after Danny's made it pretty clear to both him and Elaine that he doesn't like her. Jodie tries to get to the bottom of why Bob has been sending him rude notes, and Burt and Mary have a frank discussion about Burt's need for psychiatric help. Meanwhile, Jessica, Mallu and Chester meet the prosecutor and the judge in the case—and to think they thought the odds were stacked against them before.

Cast: Billy Crystal (Jodie), Cathryn Damon (Mary), Katherine Helmond (Jessica), Howard Hesseman (Mr. Franklin), Jay Johnson (Chuck & Bob), Charles Lane (Judge Petrillo), Robert Mandan (Chester), Dinah Manoff (Elaine), Richard Mulligan (Burt), Eugene Roche (E. Ronald Mallu), Jennifer Salt (Eunice), Ted Wass (Danny), Edward Winter (Congressman McCallam), Rod Roddy (Announcer),

Sorrell Booke (Mr. Lefkowitz), Milt Oberman (Man in hotel), Marvin Braverman (The Messenger)

Highlights. Eunice going through other people's mail in the mailroom, and her and McCallam's subsequent daydreaming about moving to an island; the entire "Bob in the fridge" scene; the delightful way Mr. Lefkowitz explains to Danny that he must marry Elaine, and Danny's "Is it too late to kill my stepfather?"; and Burt leveling with Mary about his rapidly deteriorating sanity.

Confused? You Won't Be. *'Marry Elaine or I'll blow your brains out.'*

◉ Mr. Lefkowitz has investigated Danny's family, just as Mallu did last episode.

◉ Already Susan Harris has garnered a reputation among her cast, crew and audience for being able to follow up a comedic line with a heartbreaking one. Last episode it was Jessica's appeal to Corinne; this episode we're hit with *Soap*'s best combination for the first time: Harris' dialogue and Richard Mulligan's performance. If you go back and watch the scene in which Mary mentions having Burt committed, you can actually hear the live audience guffaw at his line about losing his marbles, only to be blindsided by where Harris and Mulligan take this line of reasoning. For all of his eccentricities, the character of Burt Campbell is *Soap*'s indictment of Hollywood's own approach to mental illness. His citing of the 1957 film *The Three Faces of Eve*—one of many films that make treating psychological wounds appear as simple as healing a cut—makes this pretty clear. While the religious right was pursing its lips at the sex jokes, *Soap* was addressing the world as it was, and not as the more puritanical element wished it to be. Powerful stuff.

The Three Faces of Eve

◉ The Mr. Franklin we meet in the judge's chambers is prosecuting, and is the twin brother of the one who refused to defend Jessica (1.17), or so he says. (This one giggles incessantly, and lost a case to Mallu 10 years earlier.)

◉ Judge Petrillo's name would later be plucked for another Witt Thomas Harris character, Sophia Petrillo, on *The Golden Girls*. There's a good chance that the name is a nod to the early 20th century president of the Chicago Local 10 musician's union, James Petrillo. He was a frequent punch line on the Jack Benny radio show and its spin-offs.

$40,000: How much Judge Petrillo lost years before after Chester "invested" it for him. "My son didn't care that much about going to college. He's doing very nicely at the taco stand....After all, my father only had a couple more years on that kidney machine. Hey, he was old. Had to go sometime. See all you folks in court."

Giving Bob the Cold Shoulder

There is no shortage of classic Chuck & Bob moments. However, one of the most memorable—Jodie hiding the gay-baiting Bob in the fridge and the chaos that ensues—is a wonderful example of what can happen when cast and writer come together perfectly.

"That's one of my favorite scenes," says Jay Johnson. "I remember the genesis of that. Billy Crystal came to me one day and said, 'What would happen if Chuck didn't have Bob anymore?' We started talking about it and I think he pitched the scene. I said, 'Jeez, he'd probably try to make a puppet out of anything that he had,' so we started coming up with ways to interact that way. I think we had about 10 more of those and they cut half of them. We were usually successful about pitching ideas, and then they would write them, particularly with my character; I was real successful at getting my ideas in."

Bob's "You know, that little light stays on" was also a rare example of an ad lib on *Soap*, stage manager Carl Lauten points out. "Jay thought of that during the air show [the performance that immediately followed the taped dress rehearsal]. That wasn't written like that, he just did it when he pulled Bob out as they were leaving. I'm glad it was on mike and they didn't pull off of him because the line wasn't scripted."

Best Lines.
[Jodie stuffs Bob in the fridge before going on to make breakfast. A manic-looking Chuck enters the kitchen.]

Chuck: Jodie, have you seen Bob?

Jodie: Bob who?

Chuck: Bob. [Holds up his "Bob" hand.] My Bob.

Jodie: Oh *Bob*! No.

Chuck: I don't know what happened. I was in the bathroom, he was still sleeping and when I came back he was gone.

Jodie: Maybe he ran away.

Chuck: No, I just have this awful feeling that something awful happened to him.

Jodie: Chuck, why don't you sit down, I want to talk to you.

Chuck: I can't, Jodie. I can't sit down and talk. Bob is missing!

Jodie: Well maybe by the time we finish talking, Bob might turn up.

Chuck: You do know where he is, don't ya?

Jodie: Sit down.

Chuck: All right, all right, where is he? What did you do with him?

Jodie: Listen, Chuck. Recently I've been getting some very nasty notes like that one. [Hands him one.] That's vicious Chuck, that hurts. And they're all signed Bob Campbell.

Chuck: Oh no.

Jodie: Yes.

Chuck [tearing up the note]: Well I'll have a talk with him.

Jodie: Chuck, why are you sending me these notes?

Chuck: What are you talking about, Jodie? You just said Bob was sending these notes.

Jodie: Chuck, you *are* Bob.

Chuck: And if he is I'm going to sit down and really give him hell for it, that's for sure.

Jodie: Chuck, for God's sakes you can't talk to him, you are him! Every time I try to talk to you Bob answers, Chuck.

Chuck [making his grapefruit talk]: Hello there. I'm Grapey the Grapefruit. What's a matter Jodie, you look upset.

Jodie [freaked out]: I'd like to talk to Chuck.

Chuck [as grapefruit]: How about talking to me, I'm in season, sweet, just like Bob.

Jodie: No, no, I understand—I don't believe this, I'm having a conversation with a grapefruit here! Chuck, look Chuck. [Takes the grapefruit away.] It's food Chuck, see, watch, it's just food [starts grinding the grapefruit into a hand juicer—the grapefruit moans].

Jodie: Chuck, if you're joking, cut it out. I just would like to talk to you.

Chuck [making his banana talk]: Ole! As one fruit to another -!

Jodie [grabbing it and taking a bite]: Chuck, look, it's food, see. You need help, Chuck.

Chuck [making his muffin talk]: Hello there, I'm an English Muffin!

Jodie [grabbing the muffin]: See, it's food! [Takes a bite.] See Chuck, it's food! You really should see a doctor, Chuck!

[Chuck makes the cream dispenser burp.]

Jodie [grabbing Chuck]: For God's sakes, Chuck! Listen to me, wouldya!? [Burt enters and Jodie tries to play it cool.] Nobody wears a Windsor knot anymore.

Burt: I'm going to heat up some bagels, anybody want one?

Jodie [to Chuck]: I'll talk to you later, Chuck!

[A few minutes later, Burt opens the fridge to get some butter for his bagel and freaks out when he sees Bob in there.]

Chuck: Oh my God! Bob!!

Bob [shivering]: You're sick, you know that? You're really sick! I coulda froze in there! You coulda killed me!

Chuck: You know I wouldn't be surprised if you killed Peter!

Bob: Yeah. You tried to choke Chuck, freeze me—you're sick, you know that? [To Chuck] You know that little light stays on.

Chuck: Does it?

Bob: Yeah.

The three minds behind the 'Bob in the fridge' scene.

Burt: I'm losing it. Mary I'm losing it.

Mary: What Burt? What are you losing?

Burt: My marbles. It's like now, like right now, Mary. Everything gets so clear. I'm here, right, and you're here and we're talking and everything is good. But I can't keep it that way, it won't stay. I try Mary. I really try to keep everything right the way it is but it starts slipping. I slip. And then I go away and I can't stop it. I try, Mary, I really try. I can't help it. And then I'm gone.

Rod Roddy's Wrapup: Will Danny marry Elaine, or will he ask Mr. Lefkowitz to blow his brains out? Will Burt allow himself to be committed, and if he does, will he allow himself to be seen? Since the judge lost a lot of money, and he doesn't find it funny, and though Chester says he's sorry and the judge says not to worry, will Jessica get the chair even though it isn't fair, because the judge holds a grudge? These questions and many others will be answered on next week's episode of *Soap*.

1.21 First aired: Feb 21, 1978 • Written by Susan Harris • Directed by Jay Sandrich

Danny's brought Elaine to the Campbell house, ostensibly to let Mary and Burt meet her, but really so he can show Elaine how insane his family is in hopes that she will call off the wedding. Corinne breaks into Father Tim's retreat cabin and is overjoyed to discover that the retreat hasn't worked—he admits that he's still in love with her. And Jessica's murder trial finally kicks off; she's more worried that she and Chester will lose their newfound closeness than she is of losing her life.

Cast: Jimmy Baio (Billy), Rebecca Balding (Carol David), Diana Canova (Corinne), Billy Crystal (Jodie), Cathryn Damon (Mary), Robert Guillaume (Benson), Katherine Helmond (Jessica), Howard Hesseman (Mr. Franklin), Jay Johnson (Chuck & Bob), Gordon Jump (Chief of Police Tinkler), Charles Lane (Judge Petrillo), Robert Mandan (Chester), Dinah Manoff (Elaine), Richard Mulligan (Burt), Arthur Peterson (The Major), Eugene Roche (E. Ronald Mallu), Jennifer Salt (Eunice), Sal Viscuso (Father Tim), Ted Wass (Danny), Rod Roddy (Announcer), Ian Wolfe (Father Juniper), Tim Rossovich (Elaine's bodyguard, uncredited)

Highlights. Burt glimpsing Elaine's bodyguard when he opens the door to Danny and instantly thinking Danny's gay, too; Elaine's endearing blend of "what of it?" spunk and "meet the parents" charm; Corinne breaking into Father Tim's retreat in her cute white snowsuit, and the other priest's reaction to seeing her; and Jessica's entire courtroom appearance.

Confused? You Won't Be. *'I'm afraid you've oversold it. No family can be this crazy.'*
▶ Plans to commit Burt for psychiatric help are humming right along; he's supposed to go next week. Once again The Major has disappeared (1.7), only to turn up in love.

▶ This episode introduces Carol David, the second woman to meet the homosexual Jodie and instantly take it upon herself to "convert" him. [See "Because the *Soap* Bible Tells Us So" below.] After the perfection that was last episode, we are now entering a new phase in *Soap*, in which one story line will inevitably eclipse another in creativity or execution. In this one, Elaine meeting the Campbells far outstrips the music hall titters to be derived from the court scene.

Sheba Pfeiffer: The name of the woman who's claimed The Major's heart. Says he, "I haven't felt like this since my dear departed beloved wife, whoever *she* was."

And Introducing... Carol David, Mr. Mallu's assistant.

3 years: How long it's been since the Indian who helped Corinne up the mountain had seen a woman.

For the *Soap* Bible Tells Us So. It's hard not to take Carol as a continuation of the smoldering Nurse Nancy (1.9, 1.12); they even have the same hairdo. According to a single sentence in the *Soap* bible, there's good reason to believe that they were meant to be the same character. On P. 36, the last of the document, we are told that Dennis Phillips comes out of the closet to the sports world after his marriage falls apart. "Jodie, who is now having his first satisfactory relationship with a woman (Nancy Darwin, the candy striper), is now torn between his new and old loves."

That's it, I've had it, I'm leaving. [Finger snap.] After *Soap*, Dinah Manoff (Elaine) went on to star as one of Richard Mulligan's daughters in the Witt Thomas Harris sitcom *Empty Nest*.

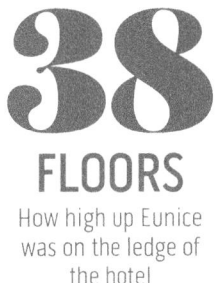

38 FLOORS
How high up Eunice was on the ledge of the hotel

1978

FEB. 15: Serial killer Ted Bundy is captured in Florida. **FEB. 16:** LA's "Hillside Strangler" (actually two people, Angelo Buono, right, and Kenneth Bianchi) kills 10th and final victim.

"Richard once told me a funny story about *Soap*," she says. "You know how Burt used to disappear on *Soap*, he'd snap his fingers and he'd disappear? Well he said when things got tough for him on the show (and don't ask me what those things were because I don't remember), he would just disappear. He would snap his fingers like Burt and he would just check out. He'd be there but not there. He'd just disappear."

Best Lines.

Danny: Elaine, this is Jodie. Jodie, this is Elaine Lefkowitz.

Elaine: Hi Jodie.

Jodie: Hi.

Danny: Jodie's a fruit.

Elaine: Well hey, whose family's perfect? My father's a gangster.

Burt: Your father's a gangster? Her father's a gangster.

Elaine: Hey, your son is a fruit!

Burt [indicating Jodie]: He's not my son, *he's* my son [points to Chuck].

Elaine: Well he's crazy.

Burt: All right, that's it, I've had it, I'm leaving. [Snaps his fingers to disappear.]

Rod Roddy's Wrapup: Will Danny marry Elaine, or will he choose the carefree life of a bachelor and have his head blown off? Will Father Tim leave the retreat to see Corinne, and if he does, will they make him pay for the window? Will Jessica be found guilty of the heinous crime that Franklin has accused her of, and what does heinous mean? These questions and many others will be answered on next week's episode of *Soap*.

1.22   First aired: Feb 28, 1978 • Written by Susan Harris • Directed by Jay Sandrich

Carol convinces Jodie to come away with her for the weekend to the cape "as friends," Burt gets to know kindly schizophrenic Harold Bronfman on his first day at the mental hospital, and Danny tells Mary the real reason why he has to marry Elaine. Billy runs

The relationship between Danny, Elaine and the Campbells might have been the most dynamic on Soap.

away from home after failing math to spare his family more tragedy, and Jessica's trial continues to be a circus that seems on the verge of being dismissed, until prosecuting counsel Mr. Franklin promises scathing testimony to come the following day.

Cast: Jimmy Baio (Billy), Rebecca Balding (Carol David), Billy Crystal (Jodie Dallas), Cathryn Damon (Mary), Robert Guillaume (Benson), Katherine Helmond (Jessica), Gordon Jump (Chief of Police Tinkler), Charles Lane (Judge Petrillo), Robert Mandan (Chester), Richard Mulligan (Burt), Arthur Peterson (The Major), Eugene Roche (E. Ronald Mallu), Jennifer Salt (Eunice), Ted Wass (Danny), Rod Roddy (Announcer), Milt Oberman (Harold Bronfman), Dick McGarvin (Dr. Resnick), Fred Iwasaki (The Chef), Cooper Neal (Hello Man), Howard Hesseman (Mr. Franklin, uncredited)

Highlights. Carol and Jodie's straightforward conversation in the Japanese restaurant and the chef's reaction; Burt using his "invisibility" finger snap after putting on Harold's top hat, and Harold copying it; Benson commandeering Tinkler's patrol car to go find Billy ("I'll tell them I'm you"); the judge's "good" upon hearing Mr. Franklin tell the jury that Chester is being investigated by the SEC; the Major's "Shoot that man" (referring to Franklin); and Franklin's final words to the judge.

Confused? You Won't Be. *'Something awful happens, just look around, I'll be in the vicinity.'*

Rebecca Balding's Carol and Fred Iwasaki's chef rescue an otherwise lackluster episode.

▶ Carol's "I finally meet a guy I really like and he hates me" is a telling line as it also sums up the predicament of that other woman dating one of Mary's sons: Elaine. In both cases, all of the trouble that is to come the way of Jodie and Danny is because they've allowed themselves to become involved with women they really don't love.

▶ Despite an underwhelming scene of Burt being left at the mental hospital, if you listen closely you can hear somebody in the audience actually say "Poor Burt."

▶ With Billy's running away from home because of a bad report card, the *Soap* producers seem torn between making fun of this typical sitcom fodder and revealing that they still have no idea how to use him, or why he's even there.

▶ Though we get both Burt in the mental hospital and some wonderful Benson in the courtroom scenes, it's surprising that it's the few minutes between Jodie and Carol at the Japanese restaurant that make this episode at all memorable.

Burt's Fellow Inmates: Harold Bronfman: a sweet paranoid schizophrenic who keeps switching hats to throw off the Argentinean police; a lady who thinks NBC is trying to kill her by shooting death rays through their broadcasts, which means no one there can watch Johnny Carson; and a guy who thinks he's the cousin of the Incredible Hulk.

Lenore Feldman: Someone on the jury Jessica finally realizes she knows. They did the hula dance at the PTA thing.

For the *Soap* Bible Tells Us So. Shortly after Burt is institutionalized following his crack-up over Peter's murder (more or less what we see in Season 1), his middle son, Michael, a charter-boat captain and smuggler, comes to visit him. In actuality, he's come to the area to kidnap Joey Nu Tate, David Tate's son [see "For the *Soap* Bible Tells Us So" under 1.19], so that he can hold the child for ransom. His goal: to get a stash of heroin from General Nu in return for the child's freedom. More importantly, Burt's committal should be doubly traumatic. According to the *Soap* bible, his father was institutionalized when Burt was 15.

The Challenge of Directing *Soap*

Says director Jay Sandrich, "Partially for me the biggest challenge was that we had a large talented cast, and there were many weeks when they only had one short scene and nothing particularly exciting to play. The hardest thing was just to keep everybody interested on the weeks that they didn't have a lot to do. I'd try to schedule the day so they didn't have to come in and hang around all day. Katherine Helmond was pretty much in most scenes or a big part of the show, but some of the other characters didn't always have a lot to do. It was tough to keep everybody happy.

"But the other thing was there were so many styles of comedy that it was always a challenge to try to keep the comedy sophisticated when that's what the scene called for, or play the drama with no laughs in a scene, or go for farce if the scene was a farce. However, it was always a pleasure to direct."

Best Lines.

Mr Franklin: Amazing recall, Mr. Benson. Absolutely amazing retention of detail.

Benson: Thank you.

Mr. Franklin: Tell me, is this some sort of "voodoo" way of knowing that you people have or what?

Mallu: I object!

Benson: I do, too...

Franklin: All right, very well Mr. Benson, keeping your eyes on me now. You would please demonstrate some more of this amazing talent. What color tie is the foreman wearing?

Benson [eyes on Franklin]: Green with red stripes.

Franklin: And the woman seated directly behind him, what is she wearing?

Benson: Yellow blouse with a blue scarf.

Franklin [uncomfortably]: And the man seated next to her?

Benson: Three piece blue suit with a blue shirt and a blue tie that clashes, and then the other guy-

Franklin: All right, all right! All right! [Benson could see the jurors reflected in the window.]

MAR. 6: *Hustler* magazine publisher Larry Flynt is shot and paralyzed by a sniper, allegedly serial killer Joseph Paul Franklin, near a Lawrenceville, Ga. courthouse. Flynt was battling obscenity charges there at the time of the shooting. Franklin, who confessed to the Flynt shooting but never stood trial for it, allegedly objected to mixed-race photos depicted in an issue of *Hustler*. **MAR. 16:** Former Italian premier Aldo Moro is kidnapped by leftist terror group the Red Brigades. He will be dead by May.

2
How many times Jessica says she slept with Peter, according to what she told the jury

Rod Roddy's Wrapup: Will Jodie and Carol go away for the weekend as just friends? What will they come back as? Will the hospital make Burt better, and if so, is invisibility covered by Blue Cross? Will Elaine change like Mary hopes, or is Danny doomed to be married to a selfish, sarcastic, loud, pushy, tactless, cruel and obnoxious person? Who is Franklin's surprise witness, and after hearing this witness' testimony, will the jury really jump over the railing and lynch Jessica on the spot? Would this be legal? These questions and many others will be answered on next week's episode of *Soap*.

1.23 First aired: Mar 14, 1978 • Written by Susan Harris • Directed by Jay Sandrich

The good news: Eunice and McCallam's blackmailer has been paid off. The bad: Marilyn McCallam's the one who bought the negatives, and promptly uses them to split the couple up. Meanwhile, Burt runs away from the mental hospital, only to come back and tell Mary the secret he's been hiding their whole marriage. Ingrid is perverting the course of justice by perverting Judge Petrillo, and Corinne's having none of it. Father Tim tells his mother that he's leaving the priesthood, and Mr. Franklin's surprise witness all but delivers on the prosecutor's threats last episode.

Cast: Jimmy Baio (Billy), Rebecca Balding (Carol David), Billy Crystal (Jodie), Diana Canova (Corinne), Cathryn Damon (Mary), Robert Guillaume (Benson), Katherine Helmond (Jessica), Howard Hesseman (Mr. Franklin), Jay Johnson (Chuck & Bob) Gordon Jump (Chief of Police Tinkler), Charles Lane (Judge Petrillo), Robert Mandan (Chester), Richard Mulligan (Burt), Arthur Peterson (The Major), Eugene Roche (E. Ronald Mallu), Jennifer Salt (Eunice), Inga Swenson (Ingrid Swenson, listed now as Svenson), Sal Viscuso (Father Tim), Ted Wass (Danny), Edward Winter (Congressman McCallam), Rod Roddy (Announcer), Doris Roberts (Flo Flotsky), Judith-Marie Bergan (Marilyn McCallam), Luis Avalos (The Doctor), Nita Talbot (Mrs. Fine)

Highlights. The speed with which McCallam dumps Eunice once Marilyn threatens his career; Burt explaining why he can't go home and finally telling Mary the secret he's been carrying all these years, and then turning himself invisible and slipping away; Corinne walking out on Ingrid after catching Judge Petrillo leaving their apartment; Carol's salacious glee over her forthcoming trip with Jodie (poor girl); and Mr. Franklin's surprise witness: Mrs. Fine.

Confused? You Won't Be. *'I killed your first husband.'*

● For the first time, Father Tim actually mentions that he's thinking of leaving the priesthood for Corinne. Depending on how we interpret what he says to his mother, he's already told his superiors in the church.

● We finally get the payoff to Mrs. Fine's constant fear that her husband would find out about her and Peter (1.5, 1.12). She tells the court Franklin came to her house and announced her affair in front of her husband when he told her she had to testify. Her husband promptly called his lawyer, grabbed his girlfriend and flew off to Acapulco.

● Doris Roberts appeared in *The Taking of Pelham 123* (1974) with her *Soap* son, Sal Viscuso.

Bessie Stevens: Jessica cut her braids off to use them to play Pocahontas in 7th Grade.

The Hotels Eunice and McCallam have Frequented: Standish Hotel in Boston; The Ritz Hotel in Hartford; The Plaza Hotel in New York. (Though *not* The Trafalgar Hotel in New Haven, Conn.)

Abigail: Walter and Marilyn's 7-year-old daughter (he calls her Amanda).

For the *Soap* Bible Tells Us So. Originally, the behavior that landed Burt in the mental hospital was supposed to be excessive buying brought on by Chuck's weird behavior, ex-wife Jewel's financial and personal demands, and the murder of Peter. As a result, he went on a shopping spree that culminated in "a buying frenzy in FAO Schwartz."

Meanwhile, McCallam [called "Alan McCormick" in the bible] was originally meant to be so besotted with Eunice, he would consider

The number of times Mallu has asked Jessica if she killed Peter

1978

MAR. 22: Karl Wallenda of the Flying Wallendas (mentioned by Burt in 1.3) falls off a tightrope and dies.

murdering his wife so they could be together. For her part, his wife, discovering that she's terminally ill, starts telling political columnists about her husband's philandering in an effort to hinder his ultimate goal: to become a presidential candidate.

Soap: On the Cutting Edge of Innovation

The writing wasn't the only aspect of *Soap* that pushed the limits of television in its day. According to director JD Lobue, his predecessor, Jay Sandrich, was one of the first to use what was known as the "4-camera iso" technique.

In a 2-camera iso (short for "isolated") setup—the norm at the time—only two out of four cameras would be hooked up to two different video recorders at any given time. If it was a two-character scene, for example, you would have tape continuously running on Jessica and Chester—each to a separate tape machine—with the technical director (TD) editing the show while taping was in progress. However, with this setup you couldn't be taping a master shot or shots of any other characters without switching which cameras were iso'd, and the TD would have to do this all on the fly.

With the 4-camera iso technique used by *Soap*, you could have four cameras feeding to four separate tape machines continuously, giving the video editor maximum coverage for assembling a completed scene in post-production. An AD would still be telling the cameramen what shots were wanted. (This is essentially the same setup you have with film work where each camera has its own film roll.)

The director would tell the associate director which of the cameras should be recording at any given time; the AD would then pass this information on to the camera operators who had to time their shots just right. Explains Lobue, "So you had to really make sure those 'isos' were switched properly so that you had the setup to a joke and the joke itself isolated so you could extend or shorten the time of those camera cuts, because you couldn't guess

Soap's 4-camera "iso" setup, unique in its day, provided maximum coverage of what transpired on stage.

how the audience was going to react. Sometimes a joke would play better in the dress shows than the air show," in part because different audiences were used for each. For instance, one camera operator had to be sure he recorded Danny setting up a joke—and whatever audience laughter that setup inspired—and the second camera had to capture Burt's response, and stay on Richard Mulligan long enough to record the extra little facial expressions or other reactions he tended to spring on his co-workers at the last moment. This gave the director and video editor enough material to splice together the best scene.*

Once *Soap* became successful, the network bought enough equipment so that all four cameras could record simultaneously, giving the editing team a lot more material from which to cut a scene together. Says Lobue, "That was new and different in terms of videotape production."

Yet for all its cutting-edge innovations, some of its methods were admirably old school.

"Most people who have looked at that show on the air swore that it was shot on film, but in fact it was shot on video tape," says associate producer Marsha Posner. "Before we started shooting, we went to Frederick's of Hollywood and bought some black stockings and we put the stockings over the lens of the camera, and that gave us the look we wanted. When people saw that show on the air, they swore up and down that it was shot on film."

Recalls Lobue, "We scrimmed the filter wheels in the cameras to give it a softer look. I didn't know they came from Frederick's (I'm sure this would have made Jerry Falwell cringe), but we knew they were like silk. We went for a film look; we did more cross key lighting and softened the look of the hard-edged video." Admits director Jay Sandrich with a laugh, "That's a new one on me."

Best Lines.

Mallu [about Jodie]: You're going away with him for a weekend?

Carol: That's right.

Mallu: But he's a homosexual.

❋ Lobue estimates that only about 25% or 30% of an episode was made of footage from the recorded dress rehearsal or "dress show." "So if you had a 2-shot [where two interacting characters appear at the same time on screen] the first time you shot it, you'd go to singles or close-ups the next time you shot it, and all that stuff was intercut." Not only did this give the editing team more material to draw from, it also acted as insurance if, for example, an actor's line was obscured by audience laughter.

A little of what was on offer from Frederick's of Hollywood in the '60s.

Carol: That's right. And he might come back a homosexual. But if he does, he is sure going to have something to compare it to.

Rod Roddy's Wrapup: Did Walter really walk out on Eunice forever? Did he also leave her with the restaurant bill? Now that Mary has learned that Burt killed her first husband, Johnny, what does Mary think of her second husband, Burt? Now that Corinne has walked out on two mothers, does that make her ineligible for the Daughter of the Year award? Has Mrs. Fine's testimony convinced the jury that Jessica's guilty? Is Jessica guilty? These questions and many others will be answered on next week's episode of *Soap*.

1.24
First aired: Mar 21, 1978 • Written by Susan Harris • Directed by Jay Sandrich

Carol has so successfully manipulated Jodie during their weekend at the Cape that she's gotten him to sleep with her....and it changes nothing, or so Jodie says. Burt tries to come home from the mental hospital, but Mary still hasn't decided if she forgives him for what he did all those years ago. Corinne has returned home just in time to see the Tates threatened by Ingrid, and Chester arrested for stock fraud by Tinkler. Finally, the defense rests its case and the jury adjourns to decide the fate of Jessica Tate.

Cast. Jimmy Baio (Billy), Rebecca Balding (Carol David), Diana Canova (Corinne), Billy Crystal (Jodie), Cathryn Damon (Mary), Robert Guillaume (Benson), Katherine Helmond (Jessica), Howard Hesseman (Mr. Franklin), Jay Johnson (Chuck & Bob), Gordon Jump (Chief of Police Tinkler), Charles Lane (Judge Petrillo), Robert Mandan (Chester), Richard Mulligan (Burt), Arthur Peterson (The Major), Eugene Roche (E. Ronald Mallu), Jennifer Salt (Eunice), Inga Swenson (Ingrid), Ted Wass (Danny), Rod Roddy (Announcer)

Highlights. Mary spraying dusting spray in Bob's face after his "play your cards right and I'll get you a date with Dirty Harry" crack; Ingrid's insane confrontation with the Tates; and Benson disarming The Major in the courtroom.

Confused? You Won't Be. *'Corinne's coming home is a good omen.'*

▶ How much Danny's changed since the beginning of the series. He's gone from trying to kill Burt himself (1.4) to telling Mary "It was my father that got killed, and I forgive him."

▶ Rebecca Balding finally gets a few minutes of screen time and manages to be by turns enchanting and infuriating, but always engaging.

▶ Mallu's closing remarks to the jury about Jessica ("a person I'm truly proud to say I'm a better man for having met") telegraphs what he will tell Jessica next episode while they're waiting for the jury to come back.

6: How old Jessica was when she shoved Mary out of a tree to see if she could fly. (She couldn't.)

8 weeks: About how long it took for Mary to be able to walk again.

Chuck & Bob's Matching Outfits

It's one of those details that most people don't think about, but in 1978 you couldn't just buy matching outfits for a ventriloquist and his puppet right off the peg.

"They would buy my size of clothes, find something that they thought I looked good in, and then they would buy my style three sizes or two sizes BIGGER than me, and those were Bob's clothes," Jay Johnson remembers. "They had a seamstress who would take that material and cut it down to the size of Bob. Occasionally I would try on a shirt that would just dwarf me, the sleeves would be hanging down. I'd go, 'What is this?' They'd go, 'Oh, that's Bob's shirt.'"

"The only other way of doing it would've been to make two shirts and we didn't have time for all of that," says costume designer Judy Evans (now Judy Evans Steele). "There's really plenty of material for that little guy to cut out of a man's shirt or sweater."

Best Friend Benson. Benson is the only one capable of disarming The Major in the courtroom.

Rod Roddy's Wrapup: Now that Jodie and Carol have been more than just friends, will she settle for less? If Burt sends Mary a dozen red roses, will she forgive him for killing her first husband, or is she really ticked off this time? Will the jury come back with a verdict of innocent? Will the jury come back with a verdict of guilty? Will the jury come back? These questions and many others will be answered on next week's episode of *Soap*.

Best Lines.

Jodie: Carol, all my life I've lived a certain way and I don't want to change. But I love you and I want you to be my friend. And what I'm afraid of is that if I don't sleep with you again, you won't be my friend anymore.

Carol: Jodie, I love you. I'll always be your friend. You think I just want ya for your body? My God, do you know how many guys have said that to *me*?

Ingrid: Vell, you haven't seen the last of me. Just wait, all of you. You think I'm finish?

Jessica: No, Swedish.

Tinkler [to Chester]: I have here a federal warrant for your arrest. It's brought by the Securities Exchange Commission on stock fraud and manipulation. I know it comes at a bad time, but I've managed to pull a few strings so that you could make bail and be at your wife's murder trial before the jury goes out. [Goes over to Corinne and Billy.] Awww. Bet you kids are going to be lonely around here come the holidays. Welp, have a nice day.

Benson [to the judge, after disarming The Major]: He doesn't use bullets. [To The Major, quietly] If you're gonna do this sort of thing, plan it right.

1.25

First aired: Mar 28, 1978 • Written by Susan Harris • Directed by Jay Sandrich

Never mind Ingrid's plans for revenge, the Tates and the Campbells seem to be suffering just fine on their own. Mr. Lefkowitz arrives to dash any hopes Danny might've had for ducking out of his marriage to Elaine, and Jessica finally learns the verdict in her murder trial, discovering that her attorney has fallen in love with her to boot. Jodie is strong-armed into saying he will move in with Carol and runs into Dennis Phillips, the lover who nearly drove him to suicide. Only Corinne and Father Tim seem to be on the road to happiness now that he has confessed his love and announced his plans to leave the priesthood.

Cast. Jimmy Baio (Billy), Rebecca Balding (Carol David), Diana Canova (Corinne), Billy Crystal (Jodie), Cathryn Damon (Mary), Robert Guillaume (Benson), Katherine Helmond (Jessica), Howard Hesseman (Mr. Franklin), Jay Johnson (Chuck & Bob), Gordon Jump (Chief of Police Tinkler), Charles Lane (Judge Petrillo), Robert Mandan (Chester), Dinah Manoff (Elaine), Richard Mulligan (Burt), Arthur Peterson (The Major), Eugene Roche (E. Ronald Mallu), Jennifer Salt (Eunice), Bob Seagren (Dennis Phillips), Sal Viscuso (Father Tim), Ted Wass (Danny), Rod Roddy (Announcer), Sorrell Booke (Charles Lefkowitz), Jon Terry (Foreman), Tim Rossovich (Bodyguard, uncredited)

Highlights. Mr. Lefkowitz meeting the Campbells; Burt going back to making himself invisible after Danny tells him that Lefkowitz threatened to kill all of them if Danny ran away before the wedding; Father Tim and Corinne's discussion after he tells her he's leaving the priesthood; Carol continuing to manipulate Jodie at dinner; and the spontaneous spot of dancing that erupts between Jessica, Mallu and Chester just before the verdict comes in.

Confused? You Won't Be. *'I think if this isn't over soon, I'm going to throw up.'*

25 YEARS
How long Jodie says he's been gay

▶ Jodie says "nice seeing you again" to Lefkowitz's bodyguard; clearly he remembers the pat down he received from him when he accompanied Elaine to the Campbell home (1.21). At his meal with Carol, he flat out says he doesn't trust her. He'll learn soon enough that he should've gone with his gut on that one (2.12 onward).

▶ We haven't seen Jodie's ex, Dennis Phillips, since 1.10, and his decision to try to pass as straight has gone about as well as can be expected. He also admits that he still loves Jodie.

▶ Chester's comforting of Jessica when she breaks down ("Nothing's going to happen, Jess. I promise. I love you far too much to let anything happen to you) demonstrates just how much his feelings toward his wife have changed, however temporarily, and hint at what is to come later (2.1).

▶ As associate producer Marsha Posner recalls, not even the cast knew the answer to the closing question "Who killed Peter Campbell?" "They had to wait all summer long until we went back into production to find out which one of them did it."

Best Friend Benson. After Billy leaves the room, Jessica doesn't even have to complete her thought before Benson tells her "Don't worry, I'll take care of him just fine." Jessica also asks Benson to sit down to breakfast with the family just this once, implying this is just in case this is the last time she's there to have breakfast, period.

8 hours. How long Mary hiccuped the last time she tried to keep herself from crying.

AC/Doocey. What Mr. Lefkowitz thinks Jodie is after he learns that he has a date with a girl.

Campbell Campbell. Burt's cousin in Australia. (Birth certificate mistake, don't ask.)

Trying to Pass as Straight

Though many in today's gay community still bristle at some of Jodie's peculiarities (including his near brush with a sex change, and his comments this episode about enjoying his encounter with Carol), it should be pointed out how groundbreaking *Soap* was in its depictions of homosexuality.

Dennis Phillips' brief return here is revolutionary in its mainstream portrayal of how disastrous it can be for a homosexual to try to live a straight life. The few lines about the football star having a short, painful marriage to a woman at the time was in direct opposition to the "ex gay" movement being promoted by various conservative groups throughout the 1970s.

One year after this episode, the book *Homosexuality in Perspective* was published by famed sex researchers William Masters and Virginia Johnson. This 14-year study of more than 300 gay men and women touted a substantial number of cases of "conversion", in which homosexual men and women were actually "cured" of those feelings in just a few weeks. Many of those who felt their homosexuality wasn't actually deep-seated experienced "reversion."

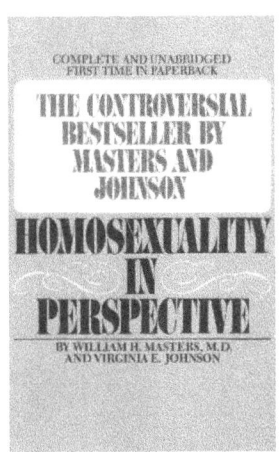

Yet, in Thomas Maier's book *Masters of Sex*, the author discovered that years later, Johnson herself suspected that Masters had cooked the books on his conclusions about homosexuality.

However, the idea that gay people can be cured remains in some parts of the U.S. today, with many organizations touting their "gay curing" services in print, and even on billboards, throughout much of the Bible belt.

'Say, Uh, Can We Meet Bob?'

It's easy to underestimate the popularity of Chuck & Bob at the time *Soap* first aired in the U.S. And outside the country...

"There were some reporters from Sweden, I think, and they'd come to the set of *Soap* to do an interview; it had just started over there and they were very excited about the show," Jay Johnson explains. "Eventually they got around to talking to me and they asked me a few questions, they weren't too probing. Then they said, 'Now, we would really like to meet the guy who does the voice for the little Bob character that you're always with. We'd like to interview him and see how that process works.' And I said, 'What do you mean? I'm a ventriloquist.' They didn't know the word, but when I told them that I was doing the

Sometimes Bob himself received interview requests.

3 WEEKS
How long until Danny and Elaine are supposed to marry

voice, suddenly the whole interview changed. They were like they had just seen a magic trick. They couldn't believe it. It was so much fun to think that someone had actually thought there was someone with a microphone behind the set doing it—a great compliment."

Best Lines.

Burt [to Mary]: It's all my fault, everything, it's all my fault. I mean I pushed some guy off a ledge and ruined everybody's life. His naturally. Danny, because Danny had to kill the man who killed his father who's me. And because he couldn't kill me he has to get married to that terrible girl who he doesn't love or else they're going to kill him. And you, your husband gets killed and you find out later on you're married to his killer. I shoulda let the guy kill me, everybody would've been better off. Except me of course because I'd be dead.

Mr. Lefkowitz [to Burt]: I can see you.

Burt: Beg your pardon?

Mr. Lefkowitz: Well aren't you the man who clicks his tongue and makes himself invisible?

Burt: No, no, it's snapping your fingers.

Mr. Lefkowitz: And you think you're not here now.

Burt: I'm here. I'm...cured.

Mr. Lefkowitz: Oh wonderful. People drop like flies from heart attacks but they've licked invisibility.

Burt: Hey, what is it with you and tongues and licking...

Corinne: You want to marry me?

Father Tim: Yeah, I want you to think about it.

Corinne: And we have to wait until we're married to uh-?

Father Tim: Oh Corinne please, give me a break. This is not nothing I'm doing.

Corinne: All right. All right, we'll wait. No lovemaking until we're married.

Sorrell Booke (Charles Lefkowitz)

Father Tim: Good.

Corinne: So what about petting?

Father Tim: Oh Corinne.

Corinne: Necking?

Father Tim: C'mon, Corinne.

Corinne: Can I hold your hand?

Jodie [to Carol]: Listen, the other night was nice, it really was and I've told you that, but I'm still gay. Hey listen, occasionally I'll have a burrito, I'm not Mexican.

Rod Roddy's Wrapup. Jessica Tate did not kill Peter Campbell. One of these five people did. [Chester, Jodie, Corinne, Benson and Burt are shown.] Who killed Peter Campbell?

And that was it. After all of the pre-premiere picketing and letter-writing campaigns and denouncements by religious leaders throughout the land, we were left with a classic whodunit, a paralegal who'd taken the sexual revolution to heart, and a former mobster trying to duck out of a wedding to a "rotten disgusting pig," as her father so tactfully put it.

Sure, we had witnessed a priest renounce his vows to be with his childhood sweetheart, though only after insisting that they get married before they ever left the handholding stage. THIS was the series that was going to open the floodgates and plunge America into the moral abyss? Even some of society's most devoted watchdogs must've felt at least a little pang of disappointment.

" I was pretty proud for winning an Olympic gold and silver medal, but when I won the *ABC Superstars* competition...! I won the first *ABC Superstars* in 1973, and then won the first *World Superstars* in '77. When I travel, I tell ya more people would see me in an airport and they'd say, 'Oh my God, I could kick your butt in a bike race or this or that.' More people recognized me from one stupid 2-hour television show of sport than anything else I'd ever done. That *Superstars* was a novel idea, but it sure made me a lot more recognized than pole vaulting ever did."

—BOB SEAGREN
(Dennis Phillips)

Season Two

After a year of being vilified as a raunchy show without cause, *Soap* this season decides to turn up the heat a notch with a randy mob boss' daughter, imagined affairs, and a coffee-cake chat that likely had ABC censors tearing their hair out. Yet Season 2 would also explore a number of more pedestrian soap-opera tropes, including amnesia and at-the-altar jiltings. (Then again, there was that devil baby!)

Through it all, Susan Harris and new permanent co-writer, Stu Silver, would deliver a strong season with laughs and heartbreak.

2.0

First aired: ?? • Written by Susan Harris • Directed by Jay Sandrich

Burt visits Jessica in jail and tells her he's still investigating the death of his son, Peter. Together they go over who in the Tate and Campbell families might have done the deed, helped along by clips galore from Season 1.

Cast. Katherine Helmond (Jessica), Cathryn Damon (Mary), Robert Mandan (Chester), Richard Mulligan (Burt), Diana Canova (Corinne), Jennifer Salt (Eunice), Jimmy Baio (Billy), Robert Guillaume (Benson), Arthur Peterson (The Major), Billy Crystal (Jodie), Ted Wass (Danny), Jay Johnson (Chuck & Bob), Rod Roddy (Announcer), Rebecca Balding (Carol David), Gordon Jump (Chief Tinkler), Charles Lane (Judge Petrillo), Rene Le Vant (Guard), Dinah Manoff (Elaine), Doris Roberts (Flo Flotsky), Eugene Roche (E. Ronald Mallu), Bob Seagren (Dennis Phillips), Sal Viscuso (Father Tim)

Highlights. Burt reacting to the way Chester dismissed Jessica's affair with Peter as cheap and sordid (it was with his son, after all); Burt not entirely certain that he didn't kill Peter himself during his crazy period; and summing up Eunice as a suspect as "the cold, silent type."

Confused? You Won't Be. *'Let's go over some of the facts about this case here.'*

▶ One of the great revelations of this "best of" is exactly how consistently manipulative Carol David has been since the day she met Jodie at Jessica's trial. When viewed in hindsight, it's hard not to consider Carol the most consistent character of the series.

▶ Though these compilation episodes seldom do more than what it says on the tin, this one in particular proves that even Richard Mulligan can only do so much when the script is so-so. Then again, where was Susan Harris supposed to find the time to write it?

Best Lines.
None.

Rod Roddy's Wrapup. Word for word his wrapup from 1.25

2.1

First aired: Sept 14, 1978 • Written by Susan Harris • Directed by Jay Sandrich

Get ready for a double-episode extravaganza. After a pot hits Chester on the head during a botched suicide attempt, he realizes that he was the one who actually killed Peter, and confesses in court just before Jessica is led away to prison. Despite Father Tim and Corinne's best efforts, his mother curses them both for their plan to marry. Mary suspects Burt of cheating on her because he comes home at 4 a.m. every night. Carol and Jodie move in together. While Carol tries to start over with Jodie for reasons we'll learn soon enough, Chester may not be staying in jail for very long as his new cellmate, Dutch, has plans to break out the next day, using Chester as a human shield!

Highlights. Burt's reaction to being told Dennis Phillips is gay while shaking his hand (with everybody nodding at him, including Dennis); Benson and Jessica's sad good-bye; Mrs. Flotsky throttling Corinne, then trying to blame it on her kidney infection; Dutch's complete terrorizing of Chester in jail; Burt telling Mary how he knows he loves her; and Carol's earnest desperation to have a relationship with Jodie, especially now that she knows she's carrying his child.

Confused? You Won't Be. *'My dad killed someone and framed my mom, but aside from that everything's fine.'*

◉ The Tate-Campbell food fight seen last season (1.3) resurfaces in the form of Danny being thrown into the snack table by Chester.

◉ Carol informs us that she's pregnant with Jodie's baby by telling him *after* he's already left the room, much the same way that Burt revealed the cause of his impotency to Mary after *she'd* left the room (1.5).

◉ Mary's initial suspicion that Burt is having an affair (thanks, Jess) foreshadows his dealings with Sally later on (2.8).

A bop on the head reveals all to Chester.

1978

SEPT. 17: Signing of the Camp David Accords. This unprecedented act of diplomacy sees Egyptian President Anwar Sadat and Israeli Prime Minister Menachem Begin sign agreements that would ultimately lead to the peace treaty between Israel and Egypt in 1979.

The number of states Dutch is wanted in (He's in for murder)

▶ Though the first two episodes of Season 1 were meant to run together, this is the first time we actually get a double episode. It's also notable for its lack of a Rod Roddy wrapup. Instead, we're treated to "coming attractions of *Soap*." In them, we get scenes of Father Tim explaining to his former church superior that he's getting married, Elaine in her underwear, and the as-yet-unintroduced Sally (Caroline McWilliams) coming on to Burt and then Danny. Clearly, after an entire season of being taken to task for questionable content, the gloves were off with Season 2.

Fresca. What Bob wants when everybody else is talking about having coffee.

Suacide. How Chester initially spells suicide in his kitchen towel suicide note.

Tank or a two-man bazooka team. What The Major thinks will be needed to bust Jessica out of jail.

The Big Home. Where Jessica says she's heading. (She means the big house.)

3B. Jodie and Carol's new apartment.

Rose Bowl Queen. Carol's charming term of endearment for Dennis.

How Burt Knows He Loves Mary. She blows her nose in instead of out, pulls all the covers off of Burt when he's asleep, takes food off his plate, and she has never ever ironed one of his shirts correctly. "And I think that is all adorable. If I didn't love you I'd have divorced you by now."

Best Friend Benson. Once again Benson brings Jessica food in jail.

Mrs. Flotsky's Curse. "May you never have a happy moment again for the rest of your life. And if you marry, may you know no such thing as peace and quiet. May you only know hardship and suffering and loss. And may you know until your dying day, whatever misfortunes happen, are on your heads."

And introducing...Dutch.

Benson and Bob. "Benson was the realist among the group and he wasn't so easily taken in, except Benson's reaction to the puppet was as if it was a real person," Robert Guillaume points out. "The other part of Benson maintained a sanity that the other characters didn't. But I remember that one scene in which the puppet was going on and on and on and Benson was in the same room, and Benson stopped what he was doing, marched directly over to the puppet, grabbed the puppet from the puppeteer's hands, and threw him out the window. At which point the puppeteer acted as if his head had been ripped off. *Soap* was such fun because it was filled with moments like that."

Best Lines.

Danny [to Bob]: You think I did it, don't ya? I know you think I did it, you've been staring at me all day!

Corinne: Please. You. Everybody's looking at me like I'm Jack the Ripper.

Jodie: Corinne, they're not looking at you, they've been looking at me.

Bob: I think it was the colored guy.

[Benson pauses for a minute, gets up, grabs Bob and throws him out the window.]

The 3 a.m. foods that get the Tate family through the night:

1) Billy: Spaghetti
2) Eunice: Chocolate mousse (which she doesn't intend to eat)
3) Corinne: Cold chili
4) Jessica: She's in the mood for turkey, but understandably doesn't prepare it.

Judge: Have you anything to say before I pronounce sentence?

Jessica: Yes, I didn't do this. I'm innocent. But if the person is here who did it, please help me. All right, I'm going to close my eyes now. Nobody will be embarrassed.

Judge: There doesn't seem to be a great traffic jam to the bench, so I'll go on. Mrs. Tate, you have what some people would perceive as certain advantages. You are white and you are rich. If the sentence is light, the court will be besieged with complaints from the poor and black. Therefore, in order not to appear prejudiced, and to be fair in arriving at a sentence, I've ignored the fact that you are white and rich and have pretended you are poor and black. I sentence you to 50 years in prison, eligible for parole in 25 years.

[Dutch goes through Chester's bag and takes his electric razor.]
Chester: Oh excuse me. That's mine.
Dutch: Not anymore it ain't.
Chester: Uh yes I see. Well what will I shave with?
Dutch: Every morning I'll rub your face against the wall.

Danny [to Jodie, explaining why his claim of impotence didn't get Elaine to break off their forthcoming wedding]: Girl knows a lot of tricks.

Rod Roddy's Wrapup is replaced by "coming attractions" from the rest of the season.

Like Living in the 'Continental Baths'

Carol's crack about living with Jodie is a pretty interesting reference for a straight sitcom of the 1970s. Opened in 1968 in the basement of New York City's Ansonia Hotel, the Continental Baths was a gay bathhouse that not only had its own disco room, saunas and cabaret lounge, but also reportedly its own STD clinic and K-Y Jelly in the vending machines. Once little known outside big city gay communities, references to gay bathhouses began to creep into magazines and newspapers throughout the '70s, perhaps most notably in Armistead Maupin's *Tales of the City* serial in the pages of *The Pacific Sun* in 1974, and later the *San Francisco Chronicle*, starting in 1976.

 To be honest, my mother was not thrilled that I was playing Corinne. She was basically very provincial for 'showfolk,' and was very unhappy that I was the one that the publicity was about… the whole Catholic thing, and the sex. Actually, there was more publicity about Billy because of Jodie being gay, but the fact that I was playing a nympho was not pleasing her one bit."

—DIANA CANOVA [Corinne], daughter of entertainer Judy Canova (above)

2.2

First aired: Sept 21, 1978 • Written by Susan Harris • Directed by Jay Sandrich

The day has finally arrived: Danny and Elaine are getting married. But little does anybody realize what Mr. Lefkowitz's final wedding gift will be. The Campbells take the day in stride, with Burt even asking Danny to become a partner in his construction business. Dutch and Chester escape from jail, and Carol finally tells Jodie that he's going to be a father. Yet as a hand clamps itself across Jessica's face in the darkness of the Tate basement, we can't help but wonder if the pregnancy rabbit will be the episode's only fatality.

Cast. Katherine Helmond (Jessica), Cathryn Damon (Mary), Robert Mandan (Chester), Richard Mulligan (Burt), Diana Canova (Corinne), Jennifer Salt (Eunice), Jimmy Baio (Billy), Robert Guillaume (Benson), Arthur Peterson (The Major), Billy Crystal (Jodie), Ted Wass (Danny), Jay Johnson (Chuck & Bob), Rod Roddy (Announcer), Rebecca Balding (Carol David), Sorrell Booke (Mr. Lefkowitz), Florence Halop (Aunt Esther), Gordon Jump (Chief of Police Tinkler), René Le Vant (Guard), Dinah Manoff (Elaine), Donnelly Rhodes (Dutch), Bob Seagren (Dennis Phillips), Tim Rossovich (Bodyguard, uncredited)

Highlights. Burt suggesting that Danny become his partner in the construction business while they're both shaving, and the cabaret that follows; Mary and Danny cracking up over Elaine being a "pig", and Jessica's left-handed compliment to Elaine; Mr. Lefkowitz's wedding toast; and Carol trying to unburden herself to Jodie through her whining.

Seems like only yesterday that Danny was trying to *kill* this guy.

Confused? You Won't Be. 'Mr and Mrs Burt Campbell are happy to announce the marriage of their son Danny... to a pig.'

⊙ In the opening moments of the show we get Burt's first mention of taking on Danny as a partner in his construction business: Campbell & Son.

Mr. Lefkowitz's Wedding Toast. "Ladies and gentlemen, I'd like to make a toast. This is an occasion I've looked forward to for a very long time. The marriage of my daughter. When my wife died, I promised her on her death bed I would take care of Elaine till the day she married, that she would never want for anything. I've kept that promise! And so I hand my daughter over to a fine young man who from now on will take care of her because I'm completely cutting her off. She'll never get another penny or hear another word from me as long as I live. Because she is a disgusting person and nothing thrills me more than to be rid of her forever, l'chaim!"

What Might Have Been

As quirky and slapstick as Chester's prison house experiences are, it bears remembering that initially these could've been even more ridiculous had the producers gone with their first idea: to have Chuck & Bob turn out to be the killers of Peter Campbell [see P. 94]. "If you remember, eventually a character is written in called Dutch, and those prison scenes were pretty much written for Chuck & Bob," says Jay Johnson. "Probably Chuck & Bob would've met Dutch rather than Bob Mandan. He got to play out those scenes of running around the country with bums and stuff like that. Bob did a great job, so I was glad that it worked out."

Best Lines.
Danny: I'm just miserable.
Mary: So am I.
Danny: I always thought I'd love the girl I married.
Mary: I always thought the girl you'd marry would be a little like me, but Elaine is...I don't know.
Danny: She's a pig.

Jessica [to Elaine]: Oh you do look lovely. You know, no one would guess you're trash.

Rod Roddy's Wrapup. Will Danny and Elaine find happiness even though he thinks she's a farm animal? Will Burt and Mary find happiness living with Danny and a farm animal? Will Jodie have to change his life once he's changing diapers? Will Sheriff [sic] Tinkler find Chester, Dutch and the other escaped criminals? And if he does find Chester, what kind of shape will he be in? What's happened to Benson, Billy, Eunice and Corinne in the basement? And what's going to happen to Jessica? These questions and many others will be answered on next week's episode of *Soap*.

The Increasingly Unpredictable Richard Mulligan

It was around the start of Season 2 that Richard Mulligan began to really push the boundaries with his acting, attempting to wring bigger and longer laughs from his scenes by amping up the absurdity of his actions.

"I have no recollection of that happening in the first year," says Ted Wass. "That first year we would literally come in two hours before the rehearsal call. We would be on the soundstage with a work light lighting us, and we'd be in the kitchen and I'd be looking for ways to kill him. Or we'd be up on the construction site beams trying to figure out how I could grab him and he could just take one step and I'd miss. With that kind of physical comedy, with that kind of timing, you can't hold anything back. And you can't, in performance, make changes; it won't work. That has to be really laid out and precisely planned. So I don't remember that so much in the first year.

"I remember it more in the second year when his character was slipping deeper and deeper into insanity after his son, Peter, had been killed, and he was doing the whole 'invisible' thing. He kind of went into his own world at that point. And at that point, all bets were off in terms of what you thought Richard might and might not do during the next take."

In other words, there was the inescapable sense that Mulligan was identifying a bit too strongly with his character.

"Sometimes the biggest problem I had with Richard, because he's so funny and so original in his thinking—the more we rehearsed the scenes, the more dramatic he'd get," says director Jay Sandrich. "So the hard job was to try to get him back to the place where the scenes that were comedic were comedic, and not serious. But when he got out in front of the audience, he'd just score. We had our difficulties. I probably had a little more tension with Richard than with any of the other actors. But after the series, I did *Empty Nest* with him and there were no problems."

1978

SEPT. 28: Pope John Paul I dies. Albino Luciani served as Pope from Aug. 26 until his death 33 days later at 65 from a heart attack. His death would go on to inspire a number of conspiracy theories, most holding that the pontiff was poisoned to prevent him from implementing radical changes.

2.3
First aired: Sept 28, 1978 • Story by Susan Harris • Teleplay by Susan Harris + Jordan Crittenden • Directed by Jay Sandrich

Dutch takes the Tate family hostage, promising a messy end for Chester if they don't do what he says. The Campbells try to enjoy their first dinner together with Elaine, but that quickly proves to be a bridge too far. Jodie tells Burt and Mary that he got Carol pregnant, and Jessica brags to Mary that she has "two killers" in her basement. Tim and Corinne finally get to the altar, only to have Tim's mother object during the ceremony. The only two having a good time this episode are Eunice and Dutch who sleep together for the first time after comparing horrible childhoods.

Cast. Katherine Helmond (Jessica), Cathryn Damon (Mary), Robert Mandan (Chester), Richard Mulligan (Burt), Diana Canova (Corinne), Jennifer Salt (Eunice), Jimmy Baio (Billy), Robert Guillaume (Benson), Arthur Peterson (The Major), Billy Crystal (Jodie), Ted Wass (Danny), Jay Johnson (Chuck & Bob), Rod Roddy (Announcer), Dinah Manoff (Elaine), Donnelly Rhodes (Dutch), Doris Roberts (Flo Flotsky), Sal Viscuso (Tim), Ian Wolfe (Father Juniper)

Highlights. The Major giving the gun back to Dutch after Benson takes it ("This man is Dutch. The Dutch are on our side!"); Mary pie-ing Elaine; Eunice and Dutch bonding over their terrible childhoods; Bob forcing Chuck to take him on his date; Cathryn Damon cracking up after Burt's "do it a few more times, you'll be hooked—it's like pretzels" line to Jodie about making love to a woman; Jessica and Mary trying to one-up each other about the big news in their lives, and Jessica's delight at revealing she has "two killers" in her basement; Corinne in her wedding dress; and Father Juniper asking Tim if priests can marry now.

Confused? You Won't Be. *'We have to learn to live together.'*

▶ Eunice was fat and had buckteeth—she looked like a blowfish, she tells Dutch. She still feels like a fat little funny looking 7-year-old girl, which explains both her fooling around with the married Congressman McCallam (1.5, etc.), and Billy's joke about his sister never having seen herself nude (1.1). She's not a prude, she just has a horrible self-image. The romance with Dutch that follows will be built on their own insecurities. Interestingly, the childlike way Eunice tells the fugitive "I like you" carries with it the same sweet innocence her sister showed when pursuing her own unavailable man, Father Tim (1.6).

▶ Once again, Mary and Jessica are trying to one-up each other with their "big news", a tradition carried over to Jessica's daughters (1.6).

1,092. The number of meals a year Burt figures they're going to have to endure with Elaine.

2 years. How long it's been since Dutch has seen a woman.

A high-strung ex-Father Tim makes Corinne's dream come true.

For the *Soap* Bible Tells Us So. We may have to take Eunice's "Butterball" explanation (see Best Lines below) at face value. According to the *Soap* bible, there may be another reason for her skittishness around the opposite sex. "Something most unfortunate happened to Eunice at a very early age—while playing in the garden, she was molested by a distant cousin. The resultant trauma left her with a distinct aversion to plants and physical contact. This was a shame because being so beautiful, Eunice was just the kind of girl you would like to kiss and send flowers to." At first glance this paragraph seems a woeful attempt to cap a serious problem with a cheap zinger, but on closer reading this is classic Susan Harris, driving home a serious point with a dose of humor: sugaring the bitter pill. One can easily see the network shooting down this explanation initially, but we'll never know if this would have been revealed in a later season. Finally, the "distant cousin" reference mercifully lets poor Jodie off the hook, refusing to fall into the scapegoating of gays as molesters that was so prevalent at the time.

Best Lines.

Eunice [grabbing a perfume sprayer]: Listen you, if you came up here intending to rape me, let me tell you right now it's not going to be any fun at all because I'll spit in your face, I'll scratch your eyes out, I'll kill you before—yeah, what?

Dutch: I happen to be a killer, not a rapist.

Eunice: Oh I love it. A killer looks down on a rapist.

[Later]

Dutch: You see when I was a kid, I had all these terrible allergies. I had asthma and hay fever and hives. You name it, I was allergic to it. I spent my whole childhood just trying to get a breath. And I was real sickly looking, too. The kids used to call me worm and beat me up! When I was 11, I changed my name to Dutch. They still called me worm, used to make me so mad!

Eunice: And so you became a killer.

Dutch: What are you crazy? I was 11.

400
The number of Swedish meatballs at the reception

Dutch & Eunice: Two damaged people find love (or merely codependency).

Eunice: Oh. Yeah.

Dutch: Worm! Can you imagine that? Being called worm.

Eunice: Well listen, they used to call me Butterball.

Dutch [Giggles]: They called you Butterball?

Eunice: Everyone except Corinne. She used to call me Lardo.

Dutch: Butterball. I think that's kind of cute.

Eunice: That is not a bit cute.

Dutch [laughing]: How you doin, Butterball?

Eunice: Knock it off, Worm! I can't believe I'm sitting here laughing with a killer.

Dutch: I can't believe I'm sitting her laughing with a rich girl.

Eunice: Well, you're really very nice.

Dutch: So are you. And you're very pretty. It's too bad I'm not a rapist.

Bob [offended that Chuck doesn't want to take him along on his date]: Yeah OK fine, fine, don't take me with you tonight. And I don't go with you to the audition tomorrow.

Chuck: Come on Bob, I mean that could be a big break for us.

Bob: Noooo. You want to be alooone. Well you can be alone there too. We'll just see how your career takes off.

Chuck: OK OK OK you can come.

Bob: Yeah?

Chuck: Yeah. But this time keep your hands off her.

Mary: Jodie is going to be a father.

Jessica [long pause as she takes this in]: DENNIS is pregnant?!

Jessica: Two killers, Mary? I mean I think two killers is bigger than a gay guy and one pregnant girl.

Rod Roddy's Wrapup. Will Danny and Elaine ever have a relationship that works? Will Chuck ever have a relationship with Bob around? What will be left of Burt and Mary's relationship living with Danny and Elaine and Chuck & Bob? What kind of relationship could

1978

SEPT. 30: Edgar Bergen, perhaps the most famous ventriloquist in America (and father of actress Candice Bergen), dies at 75. Bob is something of a descendent of Bergen's world famous puppet, Charlie McCarthy.

1978

OCT. 1: Vietnam invades Cambodia to crack down on the Khmer Rouge, sparking a war between the two countries, and setting the stage for conflict between Vietnam and China the following year.

Eunice and Dutch ever have? Will Tim's relationship with his mother destroy his relationship with Corinne? What kind of relationship can Chester and Jessica have with Chester living in the basement and Jessica living upstairs? These questions and many others will be answered on next week's episode of *Soap*.

2.4 First aired: Oct 5, 1978 • Story by Susan Harris • Teleplay by Susan Harris + Jordan Crittenden • Directed by Jay Sandrich

Married life isn't what it's cracked up to be. Corinne and Tim try to overcome the former priest's bedroom hang-ups on their wedding night; Burt feels Mary's newfound desire to go back to school will reveal to her just how stupid he is; and Danny's afraid Elaine's nonstop shopping is going to send him to the poorhouse. Even the normally frisky Chester has to turn down Jessica's advances between fainting spells, though his appreciation of the animal kingdom knows no bounds. When Chester finally collapses, the Tates park him outside the house and Dutch skips town, all to prevent themselves from being pulled into (another) messy legal situation.

Cast. Katherine Helmond (Jessica), Cathryn Damon (Mary), Robert Mandan (Chester), Richard Mulligan (Burt), Diana Canova (Corinne), Jennifer Salt (Eunice), Jimmy Baio (Billy), Robert Guillaume (Benson), Arthur Peterson (The Major), Ted Wass (Danny), Rod Roddy (Announcer), J. Pat O'Malley (Orville), Donnelly Rhodes (Dutch), Sal Viscuso (Tim)

Highlights. Jessica's marriage talk with Corinne; Orville the hotel guy blasting Father Tim for making him give up "the twins"; the Tate family trying to replace Chester's deceased rat Arnold with a turtle (Billy), a guinea pig (Eunice), a lap dog (Jessica), and former Nazi Doberman, Sigmund (The Major); Danny and Burt watching the apple fall 40 stories from the top of the building project; and the gang trying to make Chester's lifeless body look natural outside the house.

Confused? You Won't Be. *'I don't care what Gloria Steinem says, men expect certain things, you know?'*

▶ It seems like only yesterday that Jessica had to watch her daughter Corinne move out of the family home (1.19). This time, at least, it's because she's going on her honeymoon with Tim. It also seems like only yesterday that Dutch had the Tates at gunpoint—in fact it was just last episode! Now he's just like one of the family.

▶ Tim's mother continues to do her best to ruin his wedding (2.1, 2.3), this time calling their hotel room claiming to be having some kind of attack. This is the first time we get a look at the front of the Tate home (not counting stock footage), adding yet another set for what amounts to a 5-minute gag.

▶ Burt reveals himself to be a big musical lover (itself an interesting quirk considering his revulsion by all things gay), advising Danny to take a lesson from a musical called "Kiss Me, Shrew" (presumably Cole Porter's "Kiss Me, Kate") when it comes to handling Elaine. We will see Danny take this not-yet-verbalized advice—rooted in Shakespeare's *The Taming of the Shrew*—next episode.

Arnold. The rat Chester befriends in his basement, until Benson "got that mother." Possibly a nod to the 1971 horror flick *Willard*, about a misfit who befriends a murderous rat, and its sequel the following year, *Ben*. Look for Arnold the rat to get one more giggle at the beginning of the next episode.

Like Ships in the Night: The Other *Soap* writers

Though Susan Harris is rightly credited with writing most of the series, either completely on her own during most of the first year and a half, or splitting the writing duties with Stu Silver during the last couple of years—other writers did take a crack at it, too. During the first few episodes of Season 2 it was Jordan Crittenden; Tony Lang chipped in on six episodes during Season 1.

"You're talking about two enormously talented people, but as with any show, sometimes there are good fits and sometimes they're not so good," says Paul Junger Witt. "It's no reflection on the talent of the individual, it's just a matter of vision and style. Tony Lang, we had read a play of his that was just a knock out. But it didn't work at the time.

Willard, 1971

"With Jordan, he certainly was a remarkably talented guy and very funny, but our visions were slightly different, a bit askew. We didn't have time to wrestle, we had to find really good chemistry because one of the disadvantages of the form we were working with is that it's more labor intensive. You have so many story lines going and Tony, Susan and I would spend hours and hours together with index cards in which we would line out stories for as long as we could, sometimes longer than a season.

"We were flexible in that we never knew how well one story would work and another one wouldn't. We were adding characters and eliminating characters and it was just very different than standard sitcom fare at the time. Stu Silver happened to be a better fit than the previous two people. Again, and I'm not just being political, both Jordan and Tony were phenomenally talented writers, but creatively we didn't mesh as well as later on we did with Stu."

Best Lines.
Jessica [to Corinne, discussing her wedding]: …it's just a shame Bob got so drunk and hit Chuck.

Burt [after Mary tells him she wants to go back to school]: You're going to get smart.

Mary: I'm not going to get smart, Burt.

Burt: Yeah you will. You're gonna get smart and then you'll get too smart for me. You'll learn all those things I don't know. You'll start using big words when you talk like notwithstanding and heretofore—I don't understand any of that. Then you're gonna find out how really dumb I am and you'll leave me for somebody smart who you can talk with about philosophy.

Mary: Oh Burt.

Burt: It'll happen, Mary.

Mary: You're so dumb.

Burt: See, it's starting already.

Rod Roddy's Wrapup. Does Burt really have a plan to change Elaine? Does it involve surgery? Is Chester seriously ill or is he just upset about Arnold? Will Sigmund ever be housebroken? Will Dutch and Eunice get together again? Will Corinne and Tim get together? What will the police do when they discover Chester's been taken to the hospital? Will they have to wait for visiting hours to arrest him? These questions and many others will be answered on next week's episode of *Soap*.

2.5
First aired: Oct 12, 1978 • Story by Susan Harris • Teleplay by Susan Harris + Jordan Crittenden • Directed by Jay Sandrich

It's "girls, be careful what you wish for" on this episode of *Soap*. However obnoxious Elaine has been up till now, all she's ever wanted was to be loved by Danny. Danny, realizing that he can't walk out on her without arousing the ire of her mob-boss father, takes Burt's advice to "kill her with kindness." Carol, who has only ever wanted to be loved (or at least desired) by Jodie, now finds herself hit with a marriage proposal from him, and is crushed at the thought of being married to a man who "closes his eyes and pretends his wife is Arnold Schwarzenegger." The boys aren't fairing much better. Dr. Kanter discovers that Chester is suffering from a brain lesion that requires emergency surgery; Burt and Danny are both being hit on by their secretary, Sally; and Tim finally summons the courage to confront his mother, with less than encouraging results.

Cast. Katherine Helmond (Jessica), Cathryn Damon (Mary), Richard Mulligan (Burt), Diana Canova (Corinne), Jennifer Salt (Eunice), Jimmy Baio (Billy), Robert Guillaume (Benson), Arthur Peterson (The Major), Billy Crystal (Jodie), Ted Wass (Danny), Jay Johnson (Chuck & Bob), Rod Roddy (Announcer), Rebecca Balding (Carol David), Fred Iwasaki (The Chef), Jeffrey Kramer (Policeman #2), Dinah Manoff (Elaine), Caroline McWilliams (Sally), Edwin Owens (Policeman #1), Ron Rifkin (Dr. Kanter), Doris Roberts (Flo Flotsky), Sal Viscuso (Tim)

Highlights. How quickly the cops jump on Benson the moment they hear Jessica tell Dr. Kanter that he killed Arnold (the rat); Mary losing it after one insult too many from Elaine (to Burt: "Why didn't you let me kill her? I want to!"); Danny constantly ripping the clothes right off Elaine's back as he "kills her with kindness"; Jodie's pained discussion with Carol in the same Japanese restaurant they had their

> " If I'm not crazy, I think my mom's friend Brenda Vaccaro kind of helped me with the audition because I was really nervous about it."
>
> —DINAH MANOFF (Elaine)

Manoff's mother, Lee Grant (left) and Vaccaro (right) had acted together recently in the previous year's disaster flick Airport '77.

first big conversation in (punctuated by the same chef's silent kibitzing); and the sweet way Jessica and Mary comfort each other over Chester's impending surgery.

Confused? You Won't Be. *'We're going to kill her...with kindness.'*

▶ We get our first glimpse of Elaine at her makeup table. While not particularly momentous for first-time viewers of the series, on rewatching it is hard not to get a lump in the throat anticipating the speech she will give at that same table just a few episodes from now (2.7).

▶ Elaine's "Your mother needs hormone shots" to Danny after Mary tries to clobber her is one of those lines in *Soap* that speaks volumes. Elaine is referring to the progesterone shots that women were often given in the '70s to alleviate the mood swings that accompany PMS. While the joke is that Elaine is the one who wound Mary up in the first place with her cracks about her being too old to go back to school, it also acknowledges a society that seeks to shut women up during their "time of the month".

▶ It's difficult to understand what it was that Carol was expecting from Jodie after she told him she was pregnant; apparently it wasn't a marriage proposal.

▶ Ron Rifkin played another doctor in much stranger circumstances earlier this year in *Rabbit Test*, a movie starring Billy Crystal as a pregnant man, with Mrs. Flotsky herself, Doris Roberts, playing Crystal's mom.

▶ Finally, a tip of the cap to costume designer Judy Evans. Though no great slouch during Season 1, the finery sported by the female cast in particular reached new levels with this episode. Katherine Helmond has always sported custom-made outfits in the series, but the intricate number she wears at the police station, seemingly held together by a brown cord befitting the Paris Opera House curtain, is extraordinary. Rebecca Balding's Chinese-patterned red dress is stunning (and a new insight into Carol's naive vanity: "Going to a *Japanese* restaurant, gotta dress appropriately"). And even Dinah Manoff's disposable dresses are well thought out, as is the slip she wears through most of her scenes that simultaneously shows off her figure yet skirts the censors with material to spare.

And introducing...Sally. Though the character will disappear by the end of the season, actress Caroline McWilliams will go on to play the governor's secretary, Marcy Hill, on *Benson*.

"It's Benito Mussolini, You Fool." The Major ID's a picture of Dutch for the cops.

Best Lines.

Dr. Kanter [explaining Chester's dire medical status]: Well, I'm afraid my hands are tied. But there is someone here who just might be able to help. It's this lad right over here.

Billy: Me?

Jessica: I don't understand.

Dr. Kanter: Well you see Mrs Tate, there's still very little we know about the power of love. Just a few minutes ago your husband spoke his son's name and seemed to draw strength from it. And I feel if we brought this boy to his father's bedside, he just might mean the difference between life and death.

This year Ron Rifkin (left) play's Chester's doctor on *Soap* and Billy Crystal's in *Rabbit Test*.

Jessica: Well yes, certainly by all means.

Dr. Kanter [to Billy]: You must be quite a human being to have touched another person so deeply.

Billy: Thank you, sir!

Dr. Kanter: This way Arnold...

Jessica [to Eunice about her love of Dutch]: Well Eunice it's very hard for me to approve. I mean the man is a convicted killer. But then of course so is Daddy.

Carol: Why are you doing this? Guilt?

Jodie: No. It's true I think I should. But Carol what's also true is I'm actually kind of excited about having the baby.

Carol: Somehow I never pictured that.

Jodie: Well neither did I. While I'm not what Dr. Spock had in mind when he wrote his chapter "Becoming a Father," it's very hard not to be involved when you're bringing a new life into the world. Carol this is my baby, too. And since I've been a part of its beginning, I

1978

OCT. 16: Karol Józef Wojtyła becomes Pope John Paul II, the 264th pope, and the first Polish pope in history.

want to be a part of the rest of its life. It can work, Carol. We really care for each other, we love being together, and you'd never have to worry about me looking at another woman.

Carol: I don't know Jodie, I just don't know.

Jodie: Carol I promise you that if we get married I'll never touch another man again.

Chef [having overheard all this]: Excuse me please. I think I just stabbed myself.

Rod Roddy's Wrapup. Will Burt and Danny's plan really change Elaine, and if it does, what will she change into? Will Carol accept Jodie's proposal? Will Tim blame himself for his mother's death forever or just for the rest of his life? What is Sally up to, and are either Burt or Danny up to what she's up to? Will Eunice ever spend another night with Dutch, and if so, will there be passion, desire, lust, or at least some nice refreshments? Has Jessica made the right decision to go ahead with Chester's operation, and if it doesn't work out, will she find happiness living with a codfish? These questions and many others will be answered on next week's episode of *Soap*.

2.6 First aired: Oct 19, 1978 • Story by Susan Harris • Teleplay by Susan Harris + Jordan Crittenden • Directed by Jay Sandrich

Tim thinks he's cursed, Jodie finally tells Dennis what's going on with him and Carol, and Elaine and Danny make an important first step in ending the conflict that has made the Campbell home a battle zone, and Elaine's clothes scrap rags. And enter special guest stars Gloria Swanson and Gunga Din. (Scratch that, it's just Chester.)

'Gunga Din' tries to romance Jessica.

Cast. Katherine Helmond (Jessica), Cathryn Damon (Mary), Robert Mandan (Chester), Richard Mulligan (Burt), Diana Canova (Corinne), Jennifer Salt (Eunice), Jimmy Baio (Billy), Robert Guillaume (Benson), Arthur Peterson (The Major), Billy Crystal (Jodie), Ted Wass (Danny), Jay Johnson (Chuck & Bob), Rod Roddy (Announcer), Lee Bergere (Anatole Martins), Dinah Manoff (Elaine), Donnelly Rhodes (Dutch), Ron Rifkin (Dr. Kanter), Bob Seagren (Dennis Phillips), Sal Viscuso (Tim)

Highlights. The giant stuffed panda Jessica gets Tim as a "welcome to our family" present from the hospital gift shop (she bought one in red for Chester); Dennis processing what Jodie is telling him about his relationship with Carol, and his vague threat afterward; and the breakthrough Danny and Elaine have in their relationship after Mary and Burt talk to them separately.

Confused? You Won't Be. *'Well, he can't leave ya and he can't stand ya.'*

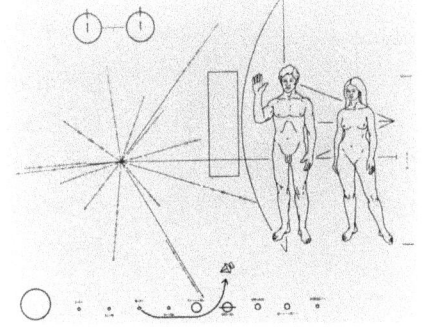

● Tim tells Corinne that he thinks he's cursed, presumably not remembering that his now-deceased mother really did curse him and Corinne not that long ago (2.1). This, combined with the falling chandelier that barely misses them all, is our first hint of what is to come. Already it's clear that the producers are having a hard time figuring out what to do with Tim now that they've worked through their "Corinne loves the priest" story line.

Line drawings on a plaque in the Pioneer spacecraft (above) were replaced with silhouettes (below) for the Voyager mission a few years later after complaints.

● Jessica tells Tim that she and Chester moved into the Tate home with her mother and father.

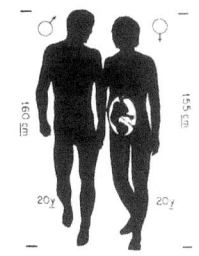

● Mary's professor, Anatole, looks a little too much like astronomer/astrophysicist Carl Sagan (below right) to be merely coincidental. Though Sagan wouldn't attain widespread fame until his 1980 PBS miniseries *Cosmos*, he was still in the news a fair amount in 1978 for winning a Pulitzer Prize for his book of that year, *The Dragons of Eden*. And also for his work in selecting the content that would be recorded on the golden phonograph records that were placed aboard Voyager 1 and 2, launched the previous year. Ironically, even these audio-visual discs fell afoul of the same American prudishness that dogged *Soap*. A simple line drawing of a naked man and woman (top right) used on a plaque placed in one of the Pioneer spacecraft in the early 1970s —an illustration meant only to explain the type of beings that had sent this message—was replaced by human silhouettes on the Voyager disc after NASA received complaints. (That said, a diagram of the human sex organs were somehow included separately. Who knows *what* those aliens think we look like.)

Carl Sagan

● The scenes between Danny and Mary in the living room, and Burt and Elaine in the dining room, and finally all four together, only give us a taste of what is to come next episode. The look on Elaine's face after she and Danny sit down together at the table as just two civilized people is unforgettable. For the first time we see *Soap*'s potential to get past the one liners and standard sitcom antics, and actually become something sublime. This is largely what makes the following, goofy scene of Chester waking up from his coma at the hospital such an anticlimax.

▶ Amnesiac Chester thinking himself Gunga Din, combined with the fact that it is Benson's voice that awakens him from his coma, suggests that whatever he's said about Benson in the past, he respects and even envies the servant who, like Gunga Din, was always the smartest person in the room, however menial his position.

Simpson. What The Major calls Benson. Well, that and "Boy".

Sidney Poitier. Who Chester thinks Benson is after he awakes from his coma.

The First Poem Mary Wrote for Her Poetry Class: To My Husband: My husband, I love him so that words merely diminish the feeling. I would not attempt to describe a rose. [Hey, she's only been going for a week.]

Meta Meta Meta. The hard time that Jodie is given by former gay lover Dennis this episode, and Carol's bigoted father Boomer the next, may be a subtle jab at the twin forces that were battering the good ship *Soap* behind the scenes at the time. While conservative groups such as the Moral Majority were castigating the show for featuring an openly gay character in the first place, the Gay Media Task Force was blasting it, and in some cases threatening protests, for the character's apparent sexual ambivalence.

The Controversy Begins…Now. This time, it won't be the conservatives crying foul. Taken on its own, Jodie's marriage proposal to Carol doesn't seem all that controversial. By now we know that Jodie generally does what he thinks is right, so marrying the woman he impregnated is perfectly in keeping with who he is. However, there were many in the gay rights community who remembered something former ABC Entertainment President Fred Silverman had said in a July 18, 1977 *Variety* article about Jodie.

6 DAYS
How long Corinne and Tim have been married

$400
The cost of the dress that Danny rips off Elaine

He was going to "meet a girl and will find there are other values worth considering." In just a few short words, he had hit two major red flags with the gay community: meeting a girl was not going to change a gay man, and the word "values" is seldom used in mixed company without the inference that the other side is lacking in them. It was the equivalent of suggesting that the local priest would drop his objections to prostitution once he met a nice working girl in his price range.

The Burden of Being Billy Tate

As the only minor on *Soap*, Jimmy Baio faced more than the usual learn-your-line hurdles; Jimmy had schoolwork.

"If you're under 18, you have to have a tutor, and if you take a GED test, you don't have to go to school but you still have to have somebody [on set]," Baio explains. "And the hours you can work are restricted unless you get a special waiver. When we were taping the show and I was under 18, I'd have to stop at 10. But if something broke down and we needed to go longer or later, you could then reason with the person and they would be fine with that."

Though he can't remember for sure, the actor believes he took most of his lessons in his dressing room with his tutor. He was enrolled in Lincoln Square Academy, one of two New York schools that cater to kids in show business (the other is Professional Children's School). One of his friends from the Academy: actor Laurence Fishburne.

Yet another teen magazine photo feature on Jimmy Baio.

"What they would do is that any time you're not in the scene, you have that time to do your schoolwork," Baio says. "You just plan it out."

Best Lines.

Billy [to Eunice, substantiating his fear that insanity runs in their family]: Our father's a murderer, our sister marries a priest, Grandpa's fighting World War II, and mom lives on Mars!

Jodie: Dennis, this is a very confusing time for her. She just found out she's pregnant and I feel responsible.

Dennis: *You* feel responsible. What about the guy who got her pregnant? Where the hell is he, huh?

Jodie [sheepishly raises his hand]: You're looking at him.

Dennis: You're kidding.

Jodie [shakes his head]: I guess you want to know why.

Dennis: I'm still wondering how.

Jodie: It just happened. It was late one night, she was crying, she was real upset, I held her in my arms and...it happened.

Dennis: It just happened. Well how does it work these days? Does she have to cry every time or can you just skip over that and go straight to the fun stuff, hm?

Jodie: Dennis, please.

Dennis: Where does that leave us?

Jodie: I don't know. I'm waiting for her answer. I asked her to marry me.

Dennis: Mary you?

Jodie: I think it could work.

Dennis: Forget it. Hey, I tried it. It doesn't work. And even if you can make it work, I'll make sure you don't.

Mary: Listen, I went with a guy once after your father died. A guy who for one reason or another I was really rotten to. I don't know why, I guess I was just going through a rotten phase. Anyhow I was rotten to him and he was nice to me. So I got rottener and he was still nice. And then I got really rotten and he still stayed nice. I finally gave up being rotten because there was no one to appreciate it. Being rotten is only satisfying if it has an effect.

Danny: So you think if I start being really, really nice she'd stop being rotten?

Mary: It's possible. It's worked before. It worked with me.

Danny: Hmm. What about the guy?

Mary: He's in the dining room; I married him.

Burt: Why you like that?

Elaine: I wasn't always like that. I used to be nice.

Burt: Well if you used to be nice, you know how to be nice. Why don't ya just be nice?

Elaine: Cause I'm scared. The people I was nice to turned out not to be so nice.

Burt: We're nice.

Elaine: I thought they were nice, too.

Rod Roddy's Wrapup. Is Tim really the kiss of death? Is Eunice ever going to see Dutch again? Is Elaine really changing? Is Mary going to have to worry about more than just grades with her professor? Is Jodie going to wind up with Carol or Dennis? Is Chester going to continue to think of himself as Gunga Din? And if so, will Jessica buy him an elephant? These questions and many others will be answered on next week's episode of *Soap*.

2.7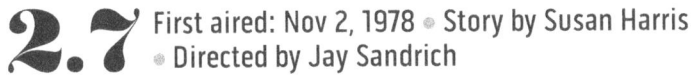
First aired: Nov 2, 1978 • Story by Susan Harris • Directed by Jay Sandrich

Chester is set to return home from the hospital, but it's the Campbell clan that's the story this week. Carol has agreed to marry Jodie (though Jodie's the one who has to break it to Carol's dad), Danny and Elaine have a heart-to-heart that finally allows them to enjoy each other's company, and Burt fends off advances, yet again, from Sally, who leaves him with the parting words "Anytime, any place, please, I'm yours." Oh, and Mary and the Tate women drown their thwarted sexual yearnings with Mary's famous apple-walnut coffee cake.

Cast. Katherine Helmond (Jessica), Cathryn Damon (Mary), Robert Mandan (Chester), Richard Mulligan (Burt), Diana Canova

(Corinne), Jennifer Salt (Eunice), Jimmy Baio (Billy), Robert Guillaume (Benson), Billy Crystal (Jodie), Ted Wass (Danny), Rod Roddy (Announcer), Rebecca Balding (Carol David), Michael Conrad ('Boomer' David), Dinah Manoff (Elaine), Caroline McWilliams (Sally), Ron Rifkin (Dr. Kanter)

Highlights. Jodie's "The princess is pregnant, Boomer" to Carol's dad; the gut punch that is Elaine's "this is why I'm awful" speech to Danny, including her confession that she loves him; Burt explaining to Mary why he works so hard; and the unprecedented coffee cake gabfest by Mary and the Tate women. Only the short hospital scene at the beginning prevents this from being a flawless episode.

Confused? You Won't Be. *'What a terrible way to live.'*

▶ Jodie's talk with Carol's father is a repeat of his discussion with Dennis Phillips last episode, from Boomer's initial confusion about who actually impregnated his daughter to his vague threat to Carol after Jodie has left. The only mystery remains who called Jodie at the restaurant that had him called away from the table in the first place?

▶ Though Mary and the Tate women attribute their eating frenzy to sublimation for the sex they're not getting, we'll learn next episode that Corinne has another reason for eating so much.

▶ This episode unspools like a show reel for the best *Soap* has to offer. It offers the smiling but bigoted Mr. David who delivers a punch line about "faggots" that is classic *Mad* magazine; the Elaine speech that is easily one of the best in the season, if not the series; and it goes for broke with its scene of Mary and the Tate women discussing sex and how perceptions have changed over the years as far as women are concerned. Plenty to bate those who detest *Soap*'s liberalism, absolutely, but a solid episode that proves just how short-sighted its detractors were.

Elaine's "Why I'm So Awful" Speech

This, the second in back-to-back sublime episodes, features one of the most memorable soliloquies in the show's four-year run. The simplicity of the scene, with Dinah Manoff saying her piece at her makeup table in the foreground while Ted Wass sits behind her slightly out of focus, belies its emotional impact.

"I remember when we did the run-through for the first time for the producers, we were sitting there watching the scene, sobbing," says associate producer Marsha Posner. "And the next day, just before we had a run-through of that scene again, the prop guys came out and handed everybody Kleenex before they started the scene."

More than 30 years later, Manoff has a hard time remembering the shooting of that scene. "I was so nervous and so intimidated by everybody in those years. I wasn't aware of the magnitude of the things happening around me, I was just aware that I wasn't getting fired that day! I was just a scared young actress; it was one of my very first jobs. I have many of those times in my career where people say, 'Oh you must've had so much fun,' and I'm like, 'Yeah, not really.' I didn't have fun until way later."

Elaine's speech this episode is arguably the high point of the series.

Best Lines.
Doctor: How are you, Mr Tate?
Chester: Fine, just fine. But the lamb chops were fatty!
Jessica: Lamb chops?
Doctor: It's a common mistake. He thinks I'm a butcher.
Benson: So do I.

Boomer [smiling]: All right, let me tell you something. If you ever bring that faggot around, I'll knock his teeth down his throat.
Carol: Well daddy, if that's the way you feel then why did you say the things you did?
Boomer: Well, a person has to be civil.

Danny: I'm giving up.
Elaine: What does that mean?
Danny: It means I don't know what to do. There's one thing I do know and that's I can't go on like this. Of course I don't have a lot of happy choices. Being with you has been murder and leaving you would literally be murder, so I don't know.

Elaine: It's that awful, huh? It's that awful being with me?

Danny: It sure has been. And the thing is that there was a time when I had the feeling that it didn't have to be. Once I think you had a day when you were nice. Just a nice normal lady and I really enjoyed you. In fact I thought we had great possibilities. But then the next day you were spitting food at me and calling me "yutz".

Elaine: I don't hate you, Danny.

Danny: Well you sure give the best damn impression of it I've ever seen.

Elaine: I know.

Danny: Well why do you do that Elaine? Why do you treat people that way?

Elaine: It's a long story.

Danny: I got time.

Elaine: I had a sister once, a couple of years older than me. Her name was Diana. She was bright and beautiful and good and kind. She was one of those people who made everybody around her feel good. When she was 16 she was killed in a car accident. On the night she died, my father in his grief said to me, "Why wasn't it you?" So my mother was dead and my sister was dead, and my father, who I loved more than anyone else in this world, wished I was dead. And I got angry. I got angry and cold, mean, and I decided then never to love anybody ever again.

Danny: Oh Elaine, I didn't know.

Elaine: I love you Danny. And maybe someday if it's not already too late, you'll love me?

Burt: I need to know I can do it. My father never did it. He tried, never did it. He was a short man, you know, not more than 5' 6". Little guy with gigantic dreams. He always figured if he couldn't be tall, he could be big. Well he was neither. He had to watch his kids grow up on potatoes. I'm lucky I've got a tooth in my head here. Never had enough to eat or rooms of our own. He was a beaten man. He always looked like something was hurting. Even when he smiled he looked like something hurt. I don't want to be my father, Mary. Every time I look in the mirror I'm afraid I'm going to see his hurting, scared little smile on my face. I need to do it for me.

Mary: You're going to keep doing it.

Burt: I gotta, Mare. What do you think?

Mary: Well I'm thinking yes, I understand you. And yes I see what you mean. I'm also thinking that tomorrow when you're driving home and some drunk jumps the center divider and you wind up dead, you will have spent the last days and nights of your life working. I'm also thinking that.

Burt: Well that's the last time I ask you what you're thinking.

Mary: So, what's going on with you three?

Jessica: Well, Eunice is depressed. And Corinne is depressed. And I was just debating whether or not to join them.

Mary: Sounds like fun.

Jessica: Actually I think I've been depressed quite a lot lately. I mean I eat a lot and I just simply cannot sit still.

Corinne: I don't think you're depressed, Ma. I think you're horny.

Jessica [thinks for a moment, then cautiously]: What is "horny"?

Corinne: What ya feel like when you're not having any sex.

Jessica: Horny?

[Corinne nods adamantly. Jessica cracks up. Mary cracks up.]

Jessica: What a funny word. Well actually I'm not having any sex because Chester is in the hospital but—Mary, I don't think not having sex could make me eat a lot.

Mary: Wrong, I have been eating like a pig.

Jessica: Burt can't again?

Mary: No he can but he's never home.

Corinne: I've gained 6 pounds since my wedding.

Mary: That makes no sense at all.

Corinne: Well when Tim's mother died, so did our sex life.

Eunice: I gained 5 pounds since Dutch left.

Mary: Dutch! You and Dutch?

Corinne: Eunice he's a criminal.

Eunice: Oh, you're going to lecture me, Mrs. Fallen Priest?

Jessica: Mary, look we've eaten all the nuts.

Corinne [eyeing the apple-walnut ring]: You know I'd love a piece of that.

1978

NOV. 4: The American Embassy in Tehran is taken over by militants supporting the Iranian Revolution. Fifty-two Americans will be held hostage for the next 444 days.

Jessica: No, now Corinne that's for daddy.

Corinne: Oh just one piece!

Mary: Look, since it's a ring I could cut out one piece and put it together.

[The women stare eagerly at the cake while Mary cuts away.]

Mary: I love sex.

Corinne: So do I.

Jessica: Well, actually I think it's pretty wonderful too, but I'm not entirely sure I should.

Eunice: Mary, could I have just a little piece of that?

Jessica: You see our mother never told us that it would be pleasant.

Mary: No, what mother said was that it was required like going to school had been. And that the best thing to do was close your eyes and make out your grocery list.

Jessica: And she also said that if you were really lucky, your husband would have a mistress and then the mistress would get stuck with it.

Corinne: What a terrible way to live.

Jessica: Well Corinne that was a long time ago before they discovered sex wasn't filth.

Corinne: It took you a long time to tell me that sex was nice.

Jessica: That's because you knew before I did.

Mary: I like it in the morning.

Jessica: I think the earliest I ever had it was noon. I don't think that could be counted as the morning.

Mary: Burt likes it in the morning, too.

Eunice: I don't like the morning because of all that light.

Corinne: What, you like it in the dark?

Eunice: Mmm hmmm.

Corinne: Not me, you never know who you're with.

Eunice: I keep track.

Corinne: What I mean is it's nice to see a person's face.

Jessica: Face? [Thinks about it a minute then dismisses it with the classic panoply of Helmond expressions.]

Mary: Well I like it in another room.

Jessica: Doesn't that make it very difficult for Burt?

1978

NOV. 7: California Proposition 6, aka the Briggs Initiative, is defeated at the ballot box. The ballot measure, inspired by victories in Dade County, Fla., by Anita Bryant's Save Our Children organization, would have banned gays and lesbians from teaching in California public schools. It's important to note that former California Governor Ronald Reagan, by most accounts a model of American conservative values, even came out against this bill, fearing it would have severely infringed upon individual rights.

Four horny women and a coffee cake.

Mary: No. With him, Jessie. With him in another room.

Jessica: Where?

Mary: Oh, the kitchen.

[Jessica drops the piece of cake she's been nibbling.]

Corinne: Outside is nice.

Jessica: Well I don't think it really matters where you do it just as long as you do it well.

Mary: Burt does it very well. With my first husband, however, it was like a news bulletin: brief, unexpected, and usually a disaster.

Jessica: Oh Mary, look what we've done.

Mary: The whole thing. We almost ate the whole thing.

Eunice: We couldn't have!

Corinne: I only had one piece.

Eunice: Me too.

Jessica: Well that's all I had.

Corinne: Eunice please. One piece, you had at least three.

Eunice: Me, oh please! Your mouth hasn't been empty for a minute.

Mary: Girls, please, don't fight. I'll make Chester another.

Eunice: Good. Anyway it's not our fault, it's theirs.

Jessica: Who's?

Eunice: The men. If we weren't so frustrated, we wouldn't be eating like this. [Gets some bread and peanut butter.]

Corinne: That's right. If I wasn't really so horny I wouldn't be eating this apple ring.

Jessica: I don't even like this apple ring. I think I had six pieces.

[The women start buttering up the bread.]

Coffee Cake Sex Talk

Today, it is extremely difficult to gauge just how daring this discussion of sex and bingeing was for its time. It was certainly the frankest discussion of sex seen on *Soap*, and proved just how far Susan Harris and Paul Junger Witt had come from their days on *Fay* just three years before.

"Actually, that famous coffee cake scene around the kitchen table was really something," says Diana Canova. "Mainly because we had to wait for the new head of ABC Entertainment, Tony Thomopoulos, to come all the way from Century City to watch the scene and give his OK as to whether it was too…risqué. He loved it, and it became a classic *Soap* scene."

"The network really couldn't have been more accommodating," Susan Harris admits. "There were weekly fights with standards and practices, but they really bent over backwards. I think they realized at a certain point that even though what we were doing was new for television, and considered it at times outrageous, that we were really going to operate within the bounds of good taste. I had a very pleasant relationship with Standards and Practices. At times you learned to negotiate and you learned to, for example, put things in the script that you don't intend to use at all, that would really give them a hard time. And then that way you'd be able to negotiate the things that you really wanted. They would say, 'You absolutely can't say this!' And you put up a fight and give in and let them win, and move on to the next thing and they'd say, 'You can't do that, either.' And I'd say, 'Listen, I just gave you this, you can't have that.' That's how it worked."

2.8

First aired: Nov 9, 1978 • Story by Susan Harris • Teleplay by Susan Harris + Stu Silver • Directed by Jay Sandrich

Ever the pragmatist, The Major enlists "Colonel" Chester in his war plans soon after his return from hospital. Jodie swings by Dennis' place to collect the last of his things and to say goodbye, and Dutch tries to break up with Eunice by rooftop, with less conclusive results. Corinne tells her mother that she's pregnant, a situation that seems less than ideal considering how depressed Tim has been about not being able to find a job. When Burt thinks he catches Mary cheating on him with Professor Martins on his couch, he goes right out and gets drunk…and arrives at the doorstep of his seemingly smitten secretary, Sally.

Cast. Katherine Helmond (Jessica), Cathryn Damon (Mary), Robert Mandan (Chester), Richard Mulligan (Burt), Diana Canova (Corinne), Jennifer Salt (Eunice), Jimmy Baio (Billy), Robert Guillaume (Benson), Arthur Peterson (The Major), Billy Crystal (Jodie), Ted Wass (Danny), Jay Johnson (Chuck & Bob), Rod Roddy (Announcer), Lee Bergere (Anatole Martins), Dinah Manoff (Elaine), Caroline McWilliams (Sally), Donnelly Rhodes (Dutch), Bob Seagren (Dennis Phillips)

Highlights. Jodie's confrontation with Dennis at his apartment; the sweet silliness of Dutch and Eunice, the star-crossed lovers, trying to break up six stories above the city; and Burt's acrobatic, drunken ramblings at Sally's place.

Confused? You Won't Be. 'Yeah, you love me so much you're leaving me.'

● Mr. Kirby, the Tates' neighbor who's borne the brunt of The Major's military operations in the past (1.1, 1.7), has his garage blown up this time by The Major *and* Chester. (He was parking his car at the time.)

● This is the episode where we begin to get some truly impressive sets. Dennis' bachelor pad with its large picture windows showing off the city at night is topped in the next scene by Dutch and Eunice on the rooftops of two brownstones.

1978

NOV. 8: Norman Rockwell, the artist who became an American icon by portraying an idealized vision of America in his *Saturday Evening Post* covers, dies.

▶ Dutch tells Eunice to meet him at his grandmother's little farm in upstate New York, and gives her written directions. Either these were for his own benefit and he thought he had pretty well memorized them, or he always intended to send Eunice there in the first place.

▶ Last episode it was Mary and the Tate women chowing down on coffee cake talking about sex; this time it's Jessica and Corinne talking about what sex leads to—a baby—over popcorn. Not surprisingly, Jessica tells Corinne that if she doesn't want a baby, she shouldn't have one, but allows the Standards and Practices department to heave a sigh of relief when she adds that she thinks Corinne *does* want her baby.

▶ It isn't just the way Elaine and Danny are kissing that demonstrates how much has changed since last episode, it's the way that Elaine calls Mary "Mare" and gives her a gentle peck on the cheek as they're leaving.

▶ Mary tells Professor Martins that the scar on her neck was the result of a duel she and Jessica had as kids with coat hangers, under the influence of an Errol Flynn movie. And her quip about being over the initial shock is a direct cribbing from an episode of the unofficial Witt Thomas Harris sitcom *Fay* (see p. 27).

Lee Bergere
(Prof. Martins)

▶ Burt's early insecurities about Mary going back to school (2.4, 2.5) have been realized with what he thinks is Mary cheating on him with Professor Martins.

And Introducing... writer Stu Silver.

Bentley, Baldwin. What Chester calls Benson.

Monica, Geraldine, Marjorie. What Chester thinks Jessica's name is.

814 Delancey St. The building rooftop Dutch is on.

816 Delancey St. The building rooftop Eunice is on.

'Conga Line'. The play Mary says she thought Danny and Elaine were rushing off too, rather than *A Chorus Line*.

AUGUST 14
Dutch's birthday

The Genius That Was Richard Mulligan

Since the early part of Season 1, Richard Mulligan had been throwing more and more physical comedy into his performances, something that reached a high point in this episode when Burt arrives at Sally's apartment thoroughly drunk. From the deadpan way he drops his glass of ginger ale on the floor to his jaw-dropping legwork atop her coffee table (in which even Caroline McWilliams has a difficult time keeping a straight face), this is Mulligan's physical comedy at its best.

"He was just unbelievable, that guy," says associate producer Marsha Posner. "He would pull things out of the air—you'd go where did that come from? When he came [to Sally's] drunk, he's on top of that table—if that's not Dick van Dyke all over again, I don't know what was. It was so incredible to watch this guy perform."

Recalls stage manager Carl Lauten, "Before a scene, no one would be within 15 feet of him. He would be in a trance behind the set going over all of his gestures, all of his actions, and I never got him on his mark until it was just that time for him to come in. He would work right up to his entrance. He was Burt Campbell once he got on the stage and started working his bits—he just needed a lot of space to be alone, and then when he came in it was killer. You watch his physical comedy, it was really something."

There was definitely a move to make Burt quirkier as the series went on, admits Susan Harris. "You have an actor like Richard and you just let him go and do his thing. Sometimes you didn't have to write for him; he would get laughs doing nothing, just being silent."

Says writer Stu Silver, "Every once in a while if Susan and I couldn't think of a blow-off for a scene, we'd say, 'Richard, just give it a little oomph!' And he'd get a laugh out of Hello."

Best Lines.
Benson (describing Jessica to Chester after he asks what she looks like): Dumpy, broad-shouldered, short black hair, nose like a fist.
Chester: What's her name?
Benson: Eric.

1978

NOV. 18: Built on the promise of establishing a Utopia where blacks and whites could live and worship side by side, Jonestown, a jungle encampment in Guayana named after the Indiana-born Rev. Jim Jones, quickly became a prison to the members of his "Peoples Temple." When California's Rep. Leo Ryan and several reporters flew to Jonestown to see whether some of Jones' followers were being held against their will, the messianic Jones ordered his flock to drink poison-laced fruit punch while some of his henchmen shot and killed Ryan and several others. In all, more than 900 people lost their lives because they wanted to believe that, following the tremendous upheavals over civil rights in the U.S., they had finally found the long-promised melting pot.

Jodie [explaining why he's marrying Carol]: Dennis, she's having my baby!

Dennis: So she's having your baby. So what? And anyway, how do you know it's yours?

Jodie: It's mine!

Dennis: It could be anybody's. It probably is.

Jodie: Dennis, come on!

Dennis: Jodie, the little slut has got more guys jumping her than the hurdles. And you're gonna be the jerk that supports her. Well I hope you're happy with spit up on your shoulder and the milkman with your wife. [Jodie decks him.]

Corinne: But ya see, when I thought of me pregnant, I kinda pictured it differently, you know. Like I pictured a little Cape Cod house with a vegetable garden and Tim going off to work and me fixing food in my little country kitchen. The only thing I got right was the food. It's just not how I pictured it.

Jessica: Nothing ever is.

Bob [about Danny and Elaine]: Well, did the Devil and Miss Jones leave? [Bob, referring to the 1973 porn flick *The Devil in Miss Jones* by *Deep Throat* director Gerard Damiano.]

Rod Roddy's Wrapup. Will Eunice be happy living on a farm with Dutch? Will Jodie be happy with Carol or will he be unhappy without Dennis? How happy will Tim be when he finds out that Corinne is pregnant? Will Burt make Sally happy? And if he does, how happy will that make Burt? Will Mary be happy studying English in the professor's class, or should she take karate instead? For the sake of everyone's happiness, should Jessica put Chester away, or should she let him go through life as a happy-go-lucky idiot? These questions and many others will be answered on next week's episode of *Soap*.

2.9

First aired: Nov 23, 1978 • Story by Susan Harris • Teleplay by Susan Harris + Stu Silver • Directed by Jay Sandrich

Burt thinks Mary cheated, Mary thinks Burt cheated, *Burt* thinks Burt cheated, and the only relationship going anyplace is between Elaine and her new mother figure, Mary. Tim continues to think he's "a jinx," and will have a hard time finding somebody to correct him after he starts and quits his job with Campbell and Son the same day. Chester now thinks he's Marlene Dietrich (thank you, Benson). Even Carol's wedding/baby shower at the Tate home ends up being an uncomfortable opportunity to study the Tate fridge when Jessica needs a few moments alone with Mary.

Cast. Katherine Helmond (Jessica), Cathryn Damon (Mary), Robert Mandan (Chester), Richard Mulligan (Burt), Diana Canova (Corinne), Jennifer Salt (Eunice), Jimmy Baio (Billy), Robert Guillaume (Benson), Arthur Peterson (The Major), Billy Crystal (Jodie), Ted Wass (Danny), Rebecca Balding (Carol David), Dinah Manoff (Elaine) Caroline McWilliams (Sally), Rod Roddy (Announcer), Sal Viscuso (Tim)

Highlights. Burt wrestling between confusion and anger when he finds himself at Sally's place; Chester's Marlene Dietrich impersonation; Jessica trying to cry after Benson gives her leave to do so; Tim's gloppy first and last day on the job; Burt's airplane on the highway story; and Jessica determining Mary has the best relationship in the room after pointing out the flaws with those of Elaine, Carol, Corinne, Eunice and herself.

Confused? You Won't Be. *'I'm confused, that's what I am, I'm confused.'* (Oops.)

▶ Frantically trying to decide what to tell Mary about why he didn't come home, Burt momentarily hits on the idea of telling her he was kidnapped, foreshadowing what is to come later (2.22).

▶ Burt's brilliant excuse to Mary about a plane landing on the highway being the reason he didn't come home last night is a call back to the excuses Chester and Corinne give in the pilot episode for not coming home after nights of fooling around. (In their cases, it was a hog truck and turkey truck accident, respectively.) And just like Chester, he casts himself as the hero, having stayed on the highway all

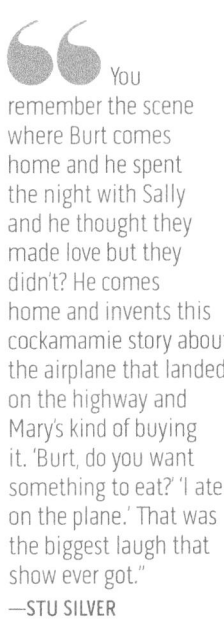

" You remember the scene where Burt comes home and he spent the night with Sally and he thought they made love but they didn't? He comes home and invents this cockamamie story about the airplane that landed on the highway and Mary's kind of buying it. 'Burt, do you want something to eat?' 'I ate on the plane.' That was the biggest laugh that show ever got."

—STU SILVER
  Writer

night helping to remove the wings from the plane so traffic could get through. Of course Burt has a much better punch line when he tells Mary he doesn't want any breakfast. "I ate on the plane."

▶ While they're giving themselves facials, Elaine tells Mary that she was 6 when her mother died. Elaine's makeup table has become a place of catharsis for the young woman. After all, it was here that she reached Danny's heart with her "why I'm awful" speech (2.7). The bonding between the Campbell women makes what is to come all the more heartbreaking.

▶ Jessica tells Mary she thinks Chester's cheating began on their honeymoon—she found the chambermaid's underwear in her suitcase.

Simpson. What The Major calls Benson.

Coffee Competition. Tim has had 11 cups, Mary 25.

Best Friend Benson. While everybody else is concerned with other things, Benson alone listens to Jessica, and tells her she's earned a good cry. After a few eye-crossing facial contortions, Jessica realizes she doesn't have to cry now because Benson's cheered her up. Says Katherine Helmond, "I think that Jessica was probably one of those kids who, when she had confusion, she crossed her eyes, and then she just never outgrew it. Her head gets scrambled with too much information and she just clears it all out of her head by crossing her eyes."

Stu Silver: The Writer Who Stayed

Though Susan Harris had been through at least two other co-writers by this point, she had yet to find an arrangement that worked. Having written the show pretty much on her own for nearly one and a half seasons, she was the only one who really understood the characters and their voices. Yet, it had also become apparent that if she continued to bang out scripts every week at this pace, she would burn out very soon.

Playwright Stu Silver, who had also been an actor in New York City for 13 years, had just moved to Los Angeles with his then-wife. He took a job as a waiter, which didn't last very long. "My wife was pregnant and I was like jeez, how do I tell my wife I just got fired from a waiter's job," Silver remembers. "We were going to have to find a new place to live because the apartment we were in didn't allow children. So as she was pulling the car into the driveway, I got a call from Tony [Thomas] asking me if I'd like to take a meeting and perhaps write the show."

Silver's old friend, director Joel Zwick (*Laverne & Shirley*), had snagged one of Silver's plays—a comedy called *Cellblock* about three old Jewish guys "complaining about whatever old Jewish guys complain about if they're at the deli"—and gave it to Harris to read. "He knew she was going crazy. She needed someone else to write with."

Whatever dynamic had been missing with Tony Lang and Jordan Crittenden she found with Silver. Harris continued to shape the story lines with Witt and Thomas as they had always done, but she no longer had to supply all the dialogue; she and Silver divided up the scenes between them, she says. "I would say I'm going to take this one and this one, Stu would say I'll take that one. It seemed to make sense. We gravitated toward different characters. Scenes between Jessica and Mary, for example, were generally my scenes. Group scenes were generally Stu's scenes. I just didn't like writing group scenes as much as I liked writing more intimate ones, so it was divided up that way."

Best Lines.
Danny: How did you get the blood on your nose?
Tim: From falling. I think from falling.
Burt: You fell?
Tim: In the cement.
Burt: How did you fall?
Tim: When the guy yelled help.
Danny: What guy yelled help?
Tim: The guy who fell first.
Burt: How did he fall?
Tim: He slipped.
Danny: How did he slip, Tim?
Tim: When the baloney dropped out of my lunch pail.
Burt: You reached out to grab him, then you fell.
Tim: Did you see it happen?
Burt: No, I've been in this business a long time, Tim.

1978

NOV. 27: Three days before Jodie gave Jessica a lesson on homosexuality throughout history, San Francisco Mayor George Moscone and openly gay City Supervisor Harvey Milk were gunned down in City Hall by former City Supervisor Dan White. Though White appeared to be more enraged by the mayor's refusal to rehire him after he resigned his seat on the board, some of his votes, especially one against anti-gay employment and housing discrimination measures, suggested to some a homophobic motive. San Francisco, already reeling from the hundreds of former Bay Area residents killed in Jonestown, Guyana, was again in mourning.

Jessica: It hurts, Mary. I know. I know. And you feel so ugly and clumsy and stupid. So self-conscious you don't even want to walk in front of him, you don't even want to talk in front of him. And you're sure he hates you and everything's all over. But it isn't. It isn't Mary.

Mary: It feels like it is.

Jessica: I know. I know. Isn't this nice?

Mary: Nice? My husband is having an affair and you call it nice?

Jessica: But you know what is nice about it, Mary? I always come running to you for help. This is the first time I have ever been able to help you.

Rod Roddy's Wrapup. Will Jodie's upcoming marriage to Carol work? How will things work out for Jessica now that Chester thinks he's Marlene Dietrich? How long will Tim's marriage to Corinne work now that he's out of work? Will Burt and Mary's marriage continue to work now that Burt thinks Mary's school work wasn't really work? And since Burt's airplane story didn't work, will Mary find out what Burt was really working on with someone from work? These questions and many others will be answered in the next episode of *Soap*.

2.10 First aired: Nov 30, 1978 • Story by Susan Harris • Teleplay by Susan Harris + Stu Silver • Directed by Jay Sandrich

There's trouble a-brewin' for the Tates and the Campbells. Chester has disappeared after breaking down over his inability to remember anything; Mary is fretting over Burt's affair; and Burt finds himself unable to hurt Sally by breaking up with her. Danny and Elaine, the only happy couple in the family (even they are marveling at how often they make love), quickly join the family's string of tragedies when Elaine is kidnapped by two masked men.

Cast. Katherine Helmond (Jessica), Cathryn Damon (Mary), Robert Mandan (Chester), Richard Mulligan (Burt), Diana Canova (Corinne), Jennifer Salt (Eunice), Jimmy Baio (Billy), Robert Guillaume (Benson), Arthur Peterson (The Major), Billy Crystal (Jodie), Ted Wass (Danny), Jay Johnson (Chuck & Bob), Rod Roddy (Announcer), Dinah Manoff

(Elaine), Caroline McWilliams (Sally), Harrison Page (Deputy Gilmore), Donnelly Rhodes (Dutch), Sal Viscuso (Tim)

Highlights. Chester struggling with the emotional trauma inflicted on him by his amnesia; Bob and Jodie trading insults in the kitchen, with Chuck only clapping his hand over Bob's mouth just before he reveals Chuck's "disgusting habits"; Jessica's disbelief that Mickey Mouse had a gay dog ("Goofy was his lover" Jodie explains); a flustered Burt hanging his full coffee cup on the coat rack before hightailing it out of the office and away from Sally; and the kidnapping of Elaine shortly after she's thanked God for letting her be so happy these last few weeks.

Confused? You Won't Be. *'This is a zoo.'*

▶ We finally get the backstory on Dutch, or what Dutch is willing to tell Jessica, anyway. He borrowed $5,000 from a loan shark after he got out of the Navy. After suffering several beatings at the hands of the goon, he shot him. (The guy who owned the loan company was the chief of police.)

▶ The Major's dog Sigmund (2.4) makes his return, though proves lousy at tracking down the missing Chester.

▶ This episode is a rarity in *Soap*: a pretty dull outing. The program's greatest innovation—the juggling of multiple story lines over an indefinite number of episodes—only works if those plots are in various stages of play. Ideally, one story should be beginning while another is in the middle of its action, and the last is reaching some kind of conclusion. In this episode, every story seems like it's just beginning: Eunice and Dutch heading off to the farm, Chester disappearing, Elaine kidnapped, Sally preparing Burt's downfall. Only Jodie's short talk with Jessica about gays in history seems to warrant the energy necessary to turn on the TV this week.

Bobbie "the Chicken" Gilmore. Benson hasn't seen the deputy since he was 8.

Fun with Chuck & Bob. In the space of just a few minutes, Bob dismisses Jodie as the "bride to be," tells Mary he wants Jodie's room, nearly spills the beans on Chuck's "disgusting" personal habits, and comes on to Jessica.

Breaking in the New Writer

After nearly a season and a half of performing material written almost exclusively by Susan Harris, there were some in the cast who had some issues with being handed lines by new writer Stu Silver, he admits.

"There was one moment when there was a little problem on the set. It was like my first week on the show, the second episode I did. The women were complaining that they didn't want me to write their scenes. They said he's a nice guy and a good writer, but he just doesn't get us. We want you [Susan] to write our scenes from now on. And Susan, without batting an eye, said 'Hey, that scene that you don't like, I wrote that scene. You got a problem, you take it up with me, don't blame Stu.' And the thing was, I *did* write that scene, but she stuck up for me. She was beautiful, talented, funny, smart, and a real mensch. And the way she stood up for me was just wonderful."

Best Lines.
Bob: Hey Jessica. Listen, when I get my own room maybe you and uh [eyes her chest] your two friends will come and see me.

Jessica: You know Jodie, when we were younger, there was no such thing as homosexuals.
Jodie: Yes there were, Aunt Jessica. The homosexuals go way back in history.
Jessica: Who?
Jodie: Alexander the Great was gay. Plato was gay.
Jessica: Plato? [Jodie nods.] Mickey Mouse's *dog* was gay?!
Jodie [after long pause]: Aunt Jessica, would you be very offended if I didn't continue this conversation?

Sally [on phone after Burt has left]: It's working. Give me a few more weeks and he'll be a broken man.

Rod Roddy's Wrapup. Will Dutch and Eunice find happiness on a farm, or will the police find them first? Will Mary tell Burt she's found out about his affair? Will Burt find out Mary didn't have the affair he thought he had found her in? Will Burt find a way to get rid of Sally, or will she find a way to destroy him? Will Chester be found? Does he want to be found? Who wants to find him? Will Danny find out who kidnapped Elaine, and will they find her? Find out the answers to these questions and many others on the next episode of *Soap*.

2.11 First aired: Dec 7, 1978 • Story by Susan Harris • Teleplay by Susan Harris + Stu Silver • Directed by Jay Sandrich

Jessica has called in the world's greatest sleuth, Detective Donohue, to search for Chester. Burt and Danny try to match wits with the kidnappers in order to get Elaine back. Corinne discovers that her pregnancy is further along than is comfortable considering she's only been with Tim for a month. And Dennis finally accepts Jodie's decision to end their relationship, but is Jodie really ready to marry Carol?

Cast. Katherine Helmond (Jessica), Cathryn Damon (Mary), Richard Mulligan (Burt), Diana Canova (Corinne), Jimmy Baio (Billy), Robert Guillaume (Benson), Billy Crystal (Jodie), Ted Wass (Danny), Jay Johnson (Chuck & Bob), Rod Roddy (Announcer), Rebecca Balding (Carol David), John Byner (Det. Donohue), Jo De Winter (The Doctor), Alex Henteloff (Mr. Peppy Flake), Bob Seagren (Dennis Phillips), Wendell Wright (Rodney Raisin)

Highlights. Bob finishing reading the ransom note before Chuck; Det. Donohue revealing his powers of deduction by casually revealing each family member's secret; Corinne's gynecological exam and her consternation over what to tell Tim about her pregnancy; the whole Raisin Flakes commercial Jodie is filming, and Carol's agitation over their forthcoming nuptials.

Confused? You Won't Be. *'This is very touching. Sick, but touching.'*
▶ From the very beginning, Donohue lets Jessica know he's only agreed to search for Chester because he likes her.

▶ Jessica suggests that maybe Corinne got pregnant from a public toilet or a swimming pool.

> "In every comedy show there are things you wish you hadn't done. I remember there was a scene where Billy Crystal is directing a commercial. I kept saying to the producers, 'This scene is never going to work, it's just stupid. It's not funny.' Of course we put it out in front of the audience and it got big laughs, so I have to admit I was wrong. In comedy, nobody knows until they try something, and from my point it didn't work, but they were sure right about that scene."
>
> —JAY SANDRICH, Director

1978

DEC. 13 The Susan B. Anthony dollar coin goes into circulation. Two days later, Cleveland becomes the first U.S. city to go into default since the Great Depression.

▶ This is the first time we've seen Jodie shooting a commercial since the introduction of Dennis Phillips (1.4), who was hawking Ball 4 at the time.

▶ According to director Jay Sandrich, there was talk around this time of creating a spin-off series about Jodie and Carol.

$250,000. How much the kidnappers initially demand for Elaine's return.

$50,000. What Danny offers them.

$25,000. What he and Burt can actually afford.

3 weeks: How pregnant Corinne thinks she is.

5 months: How pregnant the doctor tells her she is.

1 month: How long she and Tim have been married.

6 months: How long Peter's been dead.

The Controversy Begins….Now. After nearly two years of protests, pressure groups finally appear on the verge of getting the "smutty" program they've been decrying all this time. The relish with which Jessica bugs the gynecologist about a cartoon she saw concerning sperm and eggs leads into a scene of a commercial Jodie is shooting that goes through a great deal of narrative gymnastics to hit the line "don't forget to tap" (see Best Lines). As the only thing that's changed is the addition of Stu Silver to the writing desk, it's hard not to suggest he's the impish instigator.

And introducing…Det. Donohue.

John Byner: A Chance to Act

Though one of the great faces of '70s and '80s television, John Byner found himself in the unusual position on *Soap* of being one of the few actors with little theater experience playing opposite some well seasoned stage actors. "Having done impersonations of other people, I more or less did an impersonation of this character," he says of Det. Donohue. "That's what got me through. It came very easily, it was fun, and everybody around me was very supportive. Nobody treated me like the new guy in town. That helped a lot."

This glib talk of "impersonations" becomes much more significant when you realize that though Byner's ability to mimic many of the stars of his time brought him into show business, it also led to a variety of typecasting far more troublesome than that experienced by most actors. Instead of being pigeonholed as the nebbish ala Woody Allen, or the tough guy character Sylvester Stallone was locked into, Byner found himself pushed constantly to do impersonations on screen.

John Byner in *The Practice*, the series Paul Junger Witt and Tony Thomas produced shortly before *Fay*.

"That always stung me when those things would happen. Like I did a movie with Burt Reynolds called *Stroker Ace*. At one point I'm supposed to be his buddy from years and years ago. And somebody says, 'Do you sing?' Then he wants me to impersonate Johnny Mathis singing 'It's Not for me to Say.' Then that segues into a romantic scene with himself and Loni Anderson. I thought, 'Oh man, that's so Frank Gorshin, I don't want to do an impersonation.' He says, 'No, no, it's not like Frank Gorshin, it means something in the story.' So I say, 'Ohhhkay.' But it still looks like they hire you to do one little thing, you know. People would say why's Byner in this? Oh, he did Johnny Mathis, I guess that's why. Oh here we go again."

Best Lines.

Doctor: Well then, what about before your husband? When was the last time?

Corinne: Well that would've been Peter. But I'm not exactly sure when that was.

Doctor: Could Peter recall the date?

Corinne: Oh I don't think so, he's dead.

Jessica: My husband killed him.

Doctor: Is there anything unusual you've noticed lately?

Corinne: Yes there is. I know this might sound a little strange but sometimes I hear humming when there's no one else in the room. And it seems to come from my stomach.

Danny and Burt try to reason with Elaine's kidnappers.

Jessica: Oh that's hunger, Corinne. I get that, too. It kind of rumbles.

Corinne: Uh, no ma, this is different. This isn't a rumbling, this is a tune. 'Raindrops Keep Falling on My Head.'

Jessica: Maybe Burt Bacharach is the father.

Corinne: Oh dear.

Jessica: What is it?

Corinne: Well I guess this means that I have to tell Tim I'm pregnant.

Doctor: Well yes, when you go into labor I think he's going to be suspicious.

Corinne: But I've only been married a month. How can I tell him I'm 5 months pregnant?

Jessica: Well Corinne, you'll just have to tell. I mean what is he going to say?

Corinne: See ya.

Peppy Flake [singing]: Hello I'm Mr. Peppy Flake/
I used to be a schleppy flake.
My happy toes are curling and my peppy eyes are glazing/
Cause I gotta buddy pal, and his name is Rodney Raisin.

Jodie: Now remember to tap Rodney on the head after you finish the song. He can't hear you underneath all that milk, OK? Now gimme a little happy, peppy bouncing up and down. That's good, use it. Rodney, under the milk please. Here we go.

Rodney: Don't forget to tap.

Peppy [still mad about getting milk splashed in his eye]: Don't forget not to splash.

Carol [as Dennis walks on to the Raisin Flakes commercial set]: Oh just what the cereal needed. Fruit.

Rod Roddy's Wrapup. How will Burt and Danny find $50,000? And will they find $50,000 if they can't find their way out of the telephone booth? And if they can't find their way out of the telephone booth and find $50,000, how will they ever find Elaine? What will Tim do when he finds out what Corinne found out, that she is 5 months pregnant, since they've only been married a month? Will he find that difficult to believe? Now that Dennis has found out that Jodie intends to marry Carol, will Jodie find he has second thoughts? Will Det. Donohue find Chester? Does he want to find Chester? These questions and many others will be answered on the next episode of *Soap*.

2.12
First aired: Dec 14, 1978 • Written by Susan Harris + Stu Silver • Directed by Jay Sandrich

Burt and Danny arrange the ransom swap for Elaine, Eunice and Dutch discover that their country hideout may be more rustic than they'd bargained for, and Det. Donohue tells Jessica that he loves her. Jodie and Carol's wedding, the only straightforward, happy event the Tate and Campbell families have to look forward to, ends the only way it could have given the circumstances.

Cast. Katherine Helmond (Jessica), Cathryn Damon (Mary), Richard Mulligan (Burt), Jennifer Salt (Eunice), Jimmy Baio (Billy), Robert Guillaume (Benson), Arthur Peterson (The Major), Billy Crystal (Jodie), Ted Wass (Danny), Jay Johnson (Chuck & Bob), Rod Roddy (Announcer), Greg Antonacci (Dave), Ellen Blake (Lady on Phone), John Byner (Det. Donohue), Frank Coppola (Mel), Dinah Manoff (Elaine), Donnelly Rhodes (Dutch)

Highlights. Danny getting the woman off the pay phone in New York by telling her he and Burt are going to kill her, and her "Why didn't you say so?"; Eunice and Dutch's tabletop quibbling over whether it's a tarantula or a black widow spider, and Dutch's subsequent gymnastics; Danny and Jodie sharing childhood memories before they enter the chapel; and Burt and Danny wrapping their arms around a crushed Jodie as they walk him out of the church.

Confused? You Won't Be. 'We could all use a happy time right about now.'

▶ Jessica's Parker Brothers fixation, which began last episode with her playing *Monopoly* with Corinne, continues with her roping Benson into aiding her in the use of a Ouija board. (Quoth the Benson: "Forget it. It probably don't move for black people.")

▶ Det. Donohue found a bandage he believes belonged to Chester at the train station, suggesting he's headed to New York.

10 years. How long ago Dutch's grandmother died. Also, how long it's been since Det. Donohue's wife and detective agency partner ran away with most of their earnings. ("See, he was screwing around with the books, too.")

An eager Jodie awaits the inevitable.

Meta Meta Meta. Jodie's "Remember when all we used to think about was whether Susie Spivak's...were real or not" to Danny has to be a waggish call out to Susan Harris (nee Spivak). Meanwhile, Jodie's childhood dream to take New York Yankees player Mickey Mantle's job is lifted straight from the childhood aspirations of Billy Crystal himself.

Best Lines.

Jessica: If you feel the way you say you feel, how hard are you going to look for Chester?

Donohue: Very hard. I'd rather compete with a man than with a memory. Don't worry Mrs. Tate, I promise you'll get your husband. And then I'll get you.

Danny: Life was so simple then. Everything was so easy. At 6 you were going to be a fireman, and I was going to be a dog.
Jodie: That's right! Big Alfred, the collie who lived down the block.
Danny: And then a year later, I was going to be the president and you were going to take Mickey Mantle's job away from him.
Jodie: You know I'd still give five years of my life to have my face on a baseball card. [Gets up and slides into a batting stance.] Dallas, Jodie. Born New York City. Bats left, throws right. Jodie once completed four double plays in one game while wearing high heels.

Jodie [to wedding guests]: Excuse me everybody but it appears as if there's not going to be a wedding today. We seem to be missing a bride. I'm sorry. I mean you all came down here and you all got dressed up and everything and um, blew a Saturday. I wish there were something I could do. A flower girl offered to marry me and her mother said no. Listen, um, you know what I think? Uh, since we're all here anyway and uh, we sure could use a party. Why don't we go in the next room, take the dolls off the cake and get blitzed? What do ya say? OK?

Rod Roddy's Wrapup. Will the kidnappers drop Elaine off at the Campbells' after Danny and Burt make the drop, or will she have to take the bus? Can Eunice really be happy living on a farm with Dutch or will she miss Bloomingdale's? If Det. Donohue gets Chester, will he be able to get Jessica, or will she tell him to get lost? Where has Carol gone? What will Jodie do? And does this mean he has to return the wedding presents? These questions and many others will be answered on the next episode of *Soap*.

The ultra sweet Det. Donohue slyly woos Jessica.

2.13
First aired: Dec 21, 1978 • Written by Susan Harris + Stu Silver • Directed by Jay Sandrich

Elaine manages to escape from her captors, but not before being shot by one of them. Tim takes Corinne's "I'm 5 months pregnant" news about as well as she thought he would, and Burt and Mary finally come clean about their affairs...well, Burt's "affair" and Mary's attack. Jessica tries to fire Det. Donohue because of the way she feels about him, but can't bear to be away from him, much to Benson's initial concern. Still nursing their own wounds, the Campbells wait for Elaine to return, only to watch in horror as she dies in Danny's arms.

Cast. Katherine Helmond (Jessica), Cathryn Damon (Mary), Richard Mulligan (Burt), Diana Canova (Corinne), Robert Guillaume (Benson), Billy Crystal (Jodie), Ted Wass (Danny), Jay Johnson (Chuck & Bob), Rod Roddy (Announcer), Greg Antonacci (Dave), John Byner (Det. Donohue), Frank Coppola (Mel), Dinah Manoff (Elaine), Sal Viscuso (Tim)

Highlights. The way Corinne springs her news about the baby on Tim; Chuck & Bob's classic mind reading act with Danny; the sweet

180 POUNDS
What Dutch weighs, according to Eunice

flirtation between Det. Donohue and Jessica, and the man-to-man talk Benson has with him afterward; and the shocking death of Elaine Lefkowitz Dallas.

Confused? You Won't Be. *'It's all right now, Elaine. It's all right. You're home.'*

▶ Donohue and Jessica's flirtatious conversation this episode is a good preview of things to come between these two—diabetics be warned.

▶ When Mary tries to get Jodie to move back into his room, he realizes right away that she's afraid he'll try to kill himself again (1.10).

▶ Whatever temporary drop-off in quality it suffered, *Soap* has found its footing again with one more episode that is an instant classic. Particularly impressive is Ted Wass taking on a lion's share of the screen time, jumping from his amazement over Chuck & Bob's mind reading trick, to one of the saddest scenes of the series. Even worse than the death of Elaine is the viewer's realization that our brief time with Dinah Manoff is over.

George. We finally learn Det. Donohue's first name.

Danny and Bob's Special Relationship

Two and a half seasons in, it's obvious that, with the exception of Chuck, Danny is the character that talks to Bob more than any other.

"That goes back to the density of the character's thinking," Ted Wass suggests. "I think Susan Harris had a lot of fun writing Danny as somebody who was willing to believe in the puppet as being a separate person. People still talk to me about the apple-guessing bit. They'll remember that show and then they'll say, 'I remember this thing that you were doing with the puppet and he had a blindfold on and nobody was getting involved in it except you.' [Does an astonishingly accurate impression of Bob.] 'It's round, it's red, it's an apple!' My character thought it was the most amazing thing.

"And none of the other characters would do that, except the time when Bob thought he'd been shot [1.8]. Then everybody gathered around and people were holding hands and crying. 'Oh my God, Bob's dying, he's been shot!' Maybe that's why I had so much interaction with him, because I was more receptive to his taunts. I was more willing to believe he was an actual separate entity not attached to Chuck. (Isn't Jay absolutely amazing as a ventriloquist? He's really spectacular, by the way.) It's absurd but that's what she wrote, and when I think back on it, that's what made it great. That we could go from hysterical laughter—improbable-but-grounded hysterical laughter—outrageous comedy, to a tearful moment. That's pretty special. Any of the great shows can do the same thing; that's what makes them great."

Best Lines.
Chuck: Hi guys. Hey, Bob and I have been working on a new act. We thought you might like to see it.
Burt: Uh fellahs, please, we're not really in the mood now.
Chuck: I just kinda needed to practice. I thought it might break the tension around here.
Bob: The trick is I read minds.
Danny: Come on.
Bob: It's true, I do. [To Chuck] Come on, do your stuff.
Chuck [slips a sleep shade over Bob's eyes]: All right, here we go. Are you ready?
Bob: Ready!
Chuck: Danny, take something, anything, hold it up in front of Bob. [A blasé Danny holds up an ashtray.]
Bob: Uh, it's uh, round, it's uh, glass, it's an ashtray!
Danny: He's peekin'. He's gotta be peekin' in there.
Bob: No no no no no, I can't see a thing, I swear, I swear.
Burt: Wait a minute, wait a minute. [Picks up an apple.] What's that?
Bob: OK, OK, OK, I got it. It's uh, it's uh red, it's round, it's an apple!
Danny: This is amazing!
Mary: I don't believe this.

Burt: Do you know what kind of a gold mine we've got here?

Mary: Burt, Chuck can see what you're holding up.
Danny: But Bob can't!

Elaine [falls into the Campbell house, struggling to remain conscious]: I made it. I'm home. I'm home.

> Dinah was great. We loved Dinah, and we hated killing her when we did on *Soap*, but we had to for the story line."
> —SUSAN HARRIS

Danny: Don't talk babe. Save your strength.

Elaine: I love you, Danny. Do you know that I love you?

Danny: I know.

Elaine: Do you really know?

Danny: Yes, don't talk, please rest.

Elaine: You have made me so happy. I had to get back to tell you. I didn't want to die without telling you.

Danny: You're not dying, Elaine. You're not dying. [To everyone else] Do something. Somebody please do something!

Mary: I called the ambulance. They'll get here as soon as they can.

Elaine: It's all right. It's all right. It's all right.

Danny: I love you, Elaine. I love you, do you know that?

Elaine: Yes.

Danny: I've always loved you.

Elaine: Not always.

Danny: Always. Always. Even when you called me yutz. Even then I loved you.

Elaine: I never meant it.

Danny: I know. I know, silly. I know.

Elaine: Don't be sad, Danny. I don't want you to be sad.

Danny: Don't talk. Please Elaine save your strength, save your strength.

Elaine: Because it's all right. It's all right. I'm home.

Danny: You've got to save your strength, Elaine. Shhh. [Kisses her.] Shhh. Don't talk. Don't talk. I'll talk. Let me talk. I love you. I love you, and you're home now and you're going to be fine. I promise Elaine, you're gonna be fine. You're gonna be just fine.

Elaine: I am fine. Now.

Danny: You're gonna be fine, Elaine. You've got to be. You've got to be. Please, please, please be fine. Elaine? Elaine. [Realizes she's dead.] It's all right now, Elaine. It's all right. You're home. [Burt, Mary and Jodie watch in horror. Finally we hear ambulance sirens.]

Rod Roddy's Wrapup. Is it hard to believe that Elaine is dead? Does Mary really believe Burt that it was one night with an old fat lady? Does Jessica believe she can be in love with two men at the same time? What will Tim do since he doesn't believe Corinne? Do you blame him for not believing Corinne? Would you believe Corinne? These questions and many others will be answered on the next episode of *Soap*.

2.14
First aired: Jan 4, 1979 • Written by Susan Harris + Stu Silver • Directed by Jay Sandrich

Anxious to break up with Sally, Burt only succeeds in inspiring her wrath ("Someday, some way, I'm going to get you"). Jessica, Benson and Billy visit Dutch and Eunice at the farm house, but fail to throw the police off Dutch's trail. Life's not much better for the rest of the extended family. Danny's determined to hunt down Elaine's killers, and Jessica is told by Donohue that Chester boarded a train shortly before it was destroyed. Yet all is not lost as a surprisingly familiar looking hobo pops up in Toledo…

Cast. Katherine Helmond (Jessica), Cathryn Damon (Mary), Robert Mandan (Chester), Richard Mulligan (Burt), Jennifer Salt (Eunice), Jimmy Baio (Billy), Robert Guillaume (Benson), Ted Wass (Danny), Jay Johnson (Chuck & Bob), Rod Roddy (Announcer), G.W. Bailey (Hobo), John Byner (Det. Donohue), Caroline McWilliams (Sally), Donnelly Rhodes (Dutch), Richard Stahl (Officer Hickey)

Highlights. Burt's "Whew" when Sally informs him the gun she wants to buy is to kill herself, not him; Benson, Jessica and Billy ("And I'm Billy Benson") pretending to be a family to throw the cop off Dutch's scent; Chuck & Bob cooking (with matching aprons); Donohue and Benson comforting Jessica after she's told that Chester is dead; and Chester's brief conversation with the hobo.

Confused? You Won't Be. *'Life can be beautiful.' 'Life can also be a headache.'*

▶ It's been a long time since Burt has acknowledged the murder of his son Peter, but he does so here when he tells Danny that we all ask why the people in our lives get killed.

▶ The thoroughbred race horse Seattle Slew that Bob compared Elaine to won the U.S. Triple Crown of Thoroughbred Racing in 1977.

▶ Danny and Burt hitting the town, armed, in search of Elaine's killers is an odd bit of foreshadowing of their roles as lawmen starting at the end of Season 3.

▶ Donohue's explanation of how he found Chester's wallet is an echo of Tim Flotsky's story about falling into the cement (2.9).

▶ Owing to the humorous nature of the series, it's not often that you're struck by the acting chops of the cast. Yet the scene where Donohue breaks the news of Chester's "death" to Jessica is an excellent showcase for Katherine Helmond's ability to communicate an entire lifetime passing before the eyes of her character with the subtle flicker of emotion that runs through her face. Guillaume, too, accomplishes a great deal without saying very much at all. It is one of those scenes that stands testament to the power of seasoned stage actors when given free rein before the camera.

Candy and Randy. The "Benson" twins in the outhouse: they're Siamese. "They're both hoping someday to be a policeman."

$400. How much Chester's new suit cost. (Doesn't matter, it's gone now.)

Best Lines.
Burt [to Sally]: I'm not somebody you commit suicide over. I'm not somebody you even lose any sleep over.

Danny: I used to love to watch Elaine eat. She ate like a princess.
Bob: She ate like Seattle Slew.
Danny: Chuck, get Bob outta here.
Bob: Well come on Danny. Elaine's been dead for two days. I mean come on, you gotta get over it. Enough is enough. Life goes on.
Danny: Chuck...
Bob: Let's eat out.
Chuck: Good idea.
Bob: Yeah, you ruined my breakfast, he ruined my appetite. You're a real downer, Danny.

Jessica [about Chester's wallet]: Where did you get this?

Donohue: A little boy.

Jessica: A little boy?

Donohue: The boy in the mud.

Jessica: Mud?

Donohue: Mud from the flood.

Benson: There was a flood?

Donohue: Well sure, when the dam broke.

Jessica: A dam broke?

Donohue: From the weight of the bridge.

Jessica: The bridge?

Donohue: Well the bridge collapsed when the mountain fell on it.

Benson: A mountain fell down, a whole mountain?

Donohue: Well when the train blew up it jarred the mountain.

Jessica: What train?

Donohue: The train your husband was killed on, Mrs. Tate. [Jessica, stunned, turns to Benson.]

Benson: Mr. Tate's dead.

Jessica: We always used to argue, you know, about which one of us would die first. Chester always said to me, 'Jessica, I will be the first one to die, therefore I suggest you learn how to balance the checkbook.' He was right. He went first. Benson, I don't know anything about balancing the checkbook. I don't even know where the checkbook is.

Benson: I'll teach you how to balance the checkbook.

Jessica: Chester. How could Chester die? There's so many things he hasn't done yet. I mean how could Chester die?

Benson: Why don't you sit down.

Jessica: No Benson, I can't. I mean if I sat down now I'm afraid I would cry.

Benson: Do you want to be alone?

Jessica: I am alone.

Rod Roddy's Wrapup. Will Danny and Burt find Elaine's kidnappers? Will Dutch and Eunice find out that the police have found

JAN. 9: The Music for UNICEF Concert takes place to raise money for the starving people of the world, particularly children. The line-up includes ABBA, The Bee Gees, John Denver and Rod Stewart among others.

out where they're hiding? Will Burt find out what Sally is up to? Will Jessica ever find out Chester is alive? Will Chester find out who he is? Find the answers to these and many other questions during the next episode of *Soap*.

1979

Though births and deaths are usually left out of this section, we'll make an exception in this case. Jack Soo, who played Detective Nick Yamana on ABC's *Barney Miller*, died of cancer on **JAN. 11**, the same day this episode aired, at the age of 61. *Soap* and *Barney Miller* had studios beside each other, and experienced similar controversies throughout their time on air.

2.15 — First aired: Jan 11, 1979 • Written by Susan Harris + Stu Silver • Directed by Jay Sandrich

Per Chester's will, Jessica has a party where the guests are encouraged to tell all those great Chester stories, though it seems nobody has any. Later, Sally swings by the Campbell home to reveal that she's "the other woman," and that there's yet another woman that Burt's seeing (she's 18). Meanwhile in Texas, Jodie confronts Carol at her mother's house about her leaving him at the altar, only to discover she has no intention of ever letting him see their baby. The only person who seems to be having a good day is skid row Chester, who makes a breakthrough of sorts regarding his identity in a soup kitchen.

Cast. Katherine Helmond (Jessica), Cathryn Damon (Mary), Robert Mandan (Chester), Richard Mulligan (Burt), Diana Canova (Corinne), Jimmy Baio (Billy), Robert Guillaume (Benson), Arthur Peterson (The Major), Billy Crystal (Jodie), Ted Wass (Danny), Jay Johnson (Chuck & Bob), Rebecca Balding (Carol David), John Byner (Det. Donohue), Charles Hallahan (Lance), Caroline McWilliams (Sally), Peggy Pope (Mrs. David), Sal Viscuso (Tim)

Highlights. Everybody (especially Bob) trying to humor Jessica by laughing at her delightfully pointless story about Chester and the shaving cream; the overall lame stories everybody tells about the "deceased"; Sally getting hung up on the "him and me" grammar when she's explaining her affair with Burt to Mary (who presumably is still taking English classes); Mrs. David's fascination with Jodie the "homo" ("What do you people drink?") and Jodie's blowout with Carol; and finally Chester's realization that he is…Lester Pate.

Confused? You Won't Be. *'I thought it would be nice to surprise you.'*

- Billy's hammer story: When he was 5 he asked Chester to buy him a hammer so he could build a puppy of his own. (He bought him a hammer rather than a puppy.)

- Danny's funny Chester story: Chester suggested that Burt invest in rotary engine fan belts. The next day, the company went under and Burt was cleaned out.

- For the first time, the conservative elements that usually found themselves arrayed against Susan Harris and Co. over the subject of babies were faced with a far less black-and-white issue than they were used to. Jodie's anger over Carol deciding to cut him out of his baby's life was not Maude debating whether to have an abortion on the show of the same name. Granted, this is, in Mrs. David's beautifully chosen words, "a homo," but also a father wanting to care for his daughter. Not only does this scene set up the conflict between Jodie and Carol that will last pretty much the rest of the series, it also puts a new spin on Fred Silverman's placating words about prime time's first gay recurring character (see "The Controversy Begins...Now" for 2.6). Were these his "other values worth considering"?

40

The number of Chester's closest friends Jessica invited to the party (They all had headaches)

- Almost as stunning as how much Corinne is showing in her pregnancy is how little Carol is. We know there's something odd going on with the former's condition, but what's Carol's excuse?

General Mike 'Smiling Bob' Hawkins. Who The Major ends up eulogizing when he's supposed to be talking about Chester.

5 pounds. How overweight Sally says she is.

12. The number of times Mary has been on the Atkins diet. (Sally *gained* weight on it.)

Stu Silver: The Man Behind 'Soup Kitchen' Chester?

Just as some of the female actors preferred to have Susan Harris write their parts (a preference shared by Harris herself), Robert Mandan felt new writer Stu Silver occasionally had a more effective way of writing for Chester. Mandan recalls this episode in particular being a good example.

> One of my favorite scenes during this time frame was the hobo scene with this wonderful actor. We still quote that scene because it was an *acting* scene. Chester comes to him desperate. He finally says, 'Where am I, who are you?' The other guy says 'Toledo. A hobo.' And of course he's taken Chester's watch and robbed him blind. All he did was share this bottle of cheap wine called Hoop De Ha. Jay Johnson, who is a wonderful graphic artist, made me a wine bottle with a label that said Hoop De Ha on it. I still have that."
> —ROBERT MANDAN

"When Chester was off his gourd and he went into the soup kitchen, the scene absolutely did not work, and the jokes were just jokes. I didn't do this before and I never did it again on the show, but I finally said, 'I'm not doing this scene, I'll be in my room.' And because they would tend to say, 'Just do it and let them see it,' I thought why waste the afternoon? It's not working and it won't work when they see it. And then I'll be in the embarrassing position of being the lead character in that scene. So I went to my room.

"About 40 minutes later the scene came back down [from the producers' office] and it worked. I said to them, 'You're just doing jokes? Why is [Chester] there? What is his intention?' If you don't have that, you have no human interest in the scene. It came back down and it was finally very clear why he was there. And the jokes—I always have this image of a clothesline, and either the plot or the jokes are the clothespins hanging on that bit, and all the clothespins were in place, but we still had a spine to the scene: it had a beginning and a middle and an end. And it worked fine. I don't know if Stu solved that problem or not, but he just seemed to have an understanding of Chester.

"And Stu having been an actor, he knew how to find the thrust of a scene, what a scene meant. Why a scene was there. I think with comedy writers, particularly today, it's very easy to see they're just writing jokes. Some of them are funny and some of them are not, and some of them you feel like 'This sounds like a junior high jack-off film.' He just never presented a scene that was like that. His scene had a story to it rather than just a series of jokes."

Though understandably flattered by Mandan's words, Silver says usually it was hard for the actors to tell who wrote which lines. "My big contribution to the show was that I really understood those characters from day one, what to put in whose mouth. But I may have told Mandan one day, 'Actually, I did write that scene.' I may have said that to him once, especially early on when you're so grateful to have a job and so proud and happy that the work is being accepted by the actors. But also there were some scenes that Susan just didn't want to write, like those dinner scenes when the families are together. She preferred writing for the ladies and she did a great job on that. I seldom wrote for the women, like for Mary or Jessica. Susan pretty much wrote those scenes. Our writing was pretty close, Susan and me. She's the most talented writer I've ever worked with—I think she's a genius. I held my own though, for the most part."

Best Lines.

Mrs. David: We don't have homos in Texas. Live ones, anyway.

Jodie: What about the baby?

Carol: What *about* the baby?

Jodie: Well I'd like to see my child grow up.

Carol: Jodie, I don't want you to be the baby's father.

Jodie: Carol, I don't think you have that choice anymore.

Carol: I don't want you to see the baby.

Jodie: What?

Carol: Someday I hope to marry. And whoever I marry will be the baby's father.

Jodie: Carol, that's my baby. You can't do this! Carol, please. What am I gonna do? I don't stand a chance in court. I have feelings, Carol. It's my baby and I care. I don't think I've ever cared about anything quite as much.

Carol: Jodie, I know I'm right. Now I know it's hard for you but I know I'm doing the right thing.

Jodie: You mean my child will never know I'm his father?

Carol: It's better this way.

Jodie: Carol it's a mistake, it's a gigantic mistake because it's a lie. And a lie will always catch up with you later. And when it does, Carol, when my child wants his father, I'll be there.

Chester [to bum demanding the bread plate]: Please, you're beginning to pester me. [Thinks.] Pester. Nester. Mester. Lester! That's it!

Bum: Pass the plate!

Chester: Puh-Pate! I'm Lester Pate!

Bum: Pleased to meet you. Now do you pass me the bread or do I tear off your head?

Chester: Oh sir, you've helped me to remember! How could I ever repay you?

JAN. 16: The Shah flees Iran, paving the way for the Ayatollah Khomeini's takeover of the nation. **JAN. 19:** Watergate figure and former U.S. Attorney General John Mitchell is released from prison after 19 months.

Bum: Bread!

Chester: Take the bread, take my soup. I remember. Oh and I owe it all to you. You helped me gain my true self again. Good-bye.

Bum: Where ya goin'?

Chester: Home, to my family.

Bum: Oh yeah, where do they live?

Chester: I don't know. But they're out there somewhere. Somewhere there's a family of Pates waiting for their Lester, and I'll find them if I have to look in every city, in every town, I'll find them. Because when Lester Pate gets it into his head to do something, he does it! Because that's the kind of stuff we Pates are made of! I think.

Rod Roddy's Wrapup. Will Chester get his memory back, and what will Jessica do if he comes back? Now that Mary believes Sally's story, will Burt ever get her back? Can Jodie put his life back together now that he can't get Carol back? These questions and many others will be answered on the next episode of *Soap*.

2.16 First aired: Jan 18, 1979 • Written by Susan Harris + Stu Silver • Directed by Jay Sandrich

When it rains, it pours. Mary's left Burt, which leads him to drown his sorrows with Jodie, Danny, Chuck and Bob at a neighborhood bar. Tim has decided to leave Corinne to go live in a cave as a hermit; Dutch decides to give himself up when the police surround the cabin. Jodie discovers an equally depressed lesbian, Alice, when he finds himself loitering around the Triborough bridge.

Cast. Katherine Helmond (Jessica), Cathryn Damon (Mary), Richard Mulligan (Burt), Diana Canova (Corinne), Jennifer Salt (Eunice), Jimmy Baio (Billy), Robert Guillaume (Benson), Arthur Peterson (The Major), Billy Crystal (Jodie), Ted Wass (Danny), Jay Johnson (Chuck & Bob), Rod Roddy (Announcer), John Byner (Det. Donohue), Randee Heller (Alice), Richard Reicheg (Bartender), Donnelly Rhodes (Dutch), Sal Viscuso (Tim)

Highlights. Burt, Danny, Jodie, Chuck and Bob drunk in the bar; the relish with which Jodie takes on Danny's best efforts to make him throw up; and Burt telling the bartender that Bob, face down on the table with his legs dangling, will take care of the tab for the last round; Mary now believing that Burt has been sleeping with three other women (with Burt's description of Sally as old and fat now constituting a whole new lover in Mary's mind); and Mary, Donohue, Eunice and Corinne each trickling in to breakfast one by one, driving Benson crazy.

Confused? You Won't Be. *'Will you believe me when I tell you that it'll get better?'*

◉ It's always been a rule with Jay Johnson never to show Bob unless he's being animated by the ventriloquist, which is partly why the final gag of Bob passed out on the bar table works so well. (The only other time we've seen Bob separated from Chuck is when Jodie put him in the fridge in 1.20.)

◉ Once again *Soap* forces its audience to see the dilemmas that homosexual men and women face, this time with Alice's short explanation of what led her to the bridge to kill herself.

◉ Though Corinne says she's 6 weeks pregnant, next episode the doctor will say she's 5 months pregnant. This is also what she told Corinne after her exam (2.11). So desperate is Corinne to believe the baby is Tim's, she is still counting from her first time with him.

30 years. How long until Dutch would be up for parole if he went back to prison.

50. Number of state troopers surrounding the cabin.

For the *Soap* Bible Tells Us So. In its list of "Back Burner Plots," Father Tim leaves Corinne to "live a life of solitude and penance," and is gone a fair while before he discovers he left Corinne pregnant.

Best Lines.

Jodie: What about your family?

Alice: They threw me out. My father went nuts when he found out we were both dating his secretary.

1979

JAN. 29: In San Diego, 16-year-old Brenda Spencer opens fire on the Cleveland Elementary School from the window of her home across the street, killing two adults and wounding eight students and a police officer. Her reply to the question of why she did it—"I just did it for the fun of it; I don't like Mondays. This livens up the day"—inspired the No. 1 1979 UK single "I Don't Like Mondays" by the Boomtown Rats.

> [Susan Harris] was tough with executives, network people. And God bless her for that because they would ride roughshod over you and come up with the goddamedest suggestions. You'd go, 'Oh, please. Did a human write that or were they trying to get gorillas to do it?' Somebody walked by her office and she was overheard talking to New York saying, 'You can go fuck yourself, I'm not changing a fucking word!' Or words to that effect. And we all went, 'Oh right on, Susan! Go get 'em girl!'"
>
> —ROBERT MANDAN

Jodie: Really?

Alice: No. But he did throw me out.

Jodie: Why?

Alice: Why? All my life I've been a really good daughter, good student, nice person. Kind and considerate. I had really nice parents. So yesterday I decided I had to tell them about me. I figured if we talked about it, they'd understand and maybe I'd feel a little bit better about what I was. So I told them. My mother, a very reserved woman, screamed, spit in my face and stormed out of the room. My father, a noted psychiatrist, called me a sick, twisted pervert and threw me out of the house. I really loved my father.

Mary [about Burt]: He's been carrying on with his secretary, with a skinny teenager, and an old fat woman.

The Major: Hasn't he seen our training films? He'll go blind.

Jessica: Oh Mary, that's nothing.

Mary: Nothing? You call that nothing?

Jessica: Well I mean not compared to what Chester did. One time Chester was carrying on with five stewardesses—five—all on the same flight!

Mary: You always have to top me!

Rod Roddy's Wrapup. Will Danny find happiness without Elaine? Will he find her killers? Will he find happiness and her killers, or is that asking too much? Will Tim find a cave, and if he finds one, what will he find inside? Now that Jodie and Alice have found each other, what else will they find? Will Burt find Mary, and if he finds her, now that she's found out, what kind of mood will he find her in? What will they find is the reason for Corinne's advanced state of pregnancy—a good diet, or is she really a fruit fly? Find out the answers to these questions and many others on the next episode of *Soap*.

2.17

First aired: Feb 1, 1979 • Written by Susan Harris + Stu Silver • Directed by Jay Sandrich

Corinne gives birth to a baby boy shortly before Mary and Burt's marriage dies a violent death in her room back home. Burt swears that he will prove Sally is lying, at least about the 18-year-old. Meanwhile, Donohue has Jessica over for dinner with promising results, and even Jodie seems to be getting along with Alice...well, eventually. And in some backwoods burg, a middle-age fry cook realizes that he is none other than Chester Plate!

Cast. Katherine Helmond (Jessica), Cathryn Damon (Mary), Robert Mandan (Chester), Richard Mulligan (Burt), Jennifer Salt (Eunice), Jimmy Baio (Billy), Robert Guillaume (Benson), Billy Crystal (Jodie), Rod Roddy (Announcer), John Byner (Det. Donohue), Jane Daly (Midge-Ann), Jo De Winter (The Doctor), Burton Gilliam (Buck), Randee Heller (Alice)

Highlights. Mary attacking Burt in Corinne's bedroom, and Jessica and Benson's comments as they listen from the bottom of the stairs; Donohue's sweet but clumsy attempts to impress Jessica by making her dinner; Alice "Jewish mothering" Jodie; and Chester finally regaining his memory.

Confused? You Won't Be. *'Congratulations, Corinne has had a boy.'*

◉ Last episode, it was Jessica directing Billy to take people's suitcases to different rooms; this time it's Mary and the Tate women repeatedly sending him back to the coffee machine. This running gag is uncomfortably close to the situation faced by the writers over what to do with a 16-year-old character in an adult show.

◉ Mary gave birth to Jodie in the car on the way to the movies. Eunice says she wants to have Dutch's baby.

◉ The doctor insists that unlike most babies, Corinne's is beautiful.

4 hours. How long it takes for Corinne to deliver her baby boy.

14 hours. How long it took Jessica to have Eunice.

2 days. How long it took Jessica to have Billy.

FEB. 1: Patty Hearst is released from prison after President Jimmy Carter commutes her sentence. That same day, the Ayatollah Khomeini returns to Iran, kicking off a month that will end in the Islamic revolution in that country.

5 months. How long the doctor maintains Corinne was pregnant before giving birth to a 9-month-old baby.

And Introducing...Jessica and Donohue's first kiss. You crazy kids, we never knew you had it in ya.

John Byner and the Dark Side of 'Bloopers'

Det. Donohue's date with Jessica went even worse than many realized, according to John Byner. If having to learn, rehearse and perform a whole episode in front of a live audience—twice—wasn't nerve-wracking enough, the actor found himself drawing the short straw when it came to the show's bloopers—not that anybody told him beforehand.

"I was doing a scene with Katherine Helmond where I'm wooing her. She's come over to my place and I've cooked dinner and we're going to have champagne. [1971 Dom Perignon, according to the episode.] Well, what they did, which I didn't appreciate, was they played some tricks on me so they could have some bloopers. It was crummy. They're very lucky because one of the things they did was this huge magnum of champagne, they shook it up so hard that when I popped it, good thing I wasn't standing over it, because it actually flew way, way into the rafters.

Then we had these plastic champagne glasses and I'm supposed to go over and pick up a glass and offer her some champagne. What they had done was take out the stand so I just got the top of the glass—it doesn't have anything to stand on. They did this just to have bloopers for the show. There's a live audience out there and I'm looking like a jerk. I knew they were doing this to get bloopers—it just ticked me off. They pulled that on me up on *Bizarre*, too; I didn't appreciate it. I told them I didn't want to do it. We had enough bloopers up there, we didn't need this. I'll probably lose a lot of points by letting that secret out, but that's not right."

John Byner, man of a thousand impressions, became man of a thousand faces soon after *Soap* on his own series, *Bizarre*. On that show, too, they tried to get their bloopers.

Best Lines.

Mary: You told me about an old fat woman. Sally's not an old fat woman, she's a young skinny woman! I despise, loathe and detest you. Damn it! There's nothing left to throw!

Burt: Mary, Mary, no listen to me. Mary, Mary, hey it's true, I lied. But in that particular case, there was no reason to tell the truth. Don't you understand?

Mary: No. But I'm sure Nixon would.

Midge-Ann: Cookie, let me have an apple pie with cheddar on the plate. Cookie?!

Chester: Cheddar on the plate.

Midge-Ann [to Buck]: You big bully, you hurt him! Cookie, say something to me!

Chester: Cheddar, plate. Che-, Che- Chester. Chester Plate! No, no, wait, wait, wait, it's coming back to me. Chester, Che-, Tate. I'm Chester Tate! From Connecticut! I live in Connecticut! I've gotta go home. I'm Chester Tate from Connecticut. I have a loving wife named Jessica, and a fine young son named Benson. Well, it's a little murky but it's coming back.

Rod Roddy's Wrapup. What could be the reason for Corinne giving birth to a 9-month baby after a 5-month pregnancy? Lousy addition? Is something going to happen with Donohue and Jessica, and if it does, will they eat dinner first? How can Burt prove to Mary that Sally lied if Mary won't believe him because he lied? Now that Chester's on his way home, is Donohue on his way out? These questions and many others will be answered on the next episode of *Soap*.

2.18
First aired: Feb 8, 1979 • Written by Susan Harris + Stu Silver • Directed by JD Lobue

While everyone in the Tate home tries to adjust to having a new baby in the house, Burt corners Sally in her apartment and discovers the truth: not only did he not have sex with her, but that she broke up his marriage with Mary because she was being blackmailed by Corinne's real mother: Ingrid! Meanwhile, Jessica and Donohue spend their first night together, and Chester finally comes home. Yay?

Cast. Katherine Helmond (Jessica), Cathryn Damon (Mary), Robert Mandan (Chester), Richard Mulligan (Burt), Diana Canova (Corinne), Jimmy Baio (Billy), Robert Guillaume (Benson), Arthur Peterson (The Major), Billy Crystal (Jodie), Ted Wass (Danny), John Byner (Det. Donohue), Randee Heller (Alice), Caroline McWilliams (Sally), Rod Roddy (Announcer), Inga Swenson (Ingrid)

Highlights. The way Burt discovers who's behind the discord Sally has sewn between him and Mary, and Ingrid snapping a photo of Burt and Sally kissing at the last minute with her trademark "Ha!"; Danny's Burt impression for Jodie, and the whole interaction between the brothers and Alice; Jessica and Donohue's giggly review of the previous night's lovemaking; and Benson slamming the door in Chester's face the moment he sees who it is.

Confused? You Won't Be. 'I'm home.'

◉ The Major commenting on the baby crying is funnier still when you know that it is Arthur Peterson's wife who's making the baby sounds (see "Bad Baby" under the entry for 2.21).

◉ *Soap*'s longtime assistant director, JD Lobue, takes the reins here for the first time, gearing up to take over from Jay Sandrich, who will leave after 3.6.

◉ Jessica telling Mary that she didn't sleep with Donohue because she didn't want to be unfaithful to Chester is ironic, not only because of the fact that Chester isn't dead, but also because a) Chester never had a problem being unfaithful to Jessica, and b) Jessica cheated on Chester with Peter Campbell in Season 1.

◉ We finally learn that Sally was being blackmailed by that sworn enemy of the Tates and the Campbells, Ingrid, who got a hold of a porn film Sally did to earn enough money to help her sick brother. At least, that's what she told Burt. Her story is similar to the wild stories Burt, Corinne and Chester have told on previous occasions to cover up their own indiscretions, so we can't really be sure.

▶ Caroline McWilliams really shines in this episode, alternating between farcical and tragic in one of *Soap*'s most tightly crafted sequences.

▶ The scenes between Danny, Jodie and Alice not only rehabilitate the last from obnoxious Jewish mother to caring roommate, but also demonstrate that though Danny is initially freaked at his first encounter with a lesbian, he's come a long way since he and Jodie had it out over the latter's sexuality (1.8).

Benson's Baby Feeding Schedule. 1) Mary: 3 a.m.; 2) Corinne: 7 a.m.; 3) Eunice: 11 a.m.

Best Lines.
Jessica: There's something really nice about being with one person all your life. I mean you don't have to explain your scars to 'em. And you don't have to keep your chin all up all the time, you know, so it doesn't double. And you don't have to lie in the one position where nothing sags. I mean Mary, try making love propped up on one elbow with your hand behind your head.
Mary: Oh my God, you're right. And in the morning. To be seen in the morning? I mean Burt's used to me but a strange man? I mean he'd take one look at me and leave the bed in a rocket.

Ingrid: This is just the beginning. This is just practice. I will wipe out both those sisters for taking my Corinne from me. You haven't seen nothing yet.
Sally: I'm sure we haven't. Could I please just have it-
Ingrid [toying with the film she's used to blackmail Sally]: You know, I sort of hate to give it up. It's so original. Tell me, where in the world did you find all those midgets? The magic of celluloid. Here [tosses film to Sally], loved the hot tub sequence. I'm surprised you didn't drown.

Rod Roddy's Wrapup. Is this the last time Ingrid will bother the Tates and Campbells? And if not, isn't it enough already? Will Jodie and Danny be successful in getting Mary and Burt together. If they are, will Burt be successful in getting her to believe he hasn't slept with anyone? Now that Jessica and Donohue have found true love, will Chester's resurrection put a kink in their relationship? These questions and many others will be answered on the next episode of *Soap*.

2.19 First aired: Feb 15, 1979 • Written by Susan Harris + Stu Silver • Directed by John Bowab

After who knows how long away, Chester luxuriates in the pleasures of a bath in his own home, even if he has to hear from Jessica that she's given away his clothes and taken up with Det. Donohue. Meanwhile, a lonely Billy is lured away by Lisa, a classmate who tells him he could have a different life if he explores what The Church of the Golden Ray has to offer. Eunice visits Dutch in prison and tells him she's hired a lawyer who wants him to turn state's evidence. The only people who have a decent day are Burt and Mary who, thanks to the duplicity of Jodie and Danny, and the help of Sally, finally patch up their differences. Yet even as the Campbells unite, a force far more sinister than Ingrid appears to have invaded the nursery in the Tate home.

Cast. Katherine Helmond (Jessica), Cathryn Damon (Mary), Robert Mandan (Chester), Richard Mulligan (Burt), Diana Canova (Corinne), Jennifer Salt (Eunice), Jimmy Baio (Billy), Robert Guillaume (Benson), Arthur Peterson (The Major), Billy Crystal (Jodie), Ted Wass (Danny), Rod Roddy (Announcer), John Byner (Det. Donohue), Ruth Cox (Lisa), Tim McIntire (Devil Baby voice), Caroline McWilliams (Sally), Dick Miller (Prison Guard), Donnelly Rhodes (Dutch)

Highlights. Chester having a good old laugh after Jessica tells him she had an affair with Donohue; Lisa the "Sunnie" and Billy's ultra-clumsiness around her; Eunice's sparring with the prison guard; Danny and Jodie (!) both trying to sneak a peek at Sally's porn film; Jessica gibbering away at Corinne's baby, and Benson's disgusted "Why are you doing that?"; and the baby's room coming to life as soon as everyone's left.

Confused? You Won't Be. *'Some surprise. I can't wait to see what you're planning for Christmas.'*

▶ The producers gave theater director John Bowab an opportunity to direct this episode, director JD Lobue recalls. "I directed one week and the following week I stepped down to assist John. He had been observing Jay [Sandrich] for some time and [the producers] decided to give him an opportunity to direct. This was back in the day when you could observe a director and form a relationship with the production company. If they were willing, you might get an opportunity. Jay's advocacy and his unselfish mentoring were pivotal in the careers of more than a few successful television directors."

▶ Tim McIntire, who provides the growl of Corinne and Tim's "devil baby," was a prolific actor throughout his 42-year life. Among other roles, he played Gloria Bunker's husband in one of the *All in the Family* pilots that never aired. The part, of course, was later played by Rob Reiner.

▶ While much more will be said about the "devil baby" story line in the entry for the next episode, it bears emphasizing just what a departure this was for *Soap*. Even Corinne's accelerated pregnancy could've been dismissed either as a dig at the soap opera convention of accelerating pregnancies, as well as the aging of children. But once the audience saw the flying Teddy bear and the animated wardrobe, all bets were off.

▶ This episode is also a rarity so far as it has very little in the way of the sparkling dialogue we've come to expect from *Soap*. Indeed, much of it is spent tying up old story threads (Burt and Mary's estrangement) and clumsily setting up new ones (Billy and the Sunnies, and the devil baby). Though things will improve, they'll rarely reach the heights of inventiveness, heart and utter lunacy that we've seen up to this point.

For the *Soap* Bible Tells Us So. In the *Soap* bible, it is actually Eunice and Benson who ask The Major to plan Billy's rescue "by convincing him they are members of Allied intelligence plotting to rescue Audie Murphy from a Nazi stronghold." Once Billy is liberated, Tim Flotsky is tasked with deprogramming him.

Sunnies, Moonies and Scientologists

Despite the abuse *Soap* would take from the Catholic and protestant churches and the Moral Majority over its lifetime, the only religion to be treated with anything less than kid gloves was that of Korean spiritual leader Rev. Sun Myung Moon. However, though the Sunnies, the Rev. Sung Ray Sung and his Church of the Golden Ray all seem based on Moon and his Unification Church, many believe the Sunnies were instead a thinly-veiled reference to the Church of Scientology.

Though "Sunnies" leader Rev. Sung Ray Sung's name echoes that of the Moonies' Rev. Sun Myung Moon (above), the Sunnies were probably modeled on the Church of Scientology.

There's no doubt that the Sunnies were originally based on the Moonies. According to the *Soap* bible, Billy "falls under the influence of a spellbinding disciple of the Reverend Moon" while Jessica is standing trial for Peter's murder.

Yet when it came time to shoot this story line, the Sunnies were significantly influenced by Scientology. This is not so surprising considering the great reach Scientology had in Hollywood at the time. One of its biggest celebrity followers, John Travolta, converted in 1975. Scientology had also weathered numerous charges of brainwashing and aggressive strong-arm tactics. Perhaps the most blatant indication that the Sunnies are actually Scientologists is Simon saying "He's cleared" after Billy accepts Rev. Sung as his master in 3.2. "Clear" is a phrase Scientologists use to refer to someone who has successfully completed the highest levels of training.

Still, it's hard to get past the "Sunnies" name. Throughout the 1970s, the Rev. Moon gave high-profile speeches throughout the U.S., took out full page ads defending President Nixon during Watergate, and otherwise remained in the headlines.

It's also hard not to recognize in the Sunnies shades of Jim Jones and the tragedy of Jonestown, which only came to a head in November 1978.

Though the "Sunnies" name at first seems an obvious mirror of "Moonies", the Rev. Moon himself coined the term in a March 19, 1978 address. "Those who oppose us call us Moonies but we call ourselves *Sunnies*, and the spirit world will tell you that you are Kingies. You will confirm this when you go to the spirit world."

The Silly Looking Little Guy. Chester's description of Det. Donohue.

3. The number of minutes Eunice has to speak with Dutch.

5 more years. How much longer Dutch would have to stay in prison if he broke out and was caught again.

Best Lines.
Billy: I never even knew you thought I was alive.
Lisa: Well that's because I was in another world. But now I'm in Reverend Sun's world. I love it. I love everything. I love *you*.
Billy: Me?
Lisa: All things. Sunnies know how to love and feel! And you seem so troubled.
Billy: I am. Sorta. I just don't have anyone to talk to, anyone to listen to me. I mean my parents will, but they sorta have their own problems and I don't want to add to them.
Lisa: The Sunnies will listen, Billy. I'll listen.
Billy: You will?
Lisa: Come. Come with me.
Billy: But I have a class.
Lisa: I love you.
Billy:...that I can make up tomorrow.

Rod Roddy's Wrapup. Now that Jessica has a lover and a husband, what will life be like for her besides busy? Now that his high school love is going to introduce him to the Sunnies, what's in store for Billy? Now that Burt and Mary are back together, what will Ingrid Svenson do next? Now that Eunice has convinced Dutch not to break out, will she break in? And now, as if the Tates don't have enough trouble, what the devil is going on in the nursery? These questions and many others will be answered on the next episode of *Soap*.

2.20
First aired: Mar 1, 1979 • Written by Susan Harris + Stu Silver • Directed by Jay Sandrich

Chester is starting to realize that he's come home to a home that's no longer his own; Danny is still chasing Elaine's killers; and it's becoming more and more apparent that there's something terribly wrong with Corinne and Tim's baby. Corinne journeys to Tim's cave to enlist his help, and Burt watches Danny's back while he follows up a lead at a farm house, only to witness something far more shocking than a tough with a gun.

Cast. Katherine Helmond (Jessica), Cathryn Damon (Mary), Robert Mandan (Chester), Richard Mulligan (Burt), Diana Canova (Corinne), Jennifer Salt (Eunice), Jimmy Baio (Billy), Robert Guillaume (Benson), Arthur Peterson (The Major), Billy Crystal (Jodie), Ted Wass (Danny), Jay Johnson (Chuck & Bob), Rod Roddy (Announcer), John Byner (Det. Donohue), Randee Heller (Alice), Tim McIntire (Devil Baby voice), Sal Viscuso (Tim)

The number of times Benson's changed the baby today

Highlights. Benson being especially obstinate and insulting to Chester during breakfast; the three-ring circus insanity that erupts in the Campbell home around Alice's visit; Corinne and Benson freaking out when the devil baby speaks; Burt frantically trying to explain his close encounter to a disbelieving Danny.

Confused? You Won't Be. 'I go away for a few weeks and all hell breaks loose.'

◉ Jessica telling Chester that he no longer makes her feel loved or needed is one of those little bombs laid throughout the series that won't mean much until we discover how this pair got together in the first place (4.14). That one detail will explain all of Jessica and Mary's relationship problems throughout the show. And it must be pointed out that this detail was in the *Soap* bible long before the first episode had been made.

◉ Only a moment after Burt tells Danny about the spaceship he saw, Danny suggests calling the doctor he visited when he was "invisible" (1.22). This seems all the crueller when we think about all that Burt has done for Danny, from bringing him in to his business to going with him to confront Elaine's killers.

▶ Robert Mandan rewards us with a particularly nuanced performance this episode, as an obviously hurt Chester tries to find his place in a family that has moved on without him. Though *Soap* as a series has many strengths, it must be said that it, like many programs before and after, seldom gave Mandan a chance to show what he was really capable of.

9:30 p.m. The moment when Burt has his close encounter.

Robert Guillaume's Tightrope Walk

On stage or screen, Robert Guillaume was always mindful that many people saw him as a black role model.

Soap's humor may remain timeless, but the era in which it was made isn't always so easily appreciated. Now viewed as one of American television's great iconic characters, Benson in the 1970s was viewed by many black people still immersed in the civil rights struggle as a giant step backward.

In his autobiography *Guillaume: A Life*, the actor recalls a meal at which Ron O'Neal, who had directed him in the 1973 movie *Super Fly TNT*, cautioned him about taking the role. "It's insulting...You're beyond playing a cook. I'm telling you, Bob, it's a step backwards. Television is still operating in the dark ages of *Amos 'n' Andy*." The discussion between Guillaume, O'Neal and their dining companions went on like this until O'Neal's wife, Carol Tillery Banks, said to him, "And who's going to pay Bob's rent? You?"

As Guillaume told me about his performance of Benson in 2008, "I decided to avoid stereotypes by simply playing what I thought was the truth. The black people that I knew did not automatically play the fool. The people I knew were not idiots. I had never seen all this buffoonery from black people in their interaction with white people. I decided to play what I had seen and no more, and no less."

"I must say that when I first came into the show, I really had a gigantic chip on my shoulder," Guillaume admitted during the 1990 *Soap* reunion. "And everything they'd write for me I would check out assiduously. I would send it to the NAACP and these various organizations. And every time I'd say something to Tony, Paul and Susan they'd say, 'What is it now, for God's sake?! What is he talking about now?' But I must say that I have lived to see the time when I'm so happy that you guys chose me."

While Guillaume was feeling some pressure from those outside the ABC studios to ensure Benson kept his dignity, there was a feeling on set that the producers might've been having some trouble striking a balance between Benson's dignity on the one hand and being true to a comic moment on the other. While this led to some frustration for both producers and the actor, Guillaume's views were respected.

Katherine Helmond, perhaps the closest friend he made on that series, recalls him telling her, "'I have to speak up because I'm representing something that you don't have to worry about.' And I said I understand that."

"At the end of the table read, [the producers] would look to [Guillaume] to see if everything was OK, because they thought they understood black people," remembers Robert Mandan. "They would go off behind the sets and you could hear Bob going 'sfsfnnn nigger snnnnssff nigger,' and he was not about to do any slave impressions, and never did. I remember Katherine [Helmond] and I sometimes would just sit there and hear this. He would come out from behind those sets and we would immediately look to him and he'd just wink at us and go on to his dressing room because he'd won the battle." Mandan laughs. "And ended up with a show of his own."

Best Lines.
Chester: I can't believe it. You're in love with another man.
Jessica: You see Chester, he makes me feel the way you did 20 years ago. I feel loved and wanted and needed. You used to make me feel that way but you don't anymore. You see, he's not another man, you are.
Chester: I can be that way again, Jess. I know it. Give me a chance. I'll be everything I used to be, I promise.

Bob: I wear a red shirt, you wear a red shirt. I wear green trousers, you wear green trousers—I'm sick of it.
Chuck: That's for the act, Bob.

Bob: Act, shmact, you have no imagination.

Chuck: Bob!

Bob: And another thing. I'm a little sick and tired of you following me around all the time. No kidding, every time I turn around, there you are. I need my space.

Mary: Chuck, Jodie's bringing home a girl—

Bob: A girl. What's he trying to see how the other half lives?

Danny: She's gay.

Bob: Oh then I guess I can't tell my joke about Holland.

Rod Roddy's Wrapup. Will Danny ever find Elaine's kidnappers? Will Alice ever have dinner at the Campbells' again? When Tim gets home, will he find that the baby is really possessed, or will he find it just possesses a morbid sense of humor? Will Chester ever have what he used to have with Jessica, or will Donohue have what Chester used to have with her? Or does he already have it? Will anyone ever believe that Burt saw a flying saucer? Will you? These questions and many others will be answered on the next episode of *Soap*.

1979

MAR 4: The world glimpses the rings of Jupiter for the first time thanks to photos taken by the Voyager I space probe.

2.21 First aired: Mar 8, 1979 • Written by Susan Harris + Stu Silver • Directed by Jay Sandrich

The insanity is coming to a head for the Tates and the Campbells. Burt desperately tries to convince Mary that he saw a flying saucer; Tim and Corinne's devil baby is growing more powerful in its tantrums; Billy follows Lisa deeper into the Sunnies; and Jodie and Alice decide to...date?

Cast. Katherine Helmond (Jessica), Cathryn Damon (Mary), Robert Mandan (Chester), Richard Mulligan (Burt), Diana Canova (Corinne), Jennifer Salt (Eunice), Jimmy Baio (Billy), Robert Guillaume (Benson), Arthur Peterson (The Major), Billy Crystal (Jodie), Ted Wass (Danny), Jay Johnson (Chuck & Bob), Rod Roddy (Announcer), John Byner (Det. Donohue), Ruth Cox (Lisa), Randee Heller (Alice), Charles "Chip" Lucia (Larry), Maurice Marsac (The Waiter), Kit McDonough (Maxine), Tim McIntire (Devil Baby voice), Scott Mulhern (The Sunnie), Sal Viscuso (Tim)

> "I did a lot of luncheons with Katherine [Helmond] and the group. Three or four of us would go out to lunch quite often at the Gower Gulch they called it, across from the studio. Katherine always liked the Japanese sushi, and it came back and bit her because she had 26% more mercury in her body than most human beings at one point. It's not funny, but she insisted on going to that restaurant and doing sushi."
>
> —JOHN BYNER
> (Det. Donohue)

Highlights. Burt's desperate appeal to Mary to believe him about the UFO; Benson visiting Billy in the Sunnies' lair; Jodie and Alice deciding to date in a moment of jealous agitation; and Benson backing Tim up against the devil in a moment of ill-advised bravery.

Confused? You Won't Be. *'Prince of Darkness—Prince of Rudeness is more like it.'*

⏵ The "Father Carvelis" reference is most likely a mashup of "Father Karras" from *The Exorcist* and the Carvel ice cream franchise. Tim tells the others that the demon is possessing his child because it sensed his faith has been weak ever since he left the priesthood.

⏵ *Soap*, in its seeming quest to keep both left and right howling for blood, caps off several episodes that taught Danny and Burt (and America) that yes, there are indeed lesbians out there, by throwing Jodie and Alice together...as a couple.

Best Friend Benson. Benson braves the creepy Sunnies compound and their patronizing black/white speech to make sure Billy isn't being dragged into their control. Yet, when Billy defensively suggests Lisa likes him for himself, Benson doesn't belabor the point. After this, Benson volunteers to help Tim take on the devil baby, even if his bravery appears to desert him at the last minute.

Bad Baby!

There are two story lines for which *Soap* seems to be remembered more than any other; these also happen to be the two Susan Harris regrets the most: Burt's extraterrestrial encounter, and Tim and Corinne's possessed baby. While Harris concedes that she and Stu Silver were able to put the former setup to some interesting uses, she offers no such mitigation for that baby from hell.

Yet the devil baby's mama isn't nearly so hard on the tike. "My favorite story line was having the devil baby," says Diana Canova. Upon learning that Harris was less than thrilled with it, she says, "Really? She feels that way? Now that I think of it, yeah, I remember something like that. That it might be crossing a line somehow.

"I have to tell you, we had so much fun with that story line, though. The great thing about every story line she wrote was that it was so spot on and so smart. More importantly, it was clever and biting, but hugely sincere. That was why people loved us. Is there anything sillier than Burt waving his hands and thinking he was invisible? But he was so genuine and sincere about it that you loved him and people waited for Burt to do his thing."

In keeping with Tim Flotsky's own feelings about Corinne getting pregnant four months before they ever were a couple, Sal Viscuso says simply, "I hated the possessed baby. That's all, I don't want to embellish it, I hate it."

Explains Harris, "There were some choices that were made that, when we look back, even right after we made those choices, we realized they weren't the best ones to make. You've already mentioned two of them—the exorcism was kind of a low point in the show. And the aliens. Basically we wanted to keep it as real as we could. Even with Burt's invisibility, it made some sense. But the exorcism was just too much, I think."

Yet some understandably concentrate on the fun that was had behind the scenes during the filming of these few magic moments. Marsha Posner reveals that the wife of Arthur Peterson (The Major) "had a very special talent: she could cry like a baby. She would put a handkerchief up to her mouth and would make these sounds that you swore were made by a baby. So when Corinne had the baby that turned out to be possessed, any time that you heard the baby cry, that was Arthur's wife."

Posner also recalls Viscuso being strapped into the harness that propelled him through the window during the devil baby's telekinetic tantrum. "And the explosion back in the day, we had all kinds of sound effects, but they were on 8-track cartridges and that's what we used. You just stick the cartridge in, the sound guy gets the cue and hits the button, and there's the explosion."

Director Jay Sandrich recalls being less than pleased with the scene, too. "The stories and plots were a little far out but we always played a certain reality to the people, and this was before the aliens, too. That story just made it so it was not real, they were not real people,

50

The number of "kurtias" Rev. Sung sets Lisa for interrupting him ("To yourself, Lisa")

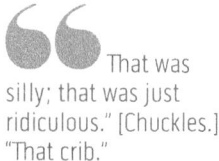

" That was silly; that was just ridiculous." [Chuckles.] "That crib."

—SUSAN HARRIS on the possessed baby story line

and it was a problem for me to direct it. That was the scene where Katherine Helmond does the exorcism; the scene just didn't play. Susan, in between shows, wrote a whole new monologue for her. That was not one of our finer moments."

Look, Harris says, "I think that was desperation. But that happens in any show because everything has to be done so quickly. You have to have a show every week, sometimes you can't help it—you just settle. We wanted to stay real within certain boundaries of aliens and exorcisms. I think we accomplished that."

Best Lines.
Burt: You think I'm crazy. You do, it's written all over your face!

Mary: No I don't, I don't think you're crazy.

Burt: Ya do, ya do, ya do. You're sitting there saying my husband, stable man. Last year invisible, this year space cadet.

Lisa: Are you here to shed your fears and rid your body and mind of stress and aggravation?

Benson: No, in my work I need my stress and aggravation. I came here to see Billy.

Lisa: Well, perhaps Billy could show you around. I have to go now to my anti-deprogramming seminar.

Benson: My mother always said to me, she said, son, look the devil in the eye and meet him straight on. You can't wrestle him to the ground unless you've got a hold of him first. [Another Satanic explosion.] My mother was a babbling fool is what she was. [Batting away smoke with his feather duster.] Major crackpot, everybody knew it. She was nuts!

Rod Roddy's Wrapup. Are Alice and Jodie falling in love? Is Billy's love for Lisa going to get him in deeper and deeper with the Sunnies? Is Jessica getting closer and closer to choosing between Chester and Det. Donohue? Does Mary think that Burt is slipping further and further from reality? Will anyone ever believe him? Do you believe him? Are Tim and the Tates prepared to take on the devil? Is the devil prepared to take on Tim and the Tates? These questions and many others will be answered on the next episode of *Soap*.

2.22
First aired: Mar 15, 1979 • Written by Susan Harris + Stu Silver • Directed by Jay Sandrich

Ah, the best laid plans. Tim and Corinne's possessed baby is still tearing the Tate home apart despite Tim's exorcism; Danny gets the drop on the guy who killed Elaine, only to lose his advantage; and Billy discovers the Sunnies aren't through with him just yet. Jessica gathers Chester and Det. Donohue together to announce her decision, and Burt returns to the area where he saw the UFO.

Cast. Katherine Helmond (Jessica), Cathryn Damon (Mary), Robert Mandan (Chester), Richard Mulligan (Burt), Diana Canova (Corinne), Jennifer Salt (Eunice), Jimmy Baio (Billy), Robert Guillaume (Benson), Arthur Peterson (The Major), Billy Crystal (Jodie), Ted Wass (Danny), Jay Johnson (Chuck & Bob), Rod Roddy (Announcer), Candice Azzara (Millie), John Byner (Det. Donohue), Frank Coppola (Mel), Ruth Cox (Lisa), Michael Delano (Rev. Sung), Randee Heller (Alice), Tim McIntire (Devil Baby voice), Sal Viscuso (Tim)

Confused? You Won't Be. *'You have come to the wrong house!'*

▸ Those present at the exorcism: The Major, Chuck & Bob, Eunice, Jessica, Chester, Jodie, Mary, Benson and Tim, who gets dragged out the window by an unseen force for his efforts. He lands in the swimming pool. (Who knew the Tates had a swimming pool?)

▸ Interestingly, the first time we ever see Tim and Corinne's still-nameless baby in the flesh is shortly after Jessica expels the devil.

▸ Chester was Florida state fencing champion.

▸ The four-photo freeze frame (showing Jessica, Billy, Danny and Burt) mimics Season 1's finale card where we're asked to decide who killed Peter.

Bolivia. Where Millie tells Danny that Mel is.

The CIA. Billy tells Rev. Sung that he's with the Agency as a last ditch effort to escape. This may also be a reference to persistent rumors that the Jonestown massacre was somehow tied to the Central Intelligence Agency.

8 hours. How long Burt has explored the field where he first saw the flying saucer before the blasted thing reappears, this time taking him with it.

Jane Espenson

The Influence of 'Soap'

Those who enjoyed *Soap* growing up went on to careers in television themselves. Jane Espenson, best known for her work on *Buffy the Vampire Slayer*, *Battlestar Galactica* and *Game of Thrones*, is one of those.

"I never consciously thought of it as an influence, but I'm sure it was," she says. "I certainly enjoy bringing gay characters into leading roles, something Susan Harris pioneered with the character of Jodie Campbell. And *Soap* included one of the best dry/sardonic observer characters of all times in Benson—that's another favorite note that I love to add to a scene. Benson is not unlike *Buffy*'s Anya in some ways.

"The show also mixed dark themes with comedy very successfully—Jodie's attempted suicide in the hospital was harrowing, and how many years prescient? And also darkly funny. I adored the earlier, more grounded seasons and lost interest when events got more surreal—I seem to recall an alien abduction and a demon baby. But those early episodes stayed with me and I'm sure they influenced my idea of what makes a compelling story and a compelling on-screen relationship."

Best Lines.

Corinne: He's here because of me.

Jessica: Don't be silly, Corinne. The devil doesn't even know you.

Corinne: It's all my fault. He's here because of me. Because I slept with everyone in town.

Mary: Oh Corinne, please. First of all you did not sleep with everyone in town.

Corinne: Yes I did.

Jessica: Oh please. Did you sleep with the mayor?

Corinne: Yeah.

Jessica and Mary: You slept with the mayor!

Jessica: Oh my goodness, the mayor! I voted for him!

Mary: I told you not to vote for him. I told you to vote for Swanson.

Corinne: I slept with him, too.

Mary: You did?

Corinne: Believe me, the best man won.

Devil baby: Accept me now. Do not resist any longer because you cannot succeed. Your soul is mine for eternity. I have won. Give up and come to me!

Jessica: We will never give up. Never! There is not a man or a spirit in this world or any other that will break my family. We've lived through too much in our lives already to give it all up to you. We've lived through sorrow and separation and death and destruction and we're still together because we love each other, and love is what holds us together. So if you intend to stay we will fight you to the end, and let me tell you we will fight, and with God's help you will never have us, and you will never have this baby! Never! You have come to the wrong house!

[The spookiness disappears, replaced by a baby crying.]

Rod Roddy's Wrapup. Now that the devil is gone, what's going to happen to Tim and Corinne's marriage? Now that Jodie and Alice are dating, what's going to happen to their relationship? Will Dutch ever get out of prison? Will Eunice wait for him? What's going to happen to Billy? Will the Sunnies take over his mind? Who will Jessica choose, Chester or Det. Donohue? What's going to happen to Danny? What happened to Burt? These questions and many others will be answered on the next episode of *Soap*.

Never before and never again will Soap *take such violent swings from conventional screwball comedy to cutting-edge parody in a single season. In many ways Season 2 was the best of the series; it certainly gave us two of* Soap's *most intriguing relationships.*

With Danny and Elaine we transitioned from put-down humor and slapstick to the blossoming of young love once a real understanding between the two was reached.

The twisted relationship between Jodie and Carol was the other standout of the season as the pair tried their darndest to change each other, and suffered terribly because of it. And of course it is that oh-so-human compulsion to change the other that has set the stage for what is to come next season.

Season Three

After two seasons of being dismissed as a simple soap-opera parody, *Soap* embraced the concept with abandon in Season 3, as it managed to work in child custody battles, philandering spouses, and not one but two fatal diseases.

However, this season would be far better remembered for alien abductions, interracial dating, a boy sleeping with his teacher, and an anticlimactic brush with a cult.

3.0 First aired: ?? • Written by Susan Harris • Directed by Jay Sandrich

Shortly before Benson is to leave for his new job at the governor's mansion, Jessica convinces him to help her rearrange the furniture in the Tate living room. While they spend a great deal of time going over what happened in Season 2, the time comes when they can put off Benson's departure no longer.

Highlights. The final moments between Jessica and Benson, and the bittersweet way Benson comes up with to avoid a long, drawn-out goodbye. (See "Best Lines".)

1978

JULY 3: Few events in the 20th century so clearly illustrated America's schizophrenic attitudes toward art and the broadcast media in particular than the *Federal Communications Commission v. Pacifica Foundation* Supreme Court decision. Stemming from a 1973 complaint to the FCC concerning the airing of George Carlin's famous "Seven Words You Can Never Say on Television" routine on WBAI in New York City, the 5-4 decision empowered the FCC to determine what constituted indecent material aired during times when children might be listening. (And for the record, those words are: ass, balls, cocksucker, cunt, fuck, motherfucker, piss, shit, tits.)

Confused? You Won't Be. *'I thought perhaps if I kept busy, I wouldn't have to think about you leaving.'*

Normally the problem with these annual compilation episodes is a lack of interesting new material and unimpressive writing for the wraparound story. This time around, we actually have the opposite problem, with our being told that Benson is going to work at the governor's mansion. To those who missed this episode, and the *Benson* pilot, it appears that Benson simply leaves the Tates after the devil baby fiasco with no explanation. The final scene should've definitely been included in the regular run of the series.

Best Lines.

Benson: We both know how much we love each other so we don't have to say it and start crying. What we're going to do instead is play a game.

Jessica: A game?

Benson: Hide and seek. Remember hide and go seek?

Jessica: Oh yes, that was my favorite game.

Benson: Well that's what we're going to do. You go around and sit down and close your eyes and count to a hundred. While you're counting to a hundred, I'll go. The only difference is when you open your eyes I won't be hiding, I'll be gone.

Jessica: Benson, I—

Benson: Mrs. Tate, please...

Jessica: OK. 1, 2, 3, 4, 5, 6, 7—goodbye Benson—8, 9, 10, 11-

Benson: Goodbye, Mrs. Tate.

Jessica: 12, 13, 14... [opens her eyes, looks miserably at the door he's just closed behind him, and continues counting].

Rod Roddy's Wrapup. Now that the devil is gone, what's going to happen to Tim and Corinne's marriage? Now that Jodie and Alice are dating, what's going to happen to their relationship? Will Dutch ever get out of prison? Will Eunice wait for him? What's going to happen to Billy? Will the Sunnies take over his mind? Who will Jessica choose: Chester of Det. Donohue? What's going to happen to Danny? What happened to Burt? These questions and many others will be answered on the next episode of *Soap*.

3.1

First aired: Sept 13, 1979 • Written by Susan Harris + Stu Silver • Directed by Jay Sandrich

Jessica, for whatever reason, has chosen Chester over Donohue, resulting in the latter's inability to leave the Tate home. Burt finds himself aboard an alien spaceship, facing the prospect of being replaced by one of his captors. Mrs. David arrives on Jodie's doorstep with his daughter, Wendy. And Benson, Chester, Donohue and The Major set out to free Billy from the Sunnies.

Cast. John Byner (Det. Donohue), Diana Canova (Corinne), Billy Crystal (Jodie), Cathryn Damon (Mary), Robert Guillaume (Benson), Randee Heller (Alice), Katherine Helmond (Jessica), Robert Mandan (Chester), Richard Mulligan (Burt), Arthur Peterson (The Major), Jennifer Salt (Eunice), Rod Roddy (Announcer), Peggy Pope (Mrs. David)

Highlights. Donohue and Chester reacting to the slips of paper Jessica's given each of them with her decision, and then switching them after she realizes she mixed them up; Burt's first encounter with the aliens and their bizarre plan to replace him with an alien double; the delightful Mrs. David trying to wrap her mind around "girl homos" ("homettes?"); The Major's speech to the rest of the family; and he, Donohue and Chester blacking up in preparation for Billy's rescue.

Confused? You Won't Be. *'It's very nice to meet you, Wendy.'*

▶ Not missing an opportunity to let any piece of pop culture go unremarked upon, the cutaway depicting the alien mothership is similar to the titular starship in *Battlestar Galactica*, which will premiere on the same network four days later.

▶ Jodie's "I think relationships are better when there's no sex to screw things up" to Alice is pretty prophetic when you consider that Billy Crystal's best-known film, 1989's *When Harry Met Sally...*, poses the question: Can men and women ever really be friends without sex getting in the way?

▶ Mrs. David tells Billy that she brought him Wendy because "Carol wanted you to see her," which we will soon learn is not really the case. She also explains that the reason she can't do math is because she was dropped on her head when she was a baby.

▶ When Jessica enthusiastically informs the family that Benson is "back," the former butler quickly sets her straight: He's only returned because they have to do something to free Billy from the Sunnies. Presumably Benson left the Tates because of his brush with the devil (2.22). Of course the character now has a show of his own, which debuted the same night as this episode.

Wendy and proud papa, Jodie.

▶ This is the first episode to give Arthur Peterson the chance to do anything of real substance, and he makes the most of his screen time here. It should also be noted just how expertly the whole "blacking up" part of this episode is handled. Though this is something that will always carry with it a certain stigma, it is John Byner's explanation to Jessica that after the rescue, they're going downtown to "pick up some white women" that does what Guillaume's "You all look alike" cannot—it defuses this longtime white view of black men so gently, it emphasizes just how gentle a show *Soap* really is.

▶ Finally, the little disco move that Alien Burt executes with Mary at the end is based on a throwaway line uttered by the lead alien in the beginning—that his race has mastered all Earth languages...and disco.

Belsen. What The Major calls Benson.

1:32 a.m.; 1:47 a.m., or 6 a.m. When Benson, The Major, Chester and Donohue set out to rescue Billy (depending on whose watch you believe).

Rod Roddy's Wrapup. Has Jessica made the right decision? Will Donohue ever feel well enough to leave the house? Now that Jodie doesn't want to let his baby daughter go, is he in for a tug of war? Will Mary realize that Burt isn't really Burt? What's going to happen to the real Burt? And after being with the new Burt, will Mary care? Will The Major's plan work? If it doesn't, can they do

The Gong Show? These questions and many others will be answered on the next episode of *Soap*.

Best Lines.

Burt: What do you mean Mary's going to think that [Alien Burt's] really me?

Alien: Yes. [The two aliens confer. Alien Burt starts skipping happily.]

Burt: Why is he jumping up and down like that?

Alien: It is nothing.

Burt: No come on, what's the matter with him?

Alien: He is just a little excited.

Burt: Yeah, about what?

Alien: Going down to Earth. Living in your house.

Burt: Oh wait, you're not gonna let him uh. I mean he's not gonna—

Alien: Sleep with your wife. [The Burt-double starts skipping excitedly again.] Why do you think he's jumping up and down? He has not had sex in 2,000 years.

One of these lucky guys gets to be Burt Campbell...

Major: Attention, damn it! Now I know sometimes you don't like to listen to me, and sometimes I can understand why, but you must all listen to me now.

Chester: Major-!

Major: Shut up. Now look here [opens box containing his war medals]. This is the silver star. It was presented to me by General Patton. This is a bronze star. I earned two of them. And this is the purple heart; Harry Truman pinned that on me himself. Now I know you think I'm a foolish old man, and sometimes I am, but that's my grandson in there. I got all these because I was a good soldier, I still am. I can get him out, I can do it. So you all had better listen to this old fool, because that's our little boy.

Jessica: All right, Daddy. We're listening.

Chester: Go ahead, sir, tell us your plan.

Major: What plan?

3 MONTHS
How long Alice and Jodie have lived together

Chester [blacked up, as is Donohue]: I don't believe this. I don't believe that I've allowed myself to do this.

Benson: Donohue, will you stop complaining.

Chester: Benson, I am not Donohue.

Benson: You're not?

Chester [gesturing to Donohue]: No Benson.

Benson: It's amazing. You all look alike.

Jessica: Oh Benson. [Sees the men blacked up.] Oh I am so sorry. I didn't know you were entertaining.

Chester: Jessica, Jessica it's me.

Jessica: Chester, you are not a Negro.

Chester: I know that dear. We're rescuing Billy.

Donohue: And then we're all going downtown to pick up some white women.

John Byner On What Passes for Comedy Today

"It's kind of frightening to turn on TV and see people I don't know. Award shows: People are walking out and I've never seen them before. I watch the news a lot and Discovery and things like that. I guess I'm just spoiled. The jokes are now obvious and there's a lot of toilet humor, and it's just not the way it used to be. It's not clever like it used to be. People talk about *30 Rock*, that's probably the most popular one I hear about on the golf course. I feel like I'm in a foreign country when I see the awards shows. I have to ask my wife: What does *she* do. She sings. Oh, OK. *Everybody* sings."

3.2 First aired: Sept 20, 1979 • Written by Susan Harris + Stu Silver • Directed by Jay Sandrich

Alien Burt and Mary are going at it like rabbits, Billy's being brainwashed by the Sunnies, and Mrs. David makes Jodie choose between baby Wendy and Alice. Meanwhile, Burt meets another abductee who reveals that he may well be stuck on the spaceship forever, and Eunice finally convinces Dutch to turn state's evidence. The only good news seems to come from the Sunnies offices, where Benson and the rest of the "Step Brothers" appear on the verge of rescuing Billy, until...

Cast. Jimmy Baio (Billy), John Byner (Det. Donohue), Billy Crystal (Jodie), Cathryn Damon (Mary), Robert Guillaume (Benson), Randee Heller (Alice), Katherine Helmond (Jessica), Jay Johnson (Chuck & Bob), Robert Mandan (Chester), Richard Mulligan (Burt), Arthur Peterson (The Major), Donnelly Rhodes (Dutch), Jennifer Salt (Eunice), Rod Roddy (Announcer), Robert Englund (Simon), Peggy Pope (Mrs. David), Jack Gilford (Saul), Scott Mulhern (Roger)

Highlights. Bob repulsed by the way Alien Burt and Mary go at it in the kitchen; Billy's last act of defiance after his torturers leave; Burt's meeting with Saul; and the entire Step Brothers routine.

Confused? You Won't Be. *'Welcome home, Burt.'*

▶ Continuing the pattern set by the first couple of episodes of Season 2, this episode in particular lunges for the "naughty" bar with references to Alien Burt and Mary's constant lovemaking, the former's lusting over Jessica the moment he meets her, and his bonding with Bob over their attraction to Mrs. Tate.

▶ *Soap* takes a new approach to the issue of homosexuality this episode. For two seasons we've been shown that gay people have feelings; this time, we get to see it all from Mrs. David's point of view. She freely admits to Jodie that she realizes her dislike of the lesbian Alice makes no sense, but she also makes him understand that her beliefs are deeply ingrained, and won't be swayed by logic. Not since Burt tried to explain his problem with gays to Jodie (see "From now on, I'll try to look at ya as a person" under 1.3) have we been presented with the other side of the issue. Considering the tightrope *Soap* walked between conservatives on one side and the gay lobby on the other, this is a brave choice, and ultimately a powerful one. Even the most liberal among us must admit that Mrs. David's ideals are as important to her as ours are to us.

▶ Though Robert Englund will realize lasting fame as horror movie icon Freddy Krueger in the *Nightmare on Elm Street* movies starting in 1984, he had already gotten his foot on the ladder of terror by the time he appeared on *Soap*. Just a couple of weeks after *Soap* premiered, he had a bit part in *Eaten Alive*, Tobe Hooper's follow-up to the now legendary 1974 classic *The Texas Chain Saw Massacre*.

4,000 years. How long Saul has been aboard the spaceship.

64. How old he was when he was taken.

Bentley, Bronson, Birnbaum. What The Major calls Benson.

'We're the Step Brothers…'

Gay characters, lusty aliens, possessed babies—*Soap* never backed away from a challenge. Yet no scene had the potential to go as flat-out badly as the "Step Brothers" routine.

The real Step Brothers (above) toured with the likes of Duke Ellington, and appeared on several variety shows right through to the 1960s…

Though at its heart a piece of slapstick, beginning as it does with Benson, The Major, Chester and Donohue fighting over which columns to hide behind in the Sunnies building, the scene is actually an extension of one from last episode. In 3.1, Harris and Silver have gotten most of "the guys have blacked up" humor out of the way, capped by John Byner's brilliantly downplayed "we're all going downtown to pick up some white women." This episode, it's all about the rescue.

When Roger the Sunnie demands to know what the men are doing there, Benson tells him they're the Step Brothers ready for an audition. What follows is a spirited recreation of the phenomenon made famous by the "Four Step Brothers": Maceo Anderson, Red Walker, Al Williams and Sherman Robertson, who toured with the likes of Duke Ellington, and appeared on several variety shows right through to the 1960s. Naturally, getting laughs by pretending three white guys are black in 1979 is a tough gig; one has to ask if such a thing could've been pulled off if the lone black man involved had been anyone but the widely respected Robert Guillaume.

"None of us used any kind of Southern voice or any of that stuff," John Byner points out. "It was guys in trouble trying to find a way out."

...while *these* Step Brothers barely managed to rescue Billy from the Sunnies compound.

Indeed, one of the main reasons the scene misses the offensive mark is because the white characters have already been portrayed as barking mad (The Major), bumbling (Donohue) and a vain heel (Chester).

Remembers Marsha Posner, "The first time we saw the runthrough of that scene, I have never seen people laugh so hard as when those four started dancing. Not in front of the audience, this is just the first runthrough for the producers. The laughter was absolutely nonstop!"

"It made me laugh so hard," director Jay Sandrich recalls. "I kept saying let's rehearse this, and they said we don't need to rehearse it. I said I know, but once we do the show I'll never see this scene again! We just had a lot of fun."

Best Lines.
Bob [about Mary and Alien Burt's night-long escapades]: I need this. I don't have enough strain with that paternity suit, I need to stay up all night.

Alien Burt [about Jessica]: It's a wonder she doesn't tip over.
Bob: She can fall on me anytime.

Mrs. David [about Alice]: Look, I know what you're thinking. If I can accept you I can accept her. I mean I know it's silly, what's another homo more or less? But Jodie I just can't help it. One homo, fine. But two homos, that's just one homo too many.

Jodie: Mrs. David, excuse me, but this is my home and Alice is my friend. Now I am very grateful to you for bringing Wendy to see me, but seeing as how Carol abandoned her, she is now my legal responsibility.

Mrs. David: Jodie if you insist on having Alice stay here, I'm going to have to take the baby back to Texas with me.

Jodie: I'll take you to court.

Mrs. David: You'll lose.

Jodie: No I won't.

Mrs. David: Two homosexuals bringing up a little baby, you won't stand a chance in court. Oh Jodie, I'm sorry, I don't want to hurt you. I don't want to keep you from your daughter. But I'm her grandmother and I can't help the way I feel.

Jodie: You're asking me to choose between my best friend and my child.

Mrs. David: If you love your child the choice is easy.

Mrs. David and Alice, AKA the 'one homo too many.'

Roger: Hey you!

All: Who?

Roger: What do you think you're doing? Who are you?

Benson: Who are we? The Step Brothers. Where's the audition?

Roger: Audition? Here?

Benson: The audition's here? OK, let's hit it fellahs. [Benson and the rest dance and clap, until Benson belts Roger, knocking him out cold.]

The Major: Good work, Bronson!

Benson [off stage]: Benson!!!

Rod Roddy's Wrapup. Will Dutch and Eunice find happiness? Will Mary ever realize that the Burt she is living with is a fake? If she does, will she keep him anyway? Is Saul right and Burt is really trapped on the spaceship forever? If so, will they do his laundry? Who will Jodie choose: his baby or Alice? What's going to happen to the Step Brothers now that they're caught? Will they be able to dance their way out of this one? These questions and many others will be answered in the next episode of *Soap*.

3.3 First aired: Sept 27, 1979 • Written by Susan Harris + Stu Silver • Directed by Jay Sandrich

Billy may have been rescued from the Sunnies, but all is hardly sweetness and light. Burt and Saul have managed to beam themselves off the spaceship, but heaven knows where they've ended up. Mary is questioning her sanity because she's convinced Burt (well, Alien Burt) isn't really Burt at all. Alice is moving out of Jodie's apartment so he can get custody of baby Wendy. Add to that the departure of Benson as he embarks on his new career as an employee of the governor, and you have what amounts to one bummer of an episode.

Cast. Jimmy Baio (Billy), John Byner (Det. Donohue), Diana Canova (Corinne), Billy Crystal (Jodie), Cathryn Damon (Mary), Robert Guillaume (Benson), Randee Heller (Alice), Katherine Helmond (Jessica), Jay Johnson (Chuck & Bob), Robert Mandan (Chester), Richard Mulligan (Burt), Arthur Peterson (The Major), Jennifer Salt (Eunice), Rod Roddy (Announcer), Jack Gilford (Saul), Robert Englund (Simon)

Highlights. Burt being turned upside down on the alien gurney (even more so when you know the story behind it; see "Behind the Scenes on the Spaceship" under this entry), and Saul's impassioned plea to the aliens to let Burt go; Chuck & Bob arm wrestling; Alien Burt continuing to come on to Jessica; Saul's attempts to beam Burt back home; and the tearful goodbye between Benson and Jessica.

Confused? You Won't Be. *'It's time to go.'*
▶ Jessica actually uses Donohue's given name, George, when she thanks him for helping to rescue Billy from the Sunnies.

▶ For the first time since Danny disappeared, somebody (Jessica) finally admits that this is cause for concern.

▶ The departure of Alice quickly brings to an end the uncomfortable idea that a gay man and a lesbian should, you know, date. Still, it seems a shame to say goodbye to such a sweet, sunny character as Alice. She credits Jodie's friendship with giving her the courage to live. If nothing else, she leaves the apartment with two suitcases, subtly underscoring her earlier joke that when she picks up her pair of extra shoes, she's all packed.

▶ The news that Benson is leaving the Tate home to go work for the governor is sprung on us here, coming out of nowhere. This is even more unusual when you consider that his new show actually premiered two weeks ago. Though we know that the governor is related to Jessica, the way she explains it here doesn't make that entirely clear.

Bernstein. What The Major calls Benson.

Denver omelette. What Burt had for breakfast on the ship.

3,783 years ago. When Saul's wife died. (He should be over it by now.)

How many months old Wendy is

Chugach National Forest. The Alaskan destination Alice has always wanted to visit.

Augusta. An aunt of Jessica and Mary's who used to have nervous breakdowns all the time.

Donohue's joke, which distracts Simon long enough for Billy to break a chair over him. "Guy walks in the doctor's office, says to the doc, Doc, I don't feel so good. The doc says well what ya got to do is exercise. What ya got to do is 5 miles a day, jog, call me back in two weeks. So the guy jogs 5 miles a day, calls the doctor back in two weeks and says Doc, I'm in Chicago, what do I do now?"

For the *Soap* Bible Tells Us So. No sooner has Billy been freed from the Sunnies than The Major completes the drafting of his maps. The psychological shock he suffers as a result finally wakens him from his World War II delusions…and deposits him in the delusion that he is, in fact, Alexander the Great. "This turn of events causes great problems for Benson, who now must learn to iron togas." Also, the bible would have us understand that the Gatlings made their fortune with the famous Gatling gun, and not in haberdashery as Jessica explains in this episode. It's possible that "the killing" her great great great grandfather made is an in-joke about what was originally intended.

Behind the Scenes on the Spaceship

As one would expect with a sitcom performed twice in front of a live audience, pulling off Burt's close encounter with the aliens aboard their ship was a tremendous feat back in 1979. But the skilled crew managed to pull it all off by getting the most out of what they already had.

This began with recruiting Det. Donohue himself, John Byner, to speak for the lead alien. "That was like the last couple of days of the show," he remembers. "I did all the voices for that in a little studio."

Next, several little people were recruited to play the aliens themselves. "Of course they built everything for them including their heads, which were these giant foam-like things," says stage manager Carl Lauten. "I don't know if anybody told you about this, when the aliens were trying to get in the door, but it's the funniest thing that I've ever seen happen. Well, it's the funniest blooper I've ever seen; if you were there it was hysterical.

"There were two grips that were in charge of doing two different things, which is fine as long as they don't get the cues confused. Richard Mulligan led a pretty party kind of life; needless to say he would not like to be upside down; and the scene called for him to start upside down, and then the gurney that rotated would take him all the way around and he would be straight up. But I wasn't going to put him into that position until the last minute. Behind him a door would open and space men would walk out and then I would bring him up so he was facing the audience in an upright position; then I would cue the door to go down again.

"So we got ready to do the scene. I cue Richard upside down, I cue the door to open to bring the space people in. About two of them come in. After the second one, I give another cue for Richard to go right side up again to start the scene, and then I would cue the door

The biggest gag took place behind Burt...

to drop behind the aliens. So I cued Richard to go down, I cued the door to go up, and then the guy told me to cue the table to go back up with Richard on it to make him upright, but he dropped the door...on the last alien. He didn't get hurt, but his helmet got stuck in the door. Here's this 3-foot guy trying to get out from under this door, and the audience is going crazy, and Richard can't see behind him what's going on, so he's doing these straight lines with Jack Gilford. Jay Sandrich is in the booth crying, he's laughing so hard, and I'm trying to get the guy to get the door up to get the alien out. Of course after it was over Richard was like I'm not going upside down again."

Best Lines.

Benson: Um, you know, I didn't take that job at the governor's mansion because I'm unhappy here.

Jessica: Oh Benson, I know that. I mean my goodness, running the governor's mansion is a wonderful opportunity for you, and they need you. I mean this side of the family has a minor snafu once in a while, but *they* have problems.

Benson: I'm glad you understand.

Jessica: That always was the screwy side of the family, the Gatlings. Very screwy and very rich. You know my great-great-great grandfather? He made a killing in haberdashery. He invented those tall hats that the pilgrims wore. [Begins to cry.]

Rod Roddy's Wrapup. Were Burt and Saul able to beam themselves home? If not, did they at least beam themselves to a warm climate? Now that Alice has gone, will Mrs. David leave the baby with Jodie? How long will Donohue live with the Tates? Will he pay rent? Will The Major's rescue team ever be called back to action? If not, will they at least be called to entertain at a bar mitzvah? Will Mary ever find the Burt she thinks isn't Burt really isn't Burt? These questions and many others will be answered on the next episode of *Soap*.

3.4
First aired: Oct 4, 1979 • Written by Susan Harris + Stu Silver • Directed by Jay Sandrich

Burt and Saul beam from crisis to crisis through space and time, while closer to home Chester puts his foot down and Jessica convinces Donohue to leave once and for all. Unfortunately, Chester quickly falls back into his cheating ways, and son Billy seems to be starting down the road of ladies man, too, with his teacher Mrs. Walker. And at last, Danny is free from Mel's clutches, but his rescuer is already talking about getting married. Dames!

Cast. Katherine Helmond (Jessica), Cathryn Damon (Mary), Robert Mandan (Chester), Richard Mulligan (Burt), Diana Canova (Corinne), Jennifer Salt (Eunice), Jimmy Baio (Billy), Ted Wass (Danny), Rod Roddy (Announcer), Candice Azzara (Millie), John Byner (Det. Donohue), Frank Coppola (Mel), Hector Elias (Federale), Jack Gilford (Saul), Marla Pennington (Leslie Walker), Mark Rhudy (Cell keeper)

Highlights. Donohue trying to get out of leaving the Tate home one last time by "fainting" again, and Jessica warmly but firmly calling him on it; the whole "Millie," "Mel," "Dannie," "Millie" scene in the barn; Chester fighting the urge to cheat on the phone with Joyce, and failing miserably; Billy cheering up his teacher Mrs. Walker, and his "Call me Bill" shortly before they kiss.

Confused? You Won't Be. *'It is always perfect in the movies, though.'*

▶ It's hard not to think that the turmoil behind the scenes—original director Jay Sandrich is about to hit the road—is negatively influencing what's on screen. The cliffhanger over Danny's fate, like the rescue of Billy, is resolved far too quickly and neatly for a show that can take as many episodes as necessary to tell its stories. Saul and Burt zipping through Rome 107 AD and Mexico in 1850, while allowing us a bit more time with the delightful Jack Gilford, seems only to be putting off Burt's inevitable return home. The only up side is the way their brush with the Mexican firing squad teases the similar circumstances that will see Jessica out of the series (4.21).

▶ It's good to have Chester the rat back after all this time, even if it is poor Jessica that has to suffer the consequences. The fact that he starts cheating the same day he insists that Jessica get rid of Donohue is a particularly nasty detail that's extremely effective.

▶ Strangely, it seems that the producers wanted to recreate the "coffee cake sex talk" between the Tate women and Mary (2.7), but couldn't pull it off, mostly because this time the characters really had nothing to say. This actually is a symptom of a much larger problem with Season 3: *Soap* is beginning to live up to its own negative publicity. This is hardly surprising since the show has been so abused in print, yanked off the air in some markets and programmed ridiculously late in others—one gets the feeling that the prevailing attitude is becoming "If you're gonna have to do the time, do the crime." Unfortunately, all of this talk about how loud Chester is in bed, and how Corinne should get Tim's engine revving, does the characters a grave disservice. Is it any coincidence that most of this began with the departure of Benson, the most civilized of the bunch? Indeed, the only shred of humanity to be had in this episode comes from Mrs. Walker. Though she ends her very first scene locking lips with her student, Billy, she expresses genuine grief over the way her divorced status and profession have virtually locked her out of ever having a social life. "Try having a kid on top of it," we can almost hear Susan Harris cry from offstage.

And introducing...Leslie Walker.

Cleveland. Where Mrs. Walker's ex-husband lives.

continued on page **266**

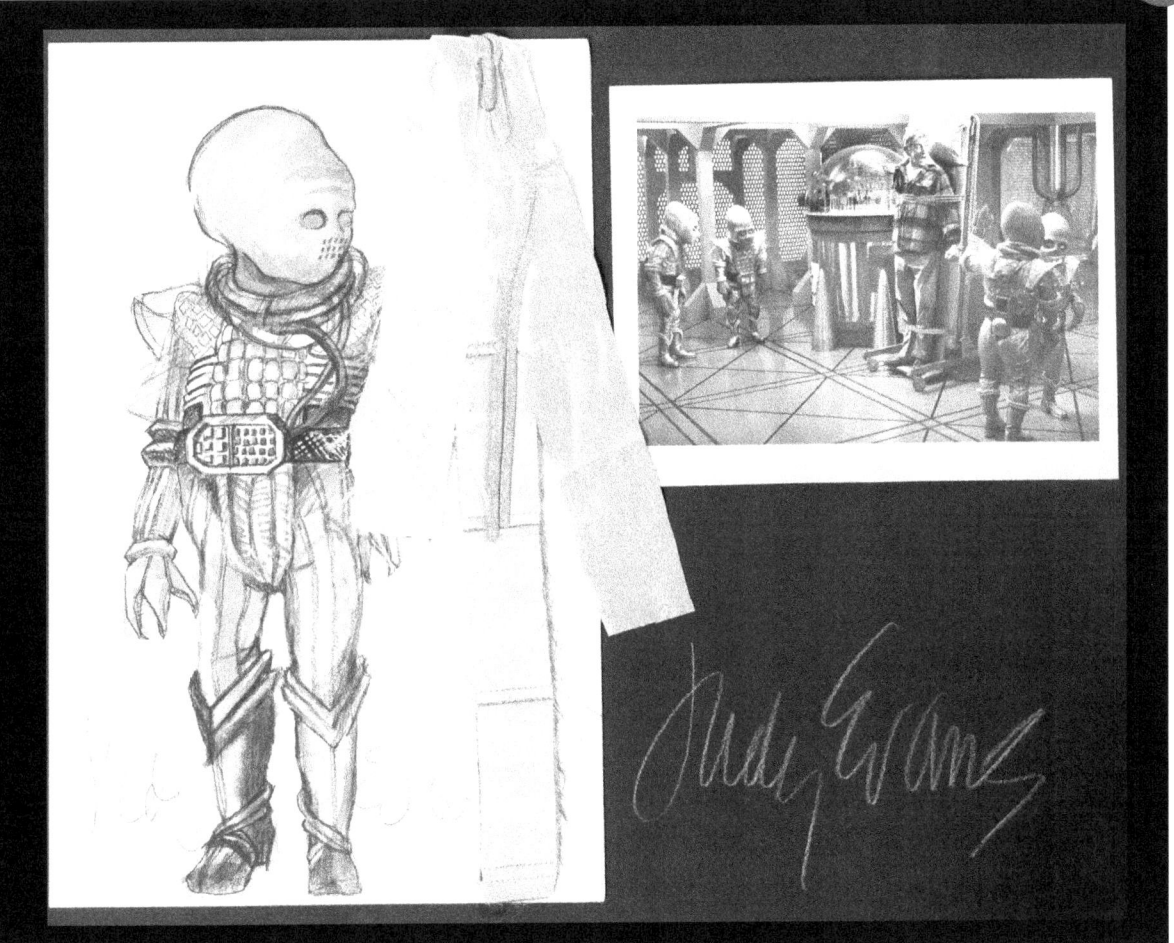

All in the (*Soap*) Family

Creating the aliens that give Burt such a hard time this season were makeup artist Ray Steele and costume designer Judy Evans. Though the pair briefly knew each other back at NBC, they worked together closely on *Soap*, and ultimately married.

Steele designed the alien heads and Evans "did the costumes with the lighted rings and blinking belts. We had the belts made so they would blink on and off and they were all on battery packs." Check out Evans' finished design for the aliens, as well as a swatch from one of their spacesuits, above.

continued from page 264

1 in 500. The likelihood of a common guppy reaching maturity, according to Billy.

Marla Pennington: From *Soap* fan to *Soap* Star

Of all the morally questionable characters to grace the *Soap* stage, that of Leslie Walker may be the one who sailed closest to the wind.

Society takes a dim view of those who would corrupt the perceived innocence of minors. The relationship that sprang up between Billy and his teacher was probably only saved from public excoriation by the gender of the teacher and the fact that the "child" in question looked like he could be her peer. Of course after more than two years of protesting every little detail about *Soap*, the squeaky wheels of society had squandered whatever political capital they might have held by the time Mrs. Walker appeared.

Like many of the guest stars who joined the series in its later years, Marla Pennington (now Marla Pennington Rowan) was a regular *Soap* viewer before she ever became involved with the production.

"I was a fan of the show and a fan of their acting," she admits. "I thought everything was very fresh. You just had to make yourself back down and do the work, and after a while you forget all about that." The character of Leslie Walker, Pennington says, was very easy to portray sympathetically.

"I think, especially at the beginning, it was just me being very vulnerable and letting that side show through so you could see how this woman of principles who'd been married before, how she could fall for this young kid who gave her her youth back and some hope. It was just keeping that vulnerable and innocent and real and we could play off of it, with comic timing and everything else that went with it."

Best Lines.
Chester [on the phone to Brockhurst Investments]: Joyce? Wuh- hi! Yeah it has been a while. Well, you know, this and that. Well, I'm

afraid I don't do *that* anymore. Excuse me? Yeah, maybe sometime, lunch sounds fine. Is Mr. Brockhurst—what? Well I admit that the offer is certainly tempting but I couldn't possibly—what? You're kidding. I didn't know they made them in leather. No, no Joyce, I really must decline. I'm a new man now, Joyce. I'm a one-girl guy. What's past is past. That's all behind me—what? You're joking. Well, what do you do with it? Oh yeah, I'll bet. Yeah well I'd really love to but I can't—what? Aw well sure, a drink sometime, absolutely. There's no harm in a little drinky-poo for old time's sake. Of course. Yeah, me too. Listen, Joyce, there's no reason to apologize. I understand completely. Sure. Yes, same here. Take care of yourself. I'll see ya in half an hour. [Starts slathering on the aftershave. Jessica enters.]

Jessica: Hello dear. Uh Chester. What are you doing?

Chester: Gotta go, Jess.

Jessica: Where?

Chester: Brockhurst Investments. They may have an opening for me.

Jessica: Oh Chester, that's wonderful. Just wonderful. What position?

Chester: I'll uh, know when I get there.

Jessica: You must be very excited.

Chester: As a matter of fact, I am.

Jessica: Chester, you could go all the way with that company.

Chester: Knock on wood. Bye dear.

Jessica: Chester. Good luck.

Leslie [explaining men's attitudes to divorced women]: Well they all think that just because you're divorced, you're an easy target.

Billy: So what do you do?

Leslie: Go home. Read. Feed the fish. Read some more. Feed the fish some more. My eyes are very weak and my fish look like Oldsmobiles.

Rod Roddy's Wrapup. Now that Det. Donohue has left, will Jessica be happy with her choice of Chester? Now that Chester is playing around again, will Chester be happy with her choice of Chester? Now that Millie has saved him from Mel, who will save

1979

OCT. 5: Blake Edwards' movie *10* starring Bo Derek and Dudley Moore premieres, launching the former to superstardom. In 3.17, Chester will refer to his fling of the moment, Gloria, as his "10"... moments before she dumps him.

Danny from Millie? What has happened to Saul and Burt in Mexico? Did they get away? Did they die? Did they have time to take in a bullfight? Will there be extracurricular activity between Billy and his teacher? These questions and many others will be answered in the next episode of *Soap*.

3.5
First aired: Oct 11, 1979 • Written by Susan Harris + Stu Silver • Directed by Jay Sandrich

It's all about starting a new life this week as a newly freed Dutch, and Millie, the former girlfriend of Elaine's kidnapper, try to fit into the Tate and Campbell families, respectively. Jodie finds himself alone with baby Wendy for the first time, and realizes it's time for him to step up as a parent. After debating whether to pursue a relationship with Billy, Mrs. Walker finally allows herself to be won over by his words. And Burt returns home…only to run into Alien Burt.

Cast Katherine Helmond (Jessica), Cathryn Damon (Mary), Robert Mandan (Chester), Richard Mulligan (Burt), Diana Canova (Corinne), Jennifer Salt (Eunice), Jimmy Baio (Billy), Arthur Peterson (The Major), Billy Crystal (Jodie), Ted Wass (Danny), Jay Johnson (Chuck & Bob), Rod Roddy (Announcer), Candice Azzara (Millie), Jack Gilford (Saul), Marla Pennington (Leslie Walker), Peggy Pope (Mrs. David), Donnelly Rhodes (Dutch), Jenna Kay Starr (Wendy)

Highlights Dutch trying to adjust to life with the Tates and away from prison; Alien Burt mistaking Millie for Jodie; the freakout meeting between Burt and Alien Burt; and Mrs. Walker trying to smarten up Billy if they're going to date.

Confused? You Won't Be. *'Home is where you tie your goat.'*
▶ Like a cross between Godot and an employee everybody knows is about to be laid off, Tim Flotsky continues to be briefly mentioned but never appears. (This time he's still in his room at the Tate house, praying.)

▶ True to form, Susan Harris interrupts Chester's bullying and buffoonery with a heartfelt appeal from Dutch to the family that he is doing his best to fit in.

▶ Bob's offhand paternity quip (2.2) reemerges as he breaks up with his girlfriend over the phone.

▶ Another rough-around-the-edges episode with none of the clever dialogue we've come to expect from *Soap*. Considering the fact that Susan Harris and Stu Silver have also written an episode of *Benson* that will appear early the following month, it's not hard to see what might've happened here.

A Timex. What Burt gives Saul as a keepsake. (Saul gives him a knob from the beaming room control panel.)

Lillian. What Billy thought Mrs. Walker's name was.

Susan Harris and Mortality

On the same day this episode aired, *Soap*'s creator was the focus of a five-page interview in *TV Guide* insightfully headlined "Susan Harris is Running as Fast as She Can." In it, writer Robert Ward initially has some fun recording how the then-37-year-old checked with Paul Junger Witt to see if she should've told him that she was toying with the idea of having a child with some willing partner because her 14-hour work days left her little time to meet a man properly.

(Harris frankly tells Ward that she's not a tactful person, which has cost her to some extent in the press; hence her checking with Witt. Three years later Harris and Witt would marry.) However reluctant she is to discuss her urge to have a second child here, it's telling that this episode Jodie finds himself alone with his daughter for the first time—a daughter who was conceived in a way not far removed from what Harris has suggested.

However, the piece quickly gives us a stunning insight into what drives *Soap*'s creator. She mentions seeing her father die of a rare neurological disease a few years before (possibly the inspiration for Jessica's brush with death at the end of this season), and admits to having "read all the books on death," citing Elisabeth Kubler-Ross' work and Ernest Becker's *Denial of Death* by name. Harris is keenly aware of her own mortality at this time, almost distractingly so, and sheds some light on the desperate sorrow lurking just beneath the laughs in *Soap*, especially now.

OCT. 14: First National March on Washington for Lesbian and Gay Rights is held, drawing between 75,000 and 125,000 gays, lesbians, bisexuals and transgendered people, urging lawmakers to pass civil rights protections for the LGBT community.

Burt's forthcoming health scare and subsequent quest to find a way to live on, even if only in the *Guinness Book of World Records*, is a prime example, and Dr. Saxon's warning to Burt that credit card companies may cancel his accounts once they figure out he has something terminal has the faintest hint of a detail gleaned from experience or research (3.16).

The result of this contemplation of annihilation is also covered in the *TV Guide* piece: Harris keeps active—extremely active. She plays racquetball three times a week; she runs 5-7 miles every morning starting at 5:30; she endures Nautilus training, skis and scuba dives. While Ward concludes from this that her inability to meet men "seems partially self-imposed," he refrains from drawing a more obvious, and in the end more meaningful, conclusion. If Susan Harris is "running as fast as she can," she is running from the grim reaper that dogs both Burt and Jessica this season, and by series end will have claimed others, too. Jodie's forthcoming court battle and globetrotting adventures to reclaim his daughter suggest that the main reason Harris wants to have another child is not simply to give son Sam a playmate, but to hedge her bets for the legacy she will ultimately leave behind.

A refreshingly frank interview with Susan Harris appeared in *TV Guide* the same day this episode aired.

Though *Soap* had garnered a great deal of publicity by this time, Harris had yet to slam it out of the park with a television hit that promised any form of longevity—*The Golden Girls* was five years away from its premiere. Having lived through the premature decimation of *Fay* five years before, she had learned from bitter experience that Hollywood only bestowed immortality on some by erasing the dreams and legacies of others.

Best Lines.
Bob: I should've married her.
Chuck: Bob, look. You did the right thing. I mean there's no way to tell if that baby's yours or not.

Bob: I don't know, I don't know. I guess I'll always wonder if it looks like me, you know. The hair. The eyes. The grain.

Mrs. David: I tried so hard to be the best mama there ever was. And what happened? My child goes and runs off with a cowboy—a fake cowboy. What do ya call a male bimbo?
Jodie: Cowboy's close.

Mrs. Walker [Gives Billy a book]: Here.
Billy: What's this?
Mrs. Walker: *Wars of the Roses*. If we're going to be seeing each other, you're gonna have to do your homework. I don't go out with dummies. OK?

Rod Roddy's Wrapup. Now that Millie's met the Campbells, will she decide a life of crime is quieter? Now that Real Burt and Alien Burt have met, will they decide it might be nice to dress alike? What will happen between Billy and his teacher, and will he get marks for it? These questions and many others will be answered in the next episode of *Soap*.

3.6 First aired: Nov 1, 1979 • Written by Susan Harris + Stu Silver • Directed by Jay Sandrich

It's fall and nymphomania is in the air. Millie tells Danny that (Alien) Burt's a nymphomaniac, Jessica suspects Chester is back to his philandering ways, and Billy and Leslie are having a secret rendezvous at the Hideaway Cafe. (Billy spots Eunice there with another man shortly after she told Corinne that she's sick to death of Dutch.) When Corinne tries to get Tim to come to bed, he practically accuses her of being a nympho too, the prelude to a much graver conversation. The only person "getting less" than Corinne is Burt, who tries to lure Mary to the drugstore to explain she's been living with his alien double, all to no avail.

Cast. Candice Azzara (Millie), Jimmy Baio (Billy), Diana Canova (Corinne), Cathryn Damon (Mary), Katherine Helmond (Jessica), Jay

1979

OCT. 14: The Iran Hostage Crisis begins with the storming of the U.S. Embassy in Tehran; 90 hostages are taken.

Candace Azzara (Millie)

Johnson (Chuck & Bob), Robert Mandan (Chester), Richard Mulligan (Burt), Marla Pennington (Leslie Walker), Jennifer Salt (Eunice), Sal Viscuso (Tim), Ted Wass (Danny), Rod Roddy (Announcer), Martin Ferrero (Waiter)

Highlights. Burt's impromptu ketchup squirt in the drugstore; Millie's asides about Burt's lascivious nature; Chester's return to telling whoppers to cover for his philandering; Eunice blurting out "boogers" at the restaurant, and she and Corinne collapsing into laughter; Chester and his date showing up at the Hideaway Cafe where Billy and Leslie are (and Chester quickly hustling her out of there when he spots Billy); and the whole funny-but-tragic give and take between Tim and Corinne in what will be Sal Viscuso's last scene on the series.

Confused? You Won't Be. *'Nympho? Is that one of the Marx Brothers?'*

▶ Watch the scene where Billy dips Leslie closely and you'll see not everything went according to plan. "He dipped me and my head hit the table and got a big laugh, but I was seeing stars," says Marla Pennington. "It hit hard! We continued with the scene, finished it, and everyone's going 'Are you OK?' And I'm going, 'Yeah, yeah, yeah, oookay.' Of course they used that take." For the rest of her scene, you can see the pain in her face.

▶ Eunice and Corinne are becoming Jessica and Mary, an idea that surely would've been explored further had the series continued.

▶ Eunice (like Jessica used to) refuses to acknowledge that Chester is in the restaurant with another woman, even though Corinne is convinced.

Reasons Jessica thinks Chester is having an affair:
1) He's been nice and caring and cheerful. 2) He's gone back to the gym. 3) He didn't come home last night. 4) When he did come home, he was reeking of perfume. (It was from his meeting with Ralph Hirshberg. Hirshberg's gay.)

Billy Sinatra. How Billy identifies himself to the waiter who's just carded him.

Goodbye, Sal Viscuso.
See you, Jay Sandrich.

Eternally grateful for the start in acting that *Soap* gave him, Sal Viscuso nevertheless wonders why Tim Flotsky was written out of the show when he was.

Whatever back room discussions were going on at the time, it seems pretty obvious that after the marriage of Tim and Corinne, the producers simply hit a brick wall with what was the one character that had garnered *Soap* the most negative publicity. Though there's the temptation to suggest they simply let him fade away to ease the pressure ABC was feeling from activists, it appears more likely that Harris, Witt and Thomas simply hadn't thought through what they could do with an ex-priest. Once he'd hung up the collar, the character was just one more in a series already glutted with them. Even the *Soap* bible, which dreamed big for every character in the series, dropped Tim's story line the moment he left Corinne to rethink his life, not realizing she is pregnant.

Yet Sal Viscuso wasn't the only one to leave *Soap* this episode. "Jay Sandrich directed every episode of mine, and as luck would have it, my last episode; that was his last episode," Viscuso recalls. "So they brought two separate cakes [to the going away party]. He's a genius. Obviously it's been a while, but it's the show that put me on the map, the show that gave me my foothold in the business, and thank God, it was a great show with great people. I'm so glad I'm known for *Soap* and *M*A*S*H*, *Barney Miller*—those are the shows people remember me for."

Best Lines.

Millie [after Bob backs up something Alien Burt says]: That's good, the dummy verifies the sex maniac's story.

Corinne [to Tim, who's reading the *Bible* aloud]: Tim.

Tim: Corinne, please.

Corinne: Look, I don't mind a little begatting but how about begatting around with me a little bit? I mean come on already, let's begin the begats!

> During the first show [Richard Mulligan] did the take as normal. Between the first and the second show, I saw him go to the camera guy and say, 'Stay on me at the end,' and I didn't know what he was doing. I saw him messing around with some ketchup and mustard bottles. And at the last take of that scene, he got up and squeezed the ketchup bottle as hard as he could and it went up in the air and over him and all over the place. They caught it because he told the camera guy to stay there. He was just so professional, but he could be spontaneous."
>
> —MARLA PENNINGTON (Leslie Walker)

35 The number of miles from the nearest town the bar is where Leslie takes Billy

❝ There were times when I'd write something and Paul or Tony would say 'that's a 1% joke', meaning that only 1% of people were going to understand it. And there would be a fight about how you can have an intellectual joke and who cares if only 1% of the audience understands it. I'd win some of those and lose some of those because we were a show that had a particular appeal, and you wanted as broad an audience as possible."
—SUSAN HARRIS

Tim: My religion is very important to me.

Corinne: You're using your religion as an excuse to avoid me and I find that detestable.

Tim: I can't help it if I'm the way I am. I have certain needs.

Corinne: And I don't?

Tim: Look at you. It looks like you're wearing a spider's web.

Corinne: Oh, so I'm cheap, is that it? I'm an over-sexed tart, right?

Tim: There doesn't seem to be anything else on your mind these days.

Corinne: Are you calling me a nympho?

Tim: No, I didn't say that!

Corinne: Well that's OK, go ahead say it. Say it, Father Flotsky. [With an Irish lilt] Corinne me dahlin', you're a cute lass but yer a nympho.

Tim: You wanted me, Corinne, and I was a priest. I wanted you, but I was a priest. So I left the church. And now I'm leaving you. I loved the church, Corinne, and I still do. And I love you just as much, but I can't have you.

Corinne: You can have me. I'm still here for you.

Tim: I can't Corinne. As much as I want to, I can't. As much as I love you, my past won't let me. I tried but I can't undo all those years.

Corinne: But I love you.

Tim: And I love you, too much to stay.

Rod Roddy's Wrapup. Will Millie and Danny ever have a meaningful relationship? What could it possibly be based on? What will Corinne do now that Tim has left her? Will it be more fun? What will happen with Billy and his teacher? Will he be tested on it? Now that the real Burt called Mary and the Alien Burt told her he didn't, what will Mary do if the real Burt calls her again? What will Corinne and Eunice do now that they've seen Chester in a restaurant with another woman? Will they tell Jessica? Will they finish lunch first? These questions and many others will be answered in the next episode of *Soap*.

3.7
First aired: Nov 8, 1979 • Written by Susan Harris + Stu Silver • Directed by JD Lobue

The Tate and Campbell families seem to have revolving doors this episode as Dutch is welcomed into the Tate family while Millie decides she'd rather be a manicurist than marry Danny. Meanwhile, Alien Burt refuses to leave the Campbell home, forcing the aliens to kidnap Real Burt once more. Corinne and Jodie come up with a mutually beneficial arrangement to look after both their babies, and Real Burt is given one last chance to convince his doppelgänger to give up the joys he has found on Earth.

Cast Candice Azzara (Millie), Jimmy Baio (Billy), Diana Canova (Corinne), Billy Crystal (Jodie), Cathryn Damon (Mary), Katherine Helmond (Jessica), Jay Johnson (Chuck & Bob), Robert Mandan (Chester), Richard Mulligan (Burt), Marla Pennington (Leslie Walker), Arthur Peterson (The Major), Donnelly Rhodes (Dutch), Jennifer Salt (Eunice), Ted Wass (Danny), Rod Roddy (Announcer), Jack Gilford (Saul), Kenneth Gilman (Charlie Walker)

Highlights. The Major hurling a pineapple through the window thinking it's a grenade, followed by a tremendous explosion (the gas main down the street blew up); Billy giving Leslie Walker's ex, Charlie, the bum's rush; Burt's "and remember now, if you see me along the way, don't you talk to me" to Mary on the phone; Corinne and Jodie's brief talk in the park; and Burt being beamed up to the spaceship at the precise moment he's explaining the procedure to Mary in the drugstore.

Confused? You Won't Be. *'Do you think our family's crazy?'*
▶ After two years of juggling multiple story lines, the producers are clearly feeling the strain. The welcome-to-the-family party for Dutch feels like a last ditch effort to remind us that Dutch is still a regular, while Billy's affair with his teacher finally makes Jimmy Baio's character interesting after long neglect.

▶ During their conversation about space aliens, Mary suggests that Burt go see Dr. Medlow again (last seen in 1.19), and for one brief moment believes that Burt has actually succeeded in making himself invisible. This is another fantastic payoff for long-time fans of the

1979

NOV. 12: President Carter imposes a halt to the importation of oil from Iran in response to the Iranian hostage crisis. Hello gas lines...

series, as the invisibility gag began in 1.17, and has popped up several times throughout Season 2 (most recently 2.21).

Timmy. We finally get the name of Corinne and Tim's baby.

X23. Alien Burt's name.

16,000. How old X23 is.

Billy's Make Believe Martial Arts Training. 4th degree black belt in Karate and 3rd degree master in Tai Chi.

And introducing… JD Lobue as director. (He took a practice run during 2.18.)

Richard Mulligan the Unpredictable

"Richard did amazing reactions to things," says Ted Wass. "Sometimes, even in the heat of rehearsal, when you're open to finding everything, sometimes you just don't find it all. I can't specifically recall a moment, but I do remember a trend of moments where, in the fire of performance with an audience there, during a take, Richard's reactions would be much bigger, much more outrageous than anything most of us had seen during rehearsal. I can't say whether it was a choice that he decided to hold back and wait to do it, or if it was something that just occurred in the moment. I think I'd rather believe it was just that inspiration took him. I feel kindly towards him. I loved Richard very much."

Best Lines.
Chester: The braces, the fat farm, the hump, the nose job…
Eunice: Daddy come on.
Chester: You're a very attractive woman, Eunice.
Eunice: Well thank you.
Chester: But it wasn't cheap.

Alien Burt [checking his memory banks upon meeting Chester]: Chester. Stock broker. Charged with embezzlement. Murdered my son. Good to see you, Chet!

Millie: You seem to be sitting there so quiet. Is something the matter?

Corinne: See my husband was a priest and he left the church for me, which made him so guilty that he went to live in a cave. But then our son was born possessed and he came back to perform the exorcism, and when it was over I thought it would change things, but no he wouldn't go near me, he wouldn't touch me and the other day he left me. I'm Corinne.

Alien Burt: You know what they got down here? They got unlimited whoopee.

Rod Roddy's Wrapup. What will happen now that Alien Burt refuses to return to the spaceship and real Burt has only one chance to talk him into going back? Can they both stay with Mary? Is there enough drawer space? Now that Dutch is living with the Tates, will his eating habits improve, or will the carpets need extra shampooing? Now that Mary thinks Burt is purposely trying to drive her crazy, what will she do? What will happen with Billy and his teacher? Will it happen before they're too old to enjoy it? These questions and many others will be answered in the next episode of *Soap*.

1.8 BENSON • First aired: Nov 8, 1979 • Written by Bob Colleary + Tom Reeder • Directed by Jay Sandrich

Meanwhile, on Benson

"Jessica" Jessica arrives at the governor's mansion to attend a state banquet he's giving. Before she knows it, she's being wined and dined by an 87-year-old French baron, causing a minor scandal in town. However, when the baron dies in her hotel room, it's up to Benson to save everybody's reputation.

Cast. Robert Guillaume (Benson), James Noble (Gov. Gatling), Inga Swenson (Gretchen Kraus), Caroline McWilliams (Marcy Hill), Lewis J. Stadlen (John Taylor), Missy Gold (Katie Gatling), Mitchell Edmonds (Farnham), Katherine Helmond (Jessica), Louis Giambalvo (Driver), Victor Hunsberger Jr. (Baron)

Highlights. Jessica's dark blue sequin opera gown; her "there", pointing to the deceased baron behind the couch, and Benson jump-

Has it taken Benson this long to realize Jessica's this crazy?

ing away in horror; Benson strapping the baron's body to a luggage cart and making it up to look alive...ish; somebody knocking the Baron onto the couch in the hotel lobby; Kraus fighting with the dead baron in the kitchen; and Benson finally calling his former employer by her first name.

Confused? You Won't Be. *'I bet you there are people in hotel rooms all over this country wheeling dead bodies around like crazy.'*

▶ This episode aired the same night as *Soap* 3.7.

▶ Anybody needing a quick lesson in how unlike a standard sitcom *Soap* is would do well to watch this episode, which contains four actors who've been on *Soap* in various capacities, and two characters from the series. And yet the age-old paint-by-numbers sitcom formula here just about sucks the life out of all involved. Particularly jarring to longtime *Soap* fans is the way Benson bites Jessica's head off several times at the hotel. Granted the man is under a lot of pressure, but the Benson we know would never be so disrespectful to Jessica, especially when she was in the middle of a crisis.

6 months: How old Katie was when Jessica saw her last.

$400 MILLION
How much horror movies have grossed this summer, according to Jessica (who read it in *Time*)

Messy Jessy and Mean Gene. Jessica and Gov. Gatling's childhood nicknames, still applicable. Gatling broke her red tricycle, she lost his catcher's mitt.

Best Lines.

Benson: Did you call the police?

Jessica: No, I wanted you to be here when they came.

Benson: Thank you. That's one of my favorite things. Standing next to the body when the police come.

Benson [interrupting Jessica's story about her hamster's death]: Woman! I don't think you understand the seriousness of the situation. We've got a dead body over here on the couch and you're talking hamsters! Now if the baron was a hamster I could put him in my pocket and we could all get the hell out of here!

Jessica: I mean there's nothing you can't do.

Benson: Well, there is one thing I can't do.

Jessica: What's that?

Benson: Stop missing you.

3.8 First aired: Nov 22, 1979 • Written by Susan Harris + Stu Silver • Directed by JD Lobue

Never mind the course of true love, the course of hanky-panky doesn't run smoothly for the Tates as Eunice and Chester cheat on Dutch and Jessica, and Billy tries to check into a hotel with Leslie. Mary's been left mentally devastated by Burt's recent display of "invisibility" ("Suddenly I was and he, not"), and Burt puts his case to Alien Burt for returning his life to him.

Cast. Jimmy Baio (Billy), Diana Canova (Corinne), Billy Crystal (Jodie), Cathryn Damon (Mary), Katherine Helmond (Jessica), Robert Mandan (Chester), Richard Mulligan (Burt), Marla Pennington (Leslie Walker), Arthur Peterson (The Major), Donnelly Rhodes (Dutch), Jennifer Salt (Eunice), Rod Roddy (Announcer), Bruce French (Hotel Clerk), Lew Palter (Claude)

Highlights. Mary's Burt-like ravings when she first arrives at the Tate house; Corinne and Eunice's good cop/bad cop approach when confronting Chester about his philandering; Jodie's reaction when Burt dials the house for him and he finds himself talking to Alien Burt; the endless parade of Billy's cheating family members at the hotel where his fling with his teacher is easily the most innocent of the bunch; and Burt's impassioned plea to Alien Burt to let him have his life back.

Confused? You Won't Be. *'Hey hey hey—this is my life!'*

▶ During his 3 a.m. visit to Jodie's apartment, Burt begins one of *Soap*'s funniest yet most understated gags when "grandpa" announces himself to baby Wendy and makes a funny face. ("Woo-hoo, grandpa.")

▶ Billy's evening with Leslie may not go quite as planned, but she does tell him she loves him for the first time.

1979

NOV. 20: The Middle East continues to be a hotbed of violence as Saudi Arabia's Juhayman al-Otaibi, the Osama bin Laden of his day, leads about 500 militants in the takeover of the Grand Mosque in Mecca for several weeks before being captured. The following day, after Iran's Ayatollah Khomeini accuses the U.S. of occupying the mosque, the U.S. Embassy in Islamabad, Pakistan is attacked, killing four.

▶ The rapid departure of Chester and his bit of fluff at the hotel is a repeat of the same gag at the Hideaway Cafe (3.6).

▶ However much Susan Harris regretted the alien story line, it gives us one of the greatest monologues of the series this episode when Burt explains to his alien double what it is to be human, and why he's fighting so hard to reclaim his life. Though Burt is best known for his insane antics and penchant for invisibility, he remains *Soap*'s resident working-man's philosopher. Compare his speech to Alien Burt with his explanation to Mary about why he works so hard (See Best Lines in entry 2.7).

Jodie's finally convinced after talking to Alien Burt by phone.

8. Dutch's former cell block.

20. How many pounds of garlic he uses for his Hungarian goulash.

Tater Jones. Billy's alias at the hotel.

Evelyn Wood. Who Billy introduces Leslie as to Dutch. (He says he's at the hotel for a speed-reading course.)

'Don't Tell Me, Tell Bob'

As if starting his first regular series wasn't hard enough, Jay Johnson quickly discovered that the Bob he had to use during Season 1 had eye controls that were opposite to the ones that he was used to. This meant that if Bob needed to look to the left at Chuck during a scene, he'd end up looking to the right.

"I remember that became an issue for the first week or so, to make sure that Bob's eyeline was where it needed to be," says Johnson. "And that's when Jay Sandrich and I came up with this: 'Don't tell me what to do, tell Bob.' Because I was having such trouble with that, if he were to say, "Bob, you need to look at Camera 4,' then I could figure that out instinctively. I can't have Jay Sandrich say to me, 'Chuck, you need to move Bob's eyes to the left…' That's too much information. So if he would just say, 'Bob, you need to play Camera 3,' I knew what that meant instinctively rather than having to think about it."

Best Lines.

Corinne [to Chester, after Eunice leaves]: I don't want to break Little Miss Muffet's heart, but if you don't get smart and stop running around trying to see what you can get, I'll tell mother, and you'll get it so bad that you'll never get it again. Got it?

Burt [to Alien Burt]: Wait a minute here, wait, you don't understand. You don't know what it's like here. But you see you spend most of your life here struggling to make money, to get along with people, to fall in love and make it good, to give your kids the best you can, and years go by while you do this, pally, years! Then one day you wake up and you realize whoah, I've arrived. Business is good. My wife and I still love each other. The kids are alive and not on drugs. Now you can enjoy it all, no more struggle. Except then you realize you haven't gotta lot of time. Well now I've been through the struggle and I don't know how much time I've got left, but I do know one thing: I didn't come this far to give up. Now give me back my life. I'm entitled!

Alien Burt: Aw you're making me feel bad.

Burt: You *should* feel bad!

Alien Burt: We don't know about bad. We don't feel bad up there. But unfortunately when they gave me your body those little morons gave me a conscience.

Burt: Good, I'm glad.

Alien Burt: You've got some conscience!

Burt: It's one of my best qualities. That and my smile.

Rod Roddy's Wrapup. Now that Alien Burt has left for good, will Real Burt be able to convince Mary she was living with Alien Burt? Is Eunice convinced Chester isn't fooling around? Is Corinne convinced he is? Has Corinne convinced him he better stop? Is he convinced? Does Dutch really believe Eunice is planning a surprise shower for him? Or is Eunice really in for a surprise? Will Billy and his teacher ever be alone long enough to have an affair? These questions and many others will be answered in the next episode of *Soap*.

3.9

First aired: Dec 6, 1979 • Written by Susan Harris + Stu Silver • Directed by JD Lobue

As the entire Tate clan seems to be having affairs, Jessica finds herself pretty much alone. After a talk with Burt, Mary realizes she hasn't been crazy after all, but also realizes that she's been sleeping with an alien. Dutch is wise to Eunice's cheating ways, and Jessica is concerned over Billy's relationship with his teacher. That quickly leaves her mind when she spots Chester stepping into a hotel elevator with a young woman. Only Danny seems to be having any luck when he makes a new friend, Polly, at the cemetery while they're communing with their dead spouses.

Cast. Jimmy Baio (Billy), Diana Canova (Corinne), Cathryn Damon (Mary), Katherine Helmond (Jessica), Robert Mandan (Chester), Lynne Moody (Polly Dawson), Richard Mulligan (Burt), Arthur Peterson (The Major), Donnelly Rhodes (Dutch), Jennifer Salt (Eunice), Ted Wass (Danny), Rod Roddy (Announcer)

Highlights. Billy and Jessica's heart-to-heart over his relationship with Leslie; Mary placing a knob from the TV set on the spaceship knob Burt showed her with a "Here, we were both on a spaceship," and her response to his concern that Alien Burt had molested her ("Nothing. Tapped me on the shoulder a lot."); Danny and Polly conferring silently with their dead spouses about whether it's OK to go get coffee together; Dutch's revenge on Eunice at breakfast; and Jessica's newfound resolve to face Chester's affairs head-on.

Confused? You Won't Be. *'Sometimes I love him and sometimes I don't.'*

▶ Jessica's seemingly random mention of Dinah Shore's talk show to Billy isn't so random if we stretch our minds back to Season 1 and her confession that she was so lonely at the time that she talked back to Dinah Shore every day the show was on (1.9).

▶ Burt's insecurity over Mary sleeping with Alien Burt mirrors Mary's reaction to his alleged affair with Sally (2.15 onwards).

▶ Jessica and Mary spotting Chester in the company of another woman at the hotel reminds us of the last time this happened (1.9).

1979

DEC. 9: The smallpox virus is officially declared eradicated.

And Introducing...Polly.

Bobby Joe James. Billy's "friend" who's having romantic problems with one of his teachers.

Mr. Magee. Jessica had a terrible crush on this algebra teacher.

Burt Reynolds and Dinah Shore. Jessica's example of a successful May-to-December romance.

"That Little Nun". How Jessica refers to Sally Field (presumably based on her title role in *The Flying Nun*.)

Cynthia. Billy's cousin was married to someone much older. She was 22, he 76. He died on the honeymoon.

6 months. How long Polly's husband has been dead.

Leavenworth porridge. Dutch's breakfast this morning. Dutch is the only one with the recipe since they executed the only other person who knew it.

"The McDonald's of psychiatry". How Mary characterizes that self-help fad of the 1970s, EST (Erhard Seminars Training).

Best Lines.
Jessica: I'm so happy to see everyone this morning. This house was like a morgue last night. I mean Billy didn't come home from school, and Chester didn't come home from the city. Eunice didn't come home from the movies, and Corinne didn't come home. Dutch was in and out all night long but he never sat down to chat. I'm just glad that it's morning so I can have a little company.

Jessica [to Mary]: I've got too much on my mind. That's why I went shopping. When I get upset I go shopping because then I can get upset about what I bought and I forget about what I got upset about in the first place. Only today I couldn't find anything that upset me in my size.

Jessica: Mary, next week are the parent teacher conferences. I mean what am I going to talk about? How Billy's doing? I mean I don't think I want to know.

Lynne Moody (Polly)

360

How many people Dutch cooks for at one time, thanks to his prison training

Mary: Dating his teacher. He'll never know what he's being graded for.

Rod Roddy's Wrapup. Will anything happen with Danny and Polly? Will they decide to meet somewhere else next time? What will Jessica find when she goes up to Chester's room? Will a Do Not Disturb sign stop her? Is Mary glad Real Burt is back? Won't there be certain things she'll miss? Will Eunice find out what's for breakfast before she fools around again? Will she at least wear a hat? These questions and many others will be answered on the next episode of *Soap*.

27
How old Leslie is

17
How old Billy is

3.10
First aired: Dec 13, 1979 • Written by Susan Harris + Stu Silver • Directed by JD Lobue

Finally catching Chester red-handed, Jessica tells him not to come home. Yet meeting Leslie Walker suggests her other big worry won't be so easily resolved. Danny, determined to track down Polly, enlists the aid of Jodie and Burt to stake out the cemetery until she turns up again. And Jodie is just beginning to get the hang of parenting when a visit from the Child Welfare Department (sparked by a "complaint") threatens to turn his life upside down.

Cast. Billy Crystal (Jodie), Cathryn Damon (Mary), Katherine Helmond (Jessica), Jay Johnson (Chuck & Bob), Robert Mandan (Chester), Richard Mulligan (Burt), Marla Pennington (Leslie Walker), Ted Wass (Danny), Rod Roddy (Announcer), Karen Austin (Chester's woman), Richard McKenzie (The Doctor), Renny Temple (Harlen Wisser)

Highlights. The whole Chester's-paramour-as-table scene; Burt demonstrating his high-rise cemetery idea while building his sandwich, and his subsequent reaction to learning that Danny wants to date a black woman; the first meeting of Leslie and Jessica in what can only be described as a "cute off"; Bob's affection for Wendy ("I love babies; they're short—as soon as they can talk back, I can't stand 'em"); and Jodie going toe-to-toe with Child Welfare Department weenie Harlen Wisser.

Confused? You Won't Be. *'Homosexuals and puppets, what kind of place is this?'*

▶ Though there's been nothing particularly wrong with *Soap* this season, the scripts have missed the clever dialogue that made the show so beloved. Much of that returns this episode with the extended scene between Burt, Danny and Jodie.

Space lag. Burt's explanation for his insomnia.

6 pounds. How much weight Burt lost during his space trip.

Peter Dawson. The name of Polly's late spouse.

Mike Finnegan. Who Jodie took to his junior prom.

Mattresses in her Blood, Acting in Her Heart

A successful television career was the last thing that was on the cards for Marla Pennington. "I was supposed to take over the Diamond Mattress Company," she admits.

Since 1946, Compton, Calif.'s Diamond Mattress Co. has been a thriving family business that's seen the Pennington family through four generations.

"I was going to be the third generation. I was taking over from my grandmother, so I was taking courses in typing and shorthand and all those things that are really boring, with a lot of girls in it. I just couldn't take it anymore. So I went to my guidance counselor and said, 'You've gotta get me out of this, it's driving me crazy. I'll take woodshop, metal shop, whatever you have—just get me out of shorthand and typing!'"

But the only alternative open at the time was acting class, so she took that. After then-17-year-old director Don Coscarelli (*Phantasm*, *John Dies at the End*) recruited her to be the lead in his first feature, *Jim the World's Greatest*, Pennington knew there was no way she was going to take up the reins of the family business. Thankfully, her

1979

DEC. 19: For the inspiration for the Jodie-Carol custody battle, look no further than the American release of tearjerker *Kramer vs. Kramer* starring Dustin Hoffman and Meryl Streep as two parents fighting over the custody of their child.

family was extremely supportive, her grandmother most of all. "Every play that I was in, she was there. When I got on TV—they didn't really have recordings then—she would take Polaroids of me on the TV!"

Looking back on her career today, Pennington appreciates just what a golden age the '70s and '80s were for actors. "You could almost overbook; there was always a job. If you didn't get the job then you knew the person who did and you were happy for them. You just kept on going and just kept on booking, be it a movie, TV or commercials."

Yet it was on the soap opera *General Hospital* (1976-79) that the actress first began getting people's attention as Samantha Chandler. "It was so funny because when I did *General Hospital* I was really famous for my smile, so they were always going 'close-up on her smile.' In the last six months, I learned to cry on cue—oh my God, I was crying and they would have a close-up on my tears coming. I have those tapes and they're just hysterical to see how I could cry so easily."

It was a talent that would stand Pennington in good stead once Leslie Walker's relationship with Billy soured.

All these years later, the actress is still recognized for her role as the spurned teacher. "Which I find so flattering because I do really like my work in *Soap*. I was at the gym and this guy who works on computers kept looking at me and looking at me, and finally he ran after me and said 'Marla Pennington, right?' I said, 'Yeah...' And he described a [*Soap*] scene, so there are still people that remember, which is nice."

Best Lines.
Chester [to woman in hotel room]: We better get started. I'm parked in the 20 minute zone.

Burt: You know we're running out of cemetery space. Now what if we took a state that nobody hardly ever uses, like North Dakota. We knock down the mountains, you got a gigantic cemetery.

Danny [trying to remember the last name on the grave of Polly's husband]: I can almost see it. Pete. Here lies Peter...

Burt: Even better than that, listen to this one here. High-rise cemeteries.

Danny: Peter and Polly...

Burt: Everybody gets a drawer. It'll look like one huge filing cabinet. Of course we've gotta be very tasteful about it. Here, just figure, see this now. This is Mr. A's slot, right? [Puts down bread.] His wife [slaps cheese down on the bread]. Your cousin Al [slaps down some baloney]. The twins [down come two pickle slices]. And old Uncle Harvey [another piece of cheese].

Danny: Dawson!

Burt: And the Dawsons, what the hell!

Burt: A black woman?!

Jodie: I don't see anything wrong with it.

Burt: Of course not, you date guys! I mean what's a black lady next to that? Nothin! You could walk in here with a goat, I wouldn't blink! First he marries a gangster's daughter, now he's in love with a black widow!

Harlen: Are you a practicing homosexual?

Jodie: I don't have to practice, I'm very good at it.

Rod Roddy's Wrapup. Is Burt's insomnia really space lag or has he just been making up for lost time? Now that Jessica has met Leslie, does teacher's pet have new meaning? Will Danny find Polly, and if he does, what will he do? Now that Jessica has caught Chester and told him he can't come home, what will he do? How will he change his underwear? These questions and many others will be answered in the next episode of *Soap*.

DEC. 24: The Soviet Union invades Afghanistan.

3.11 First aired: Dec 27, 1979 • Written by Susan Harris + Stu Silver • Directed by JD Lobue

Happy 18th birthday, Billy. Despite Chester's pleadings, Jessica refuses to have anything to do with him. Dutch is keeping a close eye (and a fistful of chopped liver) on the philandering Eunice. Mary and Burt manage to get past the latter's insecurities over what Alien

Say Ma, remember my 18th birthday…?

Burt and Mary got up to in bed, and convince Jodie to move back home so they can all look after Wendy. Yet it is Billy who gets the biggest gift of all when Leslie reveals that she's chucked in her job at the high school, meaning there's nothing keeping them from "dating" properly.

Cast. Jimmy Baio (Billy), Diana Canova (Corinne), Billy Crystal (Jodie), Cathryn Damon (Mary), Katherine Helmond (Jessica), Jay Johnson (Chuck & Bob), Robert Mandan (Chester), Richard Mulligan (Burt), Marla Pennington (Leslie Walker), Arthur Peterson (The Major), Donnelly Rhodes (Dutch), Jennifer Salt (Eunice), Ted Wass (Danny), Rod Roddy (Announcer), Nora Denney (Miss Page)

Highlights. Chester's pathetic groveling at the bedroom window; Mary and Burt's frank discussion of Alien Burt and Mary in the bedroom; Jessica immediately asking the Campbells if Chester can have Jodie's apartment right after Jodie agrees to move back home; Leslie Walker discussing her birthday present for Billy with the birthday boy—and the whole family stopping their insane fighting for a moment when he says "It's time to open my present" to Leslie—before instantly sliding back into madness.

Confused? You Won't Be. *'18 big ones huh? He still looks like jailbait to me.'*

▶ Burt continues his shtick (which began in 3.8) with Wendy, making a face at her and saying goodbye to her with a "Woow-oowoo, grandpa."

▶ This is the first time the entire Tate-Campbell clan has met Leslie.

26. How old Jodie was when he moved out.

PS 71, Class of '46. Burt's alma mater.

Mrs. Fairbanks. Billy's new history teacher, now that Leslie has taken a job at the university.

1 HOUR
How long it takes to drive from Burt and Mary's house to Jodie's apartment

Second Generation of TV Writers

Even today, Stu Silver says he would gladly write *Soap* with Susan Harris, though the benefits of hindsight have given him a better idea of where they are in the history of television.

"The first generation of TV writers basically invented television, the ones writing *My Little Margie* and *The Life of Riley* and those sitcoms. They didn't know what they were doing. They would take old vaudeville sketches out and dust them off. Susan and I were the second generation of TV writers. We wanted to do TV but we weren't into cookie-cutter TV shows. You have the fat bumbling schmuck with a beautiful wife. All these shows now all seem to come from the same format.

"I created a show called *Webster* because ABC wanted a show with a little black kid, because NBC had one [*Diff'rent Strokes*]. We also had a much smaller canvas to paint on. We couldn't say all the things you can say today. We had to be very, very imaginative if we wanted to get a certain point across because censors wouldn't let you say anything. Today you can do a fart joke and everybody laughs. I don't think we ever did anything like that. First of all, we couldn't. And even when Burt was abducted by aliens, you still believed it. It wasn't like we jumped the shark, it was absolutely believable."

Soap writer Stu Silver went on to create the sitcom *Webster* (1983).

Best Lines.

Chester: Jess please listen, I'm sick, I've got a disease.

Jessica: Well with the company you keep, I don't wonder.

Chester: No Jess. Don't you understand, I can't help it. What I do is a sickness.

Jessica: Oh really. Is that what you call it, a sickness? And the cure is bed, is it?

Chester: I'll get help, Jess, if you'll just give me another chance. I'll get help, I swear it. If I were diabetic you wouldn't throw me out.

Jessica: If you were a diabetic you would stay away from the cookies.

Mary [explaining to Burt about Alien Burt's advances]: I felt like a fly. I had to keep going or get it.

Corinne [about Dutch]: Well I can't blame him, Eunice. He practically caught you red handed in a hotel with another guy.

Eunice: Eric and I were discussing insurance premiums.

Corinne: Please Eunice. Insurance?

Eunice: Really, we had an accident. He rear ended me.

Corinne: I don't think your insurance covers that.

Leslie: You're 18. You're a man. I'm no longer bound by any legal or moral code. I can safely give you your present. And tonight I'm going to light up every candle on your cake.

Billy: I better start thinking of a wish.

Rod Roddy's Wrapup. What will happen with Eunice and Dutch? Will she keep fooling around? Will he keep throwing food? What is Leslie's birthday present to Billy? Is it safe to bet it won't come wrapped? What will happen to Jessica and Chester now that she won't talk to him? Will they write notes? Will Burt continue to be jealous of Alien Burt's lovemaking? Will Mary miss it? These questions and many others will be answered on the next episode of *Soap*.

3.12 First aired: Jan 3, 1980 • Written by Susan Harris + Stu Silver • Directed by JD Lobue

It's a time of change for the Tates and the Campbells. Jodie has moved back into the bosom of his family, Chester and Jessica seek marriage counseling, and Danny finally sees Polly again. Yet, all of these new beginnings are trumped by what may be one killer ending for Burt, who discovers that Mary is pregnant shortly before he finds out *he* has Mylar's syndrome, a fatal disease.

Cast. Billy Crystal (Jodie), Cathryn Damon (Mary), Katherine Helmond (Jessica), John Hillerman (Minister), Kene Holliday (Eddie), Jay Johnson (Chuck & Bob), Robert Mandan (Chester), Richard McKenzie (Doctor), Lynne Moody (Polly), Richard Mulligan (Burt), Colleen Riley (Gloria), Rod Roddy (Announcer), Royce Wallace (Polly's mother), Ted Wass (Danny)

Highlights. The Jodie-treat overload as Mary, Burt and Danny try to take him to Coney Island, bowling, and to a Nicks-Lakers game, and then are tempted themselves by each other's outings; the minister's Indian philosophy concerning infidelity, Chester's instant downfall when faced with the temptation that is the minister's daughter, and the minister coming on to Jessica; Eddie providing commentary from the kitchen while Polly and Danny talk in the living room, and Danny's "See you again, brother" to Eddie, complete with black power fist; and Burt's slide from jubilation over Mary's pregnancy into misery after he learns that he's dying.

Confused? You Won't Be. *'It's incredible. On the happiest day of my life you tell me I have no life.'*

▶ It is a testament to *Soap*'s creativity that it wasn't until its third season that it played the classic soap-opera card, the dying character (unless you count Jodie's suicide attempt in Season 1). That said, we will get two fatal illnesses within the span of about eight episodes (3.21).

▶ Burt's little soliloquy to Alien Burt (3.8) now appears prophetic in view of the death sentence that has just been handed to him: "Now you can enjoy it all, no more struggle. Except then you realize you haven't gotta lot of time."

58 Milburn Street. Where Polly lives.

200. The number of Dawsons in the phone book.

7. The number of Dallases in the phone book.

5 months. How long Burt has left to live.

Shooting a Two-Family Scene

Tell anyone in the business today that *Soap* did two performances of one episode each week and chances are you'll be told you must be mistaken. However that's exactly how *Soap* was shot for four years. This is perhaps most extraordinary when you consider the sheer number of actors in one of those classic Tate/Campbell get-togethers. The secret: Everybody was on the same enormous stage at once.

> ❝ There was a big buzz when Katherine [Helmond] and I had our first scene together—everyone was just so excited to see how we would react to each other. (This was the other actors and the writers and the producers.) It was really kind of cool that there would be all this chatter about it."
>
> —MARLA PENNINGTON (leslie Walker)

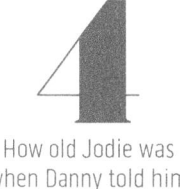

How old Jodie was when Danny told him his first dirty joke

1980

JAN. 6: Sicilian President Piersanti Mattarella is assassinated by the Mafia. **JAN. 9:** President Jimmy Carter signs a bill bailing out carmaker Chrysler Corp. to the tune of more than $1 billion in loan guarantees.

"There were times during the scene when the actors would have to hold until I got to the camera to cue them, but we never stopped a scene," says stage manager Carl Lauten. "We'd shoot a little vignette in one corner with Bob Guillaume and Katherine Helmond and Chester, then we'd cut to Danny, Mary and Burt in another part of the room. They would just hold until the camera was swung. I'd drop my arm and they'd start talking again, and some of these things lasted the whole act, and there were like 12-15 people acting in them all the time.

"We'd shoot it two times and then move on. It's just something that you don't see in this day and age. Also, if you look at the show, it's so clean how it's cut and everything else. Today you have to shoot every line four different ways in case someone else wants to play it as a two-shot or a master or a single. Back then you just kind of committed to what the show was going to be from the [directions] that the director gave. It was nothing like the required coverage today, and that's why it takes so long; you have to shoot everything 4-6 times in order to get it so everybody else can have what they want."

Best Lines.

Jessica: Chester goes through women the way an elephant goes through peanuts. See, he fools around with anything, any time, anywhere. He lies, he deceives, he sneaks around. He cheats before work, he cheats during work, he cheats after work. He cheated on our honeymoon, he cheated on our anniversary, he cheated while I was in labor in the hospital. *In the hospital.* He has cheated practically every week of every month of every year of our entire marriage. Other than that, he has been a wonderful husband.

Minister: I see. Well it sure did take you a long time to come to see me.

Chester: It took her all this time to catch me.

Minister: Of course. Well I see this sort of problem a lot. It seems to be going around. I think part of the reason is that there are no more Indians.

Chester: I beg your pardon?

Minister: You see in the olden days we had Indians to worry about. Where were the Indians? Were the Indians surrounding us?

Were the Indians angry Indians? Did the Indians want our horses? Nobody fooled around because you couldn't relax long enough. Now we got no more Indians.

Jessica: I see.

Minister: The best marriages were in the Apache territory because those were the worst Indians. Hostiles without, no hostility within. We have a lot to thank the Indians for. Happy marriages. Nice beadwork.

Jessica: What do we do now that there are no more Indians?

Minister: Aggravate some other group maybe.

Jessica: How do you keep your marriage trouble free?

Minister: Divorce. Married 16 years. My wife decided we had to have new carpeting in the family room. Guy came to lay the carpet, probably got a little confused about what he was there to lay, left me with four rolls of Bigelow shag and took off with my wife.

Jessica: How awful.

Minister: Might've been an Indian.

Rod Roddy's Wrapup. What will happen with Danny and Polly? Will her brother let it happen? Now that he's dying, what will Burt do? Will he do it quickly? Will he tell Mary? Will he pay his doctor's bill? Will Chester get himself some help with the minister's group or will Chester help himself to the minister's daughter? These questions and many others will be answered on the next episode of *Soap*.

3.13
First aired: Jan 10, 1980 • Written by Susan Harris + Stu Silver • Directed by JD Lobue

It may not be spring, but love is very much in the air. Danny and Polly celebrate their newfound love in a Laundromat after getting caught in a downpour; Billy may never leave Leslie's apartment again after discovering the joys of sex; and Burt bravely keeps his fatal illness to himself as he showers Mary with love, ostensibly because of their forthcoming child. Yet the mother-to-be suddenly realizes that Real Burt may not be the father.

> "There was a classic thing that a lot of people didn't realize, which was that soap operas, which we were a parody of, always adopted the theme of the popular movie of the day. That's why Billy [Crystal] was doing the thing with child custody—it was *Kramer vs Kramer*. *Close Encounters of the Third Kind* came out, so Burt was abducted by aliens. That was a classic soap opera move, to adopt the story lines of the big hit movies of the day. That's what they all did. And we were doing the same thing. It was a soap opera."
>
> —TED WASS (Danny)

Cast. Jimmy Baio (Billy), Billy Crystal (Jodie), Cathryn Damon (Mary), Katherine Helmond (Jessica), Jay Johnson (Chuck & Bob), Lynne Moody (Polly), Richard Mulligan (Burt), Marla Pennington (Leslie Walker), Ted Wass (Danny), Rod Roddy (Announcer), Kurtwood Smith (Guy in Laundromat)

Highlights. The complicated way Danny and Polly work out how to dry their clothes at the Laundromat, and Danny always thinking everybody's staring at them because they're a biracial couple when it turns out there are actually good reasons for them to be staring; Billy's sex-with-Leslie epiphany, followed by his flat out "you're wrong" when she says that sex isn't everything; Chuck & Bob rollerskating with Jodie, and Jodie shoving a standing Bob right out the kitchen door; and Jessica's left-field Superman reference when consoling Mary about the possibility that her child might be Alien Burt's.

Confused? You Won't Be. *'It's just not that simple.'*

▶ Harris and Silver have taken an interesting approach to the whole Danny-Polly biracial relationship here, making Danny's perceived persecution the problem, at least initially.

▶ Once again, the uber-competitive Gatling sisters (2.3) square off, this time over Mary's baby news. We learn that Jessica always knew what Mary was getting for her birthday, and even knew that Mary was getting engaged before she knew herself. (But Mary knew some things about Jessica's relationship with Chester in the beginning that Jessica didn't as we will learn in 4.14.)

▶ We get the first mention of baby Timmy in several episodes when Jessica suggests Mary's baby can have his hand-me-downs.

▶ Though Jessica telling Mary that Chester's been going to the minister's counseling sessions morning, noon and night makes us suspect he's still fooling around, we'll discover just how wrong we were next episode.

▶ The seeds for the forthcoming "flying baby" gag are planted here with Jessica's Superman talk. However, since when does Jessica accept Mary's story about Alien Burt?

Martha Black. The married neighbor down the block Mary thinks Danny is in love with at first.

The Relationship That Wasn't

Those who already had a bone to pick with *Soap*'s unusual approach to televised morality probably dropped their evening cocoa during this episode: What greater sign of the coming apocalypse than a teacher bedding her student?

The actors and producers were worldly enough to treat it as just another bit of televisual make believe, but they were also honest enough creatively to admit when something just wasn't working. However much they tried to make Billy and Leslie Walker work as a couple—Jimmy Baio was just 17, and Marla Pennington about 27—you just couldn't fake a chemistry between them.

"[Baio] wasn't all that comfortable," Pennington admits. "We did one scene that never was shown about us being in the apartment and we were kind of 'together', and it had some funny things in it, but it just didn't click. We worked all week on it, but we just couldn't make it believable that we were a couple.

"The first night together, that scene was great, but it was the scene after that when we're supposed to be comfortable and glowing so we could maybe go further—we hardly got any laughs in the

After a believable romance failed to materialize between these two characters, producers decided to take a different, funnier route.

audience. I was walking out, and I think it was Tony [Thomas] who came up and said, 'Yeah, that didn't work, did it?' He gave me a hug and said, 'Don't worry, don't worry, we're going to do something else.' That was a big hint that whatever the big plan was, wasn't going to work. Then a couple of scenes went through where I got to meet the family and there were tears when I couldn't find him. Then I realized the direction it was going."

Best Lines.

Danny: They're staring because we're a bisexual couple.
Polly: We are?
Danny: Yeah, you're black and I'm white. They're staring!

Billy [to Leslie about their lovemaking]: I'm sorry, I'm sorry. I'm just so excited. It's like discovering America or a third arm or something!
Leslie: I know.
Billy: This is the greatest thing that ever happened to me; I should have started this 10 years ago. I mean to hell with television.

Jessica: Look Mary, did Alien Burt look like Real Burt?
Mary: Exactly.
Jessica: Well then you don't have a problem because you see the baby will look like a Burt and Burt will never know.
Mary: Jessica, Alien Burt was really a little silver man.
Jessica: Well Mary if it's a little silver baby then we'll know who the father is. You know the Kents had the same problem.
Mary: Fred and Lillian Kent?
Jessica: No, Mr. and Mrs. Clark Kent.
Mary: I don't believe I know them.
Jessica: Superman and Lois Lane. If they had a baby it might fly. See Mary this isn't unusual at all. With a baby you never know what will happen. I mean will it have blue eyes, will it be left handed, will it be silver, will it fly? But whatever you have, you'll love it just the same.

Rod Roddy's Wrapup. Now that Billy has found a new pastime, will he ever do anything else again? What kind of baby will Mary have? Will she have to buy baby food or a dry cell battery? What will Danny and Polly do now that they're in love? These questions and many others will be answered on the next episode of *Soap*.

3.14
First aired: Jan 17, 1980 • Written by Susan Harris + Stu Silver • Directed by JD Lobue

Changing oneself may be the hardest thing there is. However desperate Burt is to leave his mark on society before he dies, it's clearly going to take more than some half-baked scheme to get into the *Guinness Book of World Records* to do it. And despite all of her put-downs of sister Corinne about being trampy, Eunice is incapable of being faithful to Dutch. Even when Chester fights his hardest to reform his philandering ways, circumstances (this time in the form of the minister's irresistible daughter, Gloria) find a way to lead him astray. Finally, long-standing prejudices on both sides of the racial divide seem too great to allow Danny and Polly's families to get along, no matter how much they would like to.

Cast. Diana Canova (Corinne), Cathryn Damon (Mary), Katherine Helmond (Jessica), Jay Johnson (Chuck & Bob), Robert Mandan (Chester), Lynne Moody (Polly), Richard Mulligan (Burt), Arthur Peterson (The Major), Jennifer Salt (Eunice), Ted Wass (Danny), Rod Roddy (Announcer), Kene Holliday (Eddie Coleman), Mel Stewart (Walter Coleman), Colleen Riley (Gloria), Royce Wallace (Rose Coleman)

Highlights. Danny's reaction to discovering that Burt is dying after he catches him reading *Die Without Fear* ("It's a terrible book, Danny. No laughs."), and how enthusiastically he helps Burt look for a world record he can break; how manipulative Eunice is when getting Corinne to cover for her seeing Jerry, even as she insults her to her face; Chester being seduced by Gloria, the minister's daughter (he's only human, poor devil); Polly's father and brother staring at Chuck & Bob playing cards; Mary and Rose bonding over their shared belief that Polly and Danny's relationship will never work; the sniping between Bob, Walter and Eddie; and the extreme

As with TV shows and films, *Soap* found a creative way to incorporate this other fad of the '70s & '80s.

pathos on both sides as Chester confesses his infatuation with the minister's daughter, shortly before Jessica chucks him out for the last time.

Confused? You Won't Be. *'No no no, I don't do that anymore.'*

▶ As goofy as Burt's quest to get into the *Guinness Book of World Records* is, it's also perfectly in keeping with his character. This quest to make his "mark" in the world goes right back to the reasons he gave Mary for working so hard (2.7).

▶ Though this episode isn't brimming with the clever dialogue we've come to expect from *Soap*, the combination of insane slapstick (Danny nearly putting Burt's eye out with a grape) and superb performances wrestle this one back from the edge of the ordinary. Mandan and Helmond in particular remind us what they're capable of when script and characters are in perfect alignment. And the gently biting social commentary on display in the Coleman/Campbell meeting is an apt summation of race relations at the time.

400 degrees. Highest temperature ever endured by a human.

17 years. The longest time a person has remained standing.

259 feet. The farthest distance a person has caught a grape in their mouth.

About 26 hours. How long Burt has been keeping a balloon off the ground for a record when Polly's parents come over.

Jerry. The new love of Eunice's life after Dutch scared Eric all the way to Montana (where he now herds sheep).

Bob: The Character Who Could Say Anything

Throughout *Soap*'s four year run, there were two characters who became two of the most loved of the series, yet never found themselves in a single story line: Chuck & Bob. Yet for the relatively small amount of screen time they enjoyed, their contribution to the program, and to television, was incalculable.

Simply put, Bob was the one character who could get away with the most objectionable lines on the show: Bart Simpson before there was a Bart Simpson.

"Chuck was the innocence that allowed Bob to say anything in the world," says Jay Johnson. "You had the immediate conscience of Chuck that would say, 'Oh that's not right,' or 'that shouldn't have happened,' to immediately turn it from the negative to the positive. I think that was why it was a great writing tool for Susan and the writers. Truly Bob could say anything and it could not be taken as seriously."

Part of what makes Bob so effective in scenes such as the one that takes place in this episode with Polly's family is the way Jay Johnson approached script readings. The actors saw Bob as one of their own.

The original "Bob" was donated to the Smithsonian in May 2007.

"The one thing was that when we did a readthrough and there was a scene with Bob in it, Bob was there," says Johnson. "My style of art and ventriloquism is that Bob's there, he's not a puppet. He's as much alive as anybody else, so he would become one of the guys at that point."

Says Katharine Helmond, "I think if it had been in less skilled hands than Jay Johnson it could have been a problem, but he made Bob so real and so much a part of him. It was just another piece of him. Jay Johnson is a very polite, lovely young man. And Bob is the inner voice that was the mean and vicious person that you have to subdue all your life inside of you. But it was an integral part of him. You really did feel that even though it was made of wood, it was a person.

"I think one of the things that supported that and helped that was that when we had the readthrough, Bob was right at the table reading his lines. And he would look from left to right. He had his head moving like his eyes were reading the words. You came to the point where you just believed that he was real."

Best Lines.

Bob [to Polly's family]: So, Danny here tells me that you're a family of Negroes, is that true?

Polly's family is not sure what to make of Chuck & Bob. Bob, on the other hand, will be sure to tell them what he makes of *them*.

Danny: I'm really sorry about that.

Walter: Somehow I'm not really insulted.

Danny: You're a good sport.

Walter: No, I'm a lousy sport. It's just that I can't get very upset at a person who vents his pent-up hostility through a piece of wood.

Burt: So Eddie, what do you do?

Eddie: I'm a writer.

Danny: I didn't know that.

Eddie: Well, we've never really had a chance to chit-chat.

Danny: What do you write?

Eddie: Essays, magazine articles, the plight of the black race, 400 years of oppression, the white man's disgrace.

Bob: Oh, so you're a gag writer, is that it?

Jessica: You know it's funny, I feel more stupid than anything else. I feel so incredibly stupid to have thought for one minute that you could ever change.

Chester: Jess this hurts me as much as it hurts you.

Jessica: It hurts you? It hurts you?! Nothing could hurt you, Chester Tate. You have no soul! But I will tell you one thing, and you listen to me carefully. I will never, ever, under any circumstances whatsoever, take you back again. This is the very last time, Chester. It is final and it is irreparable. Now you get out of this house! I've got a life I'm going to live!

Rod Roddy's Wrapup. Will Burt get into the world book of records? Will he live to read it? What will happen with Chester and the minister's daughter, pray tell? Now that Jessica's alone, what will she do? Will she be alone for long? These questions and many others will be answered on the next episode of *Soap*.

3.15 First aired: Jan 24, 1980 • Written by Susan Harris + Stu Silver • Directed by JD Lobue

You can't go home again, as the Tates and the Campbells learn all too well this episode. Dutch wants Eunice back but she may be too far gone, whatever psychobabble she spouts. Burt continues his quest to make his mark on the world with various world record stunts. Mary, and Polly's mother, Rose, realize that however much they love their children, they can't go back to the time before they had to face society's problem with interracial couples. Most tragic of all, Jessica discovers that the poor choice she made between Chester and Det. Donohue may have cost her the one real love of her life.

Cast. John Byner (Det. Donohue), Diana Canova (Corinne), Cathryn Damon (Mary), Katherine Helmond (Jessica), Jay Johnson (Chuck & Bob), Richard Mulligan (Burt), Arthur Peterson (The Major), Donnelly Rhodes (Dutch), Jennifer Salt (Eunice), Ted Wass (Danny), Rod Roddy (Announcer), Sandra McCabe (Shirley Slotnick Donohue), Royce Wallace (Rose Coleman)

Highlights. Burt's "other people might want to read about me while I'm at work" explanation to Mary about why he wants to be in a book; Dutch and Corinne's short talk in the baby's room; Jessica turning up one hour after Donohue got himself hitched to Shirley telling him she loves him; a dejected Jessica interrupting Rose and Mary's talk, with Rose thinking Jessica's deaf or mute, and Jessica doing nothing to disabuse her of the notion; and Dutch ripping off

> "I was in shock when I came back from doing *Soap*, and in the interim I did *Stroker Ace* and one or two other things, but I was out of the Hollywood scene. I went from *Soap* to *Bizarre* in Canada. I come back and there's an audition and the guy says, 'Have you got any video on yourself?' I say, 'Oh my God, it's over. It's me, Byner, with the voices and the things.... and the *Soap*!'"
>
> —JOHN BYNER
> (Det. Donohue)

the fridge door and hurling it through the window following his "dignity and control" speech to Eunice.

Confused? You Won't Be. *'There's something you're not telling me.'*

▶ Donohue's wine glass with no bottom is a clever wink to long-time viewers who saw how that happened in 2.17. (And be sure to read "John Byner and the Dark Side of Bloopers" in that entry for what really happened behind the scenes.)

▶ John Byner gives one of his best performances in the series during this, his swan song. Always played for laughs up till now, Det. Donohue is seen for what he is: a desperately lonely man who made the best of a bad situation. Unable to have the woman he loves, he settled for the woman who would be had.

▶ Mary and Jessica continue their long history of competitiveness (2.3, 3.13) when they compare reasons to be depressed.

▶ Eunice's confession to Dutch that she's only avoiding him because she always runs when she gets close to a guy is clearly bogus, judging by the face she pulls when he hugs her. Not only does this seem to make her out to be more of a tramp than Corinne ever was, it also sheds strong doubt on the manipulative story she told Dutch in the very beginning about being the way she is because she was fat as a child (2.3).

121. The number of quarters Burt tries to catch for the world record.

31 feet, 1 inch. The longest distance a person has spit.

1 hour. About how long Donohue's been married to Shirley before Jessica arrives.

Precious Cargo. What Donohue calls his new wife.

60. Donohue's apartment number.

Donnelly Rhodes: The Art of Playing 'Dumb'

Throughout his lengthy career, Donnelly Rhodes played tough guys and funny guys, but to the best of his recollection Dutch was the first time he played a funny tough guy. And like the rest of the characters in *Soap*, Dutch was multifaceted. He was always the man in control when he had a gun and cared nothing for the people he was around. But all of that flew out the window the moment he fell in love with Eunice. From then on, his insecurity got the best of him as he tried to fit into the upper crust Tate family, and failed miserably. But more than anything else, he was worried about coming across as dumb.

Yet behind the scenes, playing dumb had its rewards. Early on, Katherine Helmond let Rhodes in on a little trick for keeping lines in a script that he really liked. "Katherine said if you've got something that's really good, remember that the first day the writers always laugh at their own jokes," Rhodes remembers. "But they get tired of hearing them so they start messing with it. Katherine said if you get a good bit, just keep screwing it up and they'll keep telling you how to get it right. And then she says when they get to the last minute, then you get it right. You get to keep it and they all say, 'See, we told you, you just had to do that.' It was a good little clue. Just sort of pretend to be dumb and finally you get it at the last minute."

Rhodes remembers another day when he was still pretty new to the show. "The actors were all really talking about their characters' motivations and what not, and I think most everybody was from New York. And Jay Sandrich was getting kind of bored with it, he was this top-notch director. He looks over at me and he says, 'You know Donnelly, if you have anything to say just jump right in there.' And I'm sitting there thinking aw my goodness, because when you come on to a show everybody's got their own little groups. You don't want to be making any waves for anybody.

"But Katherine Helmond kind of adopted me and gave me hints and guided me through things. She was really terrific. So I'm sitting there thinking well I guess I've gotta come up with a question now. So I think of something and I put my hand up and I ask this question and Jay says, 'That's a really good question, Donnelly.

Donnelly Rhodes in *Goldenrod* (1976).

It shows you're thinking. I didn't think we were going to have that problem with you.'"

Best Lines.
Mary: She's a lovely girl.
Rose: He's a lovely boy.
Mary: They're a lovely couple.
Rose: Lovely.
Mary: We should be thrilled.
Rose: I know.
Mary: I'm going to shoot myself.
Rose: Give me the gun when you're done?

Mary [to Rose about Jessica]: She does this all the time. Watch, her depression will be bigger.

Jessica: Much bigger. I just came from Det. Donohue's. See, my husband had amnesia and he got lost so I hired Det. Donohue to find him, and what he found was that Chester had died. So I had an affair with Det. Donohue and we fell in love. And then Chester came back. Of course not from the dead because he never was really dead. And then I had to choose and I chose Chester, which was the wrong choice because Chester chose to play around and he left me for the minister's daughter. So I went to Det. Donohue's to tell him that I was his but I was too late. He's hers.

Rose: Whose?

Jessica: His wife's. My husband's gone off with a young woman, the man I love is married to someone else. My children are all grown. I've lost everyone. I'm alone. All, all alone.

Mary: She did it again. She topped me. She always does that. She always has one better.

Rod Roddy's Wrapup. Will Burt tell Mary he's going to die, or will he wait until it's too late? Will Burt be able to break a record before he dies? Will Jessica get over her depression? Will Rose and Mary get over theirs, or will they all depress each other over and over again? These questions and many others will be answered on the next episode of *Soap*.

3.16

First aired: Jan 31, 1980 • **Written by** Susan Harris + Stu Silver • **Directed by** JD Lobue

The relationship revolving door continues to spin as Carol returns (she's in town with her cowboy boyfriend for the rodeo), Eunice leaves Dutch for another man, and Billy tires of Leslie's constant attention. Burt discovers that he's not dying after all and Jessica visits a shrink, getting in touch with her pent-up anger toward Chester in the process.

Cast. Jimmy Baio (Billy), Rebecca Balding (Carol David), Diana Canova (Corinne), Billy Crystal (Jodie), Cathryn Damon (Mary), Katherine Helmond (Jessica), Jay Johnson (Chuck & Bob), Alan Miller (Dr. Alan Posner), Richard Mulligan (Burt), Arthur Peterson (The Major), Donnelly Rhodes (Dutch), Rod Roddy (Announcer), Richard McKenzie (Dr. Saxon)

Highlights. Jodie and Carol's tense, tense reunion at midnight in the Campbell living room; Dr. Posner psyching Jessica up to the point she ruptures the punching bag ("I guess I was a little angry"); the doctor explaining to Burt that since all the computers think he's dying, he'd better use cash from now on; Jessica's bizarre tuxedo-fronted blue blouse with the maroon bow tie; and the way Jessica and Corinne rally around Dutch after they've read Eunice's kiss-off letter to him.

Confused? You Won't Be. *'What's with this family and relationships?'*

▶ Dr. Posner is named after longtime associate producer Marsha Posner.

▶ Burt and Mary's doctor finally gets a name (Dr. Saxon), though it only appears in the credits.

▶ Burt's "woohoo, grandpa" to Wendy continues to get sillier.

▶ Jessica tells Dr. Posner about a distant aunt who lives in Portugal who wears a crown and thinks she's royalty; she declared war on Spain last year.

▶ This is an oddity in *Soap* history—an episode that is much better than the sum of its parts. Considering the short amount of time Carol is on screen, we get a much better reunion than we would've expected, and a true dramatist's setup for the custody battle to come. In lesser hands the first hint we'd get of trouble would be a visit from Carol's lawyer. It also makes us wonder if Carol was somehow involved in the "complaint" against Jodie to the Child Welfare Department (3.10).

▶ The disappointingly anticlimactic revelation that Burt doesn't have a fatal illness after all is capped by a pretty good joke about how credit card companies treat the terminally ill. Even the predictable running away of Eunice manages to tie in nicely with Billy's tiring of Leslie and Corinne's continued search for Mr. Right.

6 weeks. How long it's been since Burt's slept because of the baby.

Miss Warmth. Bob's term of endearment for Carol.

22 hours. How long Burt has been dribbling the basketball before the nurse slaps it out of his hands.

Irv. The Major's pigeon.

Jay Johnson and the Burden of Bob

As Jay Johnson is a world renowned ventriloquist (and with his Broadway show *The Two and Only*, a Tony-award winning one, too), audiences can be forgiven for not knowing that Johnson has acted on his own.

"I did a few episodes of *Gimme a Break* and I did a *Love Boat*, and they tried to bring back *Love American Style* and used actors that were on other series," says Johnson. "So yeah, I've done a lot of stuff with Bob and without Bob. I always preferred to do a part without Bob simply because that was a learning challenge. I always loved the idea of becoming somebody else.

"One thing that no one thinks about when you're playing that kind of part is that you're tied down; you're always holding something. So as an actor it limits your range. You can't walk in and pick up props, you can't interact with a lot of things that other actors can, so it was a challenge to find ways to stay active and still have Bob on my arm. It was odd.

1980

FEB. 2: *NBC Nightly News* reveals that the FBI has been targeting members of Congress in a corruption sting operation that would later be known to the world as Abscam. Ultimately, one senator and five members of the house will be convicted of conspiracy and bribery.

"You'll find that most of the time, if Bob and I could sit down, we were sitting. We would enter the scene and walk through it, but there wasn't a lot of Chuck & Bob standing. I remember sometimes in the background I would find a place to sit him on the mantle or someplace just for that very reason. It just gets tiring."

Best Lines.

Jodie: Carol, you come into my life like a sailor on leave. Tell me I'm going to be a father, then leave me at the altar, prevent me from seeing my child. Then you abandon her. Now here you are again and you don't understand why I'm not happy to see you? Well excuse me if you're not my choice for the woman of the year.

Jay Johnson and Bob played part of a menagerie of psychologically damaged cops in *Broken Badges* (1990).

Burt: They're ruining our lives, these computers. I had a friend once shot the computer it made him so crazy. The computers. You ever make a mistake on your bill? Forget it. Once it's in the computer, it's there for life.

Doctor: I'm glad you brought that up, Burt. See, unfortunately the computer thinks you're dying and it contacted other computers. You know, bank computers, charge card computers. See, some dying people like to charge up a storm before they go. So now since all the computers think you're dying, you've become a bad credit risk. If I were you, the next few months I'd use cash.

Corinne: It must be so nice to have someone you can spend time with.

Billy: It's the best.

Jessica: Where is she now?

Billy: Who cares?

Jessica: Billy.

Billy: I didn't mean that mom. It's just she wants to see me all the time. And I really care for her, she's a wonderful person, but I'm just too young to commit all my time to her.

Corinne: Do you believe this? Here we are dying for what you have, and you don't want it. What's with this family and relationships?

Corinne: Dutch wait. We're your family now.

Dutch: Naw. I appreciate ya saying that but that ain't true.

Jessica: Now Dutch you listen to me! You are not only a part of this family, but technically you are *the* man of the house. I mean we have just recently lost two husbands here, and I simply will not tolerate another man walking out of this house. Dinner's at 6, please don't be tardy.

Rod Roddy's Wrapup. Will seeing a psychiatrist help Jessica? Will seeing Jessica help the psychiatrist? Now that Eunice has left home, will Corinne end up with her room? Her clothes? Her man? Did Carol just drop by to see the baby or does she really want something else? Now that Burt knows he's not going to die, will finding out Mary's baby might not be his kill him? These questions and many others will be answered on the next episode of *Soap*.

3.17 First aired: Feb 7, 1980 • Written by Susan Harris + Stu Silver • Directed by JD Lobue

Overjoyed that he's not going to die, Burt finally tells Mary about his brush with mortality. And so ends the good news, this episode. Gloria abandons Chester, Polly and Danny get a taste of what to expect at a real estate office, and Dutch and Corinne wake up in bed together. Meanwhile, Dr. Posner asks Jessica out and Carol informs Jodie that she's hired a lawyer—she wants custody of baby Wendy.

Cast. Katherine Helmond (Jessica), Cathryn Damon (Mary), Robert Mandan (Chester), Richard Mulligan (Burt), Diana Canova (Corinne), Billy Crystal (Jodie), Ted Wass (Danny), Rod Roddy (Announcer), Paul Avery (Dr. Carlton), Rebecca Balding (Carol David), Alan Miller (Dr. Alan Posner), Lynne Moody (Polly), Donnelly Rhodes (Dutch), Colleen Riley (Gloria), Ted Shackelford (R.C.), Joshua Shelley (Mr. Rosen)

Highlights. Chester calling Gloria his "10" moments before she leaves him, and her list of reasons for doing so; Danny getting in the "patient" position with Dr. Stegman at the real estate office before realizing he is, in fact, his dentist; real estate agent Rosen the realist and his facts of life lecture; Corinne and Dutch freaking out moments after waking up in bed together, and Corinne's delight in being described by Dutch as soft... "like a muffin"; Jessica's wonderful powers of denial on finding them in bed together; and Jodie's furious reaction to Carol and her boyfriend after being told she wants to take Wendy from him.

Confused? You Won't Be. *'I found someone better.'*

⏵ Danny and Mary are painting Wendy's future nursery when Burt comes in to reveal that he isn't going to die after all. Mary's relief quickly turns to anger at Burt for not sharing his predicament with her. This won't be the last time she gets upset with him for keeping things from her (4.4).

⏵ Chester continues to be a more nuanced character than he was in Season 1 and most of Season 2, giving Robert Mandan more layers to work with, which he does beautifully here. As much as we love Jessica and abhor the way Chester's treated her over the years, it's hard not to cringe at the callous way Gloria tosses him aside. The implication is that she's replacing him with a younger guy, which is what Chester did to Jessica. And it's equally difficult not to read *Soap*'s constant exploration of marital strife as Susan Harris working out her own demons. As she told the crowd at her January 2011 induction into the Academy of Television Arts & Sciences Hall of Fame, "In the late '60s I was very fortunate; my husband left me for another woman. An actress." In a way, her husband's loss may have been the world's gain.

⏵ Polly and Danny's experience with Rosen the real estate agent may have been inspired in part by the creation this year of California's Department of Fair Employment and Housing. One of the agency's mandates is to crack down on housing discrimination.

⏵ There seems to be some confusion about who the "Dr. Carlton" in the credits refers to, as the only medical person encountered in the episode is Danny's run-in with his dentist, whom he calls "Dr.

FEB. 7: Italian director Ruggero Deodato's found-footage horror movie *Cannibal Holocaust* premieres depicting, among other horrors, simulated cannibalism and rape, and real-life animal cruelty and killing.

FEB. 15: Tinto Brass' infamous movie *Caligula* opens in America, financed by *Penthouse* magazine head Bob Guccione.

> "We had a flood where I lived in Topanga Canyon at the time. Our house was filled with mud and water and all of our possessions floated down this creek that had turned into a roaring river. I can remember going to work and I had no clothes left to wear. The wardrobe department gave me some jeans and prison shirts that were from the first scenes from when Dutch first came on. So I had some clothes to wear for a little while so I could get organized because we had to dig out our house and basically rebuild it."
> —DONNELLY RHODES (Dutch), on coping with what has been called the worst American flood of the century (Feb. 16, 1980.)

Stegman." Likely the name was changed at the last minute but failed to be reflected in the credits...or this is just Danny being dippy.

▶ Jessica continues to add to her family lore as she tells Dr. Posner that her great aunt was personally responsible for Freud's cocaine habit.

1 mile and 99 yards long. The longest banana split, according to Danny.

12,000. How many bananas Danny ordered to help Burt break the record.

2 days. How long Gloria's been away looking for movie magazines. ("Got lost.")

Best Lines.

Rosen [to Danny]: There's no rush, there's no rush, there's plenty of houses. All kinds of houses. Houses, houses, houses, Rosen has hundreds of houses, no rush.

Polly: See, we're together.

Rosen: I haven't got a thing.

Danny: Hey, hey, hey.

Rosen: No, joking, joking, just a little humor, please sit down. I got plenty. Sit down. Crazy kids. Crazy, crazy, crazy. What are you, crazy?

Polly: What do you mean?

Rosen: What do I mean. Look how you look. White, black. Where do you expect to live, in the land of Nod? In Oz? In Disneyworld? It's crazy, crazy.

[Later]

Polly: How did you deal with your daughter in love with a black man?

Rosen: At first I was so upset I fasted for six hours. Then I said to myself, 'Dundle, you're Jewish. There are people who are not so crazy about you, either.' And I realized hating was a disease and I was not gonna be a carrier.

Jodie: Why don't you just go punch a cow?

RC: Why don't I just punch you?

Jodie: Oh, very sensitive man you have there, Carol. He's going to make a very good witness.

RC: Better than a fag.

Jodie: I don't think I'd get so snitty if I were you. I mean after all we do shop in the same stores [eying RC's cowboy outfit].

Rod Roddy's Wrapup. Is it crazy for Jessica to date her psychiatrist? What will Jodie do now that Carol wants the baby back? Does this make her an Indian giver? Will Danny and Polly be happy living together? Will the neighbors be happy? Will Dutch and Corinne continue? Will Jessica continue to ignore them? Now that Gloria has left him, what will Chester do? Who will he do it with? These questions and many others will be answered on the next episode of *Soap*.

3.18 First aired: Feb 28, 1980 • Written by Susan Harris + Stu Silver • Directed by JD Lobue

Burt's brush with death has left him with a new ambition: to become sheriff of Dunn's River, Conn. Naturally, Danny wants to be his deputy. Meanwhile, Jodie enlists the aide of E. Ronald Mallu to fight the custody case Carol (Mallu's former assistant) is bringing over baby Wendy. And on the night Jessica finally has Dr. Posner to her house for dinner, he gets a heaping helping of family weirdness, including a tearful Leslie and the owner of the local Japanese restaurant.

Cast. Katherine Helmond (Jessica), Cathryn Damon (Mary), Robert Mandan (Chester), Richard Mulligan (Burt), Diana Canova (Corinne), Arthur Peterson (The Major), Billy Crystal (Jodie), Ted Wass (Danny), Jay Johnson (Chuck & Bob), Rod Roddy (Announcer), John Fujioka (Mr. Teshamado), Allan Miller (Dr. Alan Posner), Marla Pennington (Leslie Walker), Donnelly Rhodes (Dutch), Eugene Roche (E. Ronald Mallu)

Highlights. Sheriff Burt pulling over a speeding Danny in the living room...and it degenerating into a pretend fire fight that Mary has to break up; Mary and Jessica's Novocaine-induced high jinks at the dentist's office; the wonder that is the legal mind of E. Ronald

> [*Soap*] felt very much like a play atmosphere. They had a monitor in the back. If you weren't in the scene, everyone was gathered around the television and they're laughing hysterically. People would stay after they were released to watch other people rehearse because it was brilliant. You'd just want to be a part of it."
>
> —MARLA PENNINGTON (Leslie Walker)

Mallu; the sight of The Major sending the Tokyo Garden's kitchen staff bound and gagged down the stairs—one of the greatest visual gags in *Soap*; Burt's campaign materials; and Chester's return to Jessica...yet again.

Confused? You Won't Be. *'If there's a crack in the plaster, we'll knock down the wall.'*

▶ *Soap* takes another crack at getting the women to talk about sex, in this case Mary and Jessica at the dentist, and once again it fails to capture lightning in a bottle a second time (see "Coffee Cake Sex Talk" under the 2.7 entry).

▶ The whole "everyone falls in love with Jessica" shtick continues with Mallu, Posner and Chester all professing their feelings for her this episode. This will all come to a head shortly (3.22).

▶ Both Jessica and Rod Roddy appear to have missed the fact that technically Leslie isn't Billy's teacher anymore (3.11).

Sheriff Prentiss. The corrupt sheriff Burt seeks to usurp.

A nightstick. Bob's uncle was one, which are Bob's credentials for being a deputy.

Burt's campaign slogans: 1) Take a Gamble, Vote for Campbell. 2) Graft is Dirty, Vote for Burty. 3) Vote for Burt.

Eleanor Roosevelt. Who The Major thinks Leslie is.

Best Lines.
Mallu: OK OK. Let's see what we got here. You are a homosexual. And as I remember you once tried to commit suicide. Does anyone know that?
Jodie: Carol.
Mallu: Swell.
Jodie: It was right before my sex-change operation.
Mallu: You used to be a woman?
Jodie: No, no, no, I didn't do it.
Mallu: Too bad. Two mothers fighting over the same child. Talk about a movie!

1980

MARCH 4: The brutal Robert Mugabe is elected prime minister of Zimbabwe. That country will never be the same again.

Mallu [over intercom]: Wanda, call my fiancée and cancel my marriage.

Rod Roddy's Wrapup. What are the chances of Mary having an alien baby? Will she be able to find clothes in its size? Are Billy and Leslie really through? How will this affect his grades? Will Chester win Jessica back from the psychiatrist? Now that Mallu is back handling Jodie's case, will he be back to handle Jessica as well? Will Burt be sheriff? If Burt is sheriff, will Danny be deputy? If Burt is sheriff and Danny is deputy, will Mary be mad? These questions and many others will be answered on the next episode of *Soap*.

3.19
First aired: Mar 6, 1980 • Written by Susan Harris + Stu Silver • Directed by JD Lobue

Polly and Danny are putting up with their new psychotic neighbors, and Leslie becomes suicidal after Billy takes her to a nice restaurant only to dump her. The Campbell family can't bear the thought of losing Wendy, and Jessica finally replaces Benson with a butler called Saunders. On election night, just as Burt is fuming over the fact that his own accidental vote for his opponent might cost him the election, Jessica loses consciousness.

Cast. Katherine Helmond (Jessica), Cathryn Damon (Mary), Robert Mandan (Chester), Richard Mulligan (Burt), Diana Canova (Corinne), Jimmy Baio (Billy), Arthur Peterson (The Major), Billy Crystal (Jodie), Ted Wass (Danny), Jay Johnson (Chuck & Bob), Rod Roddy (Announcer), Rebecca Balding (Carol David), Roscoe Lee Browne (Saunders), Madelyn Cates (Mrs. Pfeiffer), John Clavin (Mr. Pfeiffer), John Medici (Waiter), Allan Miller (Dr. Alan Posner), Lynne Moody (Polly), Marla Pennington (Leslie Walker), Donnelly Rhodes (Dutch)

Introducing Sheriff Burt and Deputy Dan.

Highlights. The casual way Danny and Polly deal with their neighbors' harassment while Burt and Mary are there; Leslie's brilliant face plant in her fettuccine the moment Billy tells her he wants to break up, followed by her food freakout immediately afterward; Chester momentarily mistaking Saunders for Benson on their first meeting; and the insanity of the Tate living room as the whole family awaits the results of the election.

Confused? You Won't Be. *'We can't change anything by running away.'*

▶ Mary's reference to "grandma's old room in the attic" is intriguing. Assuming that it isn't Burt's mother, and probably not the mother of Mary's first husband, it would mean that Mary and Jessica were each looking after a parent. More importantly, Mary was looking after the woman who scuttled her romance with Chester many years ago (4.14).

▶ Burt is so distraught at the thought of losing Wendy, he can only manage a half-hearted "woohoo" for Wendy, which Mary finishes by pointing to him and saying "grandpa."

▶ Shortly after telling Billy that she's going to kill herself, Leslie begins what will become a short series of suicide, and ultimately homicide, attempts. This time around, she threatens to cut her throat...with a spoon.

▶ Saunders informs Jessica that he once served dinner for Ugandan tyrant Idi Amin; Jessica thinks he's talking about entertainer Eydie Gorme.

▶ Though Season 3 has seen some of the strongest episodes of *Soap*'s entire run, it's begun to all go horribly wrong. Though Benson has been missed, it isn't until the introduction of Saunders that we realize the Tates, and *Soap*, were doing just fine without him. As fine an actor as Roscoe Lee Browne is, the Jeeves-like Saunders from the very beginning acts as a laugh-extinguisher, the first real misstep of the series, and unfortunately not the last.

Sandy. What Dutch calls Saunders.

Jesse Owens. Who The Major thinks Saunders is.

And introducing...Saunders.

Leslie's Fettuccine Dive

Though Susan Harris and Stu Silver seldom highlighted who had written which scene, occasionally Silver just couldn't help himself when he was particularly proud of something he'd written. Leslie

Walker's face dive into her fettuccine was one of those scenes, Marla Pennington says. In fact, that's how she met Silver. "I was at a children's party and all of the sudden he comes up to me and goes, 'Aren't you Marla Pennington? Well, I wrote the most fun scene that you ever did in your entire career!'

"He was referring to the scene where I was telling Billy that I was committing totally to him, he broke up with me, and I fainted in a plate of fettuccine. Then I continued to pour marinara on me and put a plate of salad on top of my head and a bottle of red wine, and then I ate someone else's chicken leg and threw it over my shoulder.

"When I fell in my fettuccine, they laughed for two and a half minutes—it was forever. They had to cut it, and I was just laying in my fettuccine; it was crazy. And you waited until people stopped laughing—there wasn't any laugh track.

"That was also the funny thing about Stu. If he wanted you to know he'd written a particular scene, he'd tell you because he was proud of something. He'd say, 'I just wrote you something and just think Lucille Ball.' He was a little impish that way."

Best Lines.

Mr. Pfeiffer: We just wanted you to know that not everyone is like that. Not in this state and certainly not on this street! The Block Committee just wanted us to welcome you to the neighborhood and not to judge us by the acts of a few hoodlums.

Mrs. Pfeiffer: This is for you Mrs. uh

Polly: Oh, we're not—

Danny: Dallas. Polly and Danny. Thank you very much. Will you come in?

Mrs. Pfeiffer: Oh, no thank you. We should go back and put out the fire in our living room. Welcome.

Chester's new foil, Saunders.

Rod Roddy's Wrapup. Will Burt become sheriff? Now that the Tates have a new butler, will their manners improve? Will Danny and Polly continue to live where they're living? Will homeowner's insurance be a problem? Now that Billy has told her that their relationship is over, will Leslie really kill herself, or will she just have huge laundry bills? Will Jodie lose Wendy? What has happened to Jessica? These questions and many others will be answered on the next episode of *Soap*.

3.20 First aired: Mar 13, 1980 • Written by Susan Harris + Stu Silver • Directed by JD Lobue

As Jessica suffers from a mystery illness and asks Chester to look after the family while she's in hospital, Dutch and Corinne grow closer, Jodie squares off against Carol in court, and Burt becomes sheriff. His first assignment: dislodge the last sheriff who, despite being caught stuffing the ballot box, refuses to go without a fight.

Cast. Katherine Helmond (Jessica), Cathryn Damon (Mary), Robert Mandan (Chester), Richard Mulligan (Burt), Diana Canova (Corinne), Billy Crystal (Jodie), Ted Wass (Danny), Jay Johnson (Chuck & Bob), Rod Roddy (Announcer), Rae Allen (Judge Betty Small), Rebecca Balding (Carol David), Roscoe Lee Browne (Saunders), Michael Durrell (F. Peter Haversham), Allan Miller (Dr. Alan Posner), Donnelly Rhodes (Dutch), Eugene Roche (E. Ronald Mallu), Granville Van Dusen (Dr. Hill)

Highlights. Danny's unflagging determination to be Burt's deputy; Dutch's goodbye cake; the meeting of E. Ronald Mallu and F. Peter Haversham ("E!" "F!"); and Carol telling a whopper on the stand.

Confused? You Won't Be. *'We're in the crapper.'*

▶ At this point, it seems certain that Danny has grown into the son that Burt always wanted Peter to be. He may not be the brightest fellow, but he'll follow Burt anywhere.

▶ F. Peter Haversham is most likely a riff on America's most famous attorney, F. Lee Bailey, who has defended everybody from Patty Hearst to OJ Simpson.

▶ For even the staunchest *Soap* fan, it is difficult to ignore the feeling that the seeds of the series' demise were sowed in this episode, with the nadir being the weep-fest of Dr. Posner, Chester and Dutch. This is hardly surprising as the producers are now handling *Soap* and *Benson*, and are preparing to launch the Diana Canova vehicle *I'm a Big Girl Now*. That is not to say that we still don't have some wonderful individual scenes to look forward to, but from this episode on, they will be few and far between.

What Dutch's Going Away Cake Says:
Dear Corinne, This is short on account of there ain't much room on this ting. I lobe you. (He couldn't find the little chocolate "v".)

$120. The cost of Mallu's black wingtips.

The Judges Mallu challenged. 1) Hanging Henry Potkin
2) Fag-Baiting Flannigan

The Judge He Thought They'd Get. Sarah Carver (but she was arrested the night before for indecent exposure)

The Judge They Ended up With. Bad Luck Betty Small

22. The number of times Mallu humiliated Small when she was a prosecutor.

Soap and its Sets

Though production designer Edward Stephenson won an Emmy for *Soap* back in 1978, the series never really received the recognition it deserved for its set design.

"There were shows where we would have seven swing sets and [director Jay Sandrich] wanted everything in front of the audience," says stage manager Carl Lauten.

"Well, the Tate living room takes up half the stage. And so what we would do, there might be four or five sets during the course of that hour [of taping] that would roll into the Tate living room, like a float in a parade. They'd be on casters, they would have grids over

In the '70s and '80s, even a lawyer like F. Lee Bailey was a household name.

the top of them, and they were lit overhead. So they'd roll in, plug them in, and do all those scenes in the Tate living room.

"It would've been such a huge undertaking to do that today. Right now there'd be 'let's just shoot all day on Thursday' on those added scenes, and just play them back in front of the audience. But Jay and Paul and Tony and Susan's philosophy was this is [a live] audience show."

Best Lines.

Mary [about Jessica in the hospital]: Burt, they have to find out what she has.

Burt: What she has is health, Mary. And if they find it they're going to keep it.

Burt: ...This is really a breeze. This is fine. I just thought the job would be mostly parades, that's all.

Danny: Let's go.

Mary: Are you crazy? You're not going, too. Go to your room!

Danny: I don't live here anymore.

Mary: Then go home and go to your room.

Danny: Ma, I have to go. I'm the deputy. And wherever Sheriff Burt goes, Deputy Dan follows.

Carol: I asked my mother to take Wendy to New York so she could have a visit with her daddy. I just wanted her to know that whatever happened between Mr. Dallas and myself, she still had a father.

Jodie: What?!

Haversham: What happened when your mother went to pick your child up?

Carol: Mr. Dallas and a group of...

Haversham: A group of what, Miss David?

Carol: A group of homosexuals threatened to kill me if I ever came back for her again.

Jodie [shouting]: That's a lie! My God!

Rod Roddy's Wrapup. What will happen now that Carol has lied in court? Will her nose grow? Now that Sheriff Prentiss says he won't be taken alive, how will Burt take him? Or will he take Burt? Now that Dutch and Corinne are happily in love, what will happen to mess it up? And what is the doctor not telling anyone? What is the matter with Jessica? These questions and many others will be answered on the next episode of *Soap*.

3.21
First aired: Mar 20, 1980 • Written by Susan Harris + Stu Silver • Directed by JD Lobue

Chester returns home yet again, Burt and Danny resolve the Sheriff Prentiss siege situation, Mary tells Jodie that her baby may not be Burt's, and Eunice returns to complicate things further for Dutch and Corinne. However, it's Jessica who faces the biggest challenge of all when Dr. Hill tells her she isn't long for this world.

Cast. Katherine Helmond (Jessica), Cathryn Damon (Mary), Robert Mandan (Chester), Richard Mulligan (Burt), Diana Canova (Corinne), Jennifer Salt (Eunice), Jimmy Baio (Billy), Arthur Peterson (The Major), Billy Crystal (Jodie), Ted Wass (Danny), Jay Johnson (Chuck & Bob), Rod Roddy (Announcer), Rebecca Balding (Carol David), Roscoe Lee Browne (Saunders), Deborah Combs (Nurse), Allan Miller (Dr. Alan Posner), Lynne Moody (Polly), Marla Pennington (Leslie Walker), Peggy Pope (Mrs. David), Donnelly Rhodes (Dutch), Eugene Roche (E. Ronald Mallu), Granville Van Dusen (Dr. Hill)

Highlights. Leslie's latest suicide attempt (a dynamite vest that fails to detonate when she puts the wires together—it only tunes in the local radio station); Dutch's restrained delight as Corinne and Eunice fight over him; and Jessica and Dr. Hill's heart-to-heart as he tells her she has "a maximum of a few weeks, or as little as a few days" to live.

Confused? You Won't Be. 'A while longer would've been nice.'
▶ Bob's filthy joke begins "This lady walks into a bar with Ed Sullivan and a duck…" Alas, we never hear the rest.

1980

MARCH 21: President Jimmy Carter declares that the U.S. will boycott the Summer Olympics in Moscow.

▶ Mary tells Jodie that Alien Burt may be her baby's father, beating the "he might be silver" joke into the ground.

▶ Though Dutch has led us to believe that the murder he committed was a one-off, his trip down memory lane with Corinne reveals stays in reform school and the naval stockades.

▶ Once again Eunice tries to tell Dutch that the reason she treated him badly is because her love for him scared her, but he seems to be wise to her manipulation now, however temporarily. It's hard not to see the image of Corinne, Dutch and Eunice sitting up in bed together as being an homage, however brief, to the poster for the 1969 Paul Mazursky film *Bob & Carol & Ted & Alice* (left).

Rowlf. Corinne tells Eunice that the dog under the covers (actually Dutch) is named this, most likely named after the Muppets' pianist.

Meta meta meta. Jessica tells Dr. Hill she can't die because, among other things, she hasn't seen *Kramer Vs. Kramer* (which itself inspired the Wendy custody battle plotline).

Donnelly Rhodes Can Do Funny

Throughout the 1960s, the ruggedly handsome Donnelly Rhodes frequently turned up as the tough guy on a wide variety of TV shows, from *Bonanza* and *Wagon Train* to *Mannix* and *Mission: Impossible*. With so many serious shows on his résumé, it never occurred to the actor's representatives to send him to read for *Soap*. He might not have even known they were looking to cast the role of Dutch in the first place if it hadn't been for executive producer Paul Junger Witt, who asked for him personally.

"I had known Paul before that, when he was just starting out in the mail room," says Rhodes; this was probably at Columbia Pictures. "We knew each other personally so Paul knew I could be funny." Witt also had directed him in a 1969 episode of the ABC *Seven Brides for Seven Brothers* homage, *Here Come the Brides*.

When it came time to audition for *Soap*, Rhodes ended up doing two scenes: one as Menacing Dutch, another as Funny Dutch. "At one of the auditions, I actually walked into the closet instead of going out the door. I just stayed in character." He chuckles. "I was told later on I was maybe the only person in the cast who was approved by everybody, the network and all the producers."

Best Lines.
Corinne: Eunice, it's, uh, not how it looks.
Eunice: What? My boyfriend is in bed with my sister, he's going "woof woof" under the sheets, and it's not how it looks? What was he doing under there, hiding a bone? [The sustained audience reaction makes this line much funnier than it is on paper.]

Jessica: You've got something on your mind?
Dr. Hill: Yes I do.
Jessica: Wait a minute, don't say anything. Just give me a few more seconds of immortality. [Long pause.] I think you were about to tell me I'm going to die.
Dr. Hill: It's a new strain of virus and we just don't know how to combat it yet.
Jessica: How fast can you learn?
Dr. Hill: Not fast enough.
Jessica: I mean I finally replace Benson and now I'm going to die.

Rod Roddy's Wrapup. Will Leslie ever learn to kill herself? Will she kill herself trying? Now that Eunice is back, what will Dutch do? What will Corinne do? What will Eunice do? Will they do it together? Now that Chester is home, will the family stick together? Will Saunders stick around? What will Jessica do now that she knows she's dying? Does she have a lot of choices? These questions and many others will be answered on the next episode of *Soap*.

3.22 First aired: Mar 27, 1980 • Written by Susan Harris + Stu Silver • Directed by JD Lobue

Fittingly, this season finale is all about endings. While Jessica makes her peace with the people closest to her before she dies, Polly and

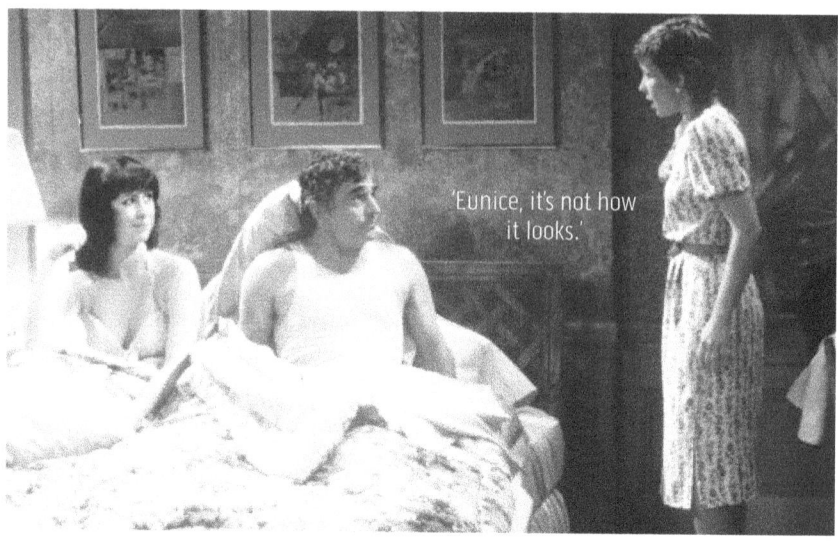

'Eunice, it's not how it looks.'

Danny's relationship appears ready to implode, arguments in Jodie's custody battle conclude, Sheriff Burt and Danny have a face to face run-in with the criminal Napoleon who runs Dunn's River, and Corinne and Eunice force Dutch to make a choice. Even Leslie gives up her suicidal rages, opting to turn homicidal instead. The only bright side is Mary finally going into labor, just moments before Jessica delivers her dying words...to Benson.

Cast. Katherine Helmond (Jessica), Cathryn Damon (Mary), Robert Mandan (Chester), Richard Mulligan (Burt), Diana Canova (Corinne), Jennifer Salt (Eunice), Jimmy Baio (Billy), Arthur Peterson (The Major), Billy Crystal (Jodie), Ted Wass (Danny), Rod Roddy (Announcer), Rae Allen (Judge Betty Small), Rebecca Balding (Carol David), Roscoe Lee Browne (Saunders), Hamilton Camp (Elmore Tibbs), Michael Durrell (F. Peter Haversham), Sheldon Feldner (Bailiff), Robert Guillaume (Benson), Kenneth Kimmins (Blind Man), Allan Miller (Dr. Alan Posner), Lynne Moody (Polly), Marla Pennington (Leslie Walker), Donnelly Rhodes (Dutch), Eugene Roche (E. Ronald Mallu), Granville Van Dusen (Dr. Hill)

Highlights. Jessica already planning on meeting men in heaven because Chester probably won't make it there; Carol's sob story on the stand and Mallu's over-the-top attack on her character; Jodie losing it in court after Mrs. David recites a preposterous story on the stand; Dutch's inspired, and very long, "Eenie Meenie Minie Moe..." when he's trying to choose between Corinne and Eunice;

Jodie's controlled-yet-passionate testimony; Danny and the blind man's interaction in the restaurant, and his spoiling his proposal to Polly by ranting at the other people there whom he thinks have been staring at them; the effortless way Saunders quiets the Tates; Jessica's wild taped message to the family, and The Major's brief moment of clarity; Burt standing up to Tibbs after he threatens to hurt Mary; and Jessica's final meeting with Benson.

Confused? You Won't Be. *'It's been a nice life…I hate to leave it.'*

▶ This is a double episode, much to its detriment.

▶ Chester's bedside talk with Jessica at the beginning gives both Robert Mandan and Katherine Helmond an increasingly rare opportunity to show us their impressive acting ranges.

▶ Jessica's throwaway line about her mother bugging her about her makeup in heaven will come back with an even better punch line later (4.1).

▶ Kudos to Susan Harris & Co. for throwing us a curveball with the Polly/Danny story line, as Polly tells Mr. "What are *you* looking at" that she doesn't think he is mature enough to handle their interracial relationship.

▶ Burt and Danny's run-in with Mr. Tibbs is a dark turn utterly out of joint with the *Soap* we've come to know. Up till now the conflicts our beloved characters have faced have been more farcical than ferocious. Between Tibbs' threats to disfigure Mary and the way he frames our bumbling pair next season, it all reeks of a mean streak heretofore unseen on what has always been a gentle show.

▶ With the exceptions of the Jodie-Carol courtroom scenes and Danny and Polly's botched restaurant outing, the episode all but sinks under the weight of its forced cliffhangers. Last season finale it was the inspired lunacy of Burt being abducted by aliens; this time it's Burt and Danny knocked out by a crime boss.

Chester's confessions of Infidelity to Jessica: 1) Maternity ward nurse (when Jessica was in labor with Eunice), 2) Chambermaid (on their honeymoon), 3) Tour guide (while Jessica was watching the changing of the guard in London)

Mary Jr. Burt's name for their baby if it's a girl.

1980

APRIL 7: The U.S. imposes economic sanctions on Iran.

APRIL 21: Rosie Ruiz wins the Boston Marathon, but is stripped of the honor shortly thereafter once it is strongly suspected that she didn't run the whole 26.2 miles. Two years later she will do jail time for embezzling $60,000 in cash from the real estate company she worked for. In 1983 she will return to jail after trying to broker a cocaine deal.

Excerpts from the Dunn's River Penal Code: 1204: Obscene behavior; 601: Disturbing the peace; 508: Lost dog; 618: Illegal entry; 412: Hitting somebody over the head when they don't want you to; 714: Liquor store holdup

Jessica's last words. Benson, you be happy. Be happy. You be happy cause that's all there really is.

Best Friend Benson…Till the Very End. How fitting that the last man Jessica speaks with before her passing is the one man who never let her down. Benson smiles through her crazy explanation of why she's glad he came. His reply: "I guess it never leaves ya. I still understand you when you talk." She then tells him what we've known all along. "You were my best friend, Benson." Says Benson, "And you are the best person that's ever been in my life."

"It was a love story," admits Tony Thomas of the Jessica-Benson story line. "Beyond her sister, obviously, Benson was her closest confidante. He protected her, cared for her—in my mind it was a love story the entire time once we got to know them. That he cared for her certainly. Her and Billy more than anybody."

Leslie and Billy, Ahead of Their Time. As farcical as poor Leslie Walker's sudden murderous hatred of Billy becomes, little did anybody realize that the weird teacher-student relationship would be reflected in the headlines on and off for many years to come. Most famously, New Hampshire teacher Pamela Smart and her 15-year-old lover, Billy Flynn, were sent to prison after being found guilty of orchestrating the murder of Smart's husband in 1990.

"Susan Harris really hit a nerve with that," says Baio. "She was ahead of her time with a lot of things. I always think about that when they make headlines, some teacher—and a lot of times it's a female teacher—and a young boy."

Best Lines.
Jessica: Now Chester I don't want to wear a lot of makeup.
Chester: When?
Jessica: When I'm dead. So tell the undertaker to take it easy on the makeup, you see, because I know I am not going to be in heaven

two seconds before my mother will say to me, 'Do you *really* think you look nice like that, Jessica?'

Mrs. David: I will tell you exactly what happened. I went to Jodie's apartment and there was this woman there with some men and she said that if I didn't get out of there in 10 seconds, they were going to beat the living hell out of me. And if I ever tried to come back and get Wendy they were going to kill me.

Mallu: Your honor, I object.

Judge: Overruled.

Mallu: OK.

Haversham: Mrs. David, would you tell the court please, who was the aforementioned woman?

Mrs. David: The woman in Mr. Dallas' apartment with that gang of homosexuals was Jodie Dallas.

Pamela Smart, the Leslie Walker of the 1990s.

Dutch [trying to choose between Corinne and Eunice]: Eenie Meenie Minie Moe, one of you has got to go. Who it is I do not know and this hurts worse than a broken toe. Once there was a guy named Joe. He fell in love with Ruth and Flo. He chose Ruth said Flo go blow, and this is going very slow. Rooti tutti hoopty hee, I love yous and yous love me. We can't stay here all us three, so one of you has got to leave. Reeva reeva fee foe fum, one of you will be mighty glum when I choose the other one, but then I'll feel like a dirty old bum...

Haversham: Mr. Dallas, what do you do?

Jodie: I direct commercials.

Haversham: I mean with a man.

Jodie: Oh please.

Haversham: Exactly what are the mechanics involved?

Jodie: That's an insulting question!

Haversham: Did you ever frequent a bar known as Barney's?

Jodie: Was that you?

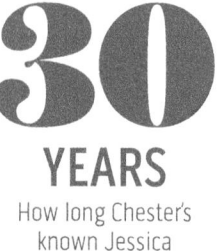

30 YEARS
How long Chester's known Jessica

Judge: Mr Dallas, I don't have to remind you that not answering the question—

Jodie: —is contempt. Fine. Because I'm not about to be humiliated and my lifestyle desecrated anymore by these examinations. I'm not going to lose my temper. I refuse to lose my self-respect. So if you want to hold me in contempt, it's fine. I've proven, at least to myself, what kind of father I am. I'd never expose Wendy to anything that was harmful or unfavorable to her health, either mentally or physically. And whether Wendy lives with me or not, at least she'll know that I've always wanted her. And that I'll always be there for her. And that's something that no one can ever take away. If you all will excuse me, I'm going home. [Leaves the courtroom.]

Mallu: Your honor, I ask you to realize the strain that my client has been under and not hold him in contempt.

Judge: Mr. Mallu, I make my decisions based on facts, not personal emotion. And may I say your client presented his case more honestly and directly than you ever have.

[Leslie hunts through her bag for her gun to kill herself.]

Billy: Look Leslie, my mother's in the hospital fighting for her life. Now if you have no regard for yours, then pull the trigger. But do us a favor, do it somewhere else. Just leave us alone.

Leslie: You're right, Billy. I can't kill myself. It wouldn't solve anything. It's just that I was so crazy with grief I didn't want to live in the same world with you.

Billy: Yeah, I know.

Leslie: And I still don't. [Points the gun at Billy.] So I'm going to kill you.

Rod Roddy's Wrapup. Will Polly marry Danny? Who will Dutch choose? What will happen to Danny and Burt? Will Leslie kill Billy? Who will get custody of Wendy? Will Mary have an alien baby? Is Jessica dead? These questions and many others will be answered on the next episode of *Soap*.

Seasons 3 began with the absurdity of Burt's abduction by aliens and Billy by a cult, and ended on a series of cliffhangers so sordid and depressing, it was pretty easy to forget by the end that Soap was in fact a comedy. The next (and final) season would not make the same mistake, but the laughs would come too few, and much, much, too late.

Season Four

Even more characters would come to inhabit the *Soap* universe in Season 4, pulling the series even further away from its greatest strength: the story of sisters Jessica & Mary. While we were given a startling bit of history about these two toward season's end, it was not enough to save the program from the inevitable. It would, at least, go out with a series of cliffhangers that still haunt viewers to this very day...

4.0 *Jessica's Wonderful Life* • First aired: Oct 28, 1980
• Written by Susan Harris + Stu Silver • Directed by JD Lobue

Jessica finds herself at the way station to heaven, pleading with Rosemary the Escort Angel to intercede on her behalf with God to let her have just a little more time on Earth. She makes her case by telling Rosemary about what's happened during Season 3 with the Tates and the Campbells.

Cast: Beatrice Arthur (Rosemary), Katherine Helmond (Jessica)

Highlights. The whole episode is made up of about 1 hour and 15 minutes of highlights from Season 3.

'I was just starting my life over,' Jessica tells Rosemary the angel.

Confused? You Won't Be. *'I can't go. I haven't finished my life yet.'*

◉ One of the Holy Grails of *Soap* fandom amongst newer *Soap* fans (owing to its lack of a DVD release), "Jessica's Wonderful Life" features a set that is impressive precisely because it is so minimal. A little fog, a riser and a faux celestial staircase and bingo: heaven.

◉ Rosemary (who died in a parking accident) tells Jessica she used to be an account executive for real-life advertising agency BBDO. (Author's note: They came up with everything from the "ring around the collar" Wisk commercial to Visa's "It's everywhere you want to be.")

◉ Sunnies don't go to heaven, according to Rosemary.

◉ Despite the writing credit for this episode, Stu Silver explains that Susan wrote all the wraparound stories (including this one) for the compilation shows. "It's like Lennon and McCartney," he laughs. "McCartney writes one song and it's 'Lennon and McCartney.'"

◉ The most striking thing about this episode is just how unexceptional the dialogue is for *Soap*. Of course with Season 4 just around the corner, *Benson* going strong, and *I'm a Big Girl Now* premiering three days from now, there wasn't a lot of time to put this one together.

1980

OCT. 21: Famous-for-being-famous socialite, Paris Hilton pal, and reality TV personality Kim Kardashian is born, paving the way for what television will become in the 21st century.

9 p.m. When heaven was expecting Jessica. (She's a few minutes early.)

White Patent Leather Loafers. What God was wearing the one time Rosemary saw him. (She only saw his feet.)

Ice cream, cookies, pasta, chocolate mousse. Just some of the things you can eat in heaven without gaining weight. (Jessica is most enthused by the last item.)

Diana Canova and *I'm a Big Girl Now*

Last year Robert Guillaume left the fold to headline the Witt Thomas Harris show *Benson*; in three days Diana Canova will follow in his footsteps with *I'm a Big Girl Now*. The series—whose story of a young woman (Canova) who moves back home to live with her doctor father sounds like a dry run for later Witt Thomas Harris series *Empty Nest*—starred Tony Thomas' father (and legendary entertainer) Danny Thomas as Canova's dear old dad.

Soap's Diana Canova and Sheree North in *I'm a Big Girl Now*.

"I said to Paul [Witt], 'I don't want to produce the show with my father—*you* give him notes,'" Tony Thomas remembers. "But I ended up giving him notes when we did *The Practice*."

We'll get back to *I'm a Big Girl Now* in a moment. First…how exactly do you give your father notes when he's *Danny Thomas*?

"He would stare me down sometimes," Tony Thomas says with a laugh. "I'd say that's good but it's got to be better, it's not funny enough. We'll do some rewriting but we think you can help us here by delivering it there. It was interesting for me, it was interesting for him, but by a few shows in he said 'I've decided to give myself the greatest compliment one man can give—I've decided to listen to my son because I've raised him well.' I said OK, thanks. It was tougher. I certainly sweated more, and I cared greatly about our work, but there was a bigger stress in making the editing of those shows as good as possible because it was my father in it."

> " I had been watching Danny Thomas all my life..."
> — DIANA CANOVA

It all comes back to family, even if that family is one forged in the service of television, as Diana Canova discovered.

"Getting my own show, having one created just for me was a big thrill," she says. "It was being produced by the same *Soap* team so I felt very comfortable. However, I do remember the last episode when Corinne had to say goodbye to Jessica [4.2] and how hard I cried as I did that last take. *Soap* was a phenomenon. Jobs like that come along once, if you're lucky. And as much as I loved the experience of *I'm a Big Girl Now* and I really did, I knew I had been part of something special and groundbreaking. The other part of it was the 'family' I had to leave. We were all very close, and as amazing as it was to be spun off, it was tough to leave the *Soap* clan.

"*I'm a Big Girl Now* was a blast. It's hard to have Marty Short in a room and not be laughing every minute. The other members of the cast were so great. I had been watching Danny Thomas all my life, and to have him play my dad was incredible. I learned so much from him and from Sheree North, who was one of the most unique, spectacular gals around. She was a tremendous talent, but also a true original and just totally cool. Rori King who played my daughter was also a find. A gifted little actress and a great kid. So yeah, it was all great."

Best Lines.
Rosemary: Those Japanese are really fantastic, you know? Calculators, TVs, cameras, brilliant people, brilliant. Still eating with sticks.

Jessica: Rosemary please, I can't go. You cannot take me with you!

Rosemary: Jessica, Jessica, if we don't take you then the next one doesn't want to go, then the one after that, and pretty soon there's nobody dead. Do you know what the world would be like? Do you want to see gas lines? I mean besides can you see the paperwork involved?

Jessica: Then you *can* do something.

Rosemary: Well occasionally we can request a delay. I mean Tito got an extra three months while Yugoslavia got in shape.

Jessica: Please, please make the request. I was just starting my life over, and my children are grown, my marriage is over, and I started dating a psychiatrist. You should understand. Rosemary you were once a woman.

Rosemary: Once?

Jessica: Well, now you're an angel.

Rosemary: But I'm still a woman.

Jessica: Then you should understand.

Rod Roddy's Wrapup. None this episode.

 **First aired:** Nov 12, 1980 • **Written by** Susan Harris, Stu Silver, Dick Clair + Jenna McMahon • **Directed by** JD Lobue

It's smiles all around as Dutch finally makes his decision, Jodie wins custody of baby Wendy, Mary has her (jaundice but not silver) baby, and Jessica recovers from the newly named "Jessica Syndrome". Yet there's trouble a brewin' as Sheriff Burt and Deputy Danny are the featured subjects of Tibbs' pornographic motel room pictures, and Carol warns Jodie that their fight over Wendy has only just begun.

Cast. Jimmy Baio (Billy), Roscoe Lee Browne (Saunders), Diana Canova (Corinne), Billy Crystal (Jodie), Cathryn Damon (Mary),

> " I used to read and type jokes for a living before I started working on all these shows. In two years I must've read and typed 20,000 to 30,000 jokes, so I have quite a file in my head for them. But Susan wrote a line that Bea Arthur said to Katherine that I still use to this day when the timing's right. Jessica's trying to convince her to let her go back to Earth. Somehow or another the Japanese come up. And Bea Arthur said something like, 'The Japanese, they think they're so smart, they're still eating with sticks.' And I thought, 'Oh jeez, I'll never forget that line.' And I've used it over and over again as if it were my own."
>
> —MARSHA POSNER, Associate Producer

Katherine Helmond (Jessica), Jay Johnson (Chuck & Bob), Robert Mandan (Chester), Allan Miller (Dr. Alan Posner), Richard Mulligan (Burt), Marla Pennington (Leslie Walker), Arthur Peterson (The Major), Donnelly Rhodes (Dutch), Eugene Roche (E. Ronald Mallu), Jennifer Salt (Eunice), Granville Van Dusen (Dr. Hill), Ted Wass (Danny), Rod Roddy (Announcer), Debbie Combs (Nurse), Sarina C. Grant (Nurse), Brian Kale (Emergency Doctor), Rae Allen (Judge Betty Small), Michael Durrell (F. Peter Haversham), Sheldon Feldner (Deputy Perkins)

Highlights. Chester and Mallu both pawing Jessica and getting blown across the room after Dr. Hill hits her with a jolt from the paddles; Burt and Danny watching the CCTV footage; Bob smoking in Mary's room; Mary's "what color is it" when she realizes she's had the baby; and Mary's "Oh thank God he's white" in front of the black nurse; Corinne telling Eunice she doesn't think Jessica's brain needs as much oxygen as other people's; Eunice's delight in Corinne's defeat; Jessica's drawn-out awakening in the hospital, followed by her gentle "Hi"; and Jessica and Mary's chat in Mary's hospital room.

Confused? You Won't Be. *'Mrs. Campbell, congratulations, you have a son.' 'Oh thank God he's white!'*

Norman Lear

◉ It's either feast or famine with the hour-long episodes. Fortunately we are in for a satisfying feast this time around.

◉ Dick Clair and Jenna McMahon, two writers that Susan Harris worked with briefly during *Fay*, join the team with this episode, and even get producing credit alongside Stu Silver.

◉ Danny's "Boy, Norman Lear really did change television" (see Best Lines) is one of the best "inside baseball" gags in *Soap*, simultaneously mocking protesters who claimed shows such as *All in the Family* would be the end of civility, and paying homage to Susan Harris' former mentor.

◉ Jessica predicted it was she, not Mary, who would be hassled about her makeup by her mother (see Best Lines under 3.22). Of course knowing Jess' devilish sense of humor since she came back from the dead, she might have changed their mother's words slightly in fun to bug Mary (see "Best Lines" for this entry).

▶ Her "I felt a whole lot weaker when I was on the Scarsdale diet" is particularly poignant considering that the diet's originator, Dr. Herman Tarnower, was shot to death by lover Jean Harris on March 10 of this year. Odder still, she originally claimed that she had taken the pistol she killed Tarnower with to his home planning to kill herself, but ended up shooting him in a jealous rage—very similar to Leslie Walker's story line in *Soap*.

Jean Harris

Arrow Motel. The sordid little place Burt and Danny wake up to find themselves in.

Jennifer. What Burt calls Danny when he's fixing his wig.

9 lbs. The weight of Mary's baby.

High-card wins. Dutch's answer to choosing between Corinne and Eunice.

10. Eunice's card

Jack. What Corinne says her card is.

3. What she actually drew. (She was bluffing.)

15 years. How long it's been since Mallu lost a case.

Charlie Graubart. Jessica's fourth-grade boyfriend. (He's a wino now.)

What We Did on Our Summer Vacation

Getting things ready for a season of *Soap* is a frenetic affair at the best of times; doing it in the middle of a strike is something else altogether. And in July, the Screen Actors Guild called a strike.

"We were all on set, we're running lines, we're getting blocked, we're working, and SAG comes and says no, you've gotta walk off," recalls Marla Pennington. "And we all just kinda go, 'Ooookay.' We gather up our stuff and we're all standing in the parking lot—now what do we do? It's just bizarre.

"And then during that strike we'd run into each other doing picket lines around Disney, where I got to meet Dick Crenna (*The Real McCoys*, *It Takes Two*) for the first time, and we walked around Disney for three hours. People would stop you and ask you for autographs and take your picture—it was otherworldly.

"Then *Soap* was nominated for Emmy awards and we couldn't go. I could've been at the Emmys other times, but I don't want to be there unless I'm there working because they're really boring if you're not working and not invested in it. And Cathryn Damon won and Richard Mulligan won and we couldn't be there. They didn't even accept the awards, it was really sad. They missed their big moments."

While Mulligan would later win an Emmy for *Empty Nest* in 1989, Damon, who was nominated in 1978 and 1981 for her work on *Soap*, never did.

The 1980 Screen Actors Guild strike was one of the longest in SAG's history.

Best Lines.
Danny: Holy cow! Look at that! She must know yoga!
Burt: Or something.
Danny: How many of them are there?
Burt: 1, 2, 3, 4, 5—there's 5. And a dachshund.
Danny: No, no, no, no, that's not a dachshund. That's some guy dressed up like a dachshund.
Burt: Good, I thought it was really sick.
Danny: What channel is this, what is this show?
Burt: And a dwarf! I forgot to count that dwarf!
Danny: Boy, Norman Lear really did change television!

Billy [reminding Leslie of the consequences of killing him]: It'll mean the chair!

Leslie: Three years tops. Then I'll write a book about it. Then Meryl Streep will star in the movie version. You know, this is starting to sound like a better idea all the time. Goodbye Billy! [She fires, Billy ducks, and the bullet grazes Saunders' temple.]

Jessica [agreeing to meet one of her mother's friends in heaven]: I'm so pleased to meet you Mr. Pasteur. Your name is on my milk.

Jessica: Mary, I have a message for you!

Mary: From whom?

Jessica: From mother.

Mary: Jessie, mother's dead

Jessica: I know. Mary, I haven't discussed this with anybody but when I died, I went to heaven. It is an incredible place, Mary. But now when you go, be sure you take electric rollers because with that mist you'll have no hairdo. Anyway Mary, when I was in heaven, I saw mother, and she told me to tell you you're wearing too much eyeliner.

Mary: It's never gonna stop.

Jessica: She says it looks cheap.

Mary: Dead, and she's still getting to me.

Jessica: She told me to stay with Chester. She said at my age I couldn't get anybody new.

Mary: And when I die, if I go to heaven, is that gonna be it? That's going to be eternal paradise, listening to her?

Jessica: Well Mary, she does have a point. I mean have you seen the competition these days? I mean they wear lipstick and roller skates and nothing in between.

Mary: Jessie, that's not competition. Teenyboppers on roller skates? What adult man would be interested in one of them? [Thinks.] You're right.

Rod Roddy's Wrapup. Now that Dutch has chosen Eunice, what will Corinne do besides get more sleep? Will Leslie be satisfied with winging Saunders or will she try to kill Billy again? Now that Jessica has a horrible disease named after her, will everybody want one? Now that Tibbs has pictures of Danny and Burt with six naked ladies, what will Danny and Burt do? When Carol said I'll make you wish you never had a daughter, was she just being a bad loser? These questions and many others will be answered on the next episode of *Soap*.

4.2 First aired: Nov 19, 1980 • Written by Susan Harris, Stu Silver, Dick Clair + Jenna McMahon • Directed by JD Lobue

This episode we see that Jessica has returned from death stronger than ever, dismissing her four suitors and gracefully accepting Corinne's decision to move to California to get away from her own misery. Burt, too, realizes that he and Danny must stand up to Tibbs' blackmail schemes, though his deputy has been laid low by Polly's news that she isn't in love with him. And the day Mary brings baby Scottie home from the hospital, Jodie discovers that somebody has kidnapped Wendy.

Jessica and the motley assortment of men (except, we hope, The Major) who would marry her.

Cast. Diana Canova (Corinne), Billy Crystal (Jodie), Cathryn Damon (Mary), Katherine Helmond (Jessica), Jay Johnson (Chuck & Bob), Robert Mandan (Chester), Allan Miller (Dr. Alan Posner), Lynne Moody (Polly), Richard Mulligan (Burt), Eugene Roche (E. Ronald Mallu), Granville Van Dusen (Dr. Hill), Ted Wass (Danny)

Highlights. Jessica's bizarre-yet-effective way of solving Dr. Hill's object-in-their-correct-holes challenge, and her telling Hill, Posner, Chester and Mallu that she's decided not to be with any of them; Jessica's philosophical talk with Corinne before she leaves for California; drunk Bob; and Burt letting Tibbs have it over the phone.

Confused? You Won't Be. *'And when they're little and they let go of your hand, they never take it again.'*

▶ Jessica's dismissal of her suitors this episode means an end to a slapstick nonsense that has been a huge drag on the series the last few episodes.

▶ The ho-hum end to Polly and Danny's relationship is particularly sad considering how much fun some of their scenes together were. Like Jodie's friend Alice before her, Polly feels like she was given the bum's rush.

▶ Though this book doesn't usually concern itself with continuity errors, Jessica does mess with history a bit when she tells Corinne this episode that her current home is only two blocks away from the one she grew up in, yet tells Eunice next episode that their current home has seen the weddings of Jessica's parents, Mary and Johnny Dallas, as well as that of her and Chester.

▶ The departure of Diana Canova is the second major one from the original cast after Robert Guillaume, and marks the beginning of the end for the series. It's all downhill from here.

Ace, King, Queen, *TV Guide*. The elements of Dr. Hill's one-of-these-objects-does-not-belong test.

Billy Crystal vs. Jodie Dallas

It had been no secret to cast and crew that Billy Crystal had been wrestling with his role on *Soap* for many years. An actor who aspired to be more of an old-school entertainer in the Sammy Davis Jr. vein than an actor *per se*, Crystal had also long since grown tired of the fruit jokes and the queen jokes that had lessened over time, but still made a regular appearance (e.g., Bob's "Well, you'd know" remark this episode after Jodie says of Wendy "the queen has arisen").

"Billy was very forthright with it, that he was tired of this show," says Marla Pennington. "I remember sitting in the prop room and there was a bunch of us around the table, and he was entertaining us as he always did, he was always naturally very funny. And his two little girls were in the dressing rooms a lot running up and down the stairs—that was the age range. But this was like one of his first big breaks, and he was ready to move on. He was tired

1980

NOV. 21 Rival network CBS scores the highest rated television episode at the time with the conclusion to its "Who Shot JR" story line on the prime time soap *Dallas*, with an estimated 83 million Americans tuning in.

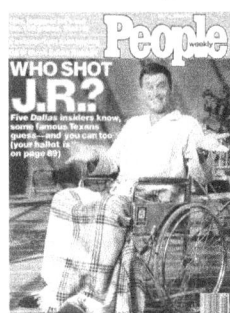

NOV. 22 Movie star Mae West, one of the few people ever to be jailed for performing comedy in the U.S. (in 1926 for her first Broadway play, *Sex*), dies.

of playing the gay guy or whatever the jokes were; it was stale to him. He didn't say it but you felt it, that he had other things to do. And he sure did."

Best Lines.

Corinne: I didn't wake you, did I?

Jessica: Oh no, Corinne, I don't sleep here. It's too dangerous. The woman in 412 went to sleep and woke up without a gallbladder. See they were supposed to take 421's gallbladder but they took 412's by mistake. And then they took 421's spleen instead of 412. And when I closed my eyes to take a nap, they took my Jello.

Rod Roddy's Wrapup. Now that Polly has left Danny for good, will Danny assume she doesn't want to see him anymore? Now that Corinne has left home for good, will she find happiness in California, or at least a terrific deli? Since Jessica has told the guys none of them can be with her, will they continue to play cards together? Will Tibbs publish the naked pictures of Burt and Danny, and if so, will they be available in wallet size? And who kidnapped Wendy, and why? These questions and many others will be answered in the next episode of *Soap*.

> "Susan may have had a story line for a whole season for a character. But after a couple of episodes she'd say I just don't like that character. Then that character was suddenly written out. Susan had a great ear and a great eye and great instincts, and would say we can't keep this character on for a whole season, or for next season. And they'd be gone in three or four episodes. Not many of them, but once in a while."
>
> —STU SILVER
> Writer

4.3
First aired: Nov 26, 1980 • Written by Susan Harris, Stu Silver, Dick Clair + Jenna McMahon • Directed by JD Lobue

Jodie vows to find Wendy after realizing the law won't help him. Jessica returns home to discover Leslie's homicidal tendencies, and to learn that Dutch and Eunice are getting married. Jessica tells Mary she's going to divorce Chester, and Mary may be right behind her in divorce court now that she's received Tibbs' motel photos of Burt and Danny. Yet even banished to the pool house, Chester soon will come up trumps.

Cast. Jimmy Baio (Billy), Roscoe Lee Browne (Saunders), Billy Crystal (Jodie), Cathryn Damon (Mary), Katherine Helmond (Jessica), Robert Mandan (Chester), Richard Mulligan (Burt), Marla Pennington (Leslie Walker), Arthur Peterson (The Major), Donnelly Rhodes (Dutch), Jennifer Salt (Eunice), Ted Wass (Danny)

Highlights. Chester accidentally strangling Billy when he was going for Dutch; Leslie's grenade attack, Dutch instantly throwing himself on top of it, and Chester having a change of heart about him; Jessica's reaction to seeing the Tibbs motel photos ("Burt is very…handsome"), and letting Mary in on how her face "falls" when she leans over; and Chester's gradual realization that his old tricks aren't going to work with Jessica now that she's made up her mind to separate.

Confused? You Won't Be. *'Things will never be the same, will they?'*

◉ It seems pretty unbelievable that the law has no problem with Carol violating Jodie's court-ordered custody of Wendy.

◉ Confronted with the prospect of Dutch marrying Eunice, Chester resorts to suicide attempts…again (2.1).

◉ Once again Mary and Jessica try to top each other's life events (2.3, 3.13, 3.15).

The 3 I's. Impotence, Infidelity, Invisibility—what Burt has put Mary through, according to Mary. (That middle one, though, applies more to her than him as Burt only *thought* he had slept with Sally, while Mary really did sleep with Alien Burt.)

'How Ignorant and Arrogant We Were as Actors'

Of all the cast and crew of *Soap*, Jennifer Salt has had one of the most unusual journeys, which has also brought with it an unusual insight into the workings of Hollywood. After starting her show-business career in 1969's *Midnight Cowboy*, she did her fair share of B-movies before breaking through with *Soap*. Yet all the while she never really felt comfortable in the role of actress.

"I think it was always iffy but I didn't acknowledge it as that," she says of her

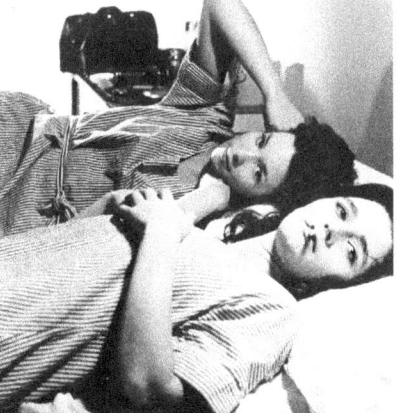

Jennifer Salt and Jon Voight in *The Revolutionary* (1970, above), and with Margot Kidder in *Sisters* (1973).

acting career. "I only realized how iffy it was when I stopped doing it and I was so happy to stop, to find what I felt comfortable doing."

What she felt comfortable doing turned out to be writing. Looking back on it now after years spent doing writing and production work on everything from the *American Horror Story* series to helping to adapt Elizabeth Gilbert's bestseller *Eat Pray Love* for the screen in 2010, Salt has some regrets.

"I think what I'm quite shocked by now that I'm a writer is how ignorant and arrogant we were as actors—it just takes my breath away. We were very critical of the writing, very resistant to their notes, very New-York-actors snobby. And I'm not just speaking of myself. We had very little awareness of what the writers were doing. It just sort of blows me away when I look back and think how there were people on that show whose names I didn't even hardly know, didn't acknowledge at the table reads. I can criticize myself, but I think others were that way as well. We were known as a difficult cast. They just thought they were too cool for school, you know."

This is not to say that the actors were particularly rude or self-aggrandizing by nature, though tempers could certainly run high, and some were harder to handle than others, according to the directors. It had more to do with the standing of television itself at the time, Salt explains. "I think it was partly the culture of that time. TV wasn't the brass ring the way it is now. I think actors sometimes felt that they were cashing in on something but it wasn't something they were massively proud of."

And like Salt herself, most of the principal actors had enjoyed at least a little time on Broadway, or at least in high-profile off-Broadway shows. Even today, most seasoned actors hold stagework in higher esteem than television and film, deeming it truer to the craft than the other mediums, which are more concerned with technical details (lighting, sound mixes, etc.) than acting itself.

"I came from New York so I was definitely part of the New York actor culture," Salt admits. "And my dad [Waldo Salt] was a screenwriter and he wrote Academy Award winning screenplays. Somehow TV didn't quite fit into the fancy plans."

Best Lines.

Leslie: Oh hi, Mrs. Tate. Oh you look wonderful.

Jessica: Thank you.

Leslie: I was so worried. I was going to send you a card but I was afraid they might try and trace it.

Jessica: Well it's a lovely thought, dear.

Leslie: Well I'm so glad you're home, welcome back. I'm gonna have to blow you up now.

Mary [on why she couldn't be in an orgy]: I could never be in a group—I'm too competitive.

Rod Roddy's Wrapup. Since Jessica has exiled Chester to the pool house, will he go crazy with grief or buy a nice pair of swim trunks? Will Leslie try to kill Billy again, or will Saunders stop her by killing her first? Now that Mary has received the porno pictures of Burt with six naked ladies, what will she do? Frame them? And what will Jodie do now that he knows the law can't help him find his kidnapped baby? These questions and many others will be answered in the next episode of *Soap*.

 First aired: Dec 3, 1980 • Written by Susan Harris, Stu Silver, Dick Clair + Jenna McMahon • Directed by JD Lobue

It's Dutch and Eunice's wedding day, but the only thing that really changes is the maid of honor, Annie, quickly shacking up with Chester in the pool house. As promised, Tibbs has the pictures of Burt and Danny published in the local paper. Yet it is Jessica, who has taken Dr. Hill's advice to seek relaxation abroad, who finds herself truly in over her head when she helps free an anti-communist revolutionary during her flight.

Cast. Jimmy Baio (Billy), Roscoe Lee Browne (Saunders), Cathryn Damon (Mary), Nancy Dolman (Annie Selig), Katherine Helmond (Jessica), Jay Johnson (Chuck & Bob), Robert Mandan (Chester), Richard Mulligan (Burt), Arthur Peterson (The Major), Donnelly Rhodes (Dutch), Jennifer Salt (Eunice), Gregory Sierra (El Puerco),

Judy Evans' original watercolor sketch for Eunice's wedding dress.

Ted Wass (Danny), Announcer (Rod Roddy), Macon McCalman (Minister)

Highlights. Dutch's delight in discussing his "blinding crazy lust" for Eunice as Chester prepares to strangle him, and the casual way Chester tosses Dutch aside when he lays eyes on Annie for the first time; everyone trying to figure out where the funeral march is coming from, and the minister producing a tape recorder; Chester propositioning Annie during the wedding ceremony ("pool house," choke); and El Puerco's hijacking of the plane Jessica's on.

Confused? You Won't Be. *'A little vacation to one of those tiny islands in the ocean.'*

▶ Annie Selig was Eunice's roommate in college, and the maid of honor at Eunice and Dutch's wedding. (An honor Eunice regrets once Annie moves into the pool house with her father.)

◉ Once again Mary gets mad at Burt not for what he's done, but for keeping his problems to himself. This time it's the whole Tibbs fiasco, last time it was his fear that he was going to die (3.17).

◉ Note the boyish, carefree manner that Chester adopts when he and Annie join the rest of the family for breakfast. (Would our Chester ever have worn a yellow sweater to the table?)

◉ The book Jessica is reading on the plane is *White House Years* by Henry Kissinger, published in October 1979; her laughter pretty much sums up the country's disgust with the previous decade's political scandals.

◉ As Tony Thomas says, by Season 4 of a series you're "tap dancing," just keeping the characters moving—something that has characterized the beginning of this season. Once again we have Burt falling out with Mary over a fooling around he wasn't conscious for; the number of funny lines has greatly diminished (check out this episode's anemic "Best Lines" section); and the only story line with any emotional weight—Jodie's missing baby—is absent. While Gregory Sierra's wonderful portrayal of El Puerco is worth the price of admission alone, even that character will gradually be tamed by season's end.

The Third Dot in from the Left. Malaguay, the island nation for which Jessica is bound, and the home of El Puerco.

Wolfies. El Puerco was captured in this restaurant in Miami the day before.

And introducing...Annie Selig and Carlos Marcela David Escobar Rodriguez Valdez: AKA El Puerco. Annie Selig is no doubt named in honor of *Soap* associate producer Andrew Selig.

Welcome to *Soap*, El Puerco
While the origins of everybody's favorite Latin American revolutionary seem to have been lost, it's a pretty good bet that the producers found their inspiration in the hijackings of U.S. planes by Cubans.

Jessica meets *Soap's* own little Fidel Castro: El Puerco.

DEC. 8: Former Beatle John Lennon is gunned down in New York City by psychotic fan Mark David Chapman. Between last month's election of a conservative U.S. president and this month's silencing of the man who sang "Imagine all the people living life in peace," the idealism born of the 1960s is all but dead.

Though U.S. aircraft were repeatedly hijacked and redirected to Cuba throughout the '60s and '70s, the Sept. 13, 1980 hijacking of a Delta Airlines plane from New Orleans to Cuba by Miguel Aguiar Rodriguez was most likely the event that inspired El Puerco's taking of Jessica's flight. This came on the heels of the Mariel boatlift, which saw thousands of Cubans set sail for the U.S. from Cuba's Mariel Harbor, from April to Oct. 31 of that year.

"I got into the office at the beginning of the last season and saw on the story board 'El Puerco,'" recalls writer Stu Silver. "I went 'Who's El Puerco?' Oh, she gets involved with this anti-communist leader who's going to free his country. I don't know if it was really inspired by Castro or anything, I just think it was just another way for Jessica to fall in love again and to give her some good story lines."

Silver also recalls that Gregory Sierra didn't take to the role immediately. "I wasn't there for the audition but apparently they had signed him, or they were in the process of doing it, and he was saying, 'I want to do the show but I don't want to do a stereotypical Latino again.' But he loved the role and the writing so much he said, 'OK, I'll do this for a season.' I got to write a lot for him, but the first few episodes he was in, Susan wrote. She was so good. As an actor, how can you turn that down?"

Best Lines
Mary [answering the phone]: No, the pervert isn't in right now. Perhaps I can help you. This is the pervert's wife.

Rod Roddy's Wrapup. Now that Chester is living with Annie in the pool house, will Eunice continue to welcome her into the family, or will she feel a twinge of bitterness from time to time? Now that the porno pictures are published and Burt and Danny have been railroaded, will the good citizens of Dunn's River run our boys out of town on a rail? And now that Jessica's vacation has been cut short by the revolutionaries, will she ever see her family again? These questions and many others will be answered in the next episode of *Soap*.

4.5

First aired: Dec 10, 1980 • Written by Susan Harris, Stu Silver, Dick Clair + Jenna McMahon • Directed by JD Lobue

Despite overpowering feelings of helplessness, various members of the Tate and Campbell family are determined to tackle their problems head-on. Jodie hires private investigator Maggie Chandler to track down Wendy, Billy leaves home to find his kidnapped mother, Burt comes up with a plan to infiltrate Tibbs' massage parlors *Serpico*-style, and Mary decides the only way to end their troubles is to go to various houses of worship.

Cast. Jimmy Baio (Billy), Roscoe Lee Browne (Saunders), Billy Crystal (Jodie), Cathryn Damon (Mary), Nancy Dolman (Annie), Katherine Helmond (Jessica), Jay Johnson (Chuck & Bob), Robert Mandan (Chester), Richard Mulligan (Burt), Arthur Peterson (The Major), Barbara Rhoades (Maggie Chandler), Donnelly Rhodes (Dutch), Jennifer Salt (Eunice), Gregory Sierra (El Puerco), Ted Wass (Danny)

Highlights. Maggie Chandler doing the Sherlock Holmes reading of Jodie shortly after he comes into her office, and her use of the term "cupcake" for Jodie; Bob helping Danny read aloud from the newspaper; the stunned silence Maggie displays on meeting the distraught Bob; Danny quickly slapping a paper bag over Bob's head when he starts hyperventilating (and nobody batting an eye); Mary's solution to heading off all the tragedy in their lives—"Everybody, go to church!"; and El Puerco convincing Jessica that the guerillas being killed in front of her are just pretending to be dead so they don't get shot again.

Confused? You Won't Be. *'Malaguay is out of my jurisdiction.'*

◗ The newspapers' attack on Burt over the Tibbs photos is a nice analog to the onslaught of overwrought moral outrage *Soap* suffered throughout its life.

◗ We begin to get a little more background on El Puerco. According to what Chester was told at the Foreign Affairs office, he is the right wing ex-dictator of Malaguay.

▶ Snapping under the weight of her family's recent misfortunes, Mary tells Burt they're cursed—a suspicion already voiced by Jessica (1.10) and Tim (2.6).

▶ This is the first time Jessica calls El Puerco "El."

And introducing…Maggie Chandler. Barbara Rhoades' performance as P.I. Maggie Chandler is one of the best we'll see this season

$75 a day plus expenses. Maggie's rates.

The Newspaper Editorial. From what depths of degradation does Sheriff Campbell and his family spring? This moral leper has flown in the face of decency and corrupted his own stepson. Can we doubt that he will corrupt our community? We have always been a liberal newspaper, but in our opinion we should bring back the ancient practice of stoning for these scoundrels.

The Houses of Worship Mary Sends Her Family to: 1) Danny: Presbyterian; 2) Burt: Baptist; 3) Chuck & Bob: Synagogue (Bob is fine with anywhere but a Catholic church—he just can't kneel.)

Pirate. What Danny wants to disguise himself as when they hit the Tibbs massage parlor. Or God. ("The wheels are always turning, Burt.")

Barbara Rhoades appeared on an episode of *The Love Boat* (1978) with singer Paul Williams.

Planning an Episode

By the end of Season 3, the writers and producers had refined their process for a task that seems impossible today.

"I would sit in the office with Susan, Paul and Tony, and we said here's what the scene needs," writer Stu Silver recalls. "Jodie's not going to get custody of the baby, Jodie's had it, he blows up in a courtroom. We have to have some funny stuff between him and Mallu. And then just let him walk out and hope we get some applause. And that, essentially, is what they'd give me. And then I would go and write the dialogue and the construction of the scene. (That was one of my favorite scenes that I wrote.) And then Susan, of course, would have the last say. She'd take my scenes and would either add to them or cut some or leave it alone as she saw fit. Her jokes were always much better than mine, so I had no problem with that."

During the last two seasons, every single episode was shot out of order, says associate producer Marsha Posner.

"So if we had a swingset of a hotel room where Chester was going to be with the minister's daughter, we would say let's shoot all those scenes this week rather than leave the set up for two weeks. Or a cast member had a problem, let's just shoot all of their scenes this week.

"So I had a big office upstairs, and I had one wall full of 5-x-7 index cards. At the top of each row was the episode number. Under each episode number I had the index cards of the scenes that were in that show. At the bottom of that card it would say what show it was actually shot in, because when you go to post production, you've got to know—well I see it on the reel that you shot this, but you say it doesn't belong in this episode? No, it belongs in next week's episode. I was the keeper of the board. Continuity was huge those last two seasons—it was just mind boggling."

Meanwhile, the actors have conflicting memories when it comes to how welcoming the producers were to their suggestions for changes. While some say it was seldom countenanced, Katherine Helmond does recall squeezing a word or phrase in there now and again.

"Occasionally when we would be rehearsing, I would throw in some kind of line just for the fun of it. If Susan laughed, it stayed in. If she didn't laugh, I didn't say it again. After all, she's the total creator of the piece, as well as the character. An example of that would be like when the revolutionary came to stay at the house and Jessica thought he was just wonderful. His name was El Puerco: 'the Pig.' One day in rehearsal I just said, 'Oh, El...' Because Jessica thought that 'El' was his first name. And Susan laughed. From then on it was in the script."

> " I loved Arthur Peterson. He was extremely loved. He was the patriarch of the whole group. He didn't have a lot to do on the show but you could always count on him for a laugh, that's for sure."
>
> —MARSHA POSNER, Associate Producer

Best Lines.

Maggie: Queens.

Jodie [defensively]: Excuse me?

Maggie: Your accent. Queens, with a touch of Manhattan mixed in. You probably play in Connecticut and you play a lot of ball. You don't smoke, you don't have any cats, and you live with your mother, correct?

Jodie: That's amazing.

Maggie: Nothing to it. See that nasal tone in your voice is a 50-50 mix of New York working man and New York intellectual, hence the Queens and Manhattan. The whiney quality is obviously Connecticut. You have the body of a second baseman, I don't smell tobacco smoke on your clothes, there's no cat fuzz on your pants, and your address is a family neighborhood. No smoking, no cats and mama.

Jodie: I whine?

Maggie [reading court transcript]: OK, mother: Carol David. Father: a cupcake.

Jodie: Excuse me?

Maggie: You're a cupcake? A fruit bowl. You're gay?

Jodie: Oh, yes.

Maggie: And you got custody?

Jodie: That's right.

Maggie: Was the judge a fruit bowl, too?

Mary: Wendy's kidnapped, you're being blackmailed. If this was a movie I'd walk out.

Danny: Sheriff Burt is burning the midnight oil and Deputy Dan is giving him a hand.

Rod Roddy's Wrapup. Now that Jodie hired a private detective to find Wendy, will they see eye to eye? Now that Billy ran off to find Jessica, can Chester still claim him as a dependant? Now that Burt told Danny he can't go to a brothel dressed as a pirate, will he go as a Dodger? Now that Jessica has been captured by revolutionaries, will she find them revolting? Will Mary ever wake up? Will Bob ever eat again? These questions and many others will be answered on the next episode of *Soap*.

4.6 First aired: Dec 17, 1980 • Written by Susan Harris, Stu Silver, Dick Clair + Jenna McMahon • Directed by JD Lobue

Burt and Danny hit one of Tibbs' brothels and locate Gwen, one of the girls from the blackmail pictures. While Danny convinces her to testify against her employer, the Tates have a cookout and deal with their sudden cashflow problem with Jessica gone. Meanwhile, Jessica begins to realize that El Puerco doesn't want to keep her as his hostage, but his wife.

Cast. Roscoe Lee Browne (Saunders), Cathryn Damon (Mary), Nancy Dolman (Alice), Katherine Helmond (Jessica), Robert Mandan (Chester), Richard Mulligan (Burt), Marla Pennington (Leslie Walker), Arthur Peterson (The Major), Donnelly Rhodes (Dutch), Jennifer Salt (Eunice), Gregory Sierra (El Puerco), Ted Wass (Danny), Jesse Welles (Gwen), Rod Roddy (Announcer), Joe Perry (Mr. Phil), Lynnda Ferguson (Hooker)

Deputy Dan wants to protect and serve Tibbs hooker Gwen.

Highlights. Danny and Burt's outlandish brothel-busting disguises (and the intriguing news that Chuck & Bob can drive!); Leslie's bittersweet explanation of her rattlesnake plan to Mary, and Burt emptying his service revolver into the beast (and Chester's foot) moments later; Jessica imitating El's pronunciation of "Connect-i-cut"; and the bashfully noble way that El Puerco brings up the possibility of marrying Jessica.

Confused? You Won't Be. 'No one owns me.'

> ❝ I'll tell you why [the Billy/Leslie romance] didn't seem silly. Because I ended up marrying my high school drama teacher, who was like 20 years older than me. So I lived it. I married him in '74, so I was 24. We were only married seven years, and I was married to him when I was doing *Soap*—I got it. I lived it."
>
> —MARLA PENNINGTON
> Leslie Walker

▶ The Tibbs brothel is called Hedley House, which was built in 1903, the third constructed in Dunn's River. (Or so Gwen tells Danny when she tries to pass herself off as a tour guide.)

▶ Tibbs told the girls that the blackmail photo shoot was for *Psychology Today* magazine, Gwen tells Danny.

▶ Having given the Moonies the business last season (2.19), *Soap* now has Gwen describe Danny's drug-induced stupor this way: "You just laid there smiling like a sleeping Scientologist."

▶ We finally get our first look at the Tate pool, and presumably the pool house, though it's hard to tell for sure what part of the Tate mansion we're looking at.

▶ The CIA promised to help El Puerco's rebels overthrow the government but they're late. "I just hope this doesn't turn out to be another Bay of Pigs here, I'll tell you that," he tells Jessica. If it all comes to naught, he and his men could go back to their marimba band.

Big Ol' Bubba Brown. Burt's alias at the brothel.

Chevron. The only card the brothel doesn't accept.

14. The age when Gwen fell under Tibbs' control.

My Little Pina Coloda and My Madonna. El Puerco's terms of endearment for Jessica.

Watercolor sketches by costume designer Judy Evans for two outfits that appear in the series.

Judy Evans' watercolors for one of Katherine Helmond's outfits (with fabric swatch).

Soap and all Those Clothes

In the television of the '70s and '80s, you would be hard pressed to find more sartorial elegance and inspiration than what was displayed each week on *Soap*. That was thanks in large part to costume designer Judy Evans (today Judy Evans Steele).

Inspired by her artist father, Evans was granted special permission to study at the Chouinard Art Institute (now the California Institute of the Arts) starting at age 11. Later, she attended USC as an undergrad, and graduated from the California Institute of the Arts with an honors degree in design.

When *Soap* associate producer Andy Selig brought her to the show, he did so with the promise that as long as she stayed in budget, she could spend that money any way she saw fit. At that time, variety shows such as *The Carol Burnett Show* had their clothing designed, but sitcoms often resorted to clothes bought off the rack.

Chester was the only male character to have some of his wardrobe made rather than bought, but the women were another story. "The women I designed for, every one of them, but you'd throw in a store bought thing here and there, and you have all your accessories and things like that, which were store bought," Evans remembers.

Not surprisingly given the flamboyant way Jessica dressed, just about everything Katherine Helmond wore on screen was designed for her.

"She would've been pretty hard to fit back then," Evans says. "You figure you're going into the '80s, she would've been hard to fit because she's very tiny, very petite, little teeny waist, but she had a figure. Katherine's things were meant to be a little more flamboyant, a little more out there. The great thing about Katherine was she could steal a scene with a scarf. You give her a wardrobe prop and all the sudden you're looking at Katherine—she's fabulous that way."

2 MINUTES
How long El's men fought valiantly and bravely before they changed sides

Best Lines.
Burt [to brothel keeper]: I'll have a dark room, a filthy girl and no view.

Hooker: First 5 minutes is 20 bucks extra. Second 5 is 30 more. Ten per minute after that. Take off your clothes, assemble your devices if that's your inclination, lie down, shut up and no smoking.
Danny: Boy, boot camp was easier than this.
Gwen: If you are a member of the police department, please state so now. Otherwise you are committing entrapment which is illegal, unethical, and may I say off the record, tacky.

Rod Roddy's Wrapup. Now that Danny's found a hooker who will testify against Tibbs, will she be afraid to open her mouth? Now that Jessica found out the revolution may last 72 years, will she have her charge account switched? Now that the Tates are out of cash, will Chester sell his sweaters? Will Billy ever find Jessica? Will anyone ever find Billy? These questions and many others will be answered in the next episode of *Soap*.

4.7  First aired: Dec 31, 1980 • Written by Susan Harris, Stu Silver, Dick Clair + Jenna McMahon • Directed by JD Lobue

After most of his rebel army deserts him, El Puerco allows Jessica to talk him into retreating to America where they can make plans for future victories. Meanwhile, Chester, desperate for money, tries to hold an estate sale, only to have it shut down by Saunders. Gwen gives her evidence to the assistant DA, who promises to put out a warrant for Tibbs' arrest, and Danny vows to protect her in the meantime. Burt and Mary address their lack of marital relations, and Maggie and Jodie check out a cowboy bar, only to discover that Carol now has a thing for circus clowns.

Cast. Roscoe Lee Browne (Saunders), Billy Crystal (Jodie), Cathryn Damon (Mary), Nancy Dolman (Annie), Katherine Helmond (Jessica), Robert Mandan (Chester), Richard Mulligan (Burt), Barbara Rhoades (Maggie), Donnelly Rhodes (Dutch), Jennifer Salt (Eunice), Gregory Sierra (El Puerco), Ted Wass (Danny), Jesse Welles (Gwen), Rod Roddy (Announcer), David Hayward (Slim), Frank Cornsentina (Tailor), Gary Epp (Cowboy), Danny Goldman (Stenographer), David Knapp (Assistant DA), Art Fleur (Bartender), Tom Lawrence (Shopper), Joe Mantegna (Juan One), Ruth Silveira (Shopper)

Highlights. Jessica being fitted for her revolutionary garb ("Lady, this is a third-world nation; what do you want, Calbin Kleins?"); the audience "wooing" at the first glimpse of the behatted shadow stalking Danny and Gwen at the police station; Maggie and Jodie sitting amidst the chaos that is the cowboy bar, and Jodie being a tough guy.

Confused? You Won't Be. *'You come to Connect-i-cut America and we'll fight the revolution from my house!'*

▶ Dutch found and lost his first job since getting out of prison, all in the same day. He was going to work at the local car wash, but he didn't know what "agua" meant.

DEC. 31: Philosopher and media critic Marshall McLuhan dies. His 1964 work *Understanding Media: The Extensions of Man* gave us the phrase "the medium is the message," which essentially said that it was the medium itself (e.g., television) that affected society rather than whatever programs a network deemed fit to broadcast. Considering the furor that surrounded *Soap*, it remains an interesting claim.

▶ Now that Corinne's left home, Eunice is the target for all the loose-woman jokes, something Annie makes clear this episode.

▶ The State Department has learned several things about Jessica's capture since it checked out El Puerco's abandoned camp. For starters, they found red hairs on the rebel leader's pillow, much to Chester's disgust. They also suggest that Jessica might possibly have been executed by the communists, foreshadowing the series finale cliffhanger (4.21).

▶ Mary's "I don't think Republicans do it" is obviously the *Soap* producers' response to the Moral Majority's obsession with sex throughout their four-year campaign against the series.

▶ A week and a half ago, Carol went off cowboys and started hanging around clowns, running off with the Farley Circus.

And introducing... Juan One.

$75. How much Chester is asking for the statue by the stairs. (It's over 200 years old...and it's chipped.)

$100. How much Chester wants for the drapes.

50 cents. How much Saunders will pay Chester to clean the oven.

Life in the 'DCLR'

It's no secret today that the *Soap* set wasn't all wine and roses. Yet, as on many other classic shows, that tension was a byproduct of the genius at work both in front of and behind the camera. While most acknowledge that Richard Mulligan's tumultuous personality could be challenging at times, Cathryn Damon, too, could make for stressful shoots at times.

"[Stage manager] Carl Lauten and I used to call the Campbells the DCLR," director JD Lobue remembers, not at all bitterly it should be said. "That was our shorthand for the 'Dreaded Campbell Living Room,' because we always knew it was going to be difficult."

Though Damon and Mulligan could be trying at times, "they were magic. And so you knew that you were in for a difficult day, that you were going to have to work a little extra in rehearsals to make things comfortable for everybody. But you also knew that ultimately it was going to be gold. It was sort of like a root canal: You know you need one and you've gotta do it."

Some of that was due to Damon having to play opposite Mulligan, Lobue thinks. In many ways no matter how good you are, Mulligan would always do something to top your performance. "They sort of fed off each other. I don't know how to explain it except that I've done some *Newharts* in my time and learned that the most difficult thing in trying to get a scene rehearsed was making sure all the cast got on stage at the same time. Nobody as an actor wants to be the second person listed on the call sheet."

'They sort of fed off each other,' says director JD Lobue of the acting between Cathryn Damon and Richard Mulligan.

Best Lines.
Saunders [after Chester threatens to deck him]: I dislike violence but I'm awfully good at it.

Burt [explaining his lack of lovemaking]: Mary I can't help it, I got two jobs here. I'm running a construction office, I'm sheriff. And public life, that really ruins your private life. Do you think it happens that presidents have problems like that? Do you think that maybe Carter and Rossalyn...stop? Or that Reagan's gonna stop?
Mary: I don't think Republicans do it.

Slim: Every man that ever tied a hog knows Carol.
Jodie: That should surprise me more than it does.

Rod Roddy's Wrapup. Now that Jessica and El Puerco have decided to escape the enemy by boat, will they remember to bring along the Dramamine? Next time Jodie and Maggie get a lead on Carol, will they remember to make reservations in advance? Will Eunice ever get along with Annie? Will Billy ever find his mother? And who is spying on Gwen and Danny? These questions and many others will be answered on the next episode of *Soap*.

4.8

First aired: Jan 7, 1981 • Story by Susan Harris, Stu Silver, Dick Clair + Jenna McMahon • Teleplay by Susan Harris, Stu Silver, Dick Clair, Jenna McMahon, Barry Vigon + Danny Jacobson • Directed by JD Lobue

42

Number of tickets Danny has given out for tailgating...during rush hour

Desperate for money, Chester finally gets back into his suit and tie and buys 80% of Burt's construction company...with an IOU. Jodie and Maggie pay a visit to a carnival and discover that Carol has taken up with Zippo the Fire Eater and they're now selling tamales in Albuquerque. Down to their last breath mint, Jessica and El Puerco are rescued at sea by Billy. And Danny, greatly bothered by Gwen's continued prostitution, gets her to promise not to do it for a while, and reveals that his interest in her may not be purely professional. But once again, a mysterious stalker lurks in the shadows.

Cast. Jimmy Baio (Billy), Billy Crystal (Jodie), Katherine Helmond (Jessica), Robert Mandan (Chester), Richard Mulligan (Burt), Barbara Rhoades (Maggie), Donnelly Rhodes (Dutch), Gregory Sierra (El Puerco), Ted Wass (Danny), Jesse Welles (Gwen), Robert Costanzo (Carny), Dan Barrow (Dr. Yalowich), Fred Smoot (Fluffy)

Highlights. Jodie and Maggie shaking down the carny for info on Carol; the surprise appearance of Billy in his scuba suit and his undisguised annoyance when confronted with El Puerco; and Gwen turning tricks with hamburger-suit-wearing Dr. Yalowich in her hotel "safe room".

Confused? You Won't Be. '*After the darkness came the dawn.*'

▶ Oddly Fred Smoot, who plays the carnival's half-man/ half-dog, Fluffy, played another canine—a man in a dog mask—in the 1986 *Benson* episode "Pardon Me."

▶ Normally *Soap*'s product placement isn't too overt, but this episode both Tic Tacs and Certs have starring roles, the former as the last bit of food Jessica and El Puerco have, and the latter as what Maggie gives Fluffy as a treat.

▶ For the second time in as many episodes we get the "Jes Jes" joke. (As in "Yes, Jes,' I have an exaggerated Spanish accent so let's make fun of that for a while.")

2. The number of murders in Dunn's River in the last four years, according to Danny. (These are Sam Ogilvy, who was killed on North Street, and Old Man Jennings on Melrose.) Either Peter Campbell wasn't killed in Dunn's River, or Danny's forgetting much of Season 1. Then again, it's Danny.

20%. How much of the construction company Burt has left after Chester invests in it. Still, Burt only sold once he made sure that Dutch would be president. What could go wrong?

My Little Chili Pepper. El Puerco's term of endearment for Jessica.

Article 2, Paragraph 1 of the Carnival Act: As long as you got prizes and patrons, you gotta let 'em play.

The Club Med Martinique. Where Billy is staying when he discovers Jessica and El Puerco.

Sobrino del Puerco. El Puerco dubs Billy "nephew of the pig."

The Susan & Stu & Dick & Jenna & Barry & Danny Show

The virtual writing-credit tsunami that the viewer is hit with at the beginning of this episode speaks to the train wreck of an episode we get. Unlike the brief run of disappointing episodes in Season 3, there are no memorable standout scenes here, nor will *Soap* bounce back much as it did then.

Susan Harris wrote the entire first season of *Soap* and it very nearly finished her off. She then tried out a couple of different writers until finding Stu Silver during Season 2, which allowed them to split the workload. However, the show continued to add cast and it was pretty clear that more help was needed. (Keep in mind that your typical television writer's room today runs anywhere from seven to 12 people!)

Soap writers Dick Clair and Jenna McMahon perform in ABC's *What's it all About, World?* (1969)

Shortly after their time on *Soap*, Dick Clair and Jenna McMahon would create *The Facts of Life* and *Mama's Family*.

Jenna McMahon and Dick Clair, whom Harris and Witt had worked with during *Fay*, were brought on at the beginning of Season 4.

"They came on as a writing team," Stu Silver remembers. "The thing is Susan brought them on because she was figuring they'd lighten the load for us a little bit." Yet it quickly became apparent that however easy Harris and Silver made it look, not just anybody could write for the Tates and the Campbells.

"I was blessed with an ear for this show, maybe no other show," Silver laughs. "I kind of understood the characters when I came in. I don't think Dick and Jenna really did, so Susan and I ended up rewriting them a lot. They were very nice people and they were good writers, but you kinda had to rewrite a lot of the dialogue because it didn't fit into the mouths of the characters. But the ideas were good."

The structure of an episode they had down perfectly, Silver says, and no wonder. Both had written for *The Mary Tyler Moore Show* and for *The Carol Burnett Show* for several years. Yet when it came to writing for the individual characters on *Soap*, the dialogue that they would write for a male character, for example, could've been written for any male character rather than specifically for Chester. Harris had created these characters and Silver had been writing for them for nearly two years at this point—for McMahon and Clair, there was simply no time to learn the nuances. Starting this episode, the writing team of Barry Vigon and Danny Jacobson were also brought in. (The former will also turn up on screen as Private Esquivo in 4.15.)

As Silver is quick to point out, all of these writers were top-notch and would go on to enjoy stellar careers. McMahon and Clair created two television mainstays of the 1980s: *Mama's Family* and *The Facts of Life*. Barry Vigon wrote for everything from *Punky Brewster* to *Martin*, and Danny Jacobson had a hit with *Mad About You* in the '90s.

Yet, self-deprecating to a fault, Silver can't pass up the opportunity to suggest that the hiring of these other writers might have made him a tad insecure, too. "I thought we were great just the two of us, and

I also thought, 'Maybe I'm not good enough. Maybe I'm making her work harder, not stepping up to the plate—maybe they need a few more Stu Silvers.' I loved that show and those people. I had nightmares about anybody else besides me and Susan writing for those actors. To them it was just another gig; to me it was everything."

Best Lines.
Burt: No Danny please, I'm talking about you have to learn how to interpret the law, all right? For example, say somebody does something wrong. Not a lot wrong, a little wrong. Now suppose the wrong doer is a right guy? Well now there's a fine line between right and wrong. And sometimes you have to let a person have the right to be wrong. Am I right or am I wrong?

Burt: I worked my whole life to have my name mean something. And today all that Campbell means is *soup*.

Danny: I'm trying to keep you safe and you're in there making love with a quarter pounder.
Gwen: He doesn't even touch me. We play a game called Fast Food. I'm the grill girl. He just lays there and I turn him over every few minutes, that's all.

Rod Roddy's Wrapup. Now that Billy has rescued Jessica and El, will they all make it home safely to Connecticut? Will Jess and Billy become bilingual? Now that Chester and Dutch are in the construction business, will it give their lives a new foundation? Now that Danny and Gwen are thinking of making love, will Danny have to throw the book at himself? Will Jodie and Maggie have any luck at the tamale stand in Albuquerque, or will they just get heartburn? These questions and many others will be answered in the next episode of *Soap*.

No, this domestic arrangement won't be awkward at all. Heck, it isn't even entirely 'domestic'. ('Hi El Puerco.')

> "You realized something was going on when more and more writers came on. It kind of lost some focus and the cast was getting bigger and bigger and bigger."
> —MARLA PENNINGTON
> Leslie Walker

4.9

First aired: Jan 14, 1981 • Story by Susan Harris, Stu Silver, Dick Clair + Jenna McMahon • Teleplay by Susan Harris, Stu Silver, Dick Clair, Jenna McMahon, Barry Vigon + Danny Jacobson • Directed by JD Lobue

Jessica and Billy return home with El Puerco and his three Juans, promptly putting Chester in his place. Danny decides to move Gwen from the motel room to the Campbell home for her own protection (and to pave the way for a future relationship). And after Jodie has too much to drink in Albuquerque, he admits to having feelings for Maggie, which she reciprocates. Meanwhile, a desperate Burt tracks down his childhood pastor to help him through his struggles with faith throughout this whole Tibbs ordeal, but the divine answer he receives suggests he will have to find another solution to his problems.

Cast. Jimmy Baio (Billy), Roscoe Lee Browne (Saunders), Billy Crystal (Jodie), Nancy Dolman (Annie), Katherine Helmond (Jessica), Robert Mandan (Chester), Richard Mulligan (Burt), Arthur Peterson (The Major), Barbara Rhoades (Maggie), Donnelly Rhodes (Dutch), Jennifer Salt (Eunice), Gregory Sierra (El Puerco), Ted Wass (Danny), Jesse Welles (Gwen), Announcer (Rod Roddy), Joe Mantegna (Juan 1), Laurie Faso (Juan 2), Chico Martinez (Juan 3), Fred Stuthman (Bishop)

Highlights. Dutch's world tour of how to say "pig" in different languages before Chester throttles him; El Puerco's dressing down of Chester and Jessica's little squeal of delight at the end—actually, every scene El Puerco is in this episode; and Burt's amazing scene with the Bishop.

Confused? You Won't Be. *'Is this your answer?'*

▶ El Puerco has made Billy a general in his rebel army.

▶ Juan 1 and Juan 2 are cousins, however Juan 2 and 3 are not related.

▶ El Puerco tells Eunice that he earned his name because of his fondness for pork.

▶ As we let the last episode have it with both barrels, it's only fair that we praise this one's strengths. While its middle is about as substantial as Twinkie filling, those scenes are bookended by El Puerco's delightful meeting of Jessica's family in the beginning, and Burt's heartbreaking *tete a tete* with his childhood pastor in the end. It isn't until this moment that we realize just how deeply Burt has been affected by recent events, mostly because there's nobody in his life he can really unburden himself to. And even though we know the moment we see the Bishop that he will probably die by the end of the conversation, it is to Susan Harris' credit that when the event does come, it is still undeniably poignant. While organized religion has spent four years mobilizing indignation against *Soap* on moral grounds, *Soap* neatly demonstrates the case against religion itself. It has no useful answer for the "Harry Alvins" of the world, and because of that, the Burt Campbells of the world must go it alone.

El Puerco and the Naming of the Family.
1) Chester: Mujeriego ("womanizer"), though El helpfully translates it as "hot trousers"; 2) Eunice: Pequeño Pajarito ("little bird"); 3) Annie: La Ramera ("slut"); 4) Francisco Franco: Who The Major thinks El Puerco is.

Henry's Hacienda. The motel where Jodie and Maggie reveal their feelings for each other.

Juneau, Alaska. Where Carol was headed when she left Albuquerque two days ago.

And introducing... Juan 2 and Juan 3.

'Richard Mulligan Was an Artist'

There are no two ways about it: Richard Mulligan could be difficult to work with. He was driven, he liked to do things his own way, and he didn't suffer fools gladly. Yet there is another side to Mulligan, one that even those who had their problems with him will readily admit: when it came to performance he was a genius.

Perhaps equally as important, "Richard Mulligan was an artist—I realize that now," says Mulligan's friend and former PR representa-

Richard Mulligan and Mariette Hartley in the short-lived series *The Hero* (1966-67). Fun fact: Jimmy Baio's brother, Joey, appeared on the series.

tive, Julian Myers. The two were on social terms from the time Myers started representing him in 1981 until the end of the actor's life in 2000. Away from the tension of the television and film sets, Myers saw the man a little differently than most.

"Richard was a very self-contained person, not one for wanting to go out to mixers or to events or parties. He was interested in reading good literature and probably dreamed of doing some important writing himself. He was quite modest, very nice and warm, but not an expansive person. Richard was a very cultured gentleman, a sweet man, but his own man, too. He wasn't much of a one to get involved with groups."

Myers' favorite memories are of Mulligan with third wife Lenore Stevens. "She was a fine, caring lady, and very protective and strong and nice for Richard. But he may not have been able to get outside of himself enough to relate well to a wife. He was so deep and sensitive, his thoughts were on other things of beauty, cultural and literary and artistic."

When it comes to assessing the actor's legacy, Myers is less certain. Though he has been on the Oscar coordinating committee since the beginning, and a member of the Academy of Arts and Sciences since its inception, he's quick to say, "Nobody has any legacy in Hollywood. When you're gone, you're gone. The nearest thing to anybody I ever worked with having a legacy in Hollywood is Marilyn Monroe."

At the entertainment public relations class he still teaches at Loyola Marymount University, his students don't recognize the names of any of the greats. "They don't know them, they don't care, except Marilyn Monroe—that name they remember. Not with great excitement, but at least they remember. When you're dead you're dead in Hollywood. And for directors and producers and writers, you're often dead before you're dead."

Best Lines.
Billy [to El]: I'm going upstairs to my quarters and plan our counter-attack on Malaguay. [To Jessica] Call me in time for *CHiPs*.

Chester: Billy, I absolutely forbid you to attack a third-world nation.

JAN. 20: Iran releases 52 hostages soon after Ronald Reagan is sworn in as president.

Billy: I'm sorry, Dad. I outrank you.

Burt [to the Bishop]: ...I tried to clean up this town and what happens? Winds up I get blackmailed, people calling me on the phone saying terrible things to me and my family. I hardly ever see my wife and baby anymore. I mean where's the sense in that, sir? Where's the logic? This all may turn out to be what I call an 'Alvin'. It's named after Harry Alvin. I know you don't know who he is. I don't know who he is either. Harry Alvin's some guy I just read about in the newspaper. He's like 40 years old and in the last year had two heart attacks, kidney failure, cerebral hemorrhage, triple bypasses and survives. And then a couple weeks ago he was riding his bike in the park, two guys jumped him, murdered him, and took his bike. I mean Harry Alvin went through a whole year of hell and winds up getting shot for a Schwinn. Where is the sense in that? Where's the logic?! That's what I call an Alvin, and who knows, this may turn out to be an Alvin, too. I don't know. What I'm saying here is that this Alvin—I don't understand. It doesn't make sense and it's making me lose faith. And that's why I came here today, sir. That's it. [Bishop slumps over.] Sir? [Goes over to check for a pulse; finds none. Speaking to God] Is this your answer?

Rod Roddy's Wrapup. Now that El Puerco and his three Juans will be living in the Tate house, will Chester learn how to tango? Since Jodie and Maggie have admitted their business relationship may be more than just business, will it hurt their relationship? Now that Danny's suggested Gwen live with the Campbells, will the shadow know? Now that Burt has bored the Bishop to death, will he go to confession? These questions and many others will be answered in the next episode of *Soap*.

4.10

First aired: Jan 21, 1981 • Story by Susan Harris, Stu Silver, Dick Clair + Jenna McMahon • Teleplay by Susan Harris, Stu Silver, Dick Clair, Jenna McMahon, Barry Vigon + Danny Jacobson • Directed by JD Lobue

Danny and Gwen are in love. Jessica and El Puerco are in love...but he won't sleep with her until they're married. Chester is engaged to

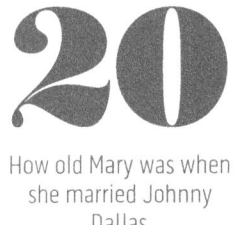

How old Mary was when she married Johnny Dallas

Annie. And amazingly Jodie and Maggie are a couple. While Leslie fails yet again to kill Billy, a mysterious gunman fires into the Tate living room, leaving Danny wounded.

Cast. Jimmy Baio (Billy), Roscoe Lee Browne (Saunders), Billy Crystal (Jodie), Cathryn Damon (Mary), Nancy Dolman (Annie), Katherine Helmond (Jessica), Jay Johnson (Chuck & Bob), Robert Mandan (Chester), Richard Mulligan (Burt), Marla Pennington (Leslie Walker), Arthur Peterson (The Major), Barbara Rhoades (Maggie), Donnelly Rhodes (Dutch), Jennifer Salt (Eunice), Gregory Sierra (El Puerco), Ted Wass (Danny), Jesse Welles (Gwen), Announcer (Rod Roddy), Joe Mantegna (Juan 1), Laurie Faso (Juan 2), Chico Martinez (Juan 3)

Highlights. Hats off to Danny for his beeper tongue twister (see "Best Lines" for this entry); Saunders' reaction to being told the man taking apart his hors d'oeuvres is looking for poison ("You mean if he finds poison he'll stop," followed by a devilish look); Danny disarming Juan 1 after he disarmed him; Eunice's delight at being patted down for "security" by the Juans; Generalissimo Billy Tate: El Puercito; Leslie trying to smuggle in various implements of destruction in her skimpy French maid outfit; Juan 1 bravely stumbling through El Puerco's full name, followed by "and here he is"; Bob's *tete a tete* with his hero the rebel leader, and Chuck telling Chester he doesn't know what they're saying because he doesn't speak Spanish; and the dueling announcements.

Confused? You Won't Be. *'You mean you're in love with a hooker that you haven't even...booked?'*

Señor Wences

▶ Though not quite up to the quality of earlier seasons, this is the closest we come to *Soap* at its madcap best during Season 4.

▶ Juan 1's "S'OK? S'alright" is a nod to that *other* master of ventriloquism, Señor Wences (1896-1999). Indeed, Mantegna admits "there probably was a little influence of that" for his voice for Juan 1. "I also have an Uncle Willy who talks like that. When I brought him to *The Simpsons* one day for a recording they laughed—they said, 'Oh my God, it's Fat Tony!' Yeah, I know. It's a variation of that."

▶ For those who missed it the first time, El Puerco's name is Carlos Marcelo David Escobar Rodriguez "El Puerco" Valdez.

C.C. Bowlers. What's written on Chuck & Bob's bowling shirts.

2. Bob's mukluk size.

Michelle. Chuck's waitress friend at the bowling alley. Or as Bob describes her, "The girl who can carry two trays without her hands."

Mary. The name of El Puerco's blessed mother.

"I want a seat from which I can see the hands of the pianist." The translation for the Spanish phrase Dutch has been working on all week.

The Party Announcements. 1) Chester announces his engagement to Annie at the party, as well as his divorce from Jessica; 2) Danny announces that he and Gwen have fallen in love; 3) Jodie announces that he and Maggie "are an item"; 4) Juan 1 announces a) dinner is ready (pork, no big surprise), and b) Juan 2 may have "bought the farm" after drinking from the punch bowl. (Scratch that.)

Best Lines.
Danny: I gotta go, ma, I'm being beeped! I've never been beeped before. Burt is beeping my beeper. Burt bought these beepers. They're the best beepers that bucks can buy. I mean when they beep, they beep. They weren't cheap beepers, either. I believe this must be big or Burt would never have beeped. I better beat it.

Juan 1 [emptying Danny's revolver]: Security! Some people may be trying to kill El Puerco.
Danny [emptying Juan 1's semi-automatic and directing his attention to Gwen]: Security! Some people may be trying to kill El Girlfriend.

Rod Roddy's Wrapup. Now that Jessica and Chester are divorced, and Chester and Annie are engaged, will Eunice give Annie a shower, or just push her into the pool? Who was the bullet that hit Danny really meant for? Is Tibbs trying to kill Danny and Burt? Was he trying to kill Gwen? Are the communist forces in Malaguay trying to assassinate El Puerco and his allies? And how badly has Danny been wounded? These questions and many others will be answered in the next episode of *Soap*.

4.11
First aired: Jan 28, 1981 • Story by Susan Harris, Stu Silver, Dick Clair + Jenna McMahon • Teleplay by Susan Harris, Stu Silver, Dick Clair, Jenna McMahon, Barry Vigon + Danny Jacobson • Directed by JD Lobue

Chester and Annie are making plans for their new life together, Jessica fails to seduce El Puerco yet again, and Gwen and the Campbells wait for news about Danny at the hospital. After four hours of surgery, it's determined that bullets passed through both of his kidneys, meaning he needs a kidney transplant soon. Just before Jodie is prepped to give him one of his, Mary reveals that he can't: Danny is only his half-brother.

Cast. Billy Crystal (Jodie), Cathryn Damon (Mary), Nancy Dolman (Annie), Katherine Helmond (Jessica), Jay Johnson (Chuck & Bob), Robert Mandan (Chester), Richard Mulligan (Burt), Gregory Sierra (El Puerco), Ted Wass (Danny), Jesse Welles (Gwen), Rod Roddy (Announcer), Richard McKenzie (Doctor Saxon)

Highlights. The complex medical conversation the doctor and Bob have over Danny's condition without the former batting an eye; Chester's "I'm fabulous" after Annie builds him up; Danny asking what happened at the party after he got shot; Burt's bedside oath to get Tibbs; and Mary's revelation about Jodie.

Confused? You Won't Be. *'Jodie, you and Danny are not brothers.'*
▶ Bob spent two years studying at Johns Hopkins.

▶ Chester's inability to perform with Annie is a first, according to him. This also affords us our first glimpse inside Chester's pool house, albeit just the bedroom. This setting will figure in one of the series finale's cliffhangers.

▶ Chester's "we'll play tennis together—you can take lessons during the day while I'm working" to Annie is a clever nod to Jessica's affair with tennis pro Peter Campbell at the beginning

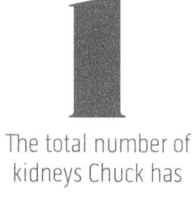

1
The total number of kidneys Chuck has

of Season 1 and, indirectly, a subtle reminder that Chester, too, was a philanderer from the beginning. Just how long can he remain faithful to Annie?

▶ Rod Roddy's Wrapup harkens back to the one for 1.12, which examined the suspects in Peter's murder. The Burt Reynolds reference is par for the course, but the image used for Mr. X resembles a (more) bizarre version of the cowled Elephant Man, no doubt inspired by the release of David Lynch's film about that gentleman the previous October. Oddly, this is the second reference to the Elephant Man in as many episodes. (Last episode, Jessica told Mary that she was trying to come up with something to cover her face to preserve her skin "without looking like the Elephant Man.")

13. How old Danny was when he jumped off a roof while wearing a cape—he was playing Superman.

4 hours. How long Danny's been in the operating room.

Hair in the shower drain…and communism. The two things El Puerco hates more than anything.

Best Lines.
Bob: OK doc, give it to me straight. What's the damage to the pancreas, colon, kidneys and duodenum?
Doctor: Well there's a lateral rupture of one kidney. There's capsular damage to the other but–
Bob: I see, so there's a possibility of uremia renal shutdown and peritonitis.
Doctor: I tend to concur.
Chuck: What are you talking about?
Bob: Shut up.

Burt [about Tibbs]: I'm gonna kill 'im, Danny. I'm going to get 'im if it's the last thing I ever do. Nobody hurts my boy like this, nobody. I'm going to get 'im and he's never gonna hurt anybody ever again.

Rod Roddy's Wrapup. Who is Danny's father? Is it his Uncle Chester, who fooled around with everyone? Did he fool around with

1981

On **FEB. 5**, Toronto police raid four gay bathhouses in the province in an initiative called, no fooling, "Operation *Soap*." The mass arrests and the protests that followed were the impetus for Toronto's Gay Pride Week. Demonstrating *Soap*'s ability to capture the times in which it was made, we'll get a scene (coincidentally) with Jodie and Maggie at a bathhouse next episode.

1981

MARCH 1: Provisional IRA member Bobby Sands starts a hunger strike in Long Kesh prison in Ireland that will end with his death on **MAY 5**, sparking a resurgence in the IRA's popularity amongst the disaffected.

his wife's sister? Is it Benson, who once worked for the family? Was some of his work not work? Is it Burt Reynolds who was in town and had nothing to do? And if it was, how could you blame her? Wouldn't you? Or was it Mr. X, a man who would shock everyone, even himself? One of these four men is Danny's father, and who he is will change the lives of the Tates and Campbells forever. Find out when *Soap* returns in its new time slot in early March.

Jodie and Maggie and a bathhouse. Surprisingly, the *least* unlikely thing to happen to them this episode.

4.12

First aired: Mar 9, 1981 • Story by Susan Harris, Stu Silver, Dick Clair + Jenna McMahon • Teleplay by Susan Harris, Stu Silver, Dick Clair, Jenna McMahon, Barry Vigon + Danny Jacobson • Directed by JD Lobue

Making good on his promise to get Tibbs, Burt attacks the crime syndicate's compound and captures Tibbs, the Godfather, and the rest of the crime bosses with a baseball bat and a pistol. Mary insists to her doctor that baby Scottie is an alien, and tells Chester that Danny is his son; if he doesn't donate his kidney, Danny will die. Jessica catches El Puerco with a hooker and realizes they will never see eye to eye on premarital sex. And Jodie and Maggie track Carol and Wendy to a Kung Fu fortress in Malibu where, Vulcan neck pinch notwithstanding, they wind up being tossed into a dungeon while Wendy is prepped for life as a "minja" warrior empress.

Cast. Billy Crystal (Jodie), Cathryn Damon (Mary), Katherine Helmond (Jessica), Robert Mandan (Chester), Richard Mulligan (Burt), Barbara Rhoades (Maggie), Gregory Sierra (El Puerco), Rod Roddy (Announcer), Earl Boen (Dr. Drell), JJ Barry (Godfather), Sandy Barry (Girl in Towel), Herb Braha (Informer), Ross Borden (Man in Towel), Hamilton Camp (Tibbs), Barbara Goodson (Nurse), HB Haggerty (Warrior No. 1), Stephanie Harker (Hooker), Joy Rinaldi (Donna), James Saito (Hiro)

Highlights. Bat-wielding Burt's insane entrance at the crime meeting and his mass arrest of the syndicate; Chester's reaction to Mary telling him that he is Danny's father; El Puerco explaining his views on men's needs and Jessica's liberated response; Mary insisting that Scottie is an alien, and fainting when Dr. Drell's beeper goes off; and Jodie and Maggie squaring off against the denizens of the Kung Fu fortress.

Confused? You Won't Be. *'He needs your kidney, Chester.'*

▶ With only a few episodes left, *Soap* covers even more ground than usual this time around as evidenced by the number, and exotic nature, of its locations: an opulent bathhouse, an equally snazzy meeting place for the crime syndicate, the more familiar restaurant where Mary lowers the boom on Chester, the Tate basement, Dr. Drell's office, and finally the Kung Fu fortress in Malibu. If nothing else, somebody was very busy going through the stock footage vaults at ABC.

▶ After years of fan service to the female viewers with Danny in various states of undress, the guys finally get a little something sent their way with the lovely Barbara Rhoades in a towel at the bathhouse.

▶ Tibbs himself finally confirms that it was one of his goons that shot Danny.

▶ Warrior No. 1 at the Kung Fu fortress is played by HB Haggerty, who specialized in playing man mountains in the '70s and '80s. He's perhaps best known as Tigerman in *Buck Rogers in the 25th Century*.

▶ Oddly, the Chester-Mary story line that *Soap* teased as a cliffhanger last episode is disposed of quietly with a scene that gives Robert Mandan the opportunity to do what he does best, but only succeeds in raising more questions than it answers: "Mary, I was forced into [marrying Jessica]. Your mother was going to have my father arrested!" What? However, with just a few lines it also gives us a new way to view Chester's recent announcement of his engagement to Annie. Despite having strong feelings for Mary, he announced his marriage to Jessica all those many years ago, which provides us with a possible excuse for his philandering. And his last scene with Annie, in which he suffers his first bout of impotence ever, may reveal that despite it all, he still loves Jessica.

Every night for two weeks. How long Mary and Chester made love prior to Chester announcing his engagement to Jessica.

1981

MARCH 11: Despot Augusto Pinochet is sworn in as president of Chile.

To dance and hold babies. Women's only needs, according to El Puerco.

19. Jodie's number at the palace. (Until he makes it 61.)

58. Maggie's.

For the *Soap* Bible Tells Us So. While this episode's revelations about Danny's parentage may seem something that came out of left field, this was one element that was planned from the very beginning, appearing on P. 5 of the *Soap* bible under the heading "Mary's Secret." Recalls associate producer Marsha Posner, "Something was going on about Danny's story line, and I remember saying to [Susan Harris] you know, Chester is Danny's real father. She looked at me and said what? I said before you started casting the show you wrote the bible. And she had completely forgotten that. So then that all came out in Season 4, but she'd actually forgotten about it because it had been so long ago."

Soap, Broad Humor and the Vulcan Neck Pinch

As Jodie and Maggie find out, this move works in Kung Fu fortresses, too.

Though most involved with the making of *Soap* will tell you it could have conceivably gone on forever had it not suffered at the hands of the pressure groups that plagued it, they also admit that its quality had suffered a bit in its final year. Little wonder. ABC had changed its time slot, its executive producers were neck deep in managing other shows—and though memories are hazy on this point—the producers probably knew *Soap* was on the chopping block during the summer hiatus before Season 4 even began.

"By year four you're tap dancing, you're trying to figure out what you're going to do next," says Tony Thomas. "Now *Soap* was an easier show to do that with because you haven't beaten every plot to death by then, and sometimes cast changes help you, and *Soap* lent itself to cast changes. And also we could make a left turn any time we wanted and start telling another story. So that was easier. But it had run its course."

Monday
9:15 PM to 10:20 PM

evangelical religion in the South. Brad Dourif, Ned Beatty, John Huston (who also directed). (1 hr., 50 min.)
9:15 ⓲ KAZOKU SOROTTE AJI JIMAN —In Japanese
9:30 ❷ HOUSE CALLS
Petty thefts around the hospital point to an odd group of suspects: a strange outpatient who harasses the staff, a recovered kleptomaniac whose mother is a hospital benefactor, and an orderly with a history of police trouble. Charley: Wayne Rogers. Ann: Lynn Reagrave. Peckler: Mark L. Taylor. Amos: David Wayne. Danny: Tony Plana. Norman: Raymond Buktenica. Kerry Selzer: Robin Haynes.
⓲ SUMO WRESTLING—In Japanese
㉞ COLORINA—Novela
10PM ❷ LOU GRANT
A tip sends Rossi (Robert Walden) to a small farm town to investigate an explosive labor dispute. Lou: Edward Asner. Donovan: Jack Bannon. Billie: Linda Kelsey. Animal: Daryl Anderson. Charlie: Mason Adams. Mrs. Pynchon: Nancy Marchand. (60 min.)
Guest Cast
Tommy Hernandez ....James Victor
Hugh Holstrum ....Jeff Corey
Paul Geyer ....Bill Lucking
Castillo ....Emilio Delgado
❺ ⓭ NEWS
❼ ㊷ SOAP
Burt (Richard Mulligan) becomes a darling of the media after his raid on an underworld meeting; Mary and Jessica (Cathryn Damon, Katherine Helmond) aren't speaking to each other; and Jodie and Maggie (Billy Crystal, Barbara Rhoades) pass the time in captivity by making love. Chester: Robert Mandan. Danny: Ted Wass. Chuck: Jay Johnson. Billy: Jimmy Baio. Dutch: Donnelly Rhodes. Eunice: Jennifer Salt. Saunders: Roscoe Lee Browne. Gwen: Jesse Welles. (60 min.)
⓲ SUEHIRO ENGEIKAI
㉔ DON'T FORGET THE KHMER —Documentary
Special: A 1980 report on the plight of Khmer (Cambodian) refugees in Thailand and an Iowa medical team's efforts to help them. Doug Brown is the program narrator. (Repeat; 60 min.)
㉞ NOCHE A NOCHE
10:20 ㉘ MEMBERSHIP-PLEDGE DRIVE

A glance at what Soap *was up against this month.*

On set, it was even more apparent that this was the case, says director JD Lobue. "Although early on the characters were well defined, by the time I took over the reins, they started writing to the character without having to develop the character, so that the scenes got a little bit more complicated, the humor got a little bit more—not more broad because the show was never overtly broad—although we had our moments."

As we have seen earlier (see 4.8 section "The Susan & Stu & Dick & Jenna & Barry & Danny Show"), what Lobue describes here is the deployment of writers new to the series who were themselves struggling with duplicating the voices of *Soap*'s distinctive characters. As the director observes, Season 4 was when *Soap* took a turn for the silly. That's quite a statement when you're talking about a show that was no stranger to alien abductions and exorcisms.

"I recall a fight scene between Jodie and a thuggish brute who was seemingly unstoppable," Lobue says. "Jodie tried everything. He even smashed the brute over the head with a 2-x-4 board with no effect." Lobue asked the writers "if the guy is impervious to pain, how do we get ourselves out of this scene? The logical solution would be for Jodie to run. But the writers had written (without specifics) that Jodie defeats the villain. In rehearsal Billy came up with the Vulcan thing where he grabs the brute's neck and the guy drops like a log. That was pretty silly I must admit, and we all knew at the time that it was. But the live audience loved it."

Best Lines.

Chester: Mary, why didn't you ever tell me?

Mary: I didn't know.

Chester: For 28 years?

Mary: When I realized I was pregnant, you suddenly announced you were going to marry Jessica.

Chester: Mary, I was forced into that. Your mother was going to have my father arrested!

Mary: Well it doesn't matter now. What matters is Danny. You're his father, Chester. You're the only one who can give him a kidney. You'll do it, of course. Chester?!

Chester: Mary, are you sure he's my son?

Mary: He is your son, Chester. Do you think that I would ask you for your kidney if he wasn't? If you weren't his father your kidney would kill him.

Chester: You realize everyone will know. If I give the kidney, it'll give it away.

Mary: Chester, without your kidney, Danny will die.

El: Now this is a man's thing, this passion. Men are all the same. Women are different. They come in two shapes. There are the ones that make love and are garbage and the ones who go to heaven when they die.

Jessica: Who says?

El: God.

Jessica: Told you personally, I suppose?

Rod Roddy's Wrapup. Now that Jodie and Maggie have been locked up in a dungeon forever, are they upset, and did they remember to bring a change of clothes? Since El Puerco has told Jessica that he fools around with other women to stop himself from fooling around with her, will Jessica start fooling around? Will they ever fool around with each other? Now that Mary has told Chester that he is Danny's real father, will Chester find it in his heart to give Danny his kidney? These questions and many others will be answered in the next episode of *Soap*.

4.13

First aired: Mar 16, 1981 • Story by Susan Harris, Stu Silver, Dick Clair + Jenna McMahon • Teleplay by Susan Harris, Stu Silver, Dick Clair, Jenna McMahon, Barry Vigon + Danny Jacobson • Directed by JD Lobue

The identity of Danny's real father is the subject of the day, and nobody's taking it very well. Mary tells Jessica and Danny the same day: Jessica is shattered by the betrayal, and Danny doesn't take it much better. Burt finds himself on the evening news after his arrest of Tibbs and company, but drops everything to be at the hospital for Danny. Just before surgery, Danny and Chester find some common ground and face their ordeal together.

Cast. Cathryn Damon (Mary), Katherine Helmond (Jessica), Robert Mandan (Chester), Richard Mulligan (Burt), Ted Wass (Danny), Rod Roddy (Announcer), Joel Brooks (Morty), Richard Brestoff (Makeup

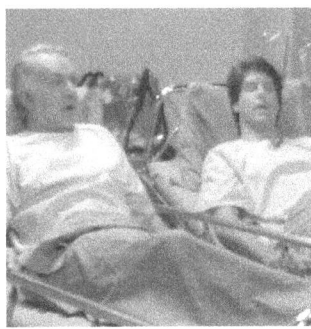

In what may be Chester's first selfless act, he donates a kidney to the dying Danny...his son.

Captain America #256. The comic that Danny's reading in the hospital.

Man), Deborah Combs (Nurse), Michael Currie (Governor), Brian Kale (Anesthesiologist), Jim McKrell (Anchorman)

Highlights. Chester parking in the 20 minute zone at the hospital when he's donating his kidney, and his delicate balance between humor and compassion with Danny; the whole wave of insanity Burt is up against before his WREQ TV interview, followed by the tsunami of insanity that takes place on air.

Confused? You Won't Be. '*We found out a lot about each other. You play guitar, I'm your father...*'

▶ While many still feel let down by the cliffhanger ending of the series, it's clear by this episode that *Soap* had found a natural ending place. The very bedrock of the series—the close relationship between sisters Jessica and Mary—was dealt a critical blow by Mary's revelation this episode. It would've taken a good season at least to bring them back to anything resembling normal.

▶ The last time Chester was worrying about being parked in a 20 minute zone was when he was cheating on Jessica with a woman in a hotel (3.10). Now the once-selfish Chester is donating a kidney.

▶ Burt's on-air sermon about why he went after Tibbs and the mob is Susan Harris' *Network* moment. Counting Paddy Chayefsky as one of her influences from the very beginning, we can see Burt Campbell as *Network*'s Howard Beale, if that agitated newsreader had been allowed to work his way through his madness to the other side, as Burt did throughout the first three seasons of *Soap*. And just as the Powers That Be do in that 1976 movie, the political and media establishment (the anchorman and the Governor) co-opt Burt's common sense heart-to-heart with the public for their own cheap political ends.

8. How old Jessica was when Mary shoved her out of a tree. (She'd put a spider in her Jello before it Jelloed.)

Christmas 1965. When Chester gave Danny a guitar.

Once and for all, is *Soap* a Soap Opera Parody or Not?

This may seem like a ridiculous question at first, but it must be said that Susan Harris has always vehemently denied that *Soap* was a straight-up parody of the genre. "It was never intended to be," she says. "It was just the form, and that's why we called it *Soap*. It was never meant as a satire."

However, *Soap* on occasion has scenes that feel like they could've been lifted right from a soap opera—take the scene between Mary and Jessica this episode. And certainly many of the actors knew their way around soap opera long before they ever set foot on the *Soap* set.

Robert Mandan in a 1961 episode of the NBC soap opera "From These Roots."

"My last actual soap before *Soap* was *Search for Tomorrow*," says Robert Mandan. "I did a short run on *Edge of Night* and did some guest spots on some other soaps when I was in New York, but I did about a four-year run on *Search For Tomorrow*. I left that and did a Broadway show, and then came to California. I probably could've stayed on that for years, I don't know. I thought to myself I've got to get off this show or go on doing soap opera. In those days, it was 'Oh, you do a soap? Oh my.'

"When I first went on [*Search for Tomorrow*], they didn't want you to have any identity other than that character and the show and the soap they were selling. So they never pushed soap stars like they do today. Some of those soap stars can go out and do personal appearances and all kinds of stuff.

"But I agree with Susan, *Soap* wasn't really a soap opera, it just had continuing story lines, that was about it. Which didn't last very long. Sometimes you thought, 'Oh, we're into a story line here,' and the very next episode it was resolved, which would not be the case in a soap opera. Those can go on for months."

Best Lines.
Jessica [to Mary]: All these years and you never told me. Practically our whole lives. I trusted you with everything. With all my thoughts and my most private fears, when you knew everything

1981

MARCH 17: Italy's illegal P2 Masonic lodge is uncovered by officials, with a membership that counts intelligence officers, government ministers and military leaders among its numbers. Ultimately, P2 will be linked to the 1982 suicide (but later ruled murder) of "God's Banker," Roberto Calvi (above), chairman of Italy's Banco Ambrosiano. The Vatican Bank was BA's primary shareholder.

about my marriage. When my marriage was everything in my life. When I let you know every corner of my soul. You kept it from me. When you sat there listening and knowing that. Oh Mary, I feel so totally, totally betrayed.

Chester: ...You need the kidney of a blood relative.

Danny: Well so that means you can't. Why not Jodie?

Chester: Well someone like your father. Close.

Danny: Don't talk about my father. He's dead. He was a crook and a murderer and he's dead.

Mary: Well, that's two out of three.

Danny: Chester's my father? The person I respect the least in the whole world has my chromotons.

Anchorman: Thank you Sheriff.

Burt: No wait a minute, wait a minute here. It's just, it's very simple. It's just that sooner or later everybody's gonna have to stand up and protect their own. I mean people are gonna have to learn, they're gonna say no, you can't take this from me or no you may not do that to me. And when people find out it's up to them to say no, then they have to make a choice. I chose to say no. There's no big deal here, there's no courage. It's just that somebody hurt my kid, my family. You can't let people go around hurting ya, or your family, so you don't—I gotta go. My kid's in the hospital, I gotta go see him. Excuse me. [Walks off.]

Anchorman: Ladies and gentlemen, you heard it here. The answer pure and simple. A modest man saying no.

Governor: That's right, Phillip. Should men like this be limited by local office? No. Men like this have too much to give our country. And that is why I have chosen that brave human being to head my war on crime. At last, a man who says no. Sheriff Bat Camp-Bull.

Anchorman: Coming up next, our special segment: schooling and why it's a good thing.

Rod Roddy's Wrapup. Now that Burt's heroism has made him a celebrity, will he continue to fight crime or will he want his own television series? What will be the outcome of Danny's operation? Will his body accept Chester's kidney? Will Chester's kidney accept Danny's body? And what about the two sisters? Will Jessica ever forgive Mary? Will Mary ever forgive herself? Or will her shocking confession destroy the Tates and Campbells forever? These questions and many others will be answered in the next episode of *Soap*.

4.14

First aired: Mar 23, 1981 • Story by Susan Harris, Stu Silver, Dick Clair + Jenna McMahon • Teleplay by Susan Harris, Stu Silver, Dick Clair, Jenna McMahon, Barry Vigon + Danny Jacobson • Directed by JD Lobue

While Danny and Chester are in surgery, the rest of the Tates and Campbells deal with the shocking news about the patients' relationship. Jessica gives Mary the cold shoulder, Mary turns to alcohol, and Burt's just happy that Danny's getting a new kidney. Finding sex boring in marriage, Eunice gets Dutch to act out her fantasies; Jodie and Maggie face execution at sunrise; and Mary reveals exactly how Jessica and Chester ended up married.

Cast. Jimmy Baio (Billy), Billy Crystal (Jodie), Cathryn Damon (Mary), Nancy Dolman (Annie), Katherine Helmond (Jessica), Jay Johnson (Chuck & Bob), Robert Mandan (Chester), Richard Mulligan (Burt), Arthur Peterson (The Major), Barbara Rhoades (Maggie), Donnelly Rhodes (Dutch), Jennifer Salt (Eunice), Jesse Welles (Gwen), Rod Roddy (Announcer), Ralph Manza (Digger)

Highlights. The crazy old lady story Jessica tells Gwen ("manya manya manya manya!"); everyone going out to get a little "air" when Burt arrives, leaving Mary to explain just what's been going on since he's been away, and Burt's wonderful reaction to what she has to tell him; The Major's WWII flashbacks merging with Dutch and Eunice acting out the beach scene in *From Here to Eternity* in a brilliant folie a trois; and the whole flashback to the Chester/Jessica engagement.

Confused? You Won't Be. *'Everything's going to be just as it was before…well, almost.'*

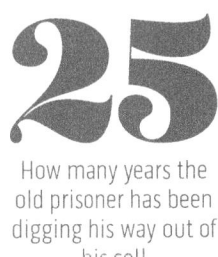

How many years the old prisoner has been digging his way out of his cell

⏵ Despite a wasted use of Chuck & Bob, a dull snippet of Jodie and Maggie, and a scene that does nothing to justify bringing back Eunice and Dutch from wherever it is they've been, we get another reason to love and respect Burt. And finally, *finally* we have the one sliver of information about the Jessica/Chester/Mary triangle that explains why the Tates and the Campbells are cursed (1.10, 1.16, 4.5). Whatever strides Jessica has made in the last two seasons toward reclaiming her life from those who would drag her down, we now know something that could devastate her beyond recovery.

⏵ Mary and Chester's two-week lovemaking ended the night before Chester asked Jessica to marry him. Even if we take him at his word that Mother Gatling blackmailed him into proposing to Jessica, when exactly did this conversation take place, and how long has Chester been sleeping with Mary realizing he must break up with her? The implication is that this whole turn of events may have led to Chester's philandering ways. However, as we also learn that Chester's father defrauded Mother Gatling, there's the possibility that cheating in affairs of the heart might also have been inherited.

⏵ Mary's parting words to Chester in her flashback—"Be good to my sister"—add a final twist of the knife as we now must see the last 4-and-a-half-seasons through Mary's eyes. All the lies, all the cheating that she and everybody else saw from Chester—this most certainly was not being good to her sister.

The *Soap* Backlash and the Black Lists

Everyone on *Soap* had their own reaction to the protests and advertiser boycotts that dogged the show, but these moves seemed eerily familiar to the actress who played Eunice. As the daughter of screenwriter Waldo Salt (*Midnight Cowboy*), whose career suffered greatly at the hands of the McCarthy-era blacklists, Jennifer Salt had seen this all before.

"I think that I had [seen it] in general a) from the blacklist experience, and b) from just the entire way I was raised, the world in which my dad lived. Even as a successful screenwriter, he had that put-upon writer's mentality," she says. "So I think the feeling 'The Man's going to get you, you gotta be careful of The Man, you

1981

MARCH 30: President Ronald Reagan and Press Secretary James Brady are shot and wounded outside a Washington hotel by John Hinckley Jr. Far more fascinating: Hinckley's family were close friends with the family of then-Vice President George HW Bush, a neighbor of Hinckley's father back in Houston.

gotta fight The Man,' has been something I grew up with for many reasons, the blacklists being one of them, and being the daughter of a Hollywood screenwriter being another. Writers never think of themselves as the privileged ones and the ones with power, or they didn't used to."

But the actress also had enough experience of the worlds of politics and Hollywood to be able to put the *Soap* protests in perspective.

"If your own government will destroy your life in the guise of protecting people with the blacklist—there was nothing about it that was rational or worthy, it was sick. So when you know that when you're really, really young, that's just part of your expectation: People are stupid and bad."

Best Lines.

Dutch [raring to make love]: Well Eunice, it's been two weeks and I've got all these little genes running around inside my body. And you had them thinking they were leaving tonight and you can't just cancel their trip.

Eunice: Maybe tomorrow, sweetie.

Dutch: They're already packed.

Growing up with a family savaged by the communist witch hunts of the '50s put some of the protest around *Soap* in perspective for Jennifer Salt.

Chester: Your mother told me I had to marry Jessica or my father would end up in jail.

Mary: For what?

Chester: Stock fraud. He cheated your mother out of a small fortune. Boy was she mad!

Mary: What does Jessica have to do with this?

Chester: Blackmail. Your mother doesn't think anybody will marry Jessica because she's so scatterbrained. This way she has a chance to marry her off.

Mary: And you're going to do it?

Chester: Oh gee whiz Mary, I have to. If I don't, my father's going to end up in jail.

Mary: I don't believe this!

Chester: And he'll cut me out of his will. Which is no small potatoes because he's loaded now that he's robbed your mother.

APRIL 12: Space Shuttle Columbia marks the first time a reusable spacecraft carrying a crew has been used; it will return to earth on **APRIL 14.**

Mary: You creep. You're disgusting. You're a disgusting, vile, opportunistic, disgusting liar.

Chester: Wow, Mary. (Hey you guys), what do you expect me to do? Run off with you? Your mother would track us down! She's determined that I marry Jessica or my father's going to end up in jail. I have no alternative, Mary. What would you have me do?

Mary: Be good to my sister.

Rod Roddy's Wrapup. Since Eunice has discovered that Dutch can make her happy by pretending to be someone else, will their lives become a Movie of the Week every week? Will Jessica ever speak to Mary again, or has Mary's childhood affair with Chester left a cold spot in Jessica's heart? And what about Jodie and Maggie? Will they be executed, or will they spend the rest of their lives in a cold dungeon? And if so, will they really care? These questions and many others will be answered in the next episode of *Soap*.

4.15 First aired: April 13, 1981 • Story by Susan Harris, Stu Silver, Dick Clair + Jenna McMahon • Teleplay by Susan Harris, Stu Silver, Dick Clair, Jenna McMahon, Barry Vigon + Danny Jacobson • Directed by JD Lobue

"Bat" Campbell is the hero of the hour, and seems to be more concerned with living up to his hero image than the feelings and well-being of his family. Chester and Jessica finally have a very difficult conversation about their beginnings as a couple, and El Puerco tries to bury the hatchet with Saunders to stay in Jessica's good graces. Danny finally gets out of hospital and proposes to Gwen. Little does he know that the woman he loves is being blackmailed into informing on ol' Bat Campbell and his deputy.

Cast. Jimmy Baio (Billy), Roscoe Lee Browne (Saunders), Cathryn Damon (Mary), Nancy Dolman (Annie), Katherine Helmond (Jessica), Jay Johnson (Chuck & Bob), Robert Mandan (Chester), Richard Mulligan (Burt), Arthur Peterson (The Major), Gregory Sierra (El Puerco), Ted Wass (Danny), Jesse Welles (Gwen), Rod Roddy (Announcer), Joe Mantegna (Juan 1), Anthony Charnota (Hood)

Highlights. Burt's little baseball-bat lapel pin, and later, the BAT emblazoned cap and bat-like baton (oh Burt); Mary pointing out that Burt has never called Bob a dummy before; the sly way Danny lets Burt know that he intends to marry Gwen, and Burt's selfish reaction; Chester and Jessica's frank discussion about why he married her; Juan 1's delight in glazing the pig, and the reason El Puerco wanted to make it.

Confused? You Won't Be. *'Burt, what's gotten into you?'*

● We've loved Burt, felt sorry for Burt, rooted for Burt, but we've never disliked Burt until now. What happened? In some ways, he's changed places with Chester, who is now one kidney lighter and sweetly trying to spare Jessica's already wounded pride over the secrets that have been revealed since Danny's operation.

● El Puerco's "then we call Israel and ask them to do it" is strangely prescient as two months from now, Israel will launch a surprise airstrike on Iraq, destroying the nuclear reactor it was constructing, setting the stage for modern preemptive strikes (the most recent Iraq War being a good example).

● Saunders tells Burt and company that he has experience in making rescue plans but refuses to go into details, nipping in the bud the one interesting aspect of his character. Like Benson before him (3.1), Saunders is the leader of the rescue mission.

'Death Valley Days'. The television show Burt tells President Reagan he "loved" him in.

Jennifer. What Chester claims he thought Jessica's name was before they met.

Joe Mantegna: Juan 1, *Soap* 1

Part of the fun in watching a program of *Soap*'s vintage comes from spotting well-known actors early in their careers. Before *Criminal Minds* and his years on *The Simpsons* as the voice of mobster Fat Tony, Joe Mantegna was El Puerco's loyal right-hand man, Juan 1.

"I haven't looked at that stuff in 30 years, but however many lines I had in that first episode couldn't have been more than one or two," says Mantegna. "But it rang something with Susan Harris who, to this day, I credit as being one of the brilliant writers of television. So she saw something in me and that character like hey, this could be fun. And I think because they had plans for developing the character of Gregory Sierra's El Puerco, they came to this conclusion: well, let's give him this guy Juan 1, and see what develops. The next thing I know, I'm in a second episode and a third and a fourth. I was happy as a clam."

Soap was Mantegna's first regular TV work since moving from Chicago (by way of New York) to Los Angeles in 1978, he remembers. Until then, he'd only played road manager Joe Esposito to Kurt Russell's Elvis Presley in the 1979 ABC TV miniseries *Elvis*.

"That was the best job I had for the next three years out here because it was a miniseries and it was a nice little part. But then after that, I did two lines in the movie *Xanadu* that actually got cut out of the movie—I still get like $10 residual checks because my name's on the credits. I was doing bit parts, bit parts, bit parts, and then the *Soap* thing came along, which again was a bit part—it was one line in one episode. I think I probably got their attention because it was hard for me to give up my look at the time, which was a beard and long hair.

"Yeah, that was my beard in the show. But luckily when I showed up for the audition, that's what they were looking for—a Maluguayan-revolutionary-looking guy—so I didn't have to put on a fake beard or anything. I looked like Che Guevara."

Joe Mantegna on his Juan 1 days: 'I looked like Che Guevara.'

Best Lines.

Bob: Oh by the way, you're speaking at the police academy tonight so get a haircut.

Burt: Look Chuck, please, this is crazy. Bob cannot be my manager. What would the president think if he thought I entrusted my career to that stupid dummy of yours?

Bob: Aw that did it. I've had it! Chuck, get up and walk out of here in a huff!

Jessica: Chester, you married me. You married me without loving me, and that's really the awful part.

Chester: But I fell in love with you, Jess. I did. You're right, not at first. At first I thought you were a nice piece, and if I had to get married, I could do a lot worse.

Chester: But I fell in love with you Jess. I swear I did.

Jessica: Chester, you certainly had peculiar ways of showing it.

Chester: Why, because I cheated? Well Jess I'll always cheat, I can't help it. I cheated on you, I cheated on the women I cheated on you with. I'll cheat on Annie. Doesn't mean that I didn't love you. I loved you, Jess. Guess I always will.

Rod Roddy's Wrapup. Will Saunders' plan to rescue Jodie and Maggie work, or does he just want some time off? Will Burt actually prevent Danny from marrying Gwen, or has someone else beaten him to it? And what is happening to Burt? Is he forsaking his family? Will Gwen forsake Danny? Will Jessica forgive Mary? These questions and many others will be answered in the next episode of *Soap*.

4.16

First aired: April 20, 1981 • Story by Susan Harris + Stu Silver • Teleplay by Susan Harris, Stu Silver, Barry Vigon + Danny Jacobson • Directed by JD Lobue

Jodie, Maggie and Wendy are rescued from the "minja" dungeon by "Bat" Campbell and his squad of insane family and associates. Jessica finally welcomes Mary back into the fold and tries to help her sister get on top of her problems: Burt's slipping away from her, Scottie may be an alien, and Mary's drinking. Gwen sends Danny a letter telling him they're through. And now that certain death has been taken off the table, Jodie tells Maggie he isn't so sure that he wants to marry her without knowing if he is "over" being gay. Not knowing what else to do, Jodie seeks help from therapist Dr. Rudolph.

Cast. Jimmy Baio (Billy), Roscoe Lee Browne (Saunders), Billy Crystal (Jodie), Cathryn Damon (Mary), Katherine Helmond (Jessica), Jay Johnson (Chuck & Bob), Richard Mulligan (Burt), Arthur Peterson (The Major), Barbara Rhoades (Maggie), Donnelly Rhodes (Dutch), Gregory Sierra (El Puerco), Ted Wass (Danny), George Wyner (Dr.

Rudolph), Rod Roddy (Announcer), Joe Mantegna (Juan 1), Nancy Bond (Nurse), Thomas Callaway (Phillip), Sheldon Feldner (Perkins), Howard George (Reporter No. 2), Fred Iwasaki (Chef), Barbara Iley (Nurse), Ralph Manza (Digger), Tom McGreevey (Reporter No. 1), Marcus Mukai (Minja Guard), Jim Staahl (Bigelow)

Highlights. Juan 1 continues to be a breath of fresh air as the Greek chorus to his beloved El Puerco (El: As I always says, when there is a maiden in distress-; Juan 1: El Puerco will get into her dress); Jodie taking Maggie to the same Japanese restaurant (with the same Japanese cook) he used to take Carol to, and the cook threatening to carve up Jodie's rude friend Phillip; and finally, Jodie's meeting with the dry-witted Dr. Rudolph.

Confused? You Won't Be. *'Is this the way it's going to be for the rest of my life?'*

George Wyner's Dr. Rudolph is one of the elements that saves this episode.

◉ Director Jay Sandrich has remarked on the occasional difficulty of working all the actors into every episode, and that was before the explosion of side characters during the last two years. The Jodie and Maggie rescue scene at the beginning emphasizes this with the use of Burt, Dutch, Billy, El Puerco, Juan 1, Saunders, The Major, Chuck & Bob (not to mention Jodie, Maggie and "Digger"), all in the same scene, the sitcom equivalent of throwing the combined equipment of the Royal Philharmonic Orchestra down a flight of stairs and hoping for something other than a cacophony.

◉ The make-up scene between Jessica and Mary in the doctor's office, despite some of the sharpest use of wardrobe for either actress in the whole series, is another disappointment. The ease with which Jessica extends an olive branch feels off, never mind how close the sisters are supposed to be. Yes, it's a sitcom, and the situation had been beaten to death, but the story line was written as a dramatic one and required an ending as serious as it began.

◉ This episode is saved by the brief reappearance of our favorite Japanese chef, and the introduction of Dr. Rudolph.

And introducing...Dr. Rudolph.

25 years. How long the old timer has been imprisoned in the dungeon.

2 or 3 years. How long Mary's been out cold if you added up all the times she's fainted in her life, according to Jessica.

Gwen's letter to Danny. Dear Danny, I can't marry you, I don't love you. I never have, you're just a good friend, that's all. —*Gwen*

Bigelow. "Nice fellow. Hates bees."

Season 4: A Marathon Year

During this season, the producers were shooting nearly two shows a week, according to director JD Lobue. "We were shooting scenes that were self-contained. I would ask the writers, 'Where is this going' after getting a script and prior to staging it. They would say, 'We don't know where it's going.' OK, so I'll just play the reality and the truth of each scene, which is what we did."

Part of the reason for this approach was because they were no longer shooting the scenes in the order in which they would be used. Before, if Scene 1 took place in the Campbell kitchen, Scene 2 in the Tate living room, and then Scene 3 was back in the Campbell kitchen, those scenes would've been shot in that order. During Season 4, they changed to shooting everything that took place in the Campbell kitchen (Scenes 1 and 3) from beginning to end, before doing the same with the Tate living room. Sometimes this meant shooting material that would be used in future episodes. "We arranged the scenes as best we could for a complete episode," says Lobue.

However, this also meant that each week they were shooting more than one week's worth of episodes. "I would say we were doing about 20 to 30 percent more than a half-hour episode a week," he says. This also meant occasionally scrapping the "dress show"—a dress rehearsal shot in front of an audience at 5 p.m. that preceded the 6:30 p.m. air show. "Sometimes we would only do an air show because it would delay us too long. It was really rigorous."

Best Lines.
Digger: Say tell me, how's President Eisenhower doing these days?
Burt: Gee I'm sorry to tell ya but Ike's passed on.

Digger: Oh my God. That means that Nixon is president!

Dr. Rudolph [to Jodie]: Let me get this straight. You have a child by one woman but you want to marry another woman and someday have children with her, and you're worried about being gay.

Dr. Rudolph: Hypnotherapy is a tool but it's not always effective, Mr. Dallas. There are dangers.
Jodie: Like what?
Dr. Rudolph: Well, it is conceivable that I couldn't bring you back. You could actually get locked into a different time period, and I'd get sued up the gi-gi.
Jodie: I'd sign a waiver releasing you of all liabilities.
Dr. Rudolph [pulling waiver forms from his desk drawer]: Then again, hypnotherapy can prove to be extremely valuable. Would you be interested in some other forms of psychiatric short cuts?
Jodie: Like what?
Dr. Rudolph: Oh, the sensory deprivation tank.
Jodie: What's this?
Dr. Rudolph: Trust me, you'll love it. Then there's LSD 25. A very fine alternative.
Jodie: No, no acid. I draw the line at hallucinogenics.
Dr. Rudolph: Great, just testing. It's illegal anyway.

Dr. Rudolph [to his secretary about Jodie]: Have we got a hot one. This guy actually signs waivers!

Rod Roddy's Wrapup. Since a psychiatrist convinced Jodie that hypnosis might help him find himself, will Jodie find anything he likes? And if not, will he still pay his doctor's bill? Now that Jessica and Mary started speaking again, will Mary stop drinking, or will she continue to find solace in a bottle? Will Burt's newfound fame cause his ego to grow, and if so, will he have to find a bigger office? These questions and many others will be answered in the next episode of *Soap*.

4.17
First aired: April 27, 1981 • Written by Susan Harris + Stu Silver • Directed by JD Lobue

After freeing Jodie, Maggie and Wendy from the Malibu fortress, the rescuers return to their lives triumphant. El Puerco has overcome his marriage fixation to finally consummate his relationship with Jessica, much to her initial disappointment. (Their subsequent talk, however, results in a new, more fulfilling relationship.) Burt prepares a political speech and further embraces the Governor, at the cost of alienating Mary, who leaves him. And Dutch is back to trying to fulfill Eunice's bedroom fantasies, to no avail. Yet the worst fate may be the one suffered by Jodie, who awakens from Dr. Rudolph's hypnotherapy…as a 90-year-old Jewish stereotype.

Cast. Jimmy Baio (Billy), Roscoe Lee Browne (Saunders), Billy Crystal (Jodie), Cathryn Damon (Mary), Nancy Dolman (Annie), Katherine Helmond (Jessica), Robert Mandan (Chester), Richard Mulligan (Burt), Arthur Peterson (The Major), Donnelly Rhodes (Dutch), Jennifer Salt (Eunice), Gregory Sierra (El Puerco), George Wyner (Dr. Rudolph), Rod Roddy (Announcer), Michael Currie (Governor), Joe Mantegna (Juan 1), Nancy Bond (Nurse), Barbara Lang (Pookie)

Highlights. Juan 1's "Oops" on finding El Puerco in Jessica's bedroom; Chester's wounded ego on learning that El and Jessica finally slept together (despite his having announced his recent marriage to Annie); Mary's "graceful" entrance into the Campbell living room where the Governor and his wife are waiting; and Eunice's sudden realization of what happened last Thursday, after talking to Dutch.

Confused? You Won't Be. *'Women don't have fun.'*

◉ Juan 1's "I tink in America this is called a home run, a grand slam for the great swine" could well be a nod to Joe Mantegna's own love of baseball, chronicled so eloquently in his successful 1977 play *Bleacher Bums* (a performance of which showed up on PBS in 1979).

◉ Ever since the classic "coffee cake sex talk" scene (2.7), the producers have been attempting to recapture the same frank-yet-gentle approach to discussing intimacy, but have only succeeded in a coarser version of that (3.4, 3.18). Jessica and El Puerco's frank conversation this episode about being a giving lover is unusual in

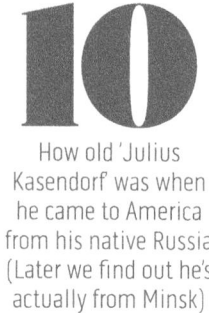

10 How old 'Julius Kasendorf' was when he came to America from his native Russia (Later we find out he's actually from Minsk)

that it hints at a return to that more subtle, nuanced approach toward sex.

▶ As the good ship *Soap* desperately strives to find a steady course during Season 4, we see subtle plays for nostalgia. Earlier (4.11) it was the "Who is Danny's Father" cliffhanger mimicking its "Who Killed Peter Campbell" heyday (1.12). This episode we get Billy being sent away from the table because Jessica still deems him too young to listen to the family's love-life discussions, and Chester going back to his moral indignation over Jessica having affairs even though he does so himself.

▶ Last episode we lost Dick Clair and Jenna McMahon from the writing credits. This episode, Barry Vigon & Danny Jacobson have been jettisoned, leaving us with the core writing team of Harris and Silver.

Yell "andele". El Puerco's euphemism for orgasm.

Pookie. The name of the Governor's wife (short for Louisa).

Rodenbach. The Governor's surname.

3 days. How long it's been since Mary's had a drink.

And introducing…Jodie as Julius Kasendorf, age 90. And the final nail in the *Soap* coffin.

Mysteries of the 'Bible': Story Lines and Details That Never Made it to Screen

The *Soap* bible that the producers presented to ABC before series launch boasts a few characters and plots we never saw, and there were some humdingers.

▶ The Major's Backstory: The fictional grandson of the very real Dr. Richard J. Gatling (who invented the Gatling gun in 1861), Seymour Gatling (aka The Major) was a quiet fellow with few standout qualities beyond his love of calves liver with ketchup, before he went off to fight in World War II. However, according to the *Soap* bible, "Seymour suffered a sever shock at the front lines when he discovered they were using real bullets." He returned from the war with a bad case of amnesia…and athlete's foot. Fortunately, his strong willed wife, Rose Pulitzer, took over the family finances and the running of the house.

▶ Chester's family dates back to the pilgrims—his ancestors "made a killing on the tall hats the pilgrims wore." This was attributed to the Gatlings in the broadcast show (P. 263). Also, Chester has three sisters: Metta, Hezza and Adja. (Place each name before the surname "Tate" for a gag that represents much of the tone of the *Soap* bible...)

▶ Burt's father, Ian Campbell, started the Campbell's soup company with his brother, Morty, who screwed him out of the business. "To this day, Burt goes crazy at the dinner table if anyone goes 'Hmmm, hmmm, good.' (Danny sometimes does this to get his goat.)" In light of this, what seems to be a simple one-liner in 4.8 carries with it an added sting. Burt confesses "I worked my whole life to have my name mean something. And today all that Campbell means is *soup*." However, as evidence suggests that Susan Harris had forgotten that the bible revealed that Danny was Chester's son (see "For the *Soap* Bible Tells Us So" under the 4.12 entry), chances are good that the soup mention was merely a happy accident.

▶ Burt first encountered Mary's first husband, mobster Johnny Dallas, when he was forced to deal with the construction union he ran.

▶ Depressed after his father's "suicide", Danny joined the Marines and went to Vietnam. When he returned, he was hired as a bodyguard/chauffeur. "He had no idea he was joining his father's organization. In fact, until the night he was asked to place a horse's ass on someone's doorstep, he had no idea he was in the Mafia." Also quite the animal lover, Danny wanted to quit the mob to open a kennel.

▶ In one of *Soap*'s most daring story lines that never made it to air, Benson's daughter, Ruby, breaks off her engagement to the son of Police Chief Tinkler (who is revealed to be a bigot) and takes up with Kimbuko Lumumba (formerly Jackson X), a black radical wanted by the FBI. Considering that Patty Hearst's sensational trial had only taken place the year before the *Soap* bible was written, it's not hard to see where some of the inspiration for this plot came from. (And let's not forget that *Patrice* Lumumba was the prime minister of the Republic of Congo until his assassination in 1961, probably with the help of the CIA.)

The *Soap* Grouse Hot Line

Whatever the public's complaints, one grievance they could never lodge was an inability to get through to the creative forces behind *Soap*. "I remember once sitting in my office and some guy got through to me, somebody from down South someplace, and said you know your show is a disgrace and all that," writer Stu Silver says. "I was on the phone with this guy for an hour, and after I got off the phone I'm like I'd really like to meet this guy. I never did. But I asked him have you ever seen the show, and he said no, I won't watch that. Well, why don't you watch an episode and then call me back. Obviously you have my number already. But he never called back. I think his wife called back and said so-and-so's not here to talk to you but I wanna tell you he's become a big fan of the show."

Best Lines.

El Puerco [in his way, promising to be a more generous lover]: Do you remember when you was a little kid and used to go to the park with your friend? At first your friend would push the swing for you and then you would push the swing for your friend? How about if now I do the pushing and you do the swinging?

Chester [to Jessica]: A fine thing. Your husband leaves the house for one night to get married and as soon as his back is turned, you fool around with the first foreigner that happens by.

Eunice: I don't know. Why don't ya just try that thing you did last Thursday.

Dutch: What thing?

Eunice: You know. When you came through the window with the stocking on your head. Now for some reason that was an incredible turn on.

Dutch: When was this?

Eunice: Last Thursday. Why don't you just get the same outfit and try it again, OK? Only this time do not really steal my jewelry.

Dutch: Eunice, that wasn't me.

Eunice [eyes wide in sudden realization]: What?

Rod Roddy's Wrapup. What will Burt do now that Mary has walked out besides have more legroom in the limo? Will Chester come back to Annie? If he does, will she take him back? Why? Now that Jodie has been hypnotized and can't be brought back, will he stay stuck forever? Will he marry Maggie or will he look for a nice Jewish girl? These questions and many others will be answered in the next episode of *Soap*.

4.18
First aired: May 4, 1981 • Written by Susan Harris + Stu Silver • Directed by JD Lobue

Everybody is fighting their worst natures, with varying degrees of success. Bob and Mary have both given up booze; Danny and Annie are fighting their mutual attraction for each other; Chester is sleeping at the YMCA to avoid killing El Puerco; and Burt…well, Burt isn't fighting too hard against the career path the Governor has laid out for him: lieutenant governor and, ultimately, senator. The only person who seems to feel at home in his skin is Julius…an old Jewish man who just happens to have taken up residence in Jodie's body.

Cast. Billy Crystal (Jodie), Cathryn Damon (Mary), Nancy Dolman (Annie), Jay Johnson (Chuck & Bob), Robert Mandan (Chester), Richard Mulligan (Burt), Donnelly Rhodes (Dutch), Ted Wass (Danny), George Wyner (Dr. Rudolph), Rod Roddy (Announcer), Michael Currie (Governor), Jay Garner (Gene), George Wendt (Counterman)

Highlights. The Governor's affable insanity, and Gene's no-nonsense talk about owning a senator; Dutch going on about Eunice's fantasies to Chester; Annie and Danny comparing disgusting habits (Danny's description of the white stuff at the corners of his mouth: "Honest to God, I look like Old Yeller right before they shot him!") and their blatant physical attraction to each other; the mounting evidence that Scottie is an alien, and Mary's reaction when Dr. Rudolph shows up at her door about Jodie ("I am not crazy, he flies!" Slam); and Burt's parting words to his whacked-out family: "Don't leave this house. Anybody. Ever."

Confused? You Won't Be. *'Burt is no longer Burt.'*

136

Burt's golf score on the front 9, compared with the Governor's 45 (Bursitis throws his game off)

▶ Despite Burt's uncharacteristic lurch toward being self-absorbed, his "I wish my father were alive to see this" after the prospect of senator is dangled before him suggests all of this is about him still trying to avoid being just another working stiff like his dad (2.7). His transformation is also a clever riff on the Alien Burt story line last season. His interstellar stand-in took over his life and nobody really noticed. He was much randier than Real Burt, but he never hurt anybody. This season "Burt is no longer Burt," but he's in control of the situation, and hurting the people closest to him.

▶ Chester's admission to Dutch that he's afraid that El Puerco being with Jessica might make him kill again hints at his part in the cliffhanger series finale (2.21). It also suggests that the medical problem that compelled him to kill Peter Campbell was never treated, which seems odd considering the seriousness of the ailment and the fortune the Tate family has access to. (He might've run away before the procedure could be done.)

▶ For many, Dutch's crass comment about missing the good old days of making love to Corinne is a reminder of one of the show's biggest losses as far as characters are concerned. On the other hand, this is also the best use of Dutch in a good two seasons at least.

▶ This episode we continue the Season 4 idea that Bob has unexpectedly specialized knowledge that Chuck does not, such as fluency in Spanish (4.10) and medical insight into Danny's doomed kidneys (4.11). As in the latter case, Dr. Rudolph finds himself in agreement with Bob's diagnosis of Jodie's problem ("Highly complicated and rare schizophrenia/multiple personality cross-over," or possibly trauma). But unlike that instance, Dr. Rudolph falls back into the usual "I'm talking to a dummy" reaction we're used to.

▶ Just before Dr. Rudolph realizes he's "talking to a dummy," he tells Bob that the therapy was a tool to help them search for the root cause of—. Presumably had he finished, he would've said "Jodie's homosexuality," which even in the 1980s might've been a bridge too far with the gay lobby being what it was.

Lt. Governor. The office the Governor offers Burt. (After one term, they'll run him for senator.)

Melvyn Douglas. Who the Governor suggests hiring to be Burt's father; he could campaign for him. Not to be confused with Mike Douglas, whose talk show Jodie—er, Julius—is going on thanks to Dr. Rudolph. [Melvyn Douglas, incidentally, will be dead by August.]

Phil's Diner: Where Chester meets Dutch.

Poppin' Fresh: Who Dutch says Chester looks like.

Evidence for Scottie Being an Alien. 1) Gets out of his crib, 2) Pushed his toy chest across the room (it was built in), 3) Made complex geometrical drawings.

Best Lines.
Gene: I need me a senator. I now own six governors, 18 congressmen, four attorney generals, 11 cars, 12 houses, but not one senator.
Burt: Uh, own?
Gene: Well, I'm just joshin' with you. You can't own people. That misguided fellow Lincoln saw to that . No, what I'm sayin is I just have a real nice relationship with a whole lotta people. What do ya say, senator?

Chester: I haven't slept. I'm staying at the 'Y' and I can't sleep a wink.
Dutch: How come?
Chester: I'm surrounded by winos and homos. The winos keep trying to steal my wallet and the homos just keep trying.

Dutch [to Chester about his love life with Eunice]: One night I'm a cop, the next night I'm a storm trooper, then I'm a forest ranger—I've got a hell of a collection of boots now, let me tell ya. Boy do I miss the good old days of screaming and scratching Corinne.

Mary [to Burt about Scottie]: 12-month-old babies don't experiment in cubism.

Rod Roddy's Wrapup. Now that Jodie is an old Jewish man, will Mary keep a kosher home? Will Burt become a senator or does [progolfer] Lee Trevino have something to worry about? Will Danny

3
The age when El Puerco started winning various fencing tournaments

ever find happiness? Will he find it with his father's wife? And will Chester stop crying and try to get Jessica back, or will he remain all choked up about her? These questions and many others will be answered in the next episode of *Soap*.

4.19 First aired: May 11, 1981 • Written by Susan Harris + Stu Silver • Directed by JD Lobue

Fearing an attack by the communists, El Puerco decides to take the fight to Malaguay. Unfortunately, he only succeeds in arranging a duel with Chester for Jessica's hand. Predictably, Annie and Danny end up in bed together and, equally predictably, Maggie is less than thrilled at the prospect of being with an old Jewish man. Meanwhile, Jessica tries to get Burt to salvage his marriage, but the sheriff cares about nothing except his speech to the Senate. The honorable gentlemen seem to ignore his words completely but embrace his political gusto, dropping Burt in the crosshairs of a political assassination plot.

Cast. Jimmy Baio (Billy), Roscoe Lee Browne (Saunders), Billy Crystal (Jodie), Cathryn Damon (Mary), Nancy Dolman (Annie), Katherine Helmond (Jessica), Jay Johnson (Chuck & Bob), Robert Mandan (Chester), Richard Mulligan (Burt), Arthur Peterson (The Major), Barbara Rhoades (Maggie), Donnelly Rhodes (Dutch), Gregory Sierra (El Puerco), Ted Wass (Danny), Rod Roddy (Announcer), Joe Mantegna (Juan 1), Raleigh Bond (Oregon Senator), Michael Fairman (Lou), Sheldon Feldner (Perkins), Pat McNamara (Chairman), Kopi Sotiropulos (NY Senator), Don Starr (Alabama Senator)

Highlights. Danny and Annie in bed together; Julius' heart-wrenching meeting with Maggie; Burt telling the Senate committee that he now manufactures the red, white and blue Bat Campbell bat ("One size hits all"); and the senators' oddball speeches.

Confused? You Won't Be. *'Sometimes when I look at myself in the mirror, I am overwhelmed that I am in the same room with me.'*
▶ Jessica's gushing over Phil Donahue and talk of what Marlo Thomas must think when she sits across the breakfast table

from him is a cute inside-baseball moment, as Marlo is executive producer Tony Thomas' sister. (Marlo Thomas and Donahue wed in May 1980.)

▶ Burt's suggestion to Jessica that the reason there was little divorce in the old days—because everyone spent hours every day walking everywhere—is remarkably similar to the minister's theory about why few people cheated on their spouses in the old days: "there were Indians to worry about." (3.12)

▶ Bob appears to have added Yiddish to his foreign language repertoire (4.10).

▶ Don Starr, who plays the Alabama senator big on killing, was a familiar face at the time as seemingly good guy turned baddie Jordan Lee on evening soap opera *Dallas*.

Above: Marlo Thomas and Phil Donahue. Below, Don Starr.

▶ In a season that has taken us in so many unsuccessful directions (including this episode's hackneyed El Puerco/Chester duel), there's the danger of glossing over some of the gambles that succeeded, however unexpectedly. Thus is the case with the Julius Kasendorf story line, if only during this episode. In it we get some of Billy Crystal's most convincing scenes in the series. While frequently praised for his portrayal of Jodie the crusading father, it is as Julius, a 90-year-old Jewish man in a 33-year-old's body, that he tackled his most difficult role, and did so with an unexpected degree of pathos. This is also Susan Harris at her best—taking an absurd situation and wringing from it a little of the heartbreak that is life. Unfortunately, like The Major's finest scene (3.1), the producers felt compelled to end this one on a joke unworthy of what came before.

Pudge, Puffy and Harriet. What The Major called Winston Churchill back in the day.

Third place. What Chester achieved in the 1965 Dunn's River Handgun Shoot for Men.

100 paces. El Puerco can shoot the eye out of a fly at this distance.

Soap and the Theater Thing

When *Soap* is praised for anything, it is usually for the writing, and rightly so. Yet something that was just as integral to its success is the fact that most of its actors were theater trained.

"It was fairly unique," admits Joe Mantegna. "In other situations you'd have one or two of the people maybe, or the lead actor would be somebody that they saw on Broadway and brought to LA. (A few years later I became one of those people.) People get discovered on Broadway and get enticed to come back to Hollywood and headline a show, then they surround them with different types of actors. But people who liked working on *Soap*, they understood theater."

Adds Robert Guillaume, "At that time, and perhaps even now, I think that stage actors bring a kind of depth to sitcom. It's my feeling that there's a depth to the performance that you don't normally encounter. But of course we had to learn how to modulate what we were presenting with the requirements of television."

This also led to a different way of directing, says JD Lobue. "Much to their credit, the cast didn't respond to the kind of direction that some TV directors utilize, telling the actor you're not on camera now, so I don't care what you're doing in the scene. Everyone in our cast had to have a through line from the beginning of the scene to the end. 'What am I doing here even though I'm not saying a line, I'm not on camera? Why?' So you're directing 25-30 people in a room and you have to have all of their motivations and movements seamlessly choreographed so that each character is where you want them to be when it's time for them to deliver their lines on camera. In the theatrical experience's weeks of rehearsal, we are required to accomplish this staging. We only had three days of rehearsal per episode, and one day of camera rehearsal."

Best Lines.
Danny: I just made it with my stepmother.
Annie: Gee I wish you hadn't said that.
Danny: We've committed inquest.

Jodie/Julius [to Maggie, about Bob]: He's a nice boy. He's made out of wood, you know.

Maggie: Jodie, don't you remember me at all?

Jodie/Julius: No. I'm sorry. I wish I did. You seem like a nice person. I've been confusing a lot of people lately and I don't wish to confuse you. I like you and I wish I didn't make you so unhappy.

Sen. Lawton of Alabama: Killin is as American as apple pie. Now we have to kill to live. If you're sick of being killed, you kill first. Nothing wrong with killin, long as you kill the right person.

Rod Roddy's Wrapup. Now that Danny and Annie are more than just friends, will they go for broke and fall in love or play it safe and just play around? Will Jodie ever become Jodie again, and if not, will Maggie convert? Who will win the duel, Chester or El? And what about Burt? Will his fame cost him his life? These questions and many others will be answered in the next episode of *Soap*.

4.20
First aired: May 18, 1981 • Written by Susan Harris + Stu Silver • Directed by JD Lobue

Gene and the Governor tell Burt that if he wants to run for senator, he will have to dump his dysfunctional family. Meanwhile, his dysfunctional sister-in-law, Jessica, is taken hostage by Malaguayan communists to lure El Puerco to his homeland and certain doom. While Mary contemplates ending it all, an understandably philosophical Julius Kasendorf tells her that if she ignores these divine "tests", God will stop piling on the heartache.

Cast. Jimmy Baio (Billy), Roscoe Lee Browne (Saunders), Billy Crystal (Jodie), Cathryn Damon (Mary), Katherine Helmond (Jessica), Robert Mandan (Chester), Richard Mulligan (Burt), Arthur Peterson (The Major), Donnelly Rhodes (Dutch), Jennifer Salt (Eunice), Gregory Sierra (El Puerco), Rod Roddy (Announcer), Michael Currie (Governor), Jay Garner (Gene), Bob Ari (Vinnie), Luis Avalos (Gen. Sandia), Michael Fairman (Lou), Joe Mantegna (Juan 1), Barry Vigon (Pvt. Esquivo)

> " It wasn't just some goofy sitcom; it was a little smarter. Susan Harris and Paul Witt and Tony Thomas, you felt that they were going to surround themselves with the best writers they could get. The closest thing I can equate it to is my 20-year now association with *The Simpsons*."
> —JOE MANTEGNA (Juan 1)

Highlights. Jessica's back and forth with the communists who capture her; the interplay between the family and Burt as he's reading the kidnappers' letter; and Julius trying to cheer Mary up.

Confused? You Won't Be. *'I have some news for you. All bad.'*

▶ Burt continues his injury-inducing performance on the tennis court that he began on the golf course (4.18).

▶ Former *Soap* writer Barry Vigon appears on screen here as Gen. Luis Sandia's assistant, Pvt. Esquivo, (Spanish for "shy" or "elusive"). Gen. Sandia's name? Spanish for "watermelon."

▶ However bonkers the scenario of Jodie as an old Jewish man, the story line is really about Mary, something emphasized in this episode. As she tells Jodie/Julius that "Jodie, Julius, young, old; ya still got the same heart," we see that Mary is the one who always accepts Jodie, whether he's gay, has a child out of wedlock, or is more or less insane. It's a quality that she has applied to everyone in her life, and one that has kept her married to Burt (we sometimes forget he killed her first husband). All of this makes what Burt is putting her through now that much more tragic.

70 degrees, winds from the North/North East. Clear skies with a 20% chance of rain. The climate in Malaguay.

Franya. Julius' first wife.

Mandan and Helmond: The Theater Reunion

Robert Mandan and Katherine Helmond got the chance to work together again on stage in 2003, though Mandan says the play wasn't up to much.

"I would do anything with her in a minute," says Robert Mandan of his working relationship with Katherine Helmond, a sentiment that came back to haunt them both in 2003, he says.

"We really got tricked into doing this play," he explains. "Somebody sent me this script and I thought this is a piece of crap. I went to the reading and it narrowed down to two other guys and me, and most of the actors there kind of knew each other. Then I got a call saying Katherine's interested in doing this if you'll do it. So I said, 'Oh well yeah, OK.' Then they called Katherine and said 'Bob wants to do it,' and she said sure. She was in the Caribbean on an island at the time and she said 'I can't get to rehearsal on Monday, I'll be there on Tuesday.' She was flying back to New York that weekend. She came in on Tuesday morning and she looked at me like 'What have we gotten ourselves into here?' But being the trooper that she is, we fought it through.

"It wasn't a play at all, it was more like a television show—13 scenes, five sets, on a little theater stage. Just awful. This writer always wrote about his mother, who was a little old Jewish lady going blind in San Diego. My character was a naval officer and they would get together and they were falling in love, older people, but then they'd have a fight and they'd split apart. We did this every single scene for 13 scenes; it was just so embarrassing.

"Now I absolutely will not do anything if it doesn't strike my intuition right, but I've done about three or four things where someone says they'll pay you good money or it'll be fun. In that instance with Katherine, they didn't pay good money and it wasn't any fun, so what the hell were we doing there?"

Best Lines.
Burt [reading from the kidnappers' letter]: ...So you give him and we give back Red to you.
Eunice: And what if we refuse?
Burt: [still reading]: If you refuse we will kill her.
Eunice: Oh my God!
Chester: Are they gonna get in touch with us?
Burt [still reading]: We are going to get in touch with you.
El Puerco: When?
Burt [still reading]: Soon. It's signed The Kidnappers.

Rod Roddy's Wrapup. Will Mary ever accept Jodie as an old Jewish man? Will they start going to temple together? Will Burt leave his family for politics? Will he live to leave them? Can Jessica survive as a hostage? Can her kidnappers survive Jessica as a hostage? How long must the family wait to find out? Will they ever see

Jessica again? These questions and many others will be answered in the next episode of *Soap*.

4.21
First aired: May 25, 1981 • **Written by Susan Harris + Stu Silver** • **Directed by JD Lobue**

Despairing over being in love with his stepmom Annie, Danny finds no comfort from Burt, who only sees him as one more political embarrassment. Jessica does her best to stall for time in Malaguay, but Gen. Sandia gently but firmly tells her that El Puerco's absence means she must die. On the eve of his duel with the Malaguayan rebel, Chester pours his heart out to Annie before discovering Danny in her bed. And though he questions why he's been tipped off about a big drug deal, Burt can't resist the urge to hit the thugs' apartment alone to make the bust, and walks right into a trap, shortly before Jessica faces a firing squad.

Cast. Jimmy Baio (Billy), Nancy Dolman (Annie), Katherine Helmond (Jessica), Robert Mandan (Chester), Richard Mulligan (Burt), Donnelly Rhodes (Dutch), Jennifer Salt (Eunice), Gregory Sierra (El Puerco), Ted Wass (Danny), Rod Roddy (Announcer), Joe Mantegna (Juan 1), Bob Ari (Vinnie), Luis Avalos (Gen. Sandia), Danny Jacobson (Informer), Paul Stolarsky (Priest), Barry Vigon (Pvt. Esquivo)

Highlights. Burt's bat leg holster and Danny's confession about his new lady love; Bob calling the Tates looking for Chuck; the gentle reluctancy of Gen. "Sandy" Sandia to execute Jessica; the bizarre way Danny chooses to hide from Chester in Annie's bed, and Chester finally pulling back the covers to reveal the truth; and finally, Jessica facing the firing squad. "Ready! Aim! Fire!" Bang.

Confused? You Won't Be. *'This is the last of the last meals.'*
◉ The last time Danny marveled at his own sexual endurance it was with Elaine (2.10), right before she was kidnapped and ultimately killed. Apparently God/karma is trying to tell him something about these boasts of his.

Scenes from the series finale

▶ For the second time in three episodes (3.19), Tony Thomas' sister, Marlo, is namechecked, this time in the 20 questions game Jessica plays with Pvt. Eskimo (no no, it's Esquivo).

▶ Once again we get a startling glimpse into the acting range of Robert Mandan in the moments after he pulls back the covers of Annie's bed to find Danny. For just a second or two between revelation and soliloquy, he oozes a kind of menace we've never before seen in Chester.

Minsk. Apparently where Julius Kasendorf is from.

36 hours. How long the Tates have to deliver El Puerco to Malaguay, or Jessica gets it.

4. The number of times Jessica sends her last meal back, prolonging the inevitable.

Joan of Arc. Jessica always thought she would die like her.

3 days. How long Danny and Annie have been...you know. (Before the bed broke.)

Meta Meta Meta. Burt's "I know you?" to the stocking-faced informer who lures Burt to his Waterloo is something of an inside joke. The man beneath the mask is former *Soap* writer Danny Jacobson.

Scenes from the series finale

The Tates, the Campbells and the Almighty

For a series that began its life with religious leaders denouncing it on the air mere moments after its debut (see P. 63), *Soap* invoked the Lord enough times to put forth a religious view of its own.

In this, its final episode, Jessica prevails upon God to look after her children after her date with the firing squad. However, the deity who rules over Dunn's River appears less the loving God of the New Testament and more the jealous, vengeful God of the Old.

Last episode, Jodie/Julius Kasendorf tried to comfort Mary by telling her about the trials his friends and family have endured, ending

Jessica prepares to meet her maker in the one series cliffhanger everybody recalls to this day.

with the advice, "Ignore God's tests, he'll stop." The irony of this may be lost on the despondent Mary, but not on us.

Jodie has been tested continuously since the pilot, by his own homosexuality and society's reaction to it; by a fickle boyfriend; and by the scheming Carol David who seduced him, left him at the altar, and then sued him for the custody of their baby whom she abandoned. He's weathered a suicide attempt and the stigma of its failure, threats by government agencies to take his baby away, and that child's subsequent kidnapping. And when he finally falls in love with Maggie Chandler (in a Malibu dungeon, no less), he seeks therapy to ensure that he can be true to his wedding vows if he goes through with his promise to marry her. God rewards his caring and decency by obliterating Jodie's personality completely, replacing it with that of the 90-year-old Jewish man Julius.

"I'm 90 and I'm a Jew, it's a hell of a combination," he tells Mary, emphasizing for us that God saw fit to make him not just any Jew, but a World War II-era Jew from the Nazi-occupied Belarusian city of Minsk.

God tests other residents of Dunn's River, too. Like Jodie/Julius, Father Tim Flotsky recognizes the particular delight the Lord takes in pushing the buttons of those He made in His image. Early on, Tim voices his concern directly to God. "I understand tests and I know you've given some humdingers in your day, but are you going to send Corinne in once a week for the rest of my life? Because if you are, I think we're going to get to a week there that could embarrass everyone..." (1.10)

And He positively seems to have it in for some of the other characters on *Soap*. Take Danny's wife, Elaine. She's given a mobster father, loses her mother at an early age, and when her sister dies, her father scars her for life by saying, "Why wasn't it you?" (2.7) On what should be the happiest day of her life, her father cuts her off without a cent moments after she marries Danny, who has been forced into this union. And after a torturous relationship with Danny and his insane family, she finally repents of her own antisocial behavior and finds in Danny true love. Of course God is not through with her yet. Mere moments after she thanks Him directly for her relationship with Danny (2.10), she is kidnapped, and ultimately killed. His ways are not so much mysterious as consistent.

Perhaps it is *Soap*'s Everyman, Burt Campbell, who comes closest to summing up the view of God that the people of Dunn's River have cultivated after years of bitter experience. "Maybe God looked down and said, 'Eh, Campbell's too happy. Let's cool him down, kill his son.'" (1.14) This not only sounds like the God of the Old Testament, but the God who occupies the world of *Soap*.

For all of this talk of the deity directly in the series, the final word on the matter should go to a character who only graced the screen for a few episodes. He may have come closest to expressing the beauty of the Supreme Being who looks over Dunn's River.

Barney Gerber does nothing to whitewash the harshness of God; indeed, he gives us a good helping of it. But he also delivers a speech that highlights why it is that human beings persevere. Though it's too lengthy to go into here (check out "Best Lines" under the entry for 1.10), he explains to a despondent Jodie why he refuses to give up on life, and why Jodie himself should stick around, whatever tests God has in store for him. Barney concludes:

"Listen, I know you don't feel so terrific right now, but wait, Jodie, wait. Someday, I guarantee you're going to hear somebody laughing, and you'll turn around…and it'll be you."

Laughter as the Lord's one enduring gift to mankind. That's the *Soap* ethos in a nutshell.

Best Lines.
Burt [to Danny, about his new love]: Nice. That's good. Nice is good here. But what's this? What is she, a hooker or what? What's the surprise on this one?
[Later]
Tennessee Williams is now writing my life.

Danny [to Annie, about their lovemaking]: This makes all the other times feel like a dental appointment.

Chester [to Danny and Annie]: Tomorrow I die. Tonight, you die.

Sandia: Would you like a blindfold?

Jessica: Oh, what colors do you have?

Esquivo: No, you see we blindfold you so you don't see the men shoot you.

Jessica: Well that's silly. If you don't want me to see them shoot me then why do you make them shoot me?

Sandia: You know, the amazing thing about it is that if you listen, she actually makes sense.

Rod Roddy's Wrapup. Can Chester really kill his son and his wife? Has Burt really walked into an ambush that he may never walk out of? Has the firing squad really shot Jessica? These questions and many others will be answered in the next episode of *Soap*.

Meanwhile, on Benson

5.03 BENSON • First aired: Sept 30, 1983 • Written by Bob Fraser + Rob Dames • Directed by Bill Foster

"God, I Need This Job" No sooner does Gov. Gatling receive a letter from the Tates saying they're going to petition the court to have Jessica declared legally dead (it's been about two years since her kidnapping) than Benson receives a visit from Jessica herself. The downside: Only he can see her. According to Jessica, she must do one good deed in order to earn her wings. But will she ever be able to say goodbye to Benson?

Cast. Robert Guillaume (Benson), James Noble (Gov. Gatling), Inga Swenson (Gretchen Kraus), Missy Gold (Katie), Rene Auberjonois (Clayton), Ethan Phillips (Pete), Didi Conn (Denise)

Highlights. The giddy delight that Jessica displays throughout her visit; invisible Jessica blowing in Clayton's ear; the governor urging Benson to release all his pent-up stresses; Clayton's story about how the health care bill ended up passing the finance committee, and its implications for Jessica's "good deed".

Confused? You Won't Be. *'I think that I am somewhere in between.'*

▶ This episode aired nearly six years to the day after *Soap* debuted, and more than two years after it ended. It also aired 12 days after Susan Harris and Paul Junger Witt were wed.

▶ At first, Jessica tells Benson she must do one good deed to get her wings and become a proper angel. Yet after she accomplishes this, she tells him that she's actually in a coma somewhere in South America, a vague and unsatisfying conclusion for any *Soap* fans who anxiously tuned in hoping for some kind of closure.

▶ Her description of heaven as being a place that "looks a lot like the MGM Grand" clashes a bit with what we saw the last time she was there (4.0).

▶ Though the continuity is probably accidental, Jessica tells Benson that she could never be an angel because of the things she's done, and the things she's thought about doing, something touched on during her pre-execution confession to the priest in her cell in Malaguay (4.21).

▶ The final scene would be moving indeed if we hadn't seen it played out several times before in *Soap* (3.0, 3.3, 3.22) and once in *Benson* (1.8). Jessica and Benson have parted so often, it's as if everybody involved is trying to get it just right.

▶ Like *Benson* 1.8, we are again reminded how crucial the writers were to *Soap*. No matter how strong the central performances by Guillaume and Helmond, they cannot stave off the status quo sitcom stagnation of the story and its dialogue.

Best Lines.
Benson: Well this really makes my day. The public utilities commission sticks it to the poor, the legislature sticks it to the elderly, and the Tates are trying to stick Jessica in the family plot. What in the world is wrong with people?

Jessica: You won't believe where I came from. First of all, you see, I was kidnapped by revolutionaries and taken to South America. And then I went to Connecticut and I was kidnapped again and taken to South America. Then I went to heaven, then I came here.

Benson: Whoah, whoah, whoah. When you say heaven, do you mean heaven or some town in Georgia?

Jessica: Heaven, you know, the real thing. God, angels, the whole ball of wax. Oh Benson, you should see heaven. It's really a lovely place.

Benson: Jessica, you haven't changed a bit.

Jessica: Oh Benson, why can't you just accept the fact that there are certain things you don't understand? That there are bonds of friendship that are so strong that their energy can send a message out through time and space.

Jessica: I don't understand it myself but I did learn one thing. I am positively not dead, I'm in a coma somewhere in South America. But don't worry, I'll get out of it all right.

Benson: I always knew you'd find a loop hole.

Jessica: I've missed you Benson. I wish we didn't have to say goodbye.

Benson: Will I ever see you again?

Jessica: Oh sure, it's a small cosmos. We'll have lunch.

Benson: Then let us not say goodbye.

Jessica: OK. I love you.

Benson: And I love you.

Soap Hung out to Dry

That's it? But, but, what happens next?

"We don't know," Susan Harris admits with a laugh. "It was canceled out of the blue, we didn't expect it. Our story lines were done sometimes a week or so in advance. We had the luxury of being able to change things, so we would leave cliffhangers at the end of each season. We really had no idea how they were going to resolve. I think we left Jessica in front of a firing squad; clearly she was not going to be killed. Whoever was in jeopardy, something would've saved them."

Despite Internet rumors to the contrary, there was no script written to tie up the loose ends at the end of Season 4. Why that is becomes a little clearer once you better understand the writing process. When you only have one or two writers on a show, "even if you start off a season with six scripts in advance, you eat them up so quickly," says Harris. "You're rewriting the script that is on the stage, and you're trying to write the next script, and you find that the lead that you've had in scripts is diminished almost immediately. Then you're doing it week-to-week. You're writing for what you're going to put on the table on Monday, you're writing it a few days before."

That said, writer Stu Silver had the answer for saving Jessica at least. "In the last scene, we had Jessica shot by a firing squad. How do we get out of that; they can't *all* miss. So I thought OK, the next scene is the shots are not coming from the firing squad, they're coming from El Puerco's men who rescue Jessica. That's the only way I could see out of it because we heard the guns fire. You had to be true to the setting. You can't just say it didn't happen next season. But outside of that no, there weren't any specific plans for Burt or for Jodie or for Chester or anybody. There was no bible for the next season."

Naturally, any discussion of *Soap*'s abrupt ending quickly turns to examining ABC's decision to pull the plug in the first place.

"I always thought it wasn't really handled well by the networks," says Robert Mandan. "We dropped a few [ratings] points and they weren't supportive, they weren't creative. They didn't say let's fix this so we can keep this on. I think we should've done seven years easy on that show instead of the four that we did, because the top shows usually do seven or nine years, or some 11. I knew almost immediately something was off. Not knowing how to do it, I couldn't step in and say listen guys, here's the answer to this problem. I've had civilians say, 'That show, it got a little weird for a while but it

> " I say this to some writers: If you paint yourself into a corner, just walk across the room. So you get some paint on your shoes, just walk out of there."
>
> —STU SILVER on the Season 4 cliffhanger

was still funny.' What can you do? If you're the singular star of a show, I think you can go in there, like Tony Danza can go in and do whatever [on *Who's the Boss*] and win your point. We were 12 in a basic cast, so that power gets spread pretty thin."

The beauty of possessing such a large cast and crew is that everyone heard something slightly different at the time. The passage of time and personal biases aside, we are still left with an approximation of what probably happened behind the scenes.

Ted Wass left behind his role as Danny to become a successful television director.

"What I always heard was that when *Soap* went on the air, it went on not fully sponsored," says Ted Wass. "The way it was explained to me was that advertising minutes that were being sold on comparably-rated shows for $120,000-$130,000 a minute, they were selling on *Soap* for $70,000 or $80,000. My understanding is that financially it never recovered from that initial controversy. I think that was probably why we didn't do a fifth year, because the network had a chance to dump a tainted show and make it seem like they weren't going to fly in the face of all the offended people anymore. But really what they were doing was just opening up the time slot to give them another chance at seeing the kinds of revenues a show like that should've made.

"The last year we were on, the last half of our last season, they combined our two half-hour episodes and we ran as an hour at 10 o'clock, and we kicked the crap out of *Lou Grant*," Wass remembers. "Everybody was set for Year 5, and then all of the sudden we were canceled, and we were like huh? Our ratings were actually stronger than ever, why would they do that? I think [the cancelation] gave them the best of both worlds." Not only did they free up the space for an untainted show, but also they could claim that they had listened to the will of the people. Everybody won... except the people involved in the making and enjoyment of *Soap*.

Yet, *Soap*'s battles with the Moral Majority were only part of the problem. Nearly everyone involved with its making agrees that the series had slipped a bit, veering off into stranger and stranger territories. Harris' regrets to the contrary, her alien story line included some powerful, astonishingly human scenes, culminating in Burt's philosophical discussion with his double (3.8). In many ways this was *Soap* at its best—equal parts hilarious and heartfelt. However, by Season 4, story lines such as that of El Puerco and Danny's dalliance with Chester's wife had strayed so far from *Soap*'s basic premise, it would've taken a Herculean effort on the part of its writers to turn the ship back to surer waters.

"My idea was to just go back to the basic story of two sisters," says Silver. "I mean that show started off with seven or eight cast members; by the time we were canceled we had about 30. We just kept picking up people along the way. El Puerco and Juan 1 and Juan 2. I think Susan would've agreed—we never had this conversation because we got canceled. Let's not try to top last year, let's go back and do a funny soap opera. But there was a lot of heat from the Moral Majority and the ratings were kind of slipping a bit, I think. I was really shocked when we got canceled—I thought we had at least one more year in us."

Admits Paul Junger Witt, "I think in Season 4, we might've drifted a little bit. We might've become a little self-conscious and started pushing to go a little further out, and I don't think we were quite as real quite as often. I think in Season 5 you would've seen a return to the form we had in Seasons 1 and 2. We still had good numbers, we still had a rabid audience. What we didn't have were sponsors. Most American corporations were still afraid. We had foreign automobile companies and Vlasic pickles. We had other things on the air at the time [including *Benson*], so we were too busy to cry in our beer, but we were devastated.

"At the same time, we had enormous respect for ABC because they kept the show on the air for four years while they were taking a loss on it. Now on the one hand, the shows that went on before and after us were beneficiaries of our high numbers, but on the other hand they're in business to make money, and they're in business to keep their affiliates happy. They kept us on longer than other networks might have at the time. It was bittersweet."

Was *Soap* ultimately punished for not being another *All in the Family*?

It's tempting to agree that yes, it was the possibly well-meaning but often-destructive pressure groups that brought down *Soap*, but there is another possibility to consider. Despite a number of expertly-written scenes and some engaging situations, *Soap* was never going to be considered in the same stratosphere as something like *All in the Family*.

"This isn't Norman Lear," says Harry Waters, the journalist credited (or blamed) for starting the *Soap* backlash in his 1977 *Newsweek* piece. "When you think of *All in the Family*, when you think of those other shows, those were *very* controversial shows. *All in the Family*—we did three covers on that show. And *Soap*, I thought it was an attempt to be controversial but in a non-witty way, and not in a well-written way. You can do all kinds of things on a show, but you have to do it in a highly intelligent way. I don't think that show measured up that way."

Perhaps Waters finally supplies us with the full equation that simultaneously explains both *Soap*'s success as well as its extinction: *Soap* was too "silly" (aliens, devil babies, Malibu "minja" dungeons) to be defended as a Norman Lear-esque treatise on the American family, and too smart a program to be easily lumped in with shows like *Happy Days* and *The Beverly Hillbillies*. It straddled the center of that perilous television highway, and was run over by the public and the media on one side, and the pressure groups on the other.

Still, the final analysis must come from the woman who gave us the Tates and the Campbells, Chuck & Bob, and yes, even that possessed baby. Nearly 40 years and several hit shows have all given Susan Harris a great deal of perspective on the hell that *Soap* was put through. There's no bitterness in her words, no regret, only a simple prediction born of experience.

"Had it not been for the Moral Majority and the pressure they put on us, I think *Soap* would've been an eight-year show. I don't think we could've run out of ideas. We had too large a cast, too many possibilities, we could've easily continued for another four years." She laughs. "But I don't know if *I* would've survived."

Biographies
+ where are they now?

On Soap, the talent both in front of and behind the camera was unrivaled by that of just about any other series at the time. The cast in particular had been hand selected from some of the finest theater-trained actors in the business, and the result was there for everyone to see week after week.

"In other shows you'd have one or two of the people maybe—or the lead actor would be somebody that they saw on Broadway and brought to LA, and then they would surround them with different types," says Joe Mantegna. "But the people who worked on Soap, *they understood theater. They would seek out those kinds of actors. If you have producers who have some degree of theater smarts, they'll load the deck with people that have that kind of background."*

Jimmy Baio (Billy Campbell).

Anyone watching television in the '60s and '70s knew the Baio name. As Jimmy remembers, it all started with a woman in their Brooklyn neighborhood who often took her child to work on commercials. Pretty soon, Jimmy's mother signed up his older brother, Joey, with the same agent representing that neighborhood child. Then, around 1972, when Jimmy was 10, his mother got him an agent, too, and he immediately started doing commercials; the same happened for his cousin, Scott, shortly thereafter.

A 1975 Broadway performance in Eugene O'Neill's *All God's Children Got Wings* opposite George C Scott led to Baio being cast in a pilot with Dick van Dyke, but it failed to go to series. However, the pilot brought him to the attention of the producers of a series about a family of Italian Americans called *Joe and Sons*. While they managed to do 15 episodes for CBS, the show was up against the first year of *Welcome Back, Kotter*, torpedoing any chance of another season. Still, his exposure on *Joe and Sons* led to a three-pilot deal with ABC.

Up until he was 18, Baio lived in Los Angeles with either his mother or his sister, Janice, who would take it in turns to fly back to New York. Once he was 18, he was on his own. Though he enjoyed some of his time in LA, he admits "LA can be a tough town when you're alone."

He was the only minor on *Soap*, but he says many in the cast often made him feel included. "Me and Ted [Wass] used to hang out a lot, and Billy [Crystal], and Katherine Helmond was so sweet to me. I had a history with Richard Mulligan because my brother did the show with him, *The Hero* (1966). When you're doing it and you're in the middle of it, it becomes very natural. But when you look back, that was really neat. I have nothing but fond memories."

And now? Baio's experience with acting was similar to on-screen sister Jennifer Salt's. Spending much of his childhood working in LA, he ultimately made the decision that the business could not make up for his feelings of isolation there. "When you've got your family in New York as I did and you're alone in California—it can get to be a very shallow town. I was very happy to move back to New York. I'm very close with my family. I'm happy here."

Cathryn "Skipper" Damon (Mary Campbell).

Throughout this book, one individual remains maddeningly conspicuous by her absence, a wispy silhouette amid the chaos of the program's creation.

"I don't think that she let people in," says director JD Lobue about Cathryn Damon. "I think Skipper was a very private person. I don't think she was comfortable allowing people in too close. For that reason, I think there were some times that you felt you weren't getting through, so you just maintained your distance. And I think she was comfortable working that way."

A lover of dance while growing up in her native Seattle, Cathryn "Skipper" Damon completed high school at 16 and studied dance at a relative's studio in New York, before spending two years with the Metropolitan Opera Ballet Company. From there she jumped ship to the musical TV spectaculars of Max Liebman, performing up to 10 numbers per 90-minute special. Finally, she made her acting debut in the hit 1962 revival of Rodgers and Hart's *The Boys from Syracuse*.

(Pretty much everybody knew Damon as "Skipper". As she once told an interviewer, "My grandmother was named Mary Centennial and she named her daughter Mary Catherine. ...When I came along they couldn't call me Cathryn because of my mother, so they used the name Skipper, which my grandfather had given me because they had wanted a boy.")

From there she applied herself to many plays, stinkers and winners alike, before taking a role in Andrei Serban's celebrated production of *The Cherry Orchard*. Between rehearsals for the Anton Checkhov classic, she auditioned for *Soap*, and was flown to California a week later to shoot the pilot.

Damon's persistent quiet, noted by many on the set of *Soap*, can probably best be explained by her quick uprooting from the New York theater world at this time. Though most on the show had substantial New York theater backgrounds, they also had been working in LA for a while; Damon had simply tried out for *Soap* at her agent's urging, and suddenly found herself a TV star thousands of miles from her friends.

As Damon told *Soap Opera Digest* in 1980, "When I first moved out here, I'd finish work on Friday and fly back to New York for the weekend. Since then I've cut down to eight trips a year, but I get a pulse in New York that I don't get in Los Angeles."

In the same interview, she told writer David Church that she had once been married before—possibly around the age of 24—and that there were children involved. Again, Damon only told people what she wanted them to know.

"I enjoyed working with her very much," says Katherine Helmond, adding that she, too, never really got to know Damon well. "I think she was really quite a private person and did not socialize that much. I think most of her socializing was with people in New York. When she wasn't working she spent all of her time there because all of her old friends were there, and her apartment was there. It was really like living two lives for her."

And now? Damon passed away in May 1987 at 56 from cancer. Recalls *Soap* stage manager Carl Lauten: "Skipper, who [as Mary] was always dressed like your basic Connecticut middle-America, married-to-a-contractor wife, was one of the most glamorous dressers off the set you can imagine. I remember during her memorial service, Richard Mulligan said, 'She was the only one I knew that would go down and have bargain finds in the Village, and celebrate it with lunch at the Russian Tea Room.'

"I really liked Skipper. I sublet her apartment when I first moved to New York when I did my first year of *The Cosby Show*." There's a pause as Lauten realizes why we're having this conversation—Damon isn't here to explain the whats and wherefores of her own life. "I worked with Madeline Kahn as well. It was so sad, both of them died before they should've, both from ovarian cancer."

Diana Canova (Corinne Tate Flotsky).

The daughter of popular film and television comedienne Judy Canova and Cuban musician Fili Rivero, Canova gained a footing in both acting and music from a very early age. At 10, she saw Angela Lansbury in *Mame* at Los Angeles City College, which further fueled her inspiration to pursue musical theater, and ultimately opera as a lyric soprano. Yet she jacked in a full voice scholarship at Cal Arts to study theater at a junior college, demonstrating an ambivalence between both sides of her artistic temperament that would express itself throughout her life.

Even as she began getting her feet wet with television work on *Happy Days*, *Chico and the Man* and *Starsky and Hutch*, Canova was also writing music. In 1981, she and music partner Steve Nelson released a 45 called "Who You Foolin'" on the 20th Century Fox label.

And now?

After *Soap*, Canova appeared in the Broadway show *They're Playing our Song* opposite *Soap*'s Ted Wass before tackling a TV movie in China called *The Peking Encounter*. In some ways the experience was like being on the *Soap* set all over again. "It was supposed to be a love story, but because of Chinese customs and modesty, I wasn't even allowed to hold my co-star's hand," she told Allentown, Penn.'s *Morning Call* newspaper in 1984. (See P. 92 for similar problems during the filming of her early scenes with Sal Viscuso on *Soap*.)

Canova ultimately found her calling beyond Hollywood. "I have been directing children's theater for over 20 years," she says. "I love it. I have coached kids to Broadway while doing it myself once in a while. I'm an adjunct professor of voice at Manhattanville College [in Purchase, NY], and I also write musicals for middle schools because I found there's not a whole lot out there that a kid's voice can handle. I have raised two boys—an actual *working* musician and a baseball player. If a show came along, I would go back to TV in a heartbeat, but on the other hand I have lived my dreams and it's all pretty OK."

Billy Crystal (Jodie Dallas).

Growing up on Long Island, NY, Billy Crystal never set out to become an actor *per se*, but an entertainer.

Growing up in his father's Commodore record store, he was surrounded by show business talent of the '50s and '60s: Sammy Davis Jr. in particular became something of a role model.

He graduated from New York University in 1970 after studying under filmmaker Martin Scorcese, and hit the stand-up comedy circuit, forming his own improv group: 3's Company. In 1975, his greatest accomplishment to date—appearing on *The Tonight Show* with Johnny Carson—was quickly followed by profound disappointment.

After weeks of preparation, Crystal's 6-minute set on the first episode of NBC's *Saturday Night* (later *Saturday Night Live*) was cut to two minutes at the 11th hour. Frustrated and unable to salvage the sketch, the young comedian walked off the project. He managed to land an episode of *All in the Family* the following year, but he found himself at a crossroads when the part of Jodie came along.

And now? Billy Crystal's career exploded after leaving *Soap*, including a triumphant return to *Saturday Night Live* during its 1984 season. He quickly became a movie star, appearing in cult favorite *The Princess Bride* (1987) before starring in what became the quintessential rom-com, *When Harry Met Sally...* (1989). The following year, he began his long association with the Academy Awards as host, and branched out into animation voice work with popular children's movies such as *Monsters Inc.* (2001), and *Cars* (2006) alongside *Soap*'s Katherine Helmond.

Perhaps his most personal accomplishment came with the 2004 Broadway premiere of *700 Sundays*, a one-man show based on his memories of his father that won him a Tony Award the following year. Jay Johnson, who went on to win the same Tony Award for Best Theatrical Event in 2007 for his own one-man (but many personalities) show *Jay Johnson: The Two and Only*, says, "I guess I'm still following him around somehow."

Robert Guillaume (Benson).

Born Robert Williams in St. Louis, Guillaume grew up desperately poor, the son of an alcoholic mother and raised by a strong grandmother. (The first chapters of his autobiography, *Guillaume: A Life*, reveal just how humble his beginnings were, and how much he managed to achieve despite them.)

After a short stint in the Army, he studied voice at St. Louis University and Washington University, before winning a nine-week classical music scholarship to an Aspen, Colo. music festival. There he met the founders of the Karamu House Theatre, who lured him to its Cleveland home. It was there that he Franco-fied his surname to Guillaume, and began taking acting lessons.

From 1959 onward, he starred in a number of dramas and musicals on the stage, culminating in *Porgy and Bess* from 1965-72. In 1968 he launched his television career with an appearance on Diahann Carroll's *Julia*, and would be a TV mainstay forever more.

And now? Despite a number of career triumphs— including taking over the part of the Phantom in Andrew Lloyd Webber's *The Phantom of the Opera* from original actor Michael Crawford in the 1990s—his greatest post-*Soap* accomplishment might have been his recovery from a stroke he suffered in 2000 while filming his sitcom, *Sports*

Night. After extensive therapy, the actor came back strong, voicing a number of animated children's films and video games, and appearing in films such as *Columbus Circle* (2012) and *Satin* (2011).

Part of what got him through it all? Visits from the friends he'd made on *Soap*. In 2004, Jay Johnson, Robert Mandan, Diana Canova, and associate producer Marsha Posner went to the actor's home…and brought the *Soap* blooper reel with them. (Sorry folks, that reel doesn't leave Marsha's sight.)

Susan Harris (Creator, writer, executive producer). *See P. 22*

Katherine Helmond (Jessica Tate).

Though Susan Harris has often claimed that none of the characters on *Soap* are modeled after anyone in real life, director Jay Sandrich accused her of being like Jessica Tate, she told *The New York Times* in 1978. "I deny being like her…although at times I don't make a lot of sense either. I often look at the world like a lovely B-movie, the way Jessica does."

The woman who would actually become the glamorous-but-ditzy face of *Soap*, itself the poster child for religious censure, was born into a Catholic home in Galveston, Texas. Katherine Helmond was raised by her mother and her grandmother, and spent most of her early life in Catholic schools.

"You're not asked in Catholic school 'Do you want to do something'; you're told what you're going to do. I was put in a lot of plays and events because I did what I was told. And so they put me up on stage and said, 'OK, you have to memorize this, and when I nod to you, you start. And when I nod at the end of it, stop, don't wiggle, and be quiet.' I would just say, 'Yes, sister.' So I fit in very well, my personality, which was quite shy. I rather blossomed when it came time to stand up and be the elephant or the donkey. In a way it was very freeing for me because it wasn't Katherine standing up. I found a great joy in the freedom that you get from that."

This led to a literal freedom as Helmond moved from community theater groups in Galveston to a professional theater in Houston 50 miles away, and finally to the thriving theater scene in off-Broadway New York at 21.

Helmond initially found herself a decent place to live because she was able to share it with a friend, but she wound up in the Bowery once her roommate left to get married. There followed a string of one-room apartments that made living trying at times. "But I had a little hope inside of me that I wouldn't live that way all my life. I figured that's just what actors did—they lived in one-room apartments in bad parts of the city."

Her inherent shyness, coupled with the trial-by-fire nature of the New York stage, helped her to develop a type of acting Zen that allowed her to find the truth in whatever character she portrayed, while keeping firmly grounded in where her work stood in the scheme of things. "I took the job seriously but it was a job," she says of her work on *Soap*. It was an attitude that made her one of the most-loved people on that show behind the scenes.

Having paid her dues on stage, her manager told her, "You're getting too old to make enough money in the theater; why don't you stay in LA and see if you can work some more in television and the movies. OK, I'll give it a try,'" is how she recalls the conversation.

"When I told my mother I was going to New York to be an actor, she said, You don't know anything about that, do you? I said, Sure, I've been doing it all along for all these years. She said, Yeah, but that's in your home town. And sure enough I managed to keep going to work on the stage in New York. And then I called one day and said I'm going to Hollywood. She said, What in the world are you going to do there? I'm going to do the play I did in New York City and see what happens—maybe television. And she said, But you don't know anything about that. And my grandmother said, Oh let her go. She's always going to do something peculiar."

No one could've predicted just how peculiar some of Helmond's roles were going to be. Though her first role would be in the television version of *Gunsmoke*, her TV and film roles would include Lizzie Borden's big sister, Emma (*The Legend of Lizzie Borden*, 1975), the wacky aunt of horror-movie hostess Elvira (*The Elvira Show*, 1993), Mrs. Ogre (*Time Bandits*, 1981), and the recipient of some extremely surreal plastic surgery (*Brazil*, 1985).

And now?

Helmond continues to be greatly in demand on stage and in television and film. She was the voice of Lizzie alongside Joe Mantegna's Grem in the animated movie *Cars 2*, and showed up in the vampire series *True Blood*. And she continues to grace the stage wherever good roles are found. "You work really quite hard in the theater and you don't make much money, but it's a joyous experience," says Helmond. "Although I love doing television and I love doing the sitcoms, I just am awfully pleased at being able to be an actor. To be able to do something throughout life that I know I can do and that gives me joy. And the cherry on the ice cream soda is that I finally made money at it, too. I never thought that I would go to Hollywood and have a big old Spanish house and live up in the Hills. That just came along with the ride in sitcoms."

Jay Johnson (Chuck & Bob Campbell).
There is the layman's temptation to attribute the unconventionality of Jay Johnson's career to his longtime struggles with

dyslexia—a condition typified by no one hemisphere of the brain taking dominance over the other. Could it be that a condition that makes reading so difficult helped him hone his ability to perform two roles at once?

Whatever the physiology, Johnson taught himself his craft from an early age. At 5 he was doing voices, at 11 he was performing as a ventriloquist. In high school he starred in his own local TV show in Dallas—there was no question he was going places, but no one predicted how far his talent would take him.

His greatest barrier early on was convincing casting directors and producers that ventriloquism isn't some simple party trick, but rather one of the most complicated forms of acting there is. "It's all about duality, about separating your brain so you can think as one character while performing as another," he explains. "They don't understand this is the most unique form of acting, and requires a more trained discipline than someone who's just trained to do one part at a time." He laughs. "I have that speech rehearsed so well because I tell it to casting people all the time."

And now? In addition to his Tony Award-winning one-man show *Jay Johnson: The Two and Only*, Johnson has continued to hone his craft, including the odd bit of television work along the way—most notably the return of Chuck & Bob in a 1999 episode of *That '70s Show*. "Ultimately my love is the stage and the live audience. It's absolutely unique. You can't recreate that audience ever, ever again. For me that's the ultimate. I love my Tony very much because that's a trophy for people who do it eight times a week in a Broadway theater where the competition is very tough, and they do it consistently. There are no retakes, there are no 'I can fix it in post,' there are no flattering angles on a certain close-up. That's what I'm all about." (You can keep up with Johnson, to the extent *anyone* can keep up with Johnson, at *bellandbayes.blogspot.com*.)

JD Lobue (Assoc. Director/Director).
John David Lobue grew up in Hammond, La., about 40 minutes north of New Orleans, just across Lake Pontchartrain. Raised on rhythm and blues and the

New Orleans sound, he got his start playing piano in rock bands throughout the south after his cousin pulled him into his own at the age of 13. After he met Jim Weatherly (who would go on to write a number of hit songs, including "Midnight Train to Georgia"), Lobue joined his band The Gordian Knot, and moved out to California with them. (The band appears briefly as themselves in the 1968 flick *The Young Runaways*.)

"We became sort of the darling of the Beverly Hills and Bel Air set," he remembers. "We played a lot of private parties for people like Frank Sinatra, we played for Tina Sinatra's wedding. We went to Vietnam with Nancy on the Boots Tour in '67."

After his son was born, Lobue decided it was time to get "a real job", starting as a page at Hollywood Video Center, an independent video facility at Sunset and Vine in LA that taped talk shows, including at least one hosted by Steve Allen. Quickly he worked his way up the ladder to become an associate director. With the help of a friend, he landed the job of music coordinator on the long-running R&B show *Soul Train*.

"He would give me a breakdown on all the songs that were going to be done on that particular weekend, and I would listen to them, write out the lyrics, break them down by time and by bar count. And since I wasn't allowed on the headset because I wasn't a DGA member, I would sit behind him in the booth and sort of bang on the console and tell him where the beats were, and where to make the camera cut." After his friend left the show, Lobue became *Soul Train*'s director, working on about 600 or 700 episodes over 20 years.

And now? After *Soap*, Lauten has continued to work steadily in television, directing everything from *Newhart* and *Herman's Head* to *Dharma & Greg* and *Living Single*. He also shot Susan Harris' short-lived sitcom *Hail to the Chief* (1985) starring Patty Duke as the first female president of the United Sates; and the more successful Witt/Thomas production *It's a Living* (1985-87), created by *Soap* scribes Stu Silver, Dick Clair and Jenna McMahon.

Robert Mandan (Chester Tate).

Mandan was born in Clever, Mo., about 5 hours from, and as many years after, the man who played his butler: St. Louis-born Robert Guillaume. The only child (save for two older brothers and a sister) in that farming town, Mandan moved to California with his family at 9. It wasn't until he was a college freshman that he started thinking seriously about chucking in his pre-legal studies to become an actor. He wangled his way onto a TV show called *So You Want to be an Actor*—a kind of acting-oriented *American Idol* in which the winner was decided by the number of postcards viewers sent in voting for each participant. He called everyone he knew to ask them to send cards, and won...a watch.

Soon he was working on soap operas in the late 1950s, including *The Edge of Night*, and enjoyed a long stint on *From These Roots*. But he put his television career on the back burner to spend a couple of years in the psychological field before coming up against a course he couldn't stand—statistics. This sent him back to television, with appearances on *One Day at a Time*, *Phyllis*, *Maude*, and many others.

And now? Mandan, too, has graced stage and television screen a great deal since *Soap*, with credits ranging from Helmond-starrer *Who's the Boss* to *Star Trek: Deep Space Nine*, *ER* and *General Hospital*. Mandan is, if anything, even more eloquent than Chester, with a stage actor's command of wit. "I've done about three or four things that I hoped would never show up, and then somebody the other day told me, 'Oh I just saw you in a [1982 movie] called *Zapped*. That was very funny.' I said, 'It was...?'

"When I was sent that script, it was still close to shows having wrapped. 'They want you to be the principal of the high school, and he was having a hot romance with somebody, and neither person knew who they were.' It turned out it was an English teacher. And they arranged a meeting in a supper club or something, and the final thing you see of him, she slides under the table and gives him a blow job. And I called my agent and said, 'I cannot do this, I'm an actor. Did you read the script? (They never read scripts.) He gets a blowjob at the end of the movie!' He said, 'So what, they're paying you good money, do the movie.' People at the time stopped me in the supermarket and said, 'I saw that movie and in that last scene she's under the table—that's very funny.' And that thing played *a lot*, and still does. We do whatever we can to pay the bills."

Dinah Manoff (Elaine Lefkowitz Dallas).

Dinah Manoff grew up with the odds stubbornly stacked against her...or under the perfect conditions for success, depending on how you look at it. Born in New York City to *Fay* star Lee Grant and screenwriter Arnold Manoff, she spent her teen years in the Malibu of the 1960s, where drinking, drug use and beach-going were the norm.

Around 15, her mother realized that her permissiveness might not be the best thing for her daughter's future, and sent her off to the California Institute of the

Arts after high school graduation. She left after a year and a half.

She broke into television with small roles in *Welcome Back, Kotter* and the TV movie *Raid on Entebbe* (1976) before landing her breakout role as the lovable Marty Maraschino in 1978's *Grease* at just 19.

And now? Manoff kept her hand in acting long after *Soap*, but gradually decided that directing theater fulfilled her more creatively. Today she and her husband have three boys, a horse, a turtle, two cats and a dog. She directs plays and teaches acting at the 245-seat Bainbridge Performing Arts center on Bainbridge Island, Wash.

"I'd like to say that fortunately I did not get the jobs that I wanted and I really started to back off of it because there's a demand when you're directing television—acting and being a mommy is very easy relative to the energy and attention you have to give; directing and being a mother is almost impossible, I think. I wasn't one of those directors who could walk away at 5 o'clock; it kept me up at night and it woke me up in the morning. So I feel that in a way I was lucky. It's irresistible to not keep taking the jobs when they're given to you because you think 'God, I'm so lucky.' Trying to please that many people in television—I wasn't cut out for it. I'm cut out for it creatively, I'm not cut out for it in terms of day-to-day dealing with people. I'm too defiant. You can't push me around a lot."

Richard Mulligan (Burt Campbell).

Of all the actors to appear on *Soap*, most would agree that it was Richard Mulligan who stole the show, even if he wasn't always the easiest person to get along with backstage. "He was a complicated guy," admits Ted Wass. "He had a lot of personal demons. And that's part of what made him so great."

One of five sons born to a Bronx cop and a housewife, Mulligan actually spent a year in seminary intent on becoming a priest before realizing he didn't have what it took to live that

kind of life. (Burt's audience with the bishop in 4.9 is a poignant coda to the actor's early clerical leanings.) Shortly after high school he joined the Navy. After a short stint in college, he took a job as a copy boy at the *Miami Herald*. In his off hours, he worked on writing plays.

After getting a flat tire one day, he pulled into a service station right across the street from the Studio M theater, where Tennessee Williams used to run through his plays. "I had some of my plays in the trunk of my car," Mulligan told *People* magazine in 1989. "Maybe this was providence."

Though no one there was interested in the one-act play he showed them, he quickly found himself cast as Andrew Mayo in the theater's production of the Eugene O'Neill drama *Beyond the Horizon*. Back to New York he went, taking classes with the legendary Lee Strasberg. Slogging through some pretty lean times, Mulligan climbed his way up the dramatic ladder, performing on and off Broadway before appearing in several films, most notably *Little Big Man* (1970) as Gen. Custer.

While the actor continued to write his own, ultimately unproduced, plays, he did so in the shadow of his successful older brother, film director Robert Mulligan, whose credits include *To Kill a Mockingbird* (1962) and *Summer of '42* (1971).

In 1981, his future publicist, Julian Myers, met the actor aboard a private plane rented from Frank Sinatra for the purposes of promoting Mulligan's latest movie, *SOB*, co-starring Julie Andrews.

That plane "didn't have any beds but it had a platform that folded out and you could sleep on it," Myers remembers. "Julie refused to take advantage of that and insisted that Richard use it, which he was reluctant to do, but he did because his health was not always so great. So we went to eight of the largest cities in the United States and Toronto. Richard and I got to know each other quite well in those two and a half days. Richard was a very cultured gentleman, a sweet man, but his own man, too."

And now? Mulligan passed away in September 2000 at the age of 67 from colorectal cancer at his home in Los Angeles. Though some found him difficult to work with during *Soap*, pretty much everyone agrees he was a genius when it came to performing. Rather than include a list of credits easily found online, let's remember him as longtime friend and publicist Julian Myers does: "Richard Mulligan was a warm, caring human being with great depth, sensitivity and love."

Arthur Peterson Jr. (The Major).

Of all the talented regulars on *Soap*, none was so sparingly used as accomplished stage performer Arthur Peterson Jr. Born in Mandan, N.D., he went on to earn a BA in theater fine arts at the University of Minnesota. (It was also there that he met poet Robert Frost, who would become the subject of a one-man show—*Robert Frost: Fire and Ice*—Peterson would co-author and perform off-Broadway in 1984.) After graduation he moved to Chicago where he met future wife Norma Ransom; they married in 1937. That same year he landed his first big role in the radio version of soap opera *The Guiding Light*, playing the wise Rev. Dr. John Ruthledge; his character was killed off in 1946. From April 1944 to May 1945, he took a leave of absence to enlist in the Third Army under General George Patton to serve in the European theater during WWII.

Following his title role in the 1949 ABC TV series *That's O'Toole*, Peterson would go on to rack up more than 100 TV credits including roles in *Barney Miller*, *Bonanza* and *I Dream of Jeanie*.

And now? Peterson died in October 1996 after battling Alzheimer's. Though he would make a handful of appearances on television and in film after *Soap*, the actor concentrated on his first love, theater. He taught acting classes at George Mason University in the Washington DC suburb of Fairfax, Va. He also spent 10 years starring opposite wife Norma in a Pasadena Playhouse production of *The Gin Game* starting in 1981. "He didn't have a lot to do [on *Soap*], but he was always right on the money," recalls associate producer Marsha Posner. "We loved him."

Donnelly Rhodes (Dutch Leitner)

Getting his start as the stage manager/jack of all trades at Theatre 77 (later the Manitoba Theater Centre) in Winnipeg for $11 a week, Donnelly Rhodes was accepted to the National Theatre School in Montreal at 21, fresh out of the Air Force. (Knowing he was broke, co-workers at Theatre 77 raised the $300 necessary to purchase a ticket for his trip...and one new suit.) From there he appeared on a few Canadian television shows before being picked up by Universal Studios in the early '60s as a contract player, becoming a frequent face on TV westerns such as *Wagon Train* and *Bonanza*.

And now? Rhodes continues to grace television and movie screens in a variety of roles. Though he's done a fair amount of work in the U.S. on such series as the rebooted *Battlestar Galactica* and the movie *Tron: Legacy*, he became something of an icon in the excellent Canadian crime drama *Da Vinci's Inquest* as Det. Leo Shannon (available on Netflix in the states).

"The reward is actually in the work itself, although it's nice to have your house paid for. I've been a very fortunate actor to survive this long. I'm [77] and I'm still going. I just finished doing an episode of a television show up here in Canada called *Heartland*, and I really enjoyed it. I get treated like I'm some kind of icon already up here; everybody was very, very nice to me. I still enjoy the process of working, that's where I'm most comfortable: on a set. To me that's not make believe, that's like reality. Once you leave the set you're in the make-believe world because now you don't know what's going to happen next. On the set I always know what's going to happen."

Jennifer Salt (Eunice Tate Leitner).

Like her *Soap* sister Diana Canova, Jennifer Salt vacillated between the disciplines of her parents throughout much of her career. Mother Mary Davenport was an actress, father Waldo Salt was a successful screenwriter (*Serpico*, *Midnight Cowboy*) who suffered at the hands of the blacklists of the 1950s.

Yet while Canova came up through the popular TV shows of the early 1970s, Salt used what she learned under Sanford Meisner at New York City's Neighborhood Playhouse to perform in a series of independent films. Though she began with the Waldo Salt-scripted *Midnight Cowboy*, she quickly fell in with thriller director Brian De Palma, appearing in his bizarre (and strangely autobiographical) student film *Hi, Mom* (1970), and his minor 1973 classic, *Sisters*, opposite her former roommate, Margot Kidder. Salt also starred in

the 1972 TV horror movie *Gargoyles*, and appeared in Woody Allen's *Play it Again, Sam* that same year. "My life had changed dramatically since *Sisters*," she says. "I was married and had a baby. Not that I had given up acting, but it had sort of been something that I put on a backburner."

And now? Salt enjoyed a nice bump in recognition from *Soap*. Yet she never really felt comfortable as an actress. "I was unhappy but I didn't know why I was unhappy. I thought maybe I should be doing theater, maybe I wasn't working hard enough, maybe I needed to go back to class, maybe I was depressed, maybe I needed a 12-step program. I had a myriad of ideas about what was wrong with me, but the idea that I was meant to be something else did not come up until quite a bit later."

That discomfort went away when she sat down to write. "I could have all this imagination and live the life of an artist but not have people looking at me." Starting in the late 1990s, she began to make a name for herself writing for television, which culminated in maximum exposure with the series *Nip/Tuck* from 2003 to 2010. In addition to adapting Elizabeth Gilbert's bestselling book of discovery, *Eat Pray Love*, for the 2010 movie of the same name starring Julia Roberts, Salt served as writer and co-executive producer on the surprise TV hit *American Horror Story*—as groundbreaking for modern television horror as *Soap* was for comedy in its day.

Jay Sandrich (Director).

Television directors are mostly journeyman types who float from show to show; it's almost exclusively writer-producers who have the name recognition in Hollywood, and with TV audiences.

One of the exceptions to this is director Jay Sandrich. Not just another product of the Hollywood director mill, Sandrich was himself the son of Mark Sandrich, one of the most successful film directors of the '30s and '40s. In addition to directing such Ginger Rogers/Fred Astaire movies as *Top Hat* and *Shall We Dance*, the senior Sandrich brought the world *Holiday Inn*, the 1942 Bing Crosby/Fred Astaire movie that unleashed the crooner's "White Christmas" upon the world.

Cutting his directing teeth on television classics such as *I Love Lucy* and *Our Miss Brooks*, it was with the megahit *The Mary Tyler Moore Show* that Jay Sandrich made his name, winning Emmys and going on to helm other hits including *The Bob Newhart Show* and *The Cosby Show*.

And now? Sandrich has been retired for about 10 years, but continues to contribute his time and insight to those who need it…including the writer of this book, who is deeply in his debt.

Tony Thomas (Executive producer)

"Laughter was in my house as far back as I can remember," says Tony Thomas. "My sisters and I were the worst at funerals and at church. We just found things to laugh at that were amusing, and that was really taught to us at home." And while the producer has had many years to boil down his storied life into a pithy soundbite, the emotion in his voice suggests that this doesn't make it any less sincere. Growing up the son of a legendary comedic actor like Danny Thomas (not to mention the younger brother of "That Girl" Marlo, and singer-songwriter Terre) meant learning the mechanics, as well as the value, of comedy.

"My father had a terrific sense of humor," he remembers. "His friends [including George Burns, Jack Benny, Milton Berle, Bob Newhart, Don Rickles, and Jan Murray, who was "one of the funniest human beings in someone's living room"] were always hanging out at our house, so it was kind of by osmosis you always 'found the funny.'"

As Thomas got older, he would spend the Catholic holidays that he wasn't in school tagging along to see his father's rehearsals for *The Danny Thomas Show* and others. "He knew where the laughs would be, where he thought the laughs would be. And the same thing with my father's stage show. He would dissect a show every night in the Sands Hotel especially, and we'd go out to breakfast at 2 in the morning. He'd talk about what worked, what didn't work, and that he was going to move that block sooner and do that segment later. Being in Vegas was like being in a whole other world. There was no 'go to bed'. That was when you could be with your father, so that's when we did it." Tony Thomas was 10.

A career in entertainment was inevitable. While he initially thought about performing in front of the camera, he quickly concentrated instead on producing, "which is where my skills truly lie because I watched those shows being produced. I watched routines and skills be crafted in a way to get certain reactions at certain times, to tell a compelling story, to find where the jokes are, make you cry when it's appropriate. I learned all of that, and so it was my biggest joy to watch that happen on *our* tape nights on all of our shows."

While working at Screen Gems Television, Thomas met producer Paul Junger Witt, who had already made his name with *The Partridge Family*. Together they partnered on the 1971 movie *Brian's Song*, based on the real-life relationship between Chicago Bears teammates Gale Sayers and Brian Piccolo, who died of cancer. From there they would jump to Spelling-Goldberg Productions, before resurrecting Danny Thomas Productions, and ultimately launching Witt Thomas and Witt Thomas Harris.

And now?
Thomas and Paul Junger Witt continue to executive produce films and television shows, including the 2011 Oscar-nominated *A Better Life*, and most recently, the reboot of their '80s TV series *Beauty and the Beast*.

Sal Viscuso (Father Timothy Flotsky)
Like many actors, Viscuso was drawn to perform-

ing in some ways as a means of mastering the pain of rejection he'd known since childhood. Born in Brooklyn, the 7-year-old Viscuso saw his parents separate, and was himself spirited away to Sacramento by his mother four years later. Over the next year he would bounce from one coast to the other, finding himself singled out because of his Brooklyn accent in California, and victimized by the teachers in the Catholic schools he inevitably found himself in back in New York.

However, it was in the Bronx that he made an important discovery. After watching new boy after new boy beaten up, he finally asked the tough kids why they had left him alone. Their reply: "Because you're funny."

"So that was one of the first times that I realized that my mouth was actually a good thing, even though in Catholic school I would get hit all the time because I couldn't keep my mouth shut."

Returning to California and enrolling in a new magnet junior high school, he found himself brushing up against the same old institutionalized ethnic insensitivity he'd encountered before. "My teacher handed me a poem of this Italian immigrant who was honoring George Washington's birthday, and another one was for baseball when baseball season started. They put me in front of the whole assembly to recite this poem. So here you've got this kid who sounds funny, dresses funny, not from Sacramento, pretending to be an Italian immigrant with a sort of Chico Marx dialect: 'The greata game is a base-a ball for young American. But ah my friend is not at all the thing for dago man.' That was the frickin' line: 'dago'. I actually said that and didn't realize how offensive that was."

He managed to win the lead in the school play his senior year of high school, but it wasn't until he saw Ivan Dixon in the TV movie *The Final War of Olly Winter* during his first year at UC-Davis that he decided acting was a way to truly touch people while working through some of his more complicated emotions.

From his first big break in the 1974 crime classic *The Taking of Pelham One Two Three* (which also starred Father Tim Flotsky's future *Soap* mother, Doris Roberts), Viscuso appeared in just about every television show you could think of, and ultimately joined a very exclusive club of actors indeed: his real name became a character name on a television show. Michael Cera plays the never seen "Sal Viscuso" who makes at least one announcement per episode on the Adult Swim comedy *Children's Hospital*, an homage to the actor's role as the PA announcer on *M*A*S*H*.

And now? Viscuso has done it all—feature films, including the cult classic *Spaceballs*—television comedies, dramas and cartoons—and the stage, including John Drouillard's 2011 production of *The Elephant Man* by Bernard Pomerance. Viscuso is also an accomplished painter and regularly volunteers his time and talent to help disadvantaged young people through a variety of creative pursuits.

Ted Wass (Danny Dallas).

As canny as Danny is clueless, Ted Wass "packed a couple of suitcases to see what [Hollywood] was like" in January 1977, and landed his first role 10 days later.

It was on the second season of the ABC drama *Family* that Wass played Sam Trask, a friend of Willie Lawrence's who had come back to town while on the run from the law. "I hid out in his guest house and went to see my father who was in the hospital dying," he remembers. "It was a big emotional thing." And six weeks later, he auditioned for *Soap*. It was something he would do five more times before he got the job.

The '70s were very good to Wass. Graduating from the prestigious Goodman School of Drama in Chicago in 1975, he went to New York and ended up playing Danny Zuko in the original Broadway production of *Grease*. And by the end of his first year on *Soap*, he would meet future wife Janet Margolin, a close friend of Wass' on-screen cousin, Jennifer Salt.

And now? Wass went off in a completely different direction from his *Soap* days. Starting in 1992, he took the directing reins on the comedy series *Blossom* (in which he played Blossom's father Nick), and forged for himself a successful television directorial career that continues to this day. From *Spin City* and *The Big Bang Theory* to *Everybody Hates Chris* and *2 Broke Girls*, he's directed for many popular series. He began to learn the craft watching the master: *Soap* director Jay Sandrich.

"I found my way into his director's booth on Episode 3 or 4 once the series was up and running, and he started showing me things and teaching me things all the way back then. I don't recall an active pursuit of directing; it was more like sure, I'll learn anything. I've always had an interest in it. Jay would see me standing in the back and he'd go, 'Hey, come sit down next to me,' and he'd show me his monitors and talk to me about the shots and show me how he wrote them down in his book. I was like a kid, 23 or 24. He'd show me stuff and I'd go, 'Well OK, thanks a lot Jay,' and he'd say come back anytime.

It was a lot of fun. Jay is a friend, and I feel he is a mentor to me."

Paul Junger Witt (Executive producer).

Born and raised in New York City, Paul Junger Witt was exposed to a great deal of theater, and always had a fascination with television and film. Like Susan Harris, he recognized the potential of television drama in the works of Paddy Chayefsky (*Network*, *Marty*), as well as the *Playhouse 90* productions of future *Twilight Zone* creator Rod Serling. Yet when it came to television comedy, few in his opinion could top Sid Caesar, who "probably had the greatest collection of comedy writers on his staff," he says.

Yet Witt pursued a pre-medical course of study his first year at the University of Virginia. "After dropping chemistry and failing math, I decided that I should find another career route." After a year of floundering, he finally ended up getting involved in the school's theater department, "partly because it was something I wanted to do, and partly because in an all-men's university, it was one of the only places where there were women."

While there, he was inspired by drama professor David Weiss to seek a career in Hollywood. (In 2010, Witt financed the creation of the "David Weiss greenroom" at UVA's Drama Building in honor of his mentor, whom he still sees occasionally.)

Of course, however keen one's interest, Hollywood seldom throws open the doors to its top jobs to new hopefuls. After slogging away in the mail room at Columbia Pictures, Witt landed at the studio's television arm, Screen Gems. Under the watchful eye of seasoned producer-director Bob Claver (*Welcome Back, Kotter*; *Mork & Mindy*), he was able to watch television writers such as Bernard Slade craft episodes of classic programs like *Bewitched* and *The Farmer's Daughter*. "I learned an enormous amount and progressed very quickly because, at that time, you could."

After producing *The Partridge Family* throughout 1970, Witt was anxious to tackle something a little more challenging. Screen Gems Vice President of Production Leonard Goldberg gave him the opportunity to produce and develop the Emmy-winning 1971 movie *Brian's Song* with Tony Thomas; the pair then left to work for the new company Goldberg started with producer Aaron Spelling.

"Of course Tony knew both men very well," Witt points out. Spelling had been Danny Thomas' business partner, and Goldberg had dated Tony's sister, Marlo. Though Witt and Thomas were happy enough at Spelling-Goldberg Productions, they both wanted to break out on their own. They took over Danny Thomas Productions for a few years before starting first Witt Thomas, then Witt Thomas Harris. "It was an era of independence," Witt says of the trio's days making *Soap*. "We wanted to be the next Tandem, the next production company with a brand of quality comedy and edgy stuff." (Tandem Productions, the film and television production company formed by Norman Lear and Bud Yorkin, was responsible for such TV classics as *All in the Family*, *Maude* and *Sanford & Son*.)

And now? Witt and Tony Thomas continue to executive produce films and television shows, including the 2011 Oscar-nominated *A Better Life*, and most recently, the reboot of their '80s TV series *Beauty and the Beast*.

Children of Soap

The following fans span several generations and backgrounds. The only thing that unites them is the feeling that *Soap*—the program that to some embodied all that was wrong with the '70s and '80s— changed their lives, and did so for the better.

Jeff Krueger: My folks had originally said the show wasn't for kids but I don't think it lived up to the controversy so they let me watch..... The third season finale had blown me away and I even taped a microphone to the TV and recorded the audio of it on the summer rerun.... I have a close family and we were anchored by our own "two sisters", my mom and my aunt. The family loved *Soap*. I could kind of relate to it as the young "Billy" of the family, wondering about the "secret lives" of my own cousins. One of my fondest *Soap* memories was (I think) Christmas Eve 1982 doing a mini-*Soap* marathon as the family was slowly arriving. We watched some episodes and had a blast. It was the episodes of Elaine's kidnapping and death and Jodie's (almost) marriage. Very much storylines about family banding together and, in retrospect, perfect.... I was working at Disneyland when *Golden Girls* hit, produced by Disney's Touchstone company. Susan Harris and I were working for the same company! And one of my teachers in college was "Beautiful Barry" Haworth, unit manager on *Soap* (because you can't let those units get out of hand). He seemed proud of having worked on the show and mentioned it on occasion. One of the assignments was to create a sitcom, so of course he also brought up Susan Harris' writing. Considering what a *Soap* fan I was (and am), I can't believe I never pressed him for *Soap* stories. But sometimes he'd wear his official *Soap* jacket and I'd look at it with awe.

The '80s was a very *Soap* decade for me and I couldn't ask for a better way to cap it off than with the reunion in early 1990 put on by the Museum of Broadcasting. My mom and my aunt, the "two sisters", went as well as a college friend from Sweden who was a big *Soap* fan and claimed to have learned English watching it. It was great to see so many fans in one place, clapping in time to the theme music and treating a TV writer like the star of the show. People hadn't forgotten.

Flash forward 20 years (yikes!). The original versions of *Soap* are on DVD, mostly uncut. My aunt died in 2010. I had given her the complete set of DVDs. She loved the show. When her son came out from St. Louis for the memorial, I gave him the DVDs because he's a fan too. *Soap* was about family and it's become part of family memories.

Gina Herlihy:
I was 7 when *Soap* premiered, I and watched it in syndication as a pre-teen. It was on at dinner time in the Boston market and my parents enjoyed it with me a second time while I watched for the first. I laughed hysterically with Chuck & Bob, sobbed the very next moment when Elaine was shot, loved Danny, thought Burt & Jessica were geniuses, but Mary... she always left me wanting more of her. In 1987 when she died I was a self-absorbed high-school student and found out after the late great "Skipper" was deceased. I remember that so clearly, I was in college and felt like I was shot. The Internet was just budding then, and I had to go to the library to find out what I could.

Since then I always tried to conduct myself with the class & decorum that she demonstrated as Mary Campbell. This tomboy, now Mom of 2 boys, seriously falls short in the lovely & graceful category, but I always thought of her. And always stop dead in my tracks when *Soap* is on TV. Recently, I showed my 7 year old Chuck & Bob and now he is begging me to watch the entire series on my DVDs and find out all about these zany characters. Ironically, he was the age I was when *Soap* premiered.

Brian Mattocks:
I watched it with my sister in the late '70s on ITV (a channel here in the UK), and as I was a young 7 or 8 year old, I never got the naughty stuff.......I never knew what infidelity was or homosexuality, or sexuality at all....but the comedy was tummy-aching funny, and 30 minutes seemed like 5 minutes. We used to try and tune into Yorkshire TV as they were a week ahead so we could watch 2 episodes sometimes. After Series 4, I assumed Series 5 never got shown here, so when it was repeated in 1986 on Channel 4 in the UK, I was stunned to find out that was really how it ended.

I was gutted.......I never knew it was so controversial either; my parents thought it was like kids TV! How funny is that? I loved that show, and still do. And I miss it. Can't they make some more anyway...?

Kyle: I was 9 years old when *Soap* premiered. We loved the Tuesday night comedies on ABC: *Happy Days*, *Laverne & Shirley*, and *Three's Company*. I usually had to go to sleep at 8:30, so I don't know if I ever saw the first season of *Soap*....

What drew me in to *Soap* was the intrigue of all the continuing stories. I specifically remember the 'Corinne's baby is possessed' story, as well as Burt's blackmail by Sally, Danny and Elaine (heartbreaking), and Chester's amnesia. I couldn't wait for the next episode and was pulled in every week.

One thing that always hooks me into a sitcom is when you can hear the studio audience laughing. If a show has more real laughs than fake, it's usually a great show. *Soap*'s first three seasons sure had that! But I was also a fan of its dramatic moments, the touching dialogue between characters. Especially, Jodie being left at the altar, Jessica and Mary discussing infidelity, and Danny and Elaine (again!). *Soap* was really the first sitcom to combine zaniness with poignancy, something a show like *Scrubs* later did successfully. *Soap* had hilarity mixed with heart, superb acting, and amazingly funny writing.

Of course, I was aware of the "adult" situations and dialogue, even though I was a kid. I didn't really pay too much attention to them. I comprehended that sex was a part of adults' lives and didn't get hung up on it, because that was just one facet of the show. In comparison, *Three's Company* was a lot racier, and the sex jokes stood out more. On *Soap*, the mature themes blended in better with the whole of the show.

I saw the show in reruns as well, which made getting the VHS tapes of *Soap* a big treat. There were so many scenes I didn't remember because they had been cut for commercials in syndication!

All in all, the characters on *Soap* seemed real to me and I cared about them.

Adam: Being only 28, I never had a chance to see *Soap* when it originally aired. However, my parents introduced me to my favorite program when it aired on Comedy Central. I always loved the concept of "To Be Continued..." TV shows so *Soap* instantly became one of my favorite shows. I was only 10 when I first watched it so I didn't fully understand all the jokes at the time, but as I grew older and rewatched the show, I gained new appreciation.

Every night we would sit down and watch Soap on Comedy Central. I remember having to wait a full weekend to find out who murdered

Peter. I can't imagine waiting an entire summer! The wackier the show got the more time I invested in it. From aliens to amnesia, I think *Soap* hit every odd and controversial storyline possible.

The only thing I wish was that one day, somebody from the show could tell us how they would have resolved the final episode! I guess those questions, and many others, won't be answered.

Steven Acevedo:
[My attitude] was one of resistance at first when one of my friends told me about [*Soap*]. But years later when I was at St. Mary's Hospital in Bayside NY for asthma prevention treatment, I looked at the series through different eyes… . I did receive some autographed pictures of some of the cast members, including Susan Harris herself, but they got lost during many moves to new homes. There *is* a framed, autographed photo of Richard Mulligan he sent me just a few years before he passed away. Others, such as Robert Mandan, were difficult to reach due to their busy schedules. My mom even tried to call up a theater he was in at the time just to find out if he got my letter… Overall *Soap* is one show I'll always remember for being so up front and honest about how things really are, even if they did exaggerate it, but it was the truth nonetheless. I'll always regard Burt, Mary, Jessica, Chester, Dutch and Corinne as the friends that got me through some very rough times.

Kristofer Woolsey:
I absolutely loved this show and have for more than 34 years. I was able to catch several episodes during its original run in the '70s (I was 11 when it premiered) when my parents would let me stay up. Most of the show flew over my head at that time but I remembered loving Chuck and Bob and the physical comedy of Burt. When I was in the 5th Grade, I convinced our English/Theater teacher that our 5th Grade play should be an "original" episode of *Soap* and that my best friend and I would write it. I was the tallest kid in the glass, and my best friend (another *Soap* fan at age 12) was the shortest. Of course, I was Chuck and he was Bob, and I'd carry him all around stage while reciting lines. I wish I still had the script….we cooked up some bizarre story lines and had all of the *Soap* regulars represented. It ran about 40 minutes and we did three shows (two for the school, one for the parents). Looking back, I can't believe they let a bunch of 12 year olds do a semi-parody of an adult, controversial sitcom. My how times have changed!

By the time I got into high school in the mid-'80s, *Soap* was syndicated and airing on local TV stations. Since it was a serialized story line, all the episodes ran in order and the local stations would get two or three complete runs done in a year. It was around then that our family got our first VCR, and I managed to record the entire series in order: I was in heaven. A year or so later, I got a second VCR and re-duped my original BETA cassettes to VHS and edited out all the commercials. I literally had *Soap* running in my room every day whether I was directly watching it or not....it served as my background noise to doing homework, cleaning, etc. After a couple years, I could recite just about any line of dialogue from the four season history of the show. I watched those tapes for *years*.

I picked up the DVDs many years ago but never got around to watching them. Then while building a Movie/TV media server for our family room a couple years ago, I thought about *Soap* again and ripped the DVDs to individual files and put them in my media server database. I spot checked the files to make sure everything was in sync, then promptly forgot about them again.

Then about two months ago, I got a hankering to watch *Soap* again in its entirety, so I put them on my iPad to take with me as I traveled for business. What a wickedly pleasant surprise.... these episodes are the entire *original* episodes as they originally aired, whereas my brain and memory was hardwired to the chopped up and edited syndicated versions of those shows that I had watched for years. Each episode has anywhere from 1 to 4 minutes of extra dialogue (often complete conversations or even mini-scenes) that I'd not seen before. And in this new context, it makes some of the seemingly abrupt editing in the syndicated episodes of the show make more sense! I'm enjoying *Soap* on a whole new level...

Ben Veenkamp:

I became a professional ventriloquist because of *Soap*, well more so because of Jay Johnson and his characters Chuck and Bob. I was spellbound as a child watching Jay with Bob. Of course I knew what Bob was, but all the more so I wanted to have that skill, and I guess (I was only a kid back then), the companionship.

So years later I am now a performing ventriloquist in Australia. I now have Jay's autograph (signed to both myself and [my puppet] MJ) framed proudly, and I still watch the episodes from time to time.

Bibliography

PUBLICATIONS

"Lee Grant Gets Last Laugh." The Miami News. Sept. 29, 1975.

Burstein, Patricia. "Katherine Helmond Cleans Up on 'Soap' While Her Sculptor Husband Takes a Sabbatical." People magazine. Dec. 12, 1977

Church, David, "Cathryn Damon: 'At This Point I'm Disinterested in Marriage...'" Soap Opera Digest, Oct. 14, 1980.

Cowan, Geoffrey. "See No Evil." Touchstone. 1978.

Guillaume, Robert with David Ritz, "Guillaume: A Life." 2002. University of Missouri Press.

Harrell, David Edwin. "Oral Roberts: An American Life." Indiana University Press. 1985.

Kaufman, Joanne and Doris Bacon. "Choosing Career Over Marriage, Workaholic Richard Mulligan Tries to Feather His Empty Nest." People magazine, 5/29/89. http://www.people.com/people/archive/article

Klemesrud, Judy. "From Rah-Rah Cheerleader, to 'Soap's' Creator." The New York Times, June 17, 1978

Maier, Thomas. "Can Psychiatrists Really "Cure" Homosexuality? "Scientific American, April 22, 2009 http://www.scientificamerican.com/article.cfm?id=homosexuality-cure-masters-johnson

Maslon, Laurence and Michael Kantor. "Make 'Em Laugh: The Funny Business in America." Twelve. 2008.

Moldea, Dan E. "Dark Victory: Ronald Reagan, MCA, and the Mob." Viking, 1986.

Montgomery, Kathryn C. "Target: Prime Time." 1990. Oxford University Press.

O'Brian, Dary. "The Hillside Stranglers." 2003. Running Press.

Shaw, Ellen Torgerson. "If he's puffing out his lips, waving his hands and making funny noises…" TV Guide. Jan. 26, 1980

Ward, Robert. "Susan Harris is running as fast as she can." TV Guide, Oct. 11, 1980.

Winfrey, Oprah. "Oprah Talks to Billy Crystal." O, The Oprah Magazine. June 2004

ONLINE

"Christian Life Commission Recommendations On Television And Morality" http://www.sbc.net/resolutions/amResolution.asp?ID=1001

Crackle's Creator Conversation: Soap's Susan Harris 8/4/2010; http://www.crackle.com/blog/crackles-creator-conversation-soaps-susan-harris/

Grant, Lee. Archive of American Television interview www.emmytvlegends.org/interviews/people/lee-grant

Sandrich, Jay. Archive of American Television interview; http://www.emmytvlegends.org/interviews/people/jay-sandrich

Mae West, 1893-1980: The Wild Woman of Film and Stage http://www.voanews.com/learningenglish/home/a-23-2008-11-22-voa2-83138367.html

EVENTS

Soap Reunion: March 22, 1990

The Museum of Broadcasting's 7th annual Television Festival: Los Angeles County Museum of Art (personal video courtesy Jeff Krueger)

Harris, Susan. Hall of Fame induction speech, Jan. 20, 2011.

Joe Mantegna, Wayne and Marsha Posner Williams, and Sal Viscuso.

Marsha with Katherine Helmond and Robert Guillaume. And below, with Diana Canova, Guillaume, Robert Mandan and Jay Johnson.

Acknowledgments

To truly give credit where credit is due for the writing of this book, the author would require a second book of similar length. I will keep it brief here, but hopefully those of you who helped this project during its long, difficult gestation, appreciate just how indebted to you I am.

In no particular order, thanks to everybody who spoke with me for this book: Paul Junger Witt, Tony Thomas, Stu Silver, Jay Sandrich, JD Lobue, Carl Lauten, Fred Silverman, Katherine Helmond, Robert Mandan, Jimmy Baio, Jay Johnson, Robert Guillaume, Jennifer Salt, Diana Canova, Ted Wass, Donnelly Rhodes, Dinah Manoff, John Byner, Bob Seagren, Marla Pennington Rowan, Joe Mantegna, Dr. Everett Parker, Julian Myers and Harry F. Waters.

Special thanks to Susan Harris for being so generous with her time and for sharing with me that Holy Grail of *Soap* research: the *Soap* bible. To Marsha Posner Williams, who never tired of answering questions, pulling strings, and otherwise sharing her memories, photos (many of which you will find in this book) and time with me. There were many times when it was her enthusiasm that convinced me to slink back to the computer to take one more swing at a chapter.

Thanks to Judy Evans Steele for sending me her original, one-of-a-kind sketches, photos, and material swatches from *Soap*, placing her trust in a fellow who just emailed her out of the blue. Thanks as well to Ellen Benjamin, the invaluable assistant to Paul Junger Witt, who imparted her wisdom to yours truly.

A big hug to Sal Viscuso, who always went above and beyond his memories of playing Father Tim to share with me just what it was like to be a young man in the '70s – you're a good man, Sal, and a hell of a painter.

Finally, many thanks to all the *Soap* fans who've encouraged me with this project over the years. Especially Jeff Krueger, for sending me DVDs of nearly-impossible-to-find *Soap* episodes (as well as episodes of the ultra-rare series *Fay*), and for allowing me access to his collection of *Soap*-related clippings. (Not to mention all those emails that made this enormous project so much easier to bear.)

Thanks to Wade Ballard and Gina Herlihy for tracking down info on Cathryn Damon; and for every single fan who's cheered this project on online. And finally to Brian Mattocks for being the first person to join the book's Facebook page, and for occasionally talking the author down from the ledge. Cheers, mate.

Index

A

ABC Movie of the Week 32, 33
ABC Superstars (TV show) 163
Academy of Television Arts & Sciences Hall of Fame 10, 309
Acevedo, Steven 439
Advertising Age 55
Allen, Rae 316, 323, 334
All Good Things (film) 124
All in the Family 19, 24, 25, 33, 45, 56, 81, 233, 334, 411, 412, 420, 435
American Family Association 56
American Film magazine 86
American Home Products 63
Anderson, Eddie 45, 84
Antonacci, Greg 211, 213
Antonowsky, Marvin 28
Archive of American Television 27
Ari, Bob 399, 402
Arnold, Danny 11
Arthur, Bea 24, 329, 333
Atkins Diet 221
Attenborough, Richard 93-94
Austin, Karen 284
Avalos, Luis 152, 399, 402
Avery, Paul 309
Azzara, Candice 243, 263, 268, 271, 272, 275

B

Bahakel, Cy 58
Bailey, F. Lee 317
Bailey, G.W. 217
Bain, Conrad 24
Baio, Jimmy 40–41, 44, 187, 295, 325, 363, 416–417
Baio, Joey 363
Balding, Rebecca 146, 149, 150, 152, 156, 157, 159, 166, 171, 181, 182, 190, 201, 207, 220, 305, 309, 313, 316, 319, 323
Banks, Carol Tillery 237
Barash, Olivia 83
Barbeau, Adrienne 24
Barney Miller 11, 41, 76, 220, 273
Barrow, Dan 358
Barry, JJ 370
Barry, Sandy 370
Battlestar Galactica 251
Benny, Jack 45, 84-85, 143, 431
Benson (TV show) 183, 269, 317, 358, 406–408
 "God, I Need This Job" (episode) 406-408
 "Jessica" (episode) 277–279
Bergan, Judith-Marie 120, 138, 152
Bergere, Lee 184, 197, 198
Berman, David 123
Berman, Susan 123–124
The Betty White Show 40
The Beverly Hillbillies 19, 33, 50
Beverly Hilton Hotel 10

Bizarre (TV show) 228
Blair, Linda 32
Blake, Ellen 211
Bleacher Bums 389
Blinn, William 26
Bob & Carol & Ted & Alice 320
Boen, Earl 370
Bond, Nancy 386, 389
Bond, Raleigh 396
Booke, Sorrell 129, 142, 159, 162, 171
Borden, Ross 370
Born Innocent 32, 36
Bowab, John 232, 233
The Brady Bunch 19
Braha, Herb 370
Braverman, Marvin 138, 142
Brestoff, Richard 375
Brian's Song 26, 31, 33, 431, 434
Broadcasting magazine 55, 58
Broken Badges (TV show) 307
Bromberg, J. Edward 29
Brooks, Joel 375
Browne, Roscoe Lee 316, 319, 323, 333, 340, 343, 347, 351, 355, 362, 366, 382, 385, 389, 396, 399
Brown, Louise 64
Bruce, Lenny 69, 89
Bryant, Anita 7, 97–98, 140, 194
Buffy the Vampire Slayer 244
Bunch, Marianne 83
Burns, Allan 21

Byner, John 40, 207, 208–209, 211, 213, 217, 220, 224, 227, 228, 230, 232, 236, 239, 240, 243, 251, 252, 254, 255, 256, 259, 263, 301, 302
 voice of alien 261

C

California's Department of Fair Employment and Housing 310
Callaway, Thomas 386
Camp, Hamilton 323, 370
Canova, Diana 43, 47, 92, 93, 170, 196, 240–241, 339, 418–419
 I'm a Big Girl Now 331–332
Canova, Judy 170
Caribe (TV show) 42
Carlin, George
 '7 dirty words' ruling 250
Carnovsky, Morris 29
Carsey, Marcy 34
Carsey-Werner Productions 34
Carson, Brandy 106
Cates, Madelyn 314
Charlie's Angels 6, 19, 33, 56
Charnota, Anthony 382
Chavez, Cesar 50
Chayefsky, Paddy 38, 376
Christian Broadcasting Network 52
Christian, David 65

"Christian Life Commission Recommendations on Television and Morality" 55
Clair, Dick 333, 334, 338, 340, 343, 347, 351, 355, 358, 359, 360, 362, 365, 368, 370, 375, 379, 382
Clavin, John 314
Cobb, Brian 59
Combs, Deborah 319, 334, 376
Conrad, Michael 190
Coscarelli, Don 285
Continental Baths 170
Coppola, Frank 211, 213, 243, 263
Cornsentina, Frank 355
Cos Cob 94
Costanzo, Robert 358
Cowan, Geoffrey 21
Cox, Ruth 232, 239, 243
Crane, Bob 57
Crenna, Dick 336
Crittenden, Jordan 174, 178, 179, 181, 184, 203
Crystal, Billy 16, 44–45, 143, 182, 212, 251, 339, 397, 419–420
Currie, Michael 376, 389, 393, 399

D

Dallas 19
  Who shot JR story line 114, 339
Daly, Jane 227
Damon, Cathryn 44, 79, 336, 356, 357, 417–418
Daniels, William 126
Danny Thomas Productions 26, 31, 37
Dark Shadows (TV show) 33
Delano, Michael 243
Denney, Nora 288
Denoff, Sam 38
Diamond Mattress Co. 285
Dinah Shore's talk show 104, 282
Dolman, Nancy 343, 347, 351, 355, 362, 366, 368, 379, 382, 389, 393, 396, 402
Donahue, Phil 396–397
Double Dare (TV show) 83
Duel (film) 33
Dunphy, Jerry 63
Durrell, Michael 316, 323, 334
Durst, Kathie 124
Durst, Robert 124
Dusen, Granville Van 316, 320, 323, 334, 338
Dyke, Dick van 199

E

Elias, Hector 263
Empty Nest 147, 174, 331, 336
Englund, Robert 255, 259
Epp, Gary 355
Equal Rights Amendment 52
Espenson, Jane 244–245
EST 283
Evans, Judy 157, 182, 265, 344, 352, 353–354
Evers, Medgar 68
Exorcist, The 32, 107, 120, 240

F

Fairman, Michael 396, 399
Falwell, Jerry 52, 98
Family Viewing Policy 20–21, 26–29, 30, 31, 32, 52, 56
Faso, Laurie 362, 366
Fay (TV show) 26–30, 33, 36, 196, 198, 209, 270, 334, 360
Federal Communications Commission 20, 30, 68, 250
Feldner, Sheldon 323, 334, 386, 396
Ferguson, Lynnda 351
Ferrero, Martin 272
Fishburne, Laurence 187
Fleur, Art 355
The Flying Nun 283
Fox, Bernard 122
Foxx, Redd 54, 60, 69
Frederick's of Hollywood 155
Freeman (TV show) 40
French, Bruce 279
Fujioka, John 312

G

Garner, Jay 393, 399
Gay Activist Alliance 50
Gay Media Task Force 186
George, Howard 386
Gilford, Jack 255, 259, 262, 263, 264, 268, 275

Gilliam, Burton 227
Gilliam, Stu 40
Gilman, Kenneth 275
Gitter, Richard 58
Go Ask Alice (film) 32
The Golden Girls 10, 75, 142, 270
Goldman, Danny 355
Goldman, William 93
Goodson, Barbara 370
Good Times 19
Gordian Knot, The 15, 16
Gordon, Steve 37
Gould, Harold 103, 106, 111, 114
Grant, Lee 26–30, 181, 425
   blacklisted 29
   Johnny Carson show appearance 28
Grant, Sarina C. 334
Green Acres 19
Group W 59
Guare, John 43
Guillaume: A Life 237
Guillaume, Robert 45–46, 131, 135–136, 169, 218, 237–238, 256, 331, 339, 398, 420–421
Guinness Book of World Records 270, 297

H

Hagen, Uta 29
Haggerty, HB 370, 371
Hallahan, Charles 220
Halop, Florence 171
Happy Bookers 108
Happy Days 78
Harker, Stephanie 370

Harrington, Pat 27
Harris, Berkeley 22
Harris, Susan 10–11, 26, 27, 31, 33, 36, 38, 43, 47, 51, 93, 94, 100, 107, 121, 139, 142, 165, 166, 179, 196, 199, 202, 203, 206, 212, 214, 216, 221, 222, 240–242, 244, 264, 274, 280, 309, 325, 330, 349, 359, 360, 363, 372, 376, 377, 383, 397, 408–409, 412
   an average day 118–119
   and mortality 269–270
   as actress 122, 124, 129
   biography 22–25
   inducted into ATAS Hall of Fame 10–11, 309
   marries Paul Junger Witt 407
   resisting network pressure 226
Hartley, Mariette 363
Hayward, David 355
Hearst, Patty 18, 391
Hee Haw 33
Heller, Randee 224, 227, 230, 236, 239, 243, 251, 255, 259
Helmond, Katherine 42–43, 44, 64, 105, 116, 124, 127–128, 135–136, 151, 202, 218, 228, 238, 240, 242, 298, 299–300, 303, 323, 349, 353, 354, 400–401, 421–423
Henteloff, Alex 207
Herlihy, Gina 437
Hesseman, Howard 129, 141, 146, 149, 152, 156, 159
Hillerman, John 290

Hillside Stranglers 5, 6, 148
Holliday, Kene 290, 297
homosexuality 161, 255
Homosexuality in Perspective (book) 161
The House of Blue Leaves (play) 43
Houser, Jerry 111
House Un-American Activities Committee (HUAC) 29
Hush, Lisabeth 23

I

If You Don't Stop It... You'll Go Blind (film) 37
Iley, Barbara 386
I'm a Big Girl Now (TV show) 317, 330, 331–332
Insight (TV show) 40
International City Racing 108
Iwasaki, Fred 149, 150, 181, 386

J

Jacobson, Danny 358, 360, 362, 365, 368, 370, 375, 379, 382, 385, 402
Jens, Salome 44
Jersey Shore 55
jiggle TV 6, 33
Johnson, Jay 46–47, 60, 62, 65, 67, 76, 92, 93, 94, 96, 121, 130, 143, 157–158, 161–162, 172, 225, 280, 299–300, 306–307, 423

Jonestown 200, 234, 244
Jump, Gordon 117, 122, 126, 129, 146, 149, 152, 156, 159, 166, 171
Justicia (pressure group) 50

K

Kale, Brian 334, 376
Kennedy, Robert F 15
Kersey, Tom 50
Kimmins, Kenneth 323
King, Rori 332
Kiss Me Kate 179
Knapp, David 355
Korman, Harvey 60
Kosner, Edward 55
Kramer, Jeffrey 181
Kramer Vs. Kramer (film) 320
Krueger, Jeff 436–437

L

Lane, Charles 141, 146, 149, 152, 156, 159, 166
Lang, Barbara 389
Lang, Tony 83, 88, 96, 99, 103, 106, 179
Lauten, Carl 66, 67, 86, 131–132, 143, 199, 261–262, 292, 318, 356
Lawrence, Tom 355
Lear, Norman 19, 24, 25, 51, 107, 334
Lefkowitz, Nat 30, 123
LeMay, Curtis 16
Libertini, Richard 77, 91, 106

Lincoln Square Academy 187
Lobue, JD 15, 16, 40, 61, 131–132, 154–156, 230, 233, 356–357, 373–374, 387, 398, 424
   takes over directing of *Soap* 275
   Vietnam draft 16
Lorre, Catharine 5
Lorre, Peter 5
Lou Grant (TV show) 410
Love American Style (TV show) 23
Love Boat, The 6
Loves Me, Loves Me Not (TV show) 38
Lucia, Charles "Chip" 239

M

Macy, Bill 24
Mad magazine 190
Magic (novel) (film) 93
Mandan, Robert 24, 41–42, 66, 78, 85, 139, 221–222, 226, 237, 238, 298, 309, 323, 371, 377, 400–401, 403–404, 409, 424–425
Manoff, Arnold 29
Manoff, Dinah 28, 29, 30, 122, 123, 129, 141, 146, 147, 159, 166, 171, 174, 181, 182, 184, 190, 197, 201, 204, 211, 213, 214, 216, 425–426
Mantegna, Joe 355, 362, 366, 382, 383–384, 386, 389, 396, 398, 399, 402
Manza, Ralph 379, 386
Marsac, Maurice 239

Marshall, Garry 23
Martinez, Chico 362, 366
Mary Hartman, Mary Hartman 60, 66
Mary Tyler Moore Show 21, 26, 33, 39, 41, 42
Mascarino, Pierrino 129
*M*A*S*H* 19, 33
Mason, Eric 103
Masters of Sex (book) 161
Mattocks, Brian 437–438
Maude 19, 24, 25, 35, 51
   abortion story line (written by Susan Harris) 25
Mayberry RFD (TV show) 19, 33
McCabe, Sandra 301
McCalman, Macon 344
McDonough, Kit 239
McGannon, Don 59
McGarvin, Dick 149
McGreevey, Tom 386
McIntire, Tim 232, 233, 236, 239, 243
McKenzie, Richard 284, 290, 305, 368
McKrell, Jim 376
McMahon, Jenna 333, 334, 338, 340, 343, 347, 355, 358, 359, 360, 362, 365, 368, 370, 375, 379, 382
McNamara, Pat 396
McWilliams, Caroline 168, 181, 190, 197, 199, 201, 205, 217, 220, 230, 231, 232
Medici, John 314
Mendillo, Stephen 77
Midnight Cowboy 20
Milk, Harvey 100, 204

Miller, Allan 305, 309, 312, 314, 316, 319, 323, 334, 338
Miller, Dick 232
The Montefuscos (TV show) 28
Montgomery, Kathryn C. 50
Moody, Lynne 282, 290, 294, 297, 309, 314, 319, 323, 338
Moonies 234
Moon, Rev. Sun Myung 234
Moral Majority 52, 98, 186
Morrison, Shelley 114
Mukai, Marcus 386
Mulhern, Scott 239, 255
Mulligan, Richard 41, 43, 142, 199, 276, 336, 356, 357, 363–364, 426–427
spaceship, behind the scenes 261–262
unpredictability 173–174
Myers, Julian 364–365

N

National Federation for Decency 56
National Gay Task Force 58
National Lampoon 14
Neal, Cooper 149
Network (film) 38, 376
Newhart 357
Newsweek 53, 54, 55, 57, 60, 64
Night Court (TV show) 83
North, Sheree 331, 332

O

Oberman, Milt 142, 149
O'Connor, Carroll 25
O'Malley, J. Pat 178
Omen, The 107
O'Neal, Ron 237
One Day at a Time 42
Ontiveros, Lupe 134
Oppenheimer, Alan 96
Owens, Edwin 181

P

Page, Harrison 205
Palter, Lew 279
Parker, Everett 67–68
Parks, Michael 23
Pennington, Marla 263, 266, 268, 272, 273, 275, 279, 284, 285–286, 288, 291, 294, 295, 311, 312, 314, 315, 319, 323, 334, 336, 339, 340, 351, 352, 362, 366
General Hospital 286
Perry, Joe 351
Persky, Bill 28
Peterson, Arthur 230, 241, 252, 349, 427–428
Petrillo, James 143
Peyton Place 30, 33
Phyllis (TV show) 41-42
Pierce, Fred 35
Planned Parenthood 51
Pope, Peggy 220, 251, 255, 268, 319
Population Institute, The 51
Posner, Marsha 36–38, 39, 57–58, 66, 100, 102, 114, 116, 155–156, 160, 191, 199, 241, 257, 305, 333, 349, 372
Power, Udana 103, 104, 114
Practice, The 38, 209, 331
Professional Children's School 187
progesterone shots 182
Pryor, Richard 69

R

Rabbit Test (film) 182
Reagan, Ronald 57
Reicheg, Richard 224
Reiner, Rob 233
Reynolds, Kathryn 83, 96, 103, 133
Rhoades, Barbara 347, 348, 355, 358, 362, 366, 370, 371, 379, 385, 396
Rhoda 21, 26
Rhodes, Donnelly 303–304, 310, 428
Rhudy, Mark 263
Richard Pryor Show, The 75
Rifkin, Arnold 47
Rifkin, Ron 181, 182, 184, 190
Riley, Colleen 290, 297, 309
Rinaldi, Joy 370
Roberts, Doris 152, 166, 174, 181, 182
Robertson, Pat 52
Roche, Eugene 133, 137, 141, 146, 149, 152, 156, 159, 166, 312, 316, 320, 323, 334, 338

Rossovich, Tim 146, 159, 171
RUN Racing 108

S

Sagan, Carl 185
Saito, James 370
Salt, Jennifer 20, 43, 44, 341–342, 380–381, 429–430
Sandrich, Jay 39, 40, 41, 42, 43, 44, 46, 47, 79, 86, 105, 124, 130, 131–132, 151, 154, 155, 174, 208, 230, 241, 257, 262, 264, 273, 280, 303–304, 386, 430
Sandrichm, Jay 233
Sanford & Son 19
Saturday Night Live 45
Save Our Children (pressure group) 98
Scarsale diet 335
Schneider, Alfred 11
Schwartz, Michael 106
Scientology 234
Screen Actors Guild strike (1980) 335–336
Screen Gems Television 26
Seagren, Bob 61, 62, 83, 88, 103, 106, 108–109, 159, 163, 166, 171, 184, 197, 207
See No Evil (book) 21, 27, 39, 59, 60
Selig, Andy 353
Sewell, Joe 96
Shackelford, Ted 309
Shelley, Joshua 309
Short, Martin 332

Siegel, Bugsy 123
Sierra, Gregory 343, 345, 346, 347, 351, 355, 358, 362, 366, 368, 370, 382, 385, 389, 396, 399, 402
Silkwood, Karen 18
Silveira, Ruth 355
Silver, Joe 26
Silverman, Fred 19, 21, 33, 34, 35, 39, 46, 47, 50, 53, 55, 58, 59, 60, 62, 63, 186, 221
Silver, Stu 165, 179, 180, 197, 198, 199, 201, 202–203, 204, 206, 207, 211, 213, 217, 220, 221–223, 224, 229, 232, 236, 239, 240, 243, 251, 254, 259, 263, 268, 271, 275, 279, 282, 284, 287, 289, 290, 293, 297, 301, 305, 308, 311, 313, 315, 316, 319, 322, 329, 330, 333, 338, 340, 343, 346, 347, 348, 351, 355, 358, 359, 360, 361, 362, 365, 368, 370, 375, 379, 382, 385, 389, 392, 393, 396, 399, 402, 409, 411
Simpsons, The 366
Smart, Pamela 325
Smith, Kurtwood 294
Smoot, Fred 358
Smothers Brothers, The 11

Soap

1990 reunion event 124, 237, 437
ad rates 64, 410
backlash (1977) 55–61
"bible" 35, 90, 94, 98, 115, 123–124, 139, 147–148, 150, 153, 175–176, 225, 233, 234, 236, 260–261, 273, 372, 390
bloopers 228
casting of 40–47

Characters

aliens
  original sketches 265
Benson
  leaves the Tates 249
  leaves the Tates…again 260
  Ruby (Benson's daughter) 391
Burt Campbell 391
  alien story line 240, 251
  invisibility 132, 136–137, 138, 147, 275–276
  mental illness 123, 132, 142, 145, 147, 150, 153, 236
  runs for sheriff 312
  world record attempts 270, 297, 298, 302, 306, 310
Mary Campbell 400
Michael Campbell (never used) 150
Chuck & Bob Campbell 143, 299–300
  matching outfits 157–158
Danny Dallas 391
  Johnny Dallas 104
Carol David 147, 150, 166
El Puerco 346, 349
  real name 345

Father Tim Flotsky 268
  name origin 89–90
Randolph Gatling 107, 122, 127
Barney Gerber 104
Julius Kasendorf 397
Elaine Lefkowitz
  origin 123–124
Mr. Lefkowitz 123–124
The Major 390–391
E. Ronald Mallu 123
Con. Walter McCallam 153
General Nu (never used) 150
Nurse Nancy Darwin 104
  and Carol David, same character 147–148
Ingrid Swenson 127
Billy Tate
  Leslie Walker relationship 295–296
Chester Tate 139, 391
  infidelities 292, 324
  on the road (amnesia) 204–229
Corinne Tate 127
David Tate (never used) 139, 150
Eunice Tate 302
  childhood abuse 175–176
Jessica Tate
  appears to Benson on his show after *Soap*'s end 406
  chooses Det. Donohue over Chester 251
Joey Nu Tate (never used) 150
Leslie Walker 264

Key Moments

Barney Gerber's speech 109
Benson visits Jessica on her death bed 324
Billy and Leslie Walker... you know 293
Billy dumps Leslie Walker 314, 315
Billy is captured by the Sunnies 235
Bob beats Danny at checkers 130–131
Burt and Alien Burt's heart to heart 281
Burt and Danny infiltrate Tibbs' brothel 351
Burt and Danny's blackmail pictures published in the local paper 343
Burt captures Tibbs and the crime syndicate 370
Burt is told he's dying 290
Burt & Jodie truce 81
Burt runs for sheriff 312
Burt's cemetery of the future 286
Burt sees a flying saucer 236
Carol leaves Jodie at the altar 212
Carol lies on the stand 319
Carol refuses to allow Jodie to see Wendy 223
Carol reveals she's pregnant 167

Carol tells Jodie she's suing for custody of Wendy 309
Chester and Annie announce their engagement 367
Chester buys into Burt's construction company 358
Chester confesses to Peter Campbell's murder 167
Chester discovers Danny and Annie in bed together 402
Chester donates his kidney to Danny 375
Chester is thought to be dead 218–219
Chester loses his memory 184
Chester proposes to Jessica 380
Chester shacks up with Annie Selig 344
Coffee Cake Sex Talk: Mary and the Tate women 196–197, 264
Corinne gives birth 227
Corinne hits on Father Flotsky in the confessional 90
Danny and Elaine get married 171
Danny and Elaine's new beginning 185
Danny forgives Burt for killing his father 157
Danny is Chester's son, Mary reveals 370
Danny is shot and wounded 366

Danny proposes to Gwen 382
Danny sleeps with Annie Selig 396
Danny tearing the clothes off Elaine 181
Dutch and Corinne sleep together 308
Dutch and Eunice get married 343
Dutch chooses between Corinne and Eunice 333
Elaine, Death of 215–216
Elaine kidnapped 204
Elaine's "Why I'm So Awful" Speech 190
El Puerco hijacks Jessica's plane 344
Eunice leaves Dutch 305
Jessica and Chester attend marriage counseling 290
Jessica and Det. Donohue's first kiss 228
Jessica arrested for murder 128
Jessica catches Chester cheating 105
Jessica faces the firing squad 406
Jessica falls ill 316
Jessica goes to heaven 329
Jessica is taken hostage by the Malaguayan communists 399
Jessica learns she's going to die 321
Jessica recovers from "Jessica Syndrome" 333
Jessica tells Corinne she's adopted 139
Jodie and Maggie become "an item" 367
Jodie and Maggie captured in the Kung Fu fortress 370
Jodie comes out to Danny 102–103
Jodie puts Bob in the fridge 143, 143–145
Julius Kasendorf, introduction of 389
Leslie Walker turns homicidal 326–327
Mary reveals Danny and Jodie are half-brothers 368
Mary tells Jessica that Chester is Danny's father 375
Peter Campbell murdered 116
Possessed baby exorcism 245–246
Step Brothers routine 256–257
Tim and Corinne's baby first shows signs of possession 232
Time and Corinne get married 174
Vulcan neck pinch, Jodie employs the 374
Wendy is kidnapped 338

Notable Dialogue

Bat Campbell, birth of 378
"Boy, Norman Lear really did change television!" 336
Burt asks Alien Burt for his life back 281
Burt's "Harry Alvins" speech to the Bishop 365
"Chester goes through women the way an elephant goes through peanuts…" 292
Chuck & Bob's mind-reading act 215
Coffee cake sex talk: Mary and the Tate women 192–195
Elaine's "Why I'm So Awful" speech 191
"…going downtown to pick up some white women." 254
"I dislike violence but I'm awfully good at it." 357
"I'm so pleased to meet you Mr. Pasteur. Your name is on my milk." 337
Jodie on the stand 326
Juan Valdez/bad beans 125
Mary's mother tells her she's wearing too much eyeliner 337
"Mickey Mouse's dog was gay?!" 206
The Peppy Flake jingle 210
"There are no more Indians…" 292
"The winos keep trying to steal my wallet and

the homos just keep trying." 395
"Those Japanese are really fantastic, you know..." 333
"Woo-hoo, grandpa." 279
"You could walk in here with a goat, I wouldn't blink!" 287
"You wear that belted!" 79

Story Lines
Possessed baby 240–242
Who killed Peter Campbell? 160
Sunnies (aka The Church of the Golden Ray) 232, 234, 330

compilation episodes 165–166, 329
creation of 33–36
East Berlin, set referred to as 76
filming innovations 154–156
flashback episode 379
"Jessica's Wonderful Life" episode 329–333
Jodie and Carol spin-off 208
Newsweek piece, damaging 1977 53–55, 412
pilot, writing of 38–39
planning an episode 348–349
Season 5? 409–410
series premiere 61–63
sets 318

shooting schedule 86–87
Sony DVD releases 7
spaceship
  behind the scenes on the 261–262
writers 359–361

Soo, Jack 220
Sopranos, The 123
Sotiropulos, Kopi 396
Southern Baptist Convention 55, 63
Spielberg, Steven 33
Staahl, Jim 386
Stahl, Richard 217
Starr, Don 396, 397
Starr, Jenna Kay 268
Steele, Ray 265
Step Brothers (real) 256
Stephenson, Edward 318
Stevens, Lenore 364
Stewart, Mel 297
St. Mary Star of the Sea 93
Stolarsky, Paul 402
Stroker Ace (film) 209
Stuthman, Fred 362
Summers, Marc 83
Super Fly TNT 237
Swenson, Inga 122, 126, 129, 134, 137, 152, 156, 230

T

Talbot, Nita 88, 114, 152
Tales of the City 170
Tandem Productions 51
Target: Prime Time (book) 50, 51, 58
Taxi Driver 123

Temple, Renny 284
Terry, Jon 159
That Certain Summer (TV movie) 31, 50
That Girl 27
The Hero (TV show) 363
Then Came Bronson (TV show) 23
Thomas, Danny 331, 332
Thomas, Marlo 66, 396–397, 403
Thomas, Tony 11, 26, 28, 31, 33, 34, 35, 36, 38, 74, 115, 203, 209, 296, 324, 331, 345, 372, 430–432
Thomopoulos, Tony 196
Thorn Birds, The 88
Three Faces of Eve, The 142
Three's Company 6, 33, 56, 66
Time magazine 67
Travolta, John 234
TV Guide 38, 269–270

U

Urich, Robert 44, 74, 80, 83, 88, 91, 111, 114, 115

V

Vaccaro, Brenda 181
Vant, René Le 166, 171
Variety 55
Veenkamp, Ben 440
Vietnam 11, 16, 49, 52, 92, 94, 140
Vigon, Barry 358, 360, 362, 365, 368, 370, 375,

379, 382, 385, 399, 400, 402

Viscuso, Sal 16–18, 28, 63, 88, 90, 91, 92, 93, 106, 114, 117, 134, 146, 152, 153, 159, 166, 174, 178, 181, 184, 201, 205, 213, 220, 224, 236, 239, 241, 243, 272, 273, 431–432

Vonnegut Jr., Kurt
letter to book-burners 65

W

Wallace, Royce 290, 297, 301
Waltons, The 28
Wass, Ted 61, 101–102, 173, 214, 276, 293, 410–411, 433–434
Waters, Harry F. 53–55, 60, 412–413
Weatherly, Jim 15
Weather Underground 98
Weaver, Lee 129
Webster, Byron 88, 103, 137
Webster (TV show) 289
Welles, Jesse 351, 355, 358, 362, 366, 368, 379, 382
Wences, Señor 366
Wendt, George 393
Werner, Tom 34
What's it all About, World? (TV show) 359
When Harry Met Sally... (film) 251
White, Betty 39
Wildmon, Donald 56, 57

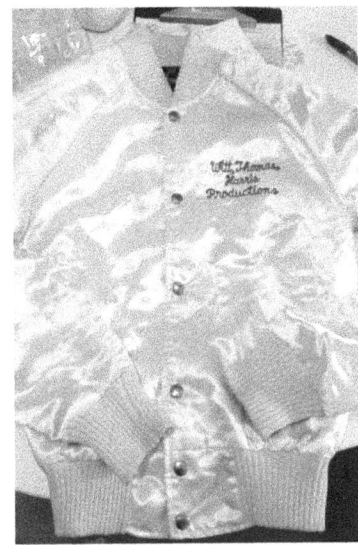

Windsor, Walter 59
Winfrey, Oprah 16
Winter, Edward 120, 129, 137, 141, 152
Winter, Jo De 207, 227
Witt, Paul Junger 11, 26, 27, 31, 33, 34, 36, 38, 44, 53, 70, 112, 121, 179, 196, 209, 269, 411, 434–435
Witt Thomas Harris 31, 34, 39, 57, 64
WLBT-TV 68
Wolfe, Ian 91, 146, 174
Wonder Woman (TV show) 19
Woolsey, Kristofer 439–440
Wright, Wendell 207
Wyner, George 385, 389, 393

X

Xanadu (film) 384

Y

Yorkin, Bud 19

Z

Zwick, Joel 203

www.ingramcontent.com/pod-product-compliance
Ingram Content Group UK Ltd.
Pitfield, Milton Keynes, MK11 3LW, UK
UKHW051248180426
11947UKWH00020B/1600